CALIFORNIA STATE UNIVERSIT

This book is due on the last date stamped
Failure to return books on the date due will
~ fees.

D0768889

THE CONTEXTURE
OF FEMINISM

CAROLYN A. DURHAM

The Contexture of Feminism

Marie Cardinal and Multicultural Literacy

UNIVERSITY OF ILLINOIS PRESS
Urbana and Chicago

Publication of this work was supported in part by a grant from The
Henry Luce III Fund for Distinguished Scholarship at the College of
Wooster.

Manufactured in the United States of America

I 2 3 4 5 C P 5 4 3 2 I

This book is printed on acid-free paper.

Library of Congress Cataloging-in-Publication Data
Durham, Carolyn A.
    The contexture of feminism : Marie Cardinal and multicul-
tural literacy / Carolyn A. Durham.
        p.   cm.
    Includes bibliographical references and index.
        ISBN 0-252-01811-7 (alk. paper).—ISBN 0-252-06184-5
(pbk.)
        1. Cardinal, Marie—Criticism and interpretation.   2. Femi-
nism and literature—France—History—20th century.   I. Title.
    PQ2663.A7Z65   1992
    843'.914—dc20   91-388
                                                                  CIP

For my mother and father
and for Henry—
with love

CONTENTS

ACKNOWLEDGMENTS

I am grateful to the College of Wooster for supporting the research leave in 1985–86 that allowed me to begin work on this project and for providing additional funding from the Henry Luce III Fund for Distinguished Scholarship to enable me to devote the spring semester of 1988 to the completion of a first draft of this book. I thank my colleagues and students for the many ways in which they have challenged and encouraged my thinking and my scholarship.

I owe particular thanks to the Camargo Foundation in Cassis, France, where I spent the spring of 1988. Not only did that fellowship result in one of the most productive five months of my professional life, but it also provided an experience of intercultural dialogue that had an important influence on the direction this book has taken. I thank my co-fellows for the stimulation of Friday afternoon project presentations; and I am especially grateful to my neighbors, Phyllis Stock and Scott Morton, for their warm friendship and constant support. Michael Pretina has my particular gratitude for his efficient, sensitive, and intelligent direction of the Camargo Foundation.

I wish to recognize the editors of *French Review, Tulsa Studies in Women's Literature,* and *Women's Studies* for their willingness to publish earlier versions of portions of the analyses of *Une Vie pour deux* and *Le Passé empiété* that appear in chapters 1 and 3. Conferences sponsored by the University of Louisville, the University of Pennsylvania, Wichita State University, and the Midwestern and Southeastern Modern Language Associations also provided a forum for presenting work in progress. I thank the members of the editorial staff of the University of Illinois Press—and Ann Lowry, Theresa Sears, and Sam Cogdell, in particular—for the encouragement and remarkably efficient assistance they provided at all stages of the editing process.

This book could not have been written without the support of some very special friends. Diane-Marie Decharme first introduced me to the work of Marie Cardinal many years ago. Germaine Brée's example and constant encouragement have played a significant role in my professional development. Conversations with Ginette Adamson and Yolanda Patterson, despite the distance that usually separated us, always provided an affectionate and stimulating context for sharing ideas. Closer to home, John and Rena Hondros, Carolee Taipale, and Joanne Frye offered me the many pleasures of close friendship on a daily basis. Most of all, I am grateful to Henry Herring, whose commitment to ideas, standard of excellence, quality of mind, respect for others, and capacity for love will always represent the ideal against which I measure my own achievement and worth.

If you ask a woman, "What happened?" suggests Suzanne Ju-hasz, she will provide you with an abundance of circumstantial detail. A man, on the other hand, will focus immediately on "the gist, the result, the *point* of the event" (Jelinek 223). The experiential evidence on which Juhasz bases her generalizations about the en-gendering of narrative finds empirical support in Carol Gilligan's interviews with women who speak "in a different voice," reflective of "a mode of thinking that is contextual and narrative rather than formal and abstract" (19). By chance, this repetition of difference announces my own recurrent interest in the question of gender specificity.[1] More immediately, it identifies a pattern of expression that I find particularly compelling as I attempt to articulate the multiple, diverse, and interrelated events that have informed the origin and the shape, the "what happened," of this book.

Although I shall speak of Marie Cardinal in these pages with a frequency that makes it imperative to name her at once, I do not regard her text as the kind of "primary source" to which literary criticism has traditionally devoted its attention. Nor do more recent amalgams such as "(con)text" or "text/context" fully reflect my intentions, since they continue to imply that "text" and "context" could function as separate and autonomous entities.[2] Rather, the central object of my analysis is what might be called a "primary context," a term that I use to refer both to Cardinal's work in particular and to feminist writing in general. I believe that the texts of feminism, on the model of those of Marie Cardinal, are most accurately characterized as a context, the locus of the complex intersections—at once intergenderal, intertexual, and interdisciplinary—of modern thought. From this perspective, the gesture by which I seek to transform Cardinal's text into the context for an exploration of the current situation of written feminism is meant to be both enabling and metaphoric. Literally speaking, then, I do define Cardinal's work as a "primary source"; her text functions not as the final, passive object of theory and criticism but as both their initial, productive "origin" and "an essential part of the organized whole" all three constitute together.[3]

I am aware that what I describe as a feminist gesture of contexture could be interpreted as a colonialist act of appropriation—to put it in the worst terms possible, those that often serve Cardinal to characterize an ever-present temptation of Western ideology. To the extent that the objection that I am "using" Cardinal arises from the belief that underlies a traditional commitment to the "primary source," namely, that respect for the autonomy and the integrity of the text automatically ensures the accuracy and the fidelity of any interpretation that it informs, the charge can be readily dismissed. Feminist scholarship as a whole has long since exposed the politics of objectivity. Still, even for those who will readily acknowledge that we inevitably ask the texts of others to serve our own and larger purposes (who will agree, in other words, to let the text act as context), the choice to include textual analysis at all, and, more importantly, the particular choice of Cardinal, will be controversial at best.

Marie Cardinal is extremely well known in France, an immensely popular writer in every sense of the term; her books appeal to a general audience—one, moreover, that is assumed to be predominantly female. Everyone whom I have met in the last few years has heard of her (and thanks to Bernard Pivot's *Apostrophes,* most of them have formed a visual image—and an opinion—as well); more importantly, almost everyone whom I meet has read at least one of her books. I must confess that I find this situation rather disconcerting at times: I am not accustomed to discussing my scholarship while I have my hair cut, even in Paris. Moreover, if this public accepts my interest in Cardinal without question, it also consistently denies me any particular authority as reader.

In a rather curious coincidence, those who do pause to reflect on the difference that might exist between reading Cardinal's books and writing a book about Cardinal consistently arrive at the same conclusion: either they express the wish that I had chosen to write about Marguerite Duras or they make the suggestion that I should. From this I deduce two things, one more encouraging than the other. On the one hand, I think it safe to infer that an awareness of the significance of gender, however differently it may be understood in each *particular* instance, is nonetheless in *every* instance a key factor in mediating the substitution of Duras for Cardinal. On the other hand, I am also forced to conclude that general readers—women, specifically, in the case at hand—do not consider their own reading habits an appropriate standard for determining which writers merit critical attention.

From a feminist perspective, I find these two conclusions to be unacceptably contradictory. To date, we have perhaps played it safe in defining the terms of our challenge to the literary canon. We have sought the inclusion of women writers from a past sufficiently distant to support a convincing argument about their historical importance, if not their literary merit. Moreover, when the latter has clearly been at issue, we have neatly sidestepped it in any of a number of ways: we have read these women's texts as documents of social realism; we have thrown vast numbers of them in with better-known writers to serve as the supporting evidence for a female literary history or tradition; we have made their appeal dependent on that of a genre whose rigid formulae eliminate any question of personal initiative or responsibility.[4]

What we have not done, however, is to devote many books to an individual, contemporary, woman writer whose claim on our attention comes not from her preestablished critical reputation but from her popularity with female readers and whose diverse publications disallow her reduction in stature to the representative of a particular genre. While I understand how such a project could seem antithetical to the collective goals of feminism (I too find painful any reminiscence of *l'homme et l'oeuvre*), I also suspect that the literary critical establishment might find such an undermining of its rules from within far more disruptive than it has so far found their redefinition from without. Moreover, an objectionable focus on an individual writer, for which the collective response of her female readers would surely compensate, cannot really lie at the source of either their prohibition or our own.

The concern of those readers who find Cardinal's work interesting and important, but who are nonetheless troubled to discover their judgment reflected in mine, centers on the quality of her *écriture*. My initial temptation to interpret this response as the result of a traditional French education, one in which the emphasis on the intricacies of *explication de texte* has always served to support a distinctly male literary canon of sophisticated stylists, no doubt underestimates a significant change that has taken place in modern France. The attention that French intellectuals have devoted to *écriture* in the last fifty years—beginning with Saussurian linguistics, continuing through structuralism and deconstruction, and embracing, notably, *écriture féminine*—has resulted in a depersonalization of the notion of writing that now allows the general public to think of *Ecriture* as it once did Flaubert or Proust. Thus, the removal of sex as obstacle theoretically (and paradoxically) makes room for the consideration of gender. Hence, Duras. But (still) not Cardinal.

I think a not dissimilar dynamics divides the consciousness of feminist critics. Many of us also continue to believe that some people write better than others; if aesthetic value has never functioned (or, at the very least, no longer functions) as a sufficient criterion to arouse our interest, it remains a necessary one. Ellen Messer-Davidow has proposed a particularly radical solution to the "intractable problems" (71) that she finds inherent in the feminist attempt to reconcile the politically acceptable and the aesthetically satisfying; she would simply eliminate literature from the scope of our inquiry: "the subject of feminist literary criticisms appears to be not literature but the feminist study of ideas about sex and gender that people express in literary and critical media" (77).[5] Perhaps Messer-Davidow is right that nothing less dramatic than a final divorce could free us from the contradictions that I, in any case, fully share. For if part of me seeks to challenge the aesthetic criteria by which a writer such as Cardinal is deemed unworthy of attention, there is another part of me that believes, and is determined to prove, that she does in fact meet those criteria. That my conflicting desires both confirm the need for Messer-Davidow's solution and virtually guarantee that I will reject it points up in passing the potential contradictions in her own position as well.

By coincidence, when I asked Cardinal which writers she likes to read, she named only one: Duras—"because of the writing [*l'écriture*], she makes me want to write in turn" (personal interview, 23 Nov. 1987).[6] This repetition of the same series of associations—Cardinal, Duras, *Ecriture*—in a new context that substitutes affiliation for alienation suggests that I may have been too hasty to position *écriture féminine* within a general transformation of the notion of *Ecriture*. In that event, I may have overestimated the significance of that transformation as well. If a newly independent *Ecriture* potentially destabilizes the relationship of the French people to language in general, it simultaneously reinforces their peculiar relationship to their own language in particular.

Allow me to indulge in overgeneralization for a moment, in the interest of identifying broad cultural patterns. On the one hand, the French lament the declining international importance of their language, an effect largely attributed to an increase in speakers of English, and they actively support policies designed to encourage the teaching of the French language throughout the world. On the other hand, at home, the French regularly thwart the efforts of foreigners to speak (and therefore to learn) their language by insistently responding to them in an English that they often command far less well than the foreigners do French. Some years of pondering such a persistent contradiction between foreign and domestic policy, between theory and practice, have led me to the only logical conclusion: the inevitable duality of linguistic interaction in the modern world, by virtue of which every language is simultaneously native and foreign, breaks down in France where native speakers do not and cannot accept "foreign French."

Now, to the extent that women's access to language has been historically limited, making them outsiders in their own culture, and to the extent that they continue to speak "in a different voice," this is a feminist issue quite as much as a linguistic one. I doubt that the prevalence in French feminist texts of images of women who speak the language of their own culture as if it were a foreign tongue can be entirely explained either by chance or by the linguistic focus of Lacanian psychoanalysis. As is often the case in women's writing, such metaphors appear to be solidly grounded in cultural ideology and experiential reality. Certainly this is true for both Cardinal and Duras, whose colonial upbringings caused each to learn a "foreign" French and whose sense of themselves as foreigners within the culture of France has become increasingly identified with their sense of themselves as women.

If a newly gendered notion of language, an *écriture féminine*, might establish a connection between Cardinal and Duras, the idea of a specifically female discourse has been a major source of divisiveness between and among Anglo-American and Francophone feminists. Yet, Americans too have a curious relationship to foreign languages, to the foreignness of language, which, however different it may be from that of the French, also has clear consequences for feminist scholarship. In the United States, where the academic community does not impose quite such stringent limits on what is worthy of scholarly attention and where feminist work has often been devoted to the discovery of unknown women writers, Cardinal has been the subject of several essays and one book (see Durham, Lionnet, LeClézio, Martin, and Yalom). All of these have focused almost exclusively on *Les Mots pour le dire* (The words to say it), the only one of Cardinal's novels available at the time in English translation.[7] Admittedly, the publication of certain articles, Elaine Martin's for example, predates that of the translation (indeed, the possibility of a causal connection suggests that an alliance between feminist critics and other women readers might prove multiply and mutually beneficial). But this apparent contradiction does not in fact diminish the role that language plays here, for without exception every study of Cardinal published by an American scholar has been comparative in nature; *Les Mots pour le dire* is always read in conjunction with one or more companion novels written in English.[8]

To restore balance by overgeneralizing about my own culture for a moment, I would suggest that Americans' ready acceptance of "foreign English," of accented speech, reflects to some extent a far less admirable readiness to colonize, to homogenize, to eliminate foreignness even as we embrace it.[9] Moreover, feminist scholars in the United States appear to share something of this penchant for domestication. When they do not focus their attention exclusively on English-language texts, the latter nonetheless often implicitly constitute, as in the case of the scholarship on Cardinal, a privileged means of access, a standard by which to judge. Furthermore, translation into English has been American feminism's preferred approach to French texts from Elaine Marks and Isabelle de Courtivron's edited volume *New French Feminisms* (1980) to Claire Duchen's *French Connections* (1987). Translation is by definition a curiously contradictory process, since it introduces cultural difference and erases it at one and the same time. This inevitable paradox may well be particularly intense in the case of feminist scholars whose emphasis on gender identity has tended to minimize individual, racial, and cultural differences. Indeed, the comparative studies in which Cardinal figures illustrate how the simple act of remaining silent on the question of cultural specificity can result in the implicit valorization of gender commonality.

Still, I realize that to write a book that pays close and consistent attention to an *écriture* that is approximately as unknown in the United States as it is well known in France and that, moreover, *cannot be known* in most cases, since there are no available translations, must appear an incredible gamble. My conviction that it is a wager worth making stems not only from a commitment to context but, more specifically, to a multicultural context. To repeat myself, but more completely, written feminism functions as the locus of the complex intersections—at once intergenderal, intertextual, interdisciplinary, and *intercultural*—of modern thought.

This introduction was first drafted at the Camargo Foundation in Cassis, France, a place to which I had originally gone out of a desire to experience Cardinal's personal understanding of the intercultural. Always in exile from Algeria, where she was raised, never quite at home in France, where she has been widely published and read, still in transit as the newly naturalized citizen of Québec, where for years she spent only vacations, Cardinal merges cultures and emerges culturally whole as a "Mediterranean." This notion, so deeply rooted for Cardinal in the particularities of climate and decor and so closely linked to her sense of herself as a woman, drew me to the sea. There, the subtle but constant shifts in color and motion that the sky and the water display against the monochromatic background of the Mediterranean landscape taught me a new awareness of nuance, a heightened sensitivity to and appreciation of difference, that might indeed support a view of self and world as a harmonious balance of multiplicity and diversity.

The Camargo Foundation itself also turned out to provide an unexpectedly appropriate context for the intercultural focus of my own work. An enclave of predominantly Anglophone scholars in an intellectually rich Francophone setting, it combines the best of both worlds. In a similar fashion, texts written in French and in English meet at the major cultural intersection of contemporary feminism. Crossing intersections can, of course, be a harrowing experience in any country, though there are clear cultural differences. In New York, one has the right of passage, but one's path is often blocked by an endless stream of cars, backed up end to end. In Paris, where the de facto, if not the legal, right-of-way always belongs to cars, the path is often clear but the passage is constantly fraught with danger. Forced to stand still in New York, one runs for one's life in Paris. Perhaps it is inevitable, then, that at the intersection of Anglophone and Francophone feminist writing, the passage seems at once open and forbidden, progress both halting and hurried, safe arrival simultaneously assured and uncertain.

I am far from the first to venture forth into the Franco-American intersection of contemporary feminism.[10] Before proceeding, however, I must reflect for a moment on the difficulties of naming the passage. The intercultural seems, almost by definition, to invite a certain amount of linguistic hybridization. But if such terminology has a high degree of formal accuracy, its content consistently tends to omit part of what it should include. To the greatest extent possible, then, even in those cases where *American* and *French* would adequately designate that which intersects, I prefer the terms *Anglophone* and *Francophone,* both because language itself will be a subject of constantly recurrent, if not constant, interest in the pages ahead and because there are close ties between the feminist texts of the United States and Britain, on the one hand, and those of France and Québec, on the other. If the first of these connections has been regularly acknowledged, since American criticism often includes textual analysis of British writers, the second, dependent on a similar theory and practice of *écriture féminine,* has been persistently occulted.[11] Still, the intersection into which others have preceded me, and to which I now return, has in fact been predominantly *Franco-American.*

To the extent that a hyphen suggests reciprocity and, in the case at hand, similar and equal activity on each side of it, this particular hybrid raises additional questions. At least the relative importance of the prefix in relationship to the root seems exact, since the careful attention that Anglophone scholarship has been paying to Francophone theory has not yet been returned in kind. If my hypothesis about a different cultural relationship to foreign language is not causal, it is at least consistent with the fact that virtually none of the feminist literary commentary published in the United States over the past two decades is available in French translation. One can hope that the recent success of the French edition of Shari Benstock's *Women of the Left Bank* may help to alter this situation. Even if the initial appeal of Benstock's book originates in the geographical and ideological context that its title identifies, French readers will nonetheless encounter therein Anglo-American writers and a theoretical and critical discourse informed by the concerns of American feminism.

Of similar interest is Toril Moi's *Sexual/Textual Politics.* To the extent that Moi speaks from a position outside American and French feminism, she offers a reasonably balanced appraisal and critique of both. But since she writes as a feminist, without any claim to an impossible objectivity, the fact that her personal views most often coincide with those of the French also provides a valuable counterpoint to most comparative analyses. I do not mean to imply that Anglo-American feminists approach Francophone theory solely, or even most frequently, from a critical perspective. I do mean to signal what may be yet another consequence of the difficulty of hearing the foreign: the virtual absence of any comparative studies done from a French perspective. Moreover, even those Americans who most fully embrace Francophone theory—Jane Gallop and Alice Jardine, for example—most often situate their collective identity, their "we," within Anglophone feminism.

The significance of such new textual conjunctures as those of Benstock and Moi relates to the now conventional distinction between Francophone feminist *theory* and Anglo-American feminist *criticism* (see, for example, Moi 97 and Jardine 19). According to this configuration, feminist literary scholars in the United States have produced primarily textual commentaries and revisionary studies of literary history, while their counterparts in France have developed a far more abstract and speculative discourse strongly informed by the linguistic, philosophical, and psychoanalytic currents of modern European thought. To accept for the moment an assumption that I will eventually challenge—namely, that such a contrast is accurate and, more to the point, useful—it initially seems to reflect a different understanding of and relationship to the text as "primary source."

If modern Anglophone feminism, particularly during its early stages, included a certain amount of purely descriptive, historical, or evaluative criticism that approached the text as an autonomous object, the distinction no longer seems pertinent at a time when Anglophone and Francophone feminists clearly share the belief that text and textual commentary are in constant dialogue. The philosophy that informs, respectively, Luce Irigaray's interrogation of Freud's text (*Speculum*) and Margaret Homan's literalization of Virginia Woolf's (*Bearing*) does not, for example, strike me as fundamentally different, since, in both cases, the reading of another's text engenders the writing of one's own. Perhaps the controversy originates instead in the difference between Freud and Woolf. Yet, here again, the argument that Francophone feminists read the texts of men while Anglophone feminists read those of women has surely become less convincing at present, given the purposes to which feminists in the United States are putting Bakhtin, for example (see Frye, Yaeger, and Fink). Moreover, the influence of Derrida and Lacan has hardly been limited to Francophone feminists—nor, for that matter, to Anglophone feminists working in the field of French literature or culture.

Similarly, the generic distinction that Freud and Woolf might represent, defining and separating the respective objects of theory and of literary criticism, has also blurred, given, on the one hand, Hélène Cixous' current interest in the fiction of Clarice Lispector and, on the other, the frequent discussion of Nancy Chodorow in Anglophone textual commentary. Indeed, intercultural contact within feminism clearly reflects this shift. If essays by Elaine Showalter ("Feminist") and Margaret Homans ("Her Very"), for example, explicitly relate their discussion of Anglophone and Francophone feminist writing to the study of literature, a number of more recent essays in collections such as those edited by Teresa de Lauretis (*Feminist Studies, Critical Studies*) and by Gayle Greene and Coppélia Kahn (*Making a Difference: Feminist Literary Criticism*) directly engage the psychoanalytic and epistemological assumptions of feminist thought.

Increasingly, the issue appears to have much less to do with *what* is being said in different locales than in *how* (in what language) it is being said. The Anglo-American tendency to group all of Francophone feminist writing under the rubric *écriture féminine,* though factually inaccurate, has the merit of identifying that which is crucial and which therefore colors—both stains and fades into—all other issues. To begin with, it further complicates my efforts to understand those distinctions that are most consistently assumed, particularly that of a commitment to or a betrayal of one's own sex. Francophone feminists may have a much stronger tendency to repeat the *ideas* of a certain male canon, but Anglophone feminists reject or ignore those ideas in the canon's own *language.*[12]

As always within feminism, the linguistic issue reflects an ideological one. On several occasions in the last few pages, I have committed an error that I have left uncorrected because of what I believe to be its origin and its significance. Having explicitly come to terms with my own lexical preferences, I proceeded to undermine them almost at once by a nonparallel usage of *Anglo-American* and *Francophone.* My linguistic inconsistency signals a complex problematic that this time, I think, really does identify a significant intercultural difference. I have not only positioned the issue of language—specifically, that of *écriture féminine,* of a distinctly female discourse—within French(-Canadian) feminism alone. (Indeed, I am forced to wonder whether my commitment to the term *Franco*phone might not initially have had as much or more to do with the visibility that it grants to the fact of language itself as with my professed desire to define more accurately the boundaries of any particular language.) But, in addition, I have simultaneously revealed the absence of attention to language—the assumption of its invisibility, its transparency—that has often been cited as characteristic of the Anglo-American side of the cultural equation.

Throughout all of its working drafts, this book (and each of its chapters) had a bilingual title to whose metaphorical value I remain deeply attached, for it figured not only the origin and the nature of perhaps the most persistent division within feminist theory but the contradictions, both literal and theoretical, of my own position. It is not just that I am an American reading a Francophone writer, nor that I am writing in English about texts composed in French, although I do think that the close ties that bind all feminist texts (whether theoretical, critical, fictional, or autobiographical) to political and material reality may make even these choices more controversial than in other cases. More to the point, I am simultaneously recontexualizing Anglophone theory through work produced within a Francophone context and Francophone theory through a writer who has often expressed profound skepticism about a great many of its most important ideas, including, in particular, the concept of *écriture féminine*. (While I am convinced of both my right and the need to do so, I must admit that I find it somewhat difficult to grasp the logic of Nelly Furman's assertion that the decision to ignore authorial intention constitutes a specifically feminist act of revolt.)[13]

My decision to interpret Marie Cardinal's work as one exemplary context within which to explore contemporary written feminism arises from the hope—and the expectation—that because her writing consistently embodies the concerns of Francophone and Anglophone feminists (in part, no doubt, because of her multicultural background), it can also point the way to their theoretical and textual *reconciliation*. I use this term only in its primary sense—the effort "to reestablish friendship"—but I have chosen it because its multiple and, for me, contradictory meanings reflect the hazards of the venture: the risk of erasing difference ("to make compatible or consistent"), of imposing sameness ("to settle or resolve"), and of choosing sides ("to bring to acquiescence"). Etymologically, *re*conciliation (to bring together *again*) situates my project within the developing history of feminist thought, marking it as yet another, and surely not the last, in a series of repetitions.[14]

Since I have committed my own text to a certain repetition of Cardinal's, I need to repeat (to go back to) and to reconcile (to bring together again) the different kinds of texts that make up written feminism. My decision to grant fiction and autobiography a central role does not stem from some notion of a textual hierarchy in which critical or theoretical writings would be of lesser significance; indeed, given the explicitly interdisciplinary nature of feminist scholarship, the opposite position would be easier to argue. Yet, I do agree, though for very different reasons, with Elaine Showalter's assertion that "no theory, however suggestive, can be a substitute for the close and extensive knowledge of women's texts which constitutes our essential subject" ("Feminist" 205). Unfortunately, by casting *theory* and *women's texts* as opposing terms of a dichotomy, simultaneously informed by gender and by genre, Showalter defines all theory as "men's texts" and all writing by women as "not theory," that is, as (only) literature. It then follows that since text and theory are diametrically opposed, they cannot coexist; one must be sacrificed to the other. A more accurate and useful interpretation would emphasize the dynamic interaction of theory and text: since the analysis of a given textual practice can be expected to generate a new theory of the text (which can then inform textual analysis in its turn), writing and reading cannot be contained by the boundaries of genre any more than by those of gender.

In addition, Showalter's formulation appears to undermine intercultural exchange. Her hierarchical model reiterates the conventional distinctions between Anglophone and Francophone feminist practice in a form that could be read as outright feminist xenophobia. Showalter not only limits Francophone feminist theory to a decidedly secondary role—at best, Anglophone feminists reading (real) women's texts may find it "suggestive"—but her association of "men" with "theory" literally denies women the possibility of producing theoretical writing and reduces women's work to mere repetition of male theory.[15]

And yet, in another sense, my own decision to begin with what Showalter calls "women's texts" stems from a certain degree of acceptance of her assumptions about gender and genre. If one begins with the theory rather than the text, one does indeed tend to begin with the male rather than the female, and, in that case, there appears to be some justification for believing that one may never (or, at the very least, not very soon) get around to the female text. Such diverse books as Susan Lanser's *Narrative Act* and Alice Jardine's *Gynesis,* both of which figure among the most important works that feminist scholarship has produced, nonetheless leave us vaguely dissatisfied (*sur notre faim,* as the French say), in large part, no doubt, because Lanser and Jardine allow their own *déception* (both disappointment and self-deception) to show through by explicitly pointing out the discrepancy between their original intentions and their final results. Lanser, whose work originates in the desire to develop a new theory designed to read the differences of female narrative practice, must settle for a description of the inadequacies of current theory. Jardine's projected exploration of the specificity of *écriture féminine* never gets beyond the analysis of the male discourse from which women's writing is assumed to differ. Although each book ends by announcing another to be devoted to the original project, Lanser's and Jardine's need to explain the delay suggests that beyond the realization of the unexpected intricacies of their endeavor may lie the suspicion that they might have gone about it differently.

Or perhaps I only like to think that self-doubt—that which, in my more confident moments, I call the awareness of complexity—characterizes feminist scholarship as a whole, because it plays such a critical role in my own thinking. What I can say and think at any given time is limited not only by *what* I have read but, far more significantly perhaps, by *how* I have read it. To repeat with Dorothy Dinnerstein that "I *believe* in reading unsystematically and taking notes erratically" and to concur in her dismissal of any claim to a more "rational" procedure as a "self-deluded exercise in pseudomastery" (viii-ix) gives me a false sense of pleasure and power, since Dinnerstein does not in fact provide me with an exact description of my own politics of reading. I would not precisely wish to assert that I *believe* in reading systematically and taking notes purposefully, but this version of events does provide a far more accurate picture of what actually happens, at least in my own case. My reading in literary theory and criticism and in Women's Studies as a whole always takes place within a very specific context that is determined by my textual interests at the time. Thus, the notes that currently surround me will surely appear erratic if they are confronted with the books from which they have been taken; the reading that I have done in the last few years will certainly seem unsystematic if its unity is sought within those same books. Yet, when considered in light of my interest in Marie Cardinal, this identical activity will appear perfectly consistent and coherent.

Clearly such a procedure does a great injustice to most of what I read; read at a different time, and out of a different context, the same books would find their content totally transformed. On the other hand, this practice may help to explain why the critical and theoretical work that I find most interesting, to the extent that I can discern a second common pattern, tends to devote some attention to textual analysis. Since I do not in fact believe that my reading habits are unique, such works, due to their ability to make visible the relationship between thought and the context in which it develops, potentially offer an important illustration of how women's writing and our reading of it can generate their own theoretical paradigms. I assume that this focus on process as well as product also explains why my reading pleasure does not depend on a prior and independent knowledge of the specific texts that inform the analysis. Indeed, to the extent that I have such knowledge, my attention tends to be diverted away from the analysis that I am reading to the text being read; I lose some sense of context.

Although I think that the interest of this particular book does not require familiarity with the work of Marie Cardinal, I do not mean to suggest that we should stop reading criticism and theory informed by texts that we know, nor that we should select books to read by virtue of our ignorance of their subject matter. On the other hand, the interdisciplinary, intercultural, and intertexual nature of feminist writing has to some extent required, trained, and encouraged us to do just that. In any given issue of a feminist journal and in every collection of feminist essays (by far the preferred format of feminist scholarship), there are essays that inevitably discuss data, whether factual or fictional, with which we are totally unfamiliar. Most of us choose to read a broad spectrum of these articles (which we would skip over in a more specialized journal), precisely because they allow us to understand the multiple contexts that inform feminism—and that feminism informs—and so the context, the contexture, that *is* feminism.

My argument grants an unusual degree of power and thus importance to the choice of context. If, in one sense, this provides a particularly strong incentive to fulfill traditional expectations that an introduction will outline the content and the structure of the book to come, such a procedure also directly contradicts every assertion that I have made so far about the contextual nature of my own thought and of written feminism in general. Contexts are spatial structures that do not lend themselves easily to linear development. Their exploration proceeds in the manner of a spiral, an image characteristic of women's studies as a whole: the construction of knowledge from an interdisciplinary perspective requires that we return repeatedly to the same questions, only to discover that they are no longer the same but have been altered by virtue of the repetition itself.

In the words of T. S. Eliot, "We shall not cease from exploration / And the end of all our exploring / Will be to arrive where we started / And know the place for the first time" ("Little Gidding" 5.26–29). At the beginning of this (ad)venture, then, I shall note only that Cardinal provides a context that allows us to explore written feminism in relation to culture, language, narration, and psychoanalysis. She asks us to be inclusive, to enlarge the boundaries of discussion, to unsettle distinctions, to overcome divisions, and to make new connections. No doubt this is why my "we" remains, depending on your perspective, so slippery or so fluid, so contradictory or so adaptable; why I can simultaneously agree and disagree with the other feminist voices that have and will intersect with mine; why I can express equal concern, as in the case of translation or comparativism, about the presence and the absence of an identical critical practice; why I have so far declined either to define *textual* and *feminist* or to deny these terms to any female text and to any woman writer yet encountered.[16]

NOTES

1. When I speak of *gender specificity*, I refer only to the historical fact that men and women have had distinctive societal experiences. Although these have often mediated physiological differences as well, my own concern is never with biology or anatomy as such. Since I am also not engaged in a comparative study of male and female writing, I do not mean to suggest that textual practices that seem to be "characteristic" or "typical" of women do not and might not also appear in the texts of men.

2. For example, the editors of the *Yale French Studies* (62) devoted to "Feminist Readings: French Texts/American Contexts" introduce division into feminism itself by separating "text" and "context" along national and linguistic lines.

3. Unless otherwise specified, all future definitions and etymologies are cited from *The American Heritage Dictionary of the English Language*. Not

only does this dictionary carefully address its own ideological premises (one of which leads to the important inclusion of an index to Indo-European roots), but it was among the first to confront the problem of sexism in its definitions and examples. In the case of French, all similar references are to *Le Grand Robert*.

4. See, for example, Elaine Showalter, *A Literature of Their Own* and Janice Radway.

5. Similarly, in Gayle Greene and Coppélia Kahn's introduction to *Making a Difference: Feminist Literary Criticism,* they define feminist literary criticism as "one branch of interdisciplinary inquiry which takes gender as a fundamental organizing category of experience" (1).

6. All translations from the French are my own, unless otherwise indicated.

7. Yalom also devotes a chapter to *La Souricière,* but this early novel is of interest to her only in relation to *Les Mots pour le dire,* of which she argues it constitutes an alternative version. (*Devotion and Disorder,* the English translation of *Les Grands Désordres,* appeared in the fall of 1990.)

8. In point of fact, my own article in *Tulsa Studies in Women's Literature* does constitute a (double) exception; the only literary text that I consider is Cardinal's *Une Vie pour deux.* Marguerite LeClézio's and Françoise Lionnet's articles on *Les Mots pour le dire* also differ from the norm in that they use other Francophone texts (Jeanne Hyvrard's *Mère la mort* and Marie-Thérèse Humbert's *A l'autre bout de moi*) as their comparative base. Since LeClézio and Lionnet are of Francophone origin, however, their critical acts of appropriation simply offer a mirror image of those of American critics.

9. Alice Jardine (*Gynesis*) also notes that the "comparativism" that has been much promoted in American interdisciplinary study can lead to a critique of cultural ideology but may operate "concretely as well—most notably in the forms of racism and colonialism" (14).

10. To cite only the work of individual authors, see, for example, Alice Jardine, Jane Gallop, Nancy K. Miller, Shoshana Felman, Shari Benstock, and the introduction to Elissa Gelfand and Virginia Thorndike Hules's recent bibliography of French feminist theory. Although their textual focus is very different from mine, Jardine shares my concern with the problematic interaction of text and context (15) and Felman my interest in fusing Francophone and Anglo-Saxon contexts into "a plural place" and "a dialogic perspective" (19).

11. Gelfand and Hules, however, very carefully include the work produced by both Belgian and Québecois women in their annotated bibliography of French feminist theory. As they note, the decision to focus on a commonality of concerns and approaches inevitably underplays "the historical and cultural factors that do contribute a unique tonality to these other Francophone voices" (xliv, note 2). This important question of difference (already fully present within the respective contexts of either American or French feminism) seems to me to

be somewhat less problematic when considering contemporary *written* feminism, divorced, however falsely, from the political action of the women's movement. Of course, French and English are also spoken (and written) in other parts of the world by a great many women whose words will not be taken into account here.

12. On the issue of the dependence of feminist theoreticians on the patriarchal authority of "male models," Laurie Fink argues that the Anglophone feminist critique of "theory" should be understood as an explicit attack on the "*particular* theories, primarily those emerging from France since the early 1960's" (262) that have informed Francophone feminist writing.

13. Furman's argument depends on an identical interpretation of authorial intention in women and men writers; it therefore fails, in my view, to take gender into account: "When a textual reader steadfastly ignores an author's presumed intentions or the assumed meaning of a literary work, it is a serious act of insubordination, for it puts into question the authority of authors, that is to say the propriety of paternity. . . . Betrayal of authorial trust therefore implies denial of patriarchal rule" (71).

14. Indeed, the "repetitiveness" of feminist criticism and theory, its interdependence and interconnections that create a strong and supportive sense of collective thought, makes the writing of "Notes" among the most difficult of critical tasks. The extensive footnotes in *Signs* may best exemplify the pattern of sisterhood that feminist scholarship appropriately claims as its own. Despite the convenience of the MLA's recent substitution of "Works Cited" for a more extensive listing of bibliographical sources, such a limited reference system inevitably renders it impossible to credit the many and diverse works that have informed all of our thinking in the last fifteen years. I apologize in advance for my inevitable failure to "cite" a great many of the women (and men) who have influenced me.

15. I am not alone in discerning a pronounced pro-American bias in Showalter (nor will this be the last instance I will need to point out). See, for example, Moi 75; see also note 12.

16. Notably, I shall characterize Cardinal's work as "feminist" throughout this study, although she, like many other Francophone writers such as Hélène Cixous (whom I shall similarly qualify), consistently rejects this description. In Cardinal's case, her hostility to the term seems to result from semantics (a very particular definition by virtue of which feminism would exclude men) and from personal circumstances (dissatisfaction with the political activities of certain French feminist groups in the mid-seventies.) Although I do not wish to limit my own sense of "feminism" by the potential overprecision of definition, I assume that feminist scholarship includes the following: a focus on issues of gender, including a reconsideration of traditional gender roles; a commitment to the interdisciplinary nature of knowledge; and a belief that women's texts and

the reality of women's daily lives are in some way connected. Although I will often use *feminism* in the singular, I always conceive it pluralistically as *feminisms*. Thus, if I am quite willing to apply it to people who might prefer that I not do so, I am, on the other hand, quite unwilling to use it for purposes of exclusion. My problems with the term *textual* stem less from the word itself than from my original desire to substitute it consistently for *literary*. Since, however, this has quickly proved to be an unwieldy and (overly) repetitive solution to my doubts about the second term, I use *literary* in its etymological sense (from Latin *litterarius,* of writing) as a synonym for *textual.* When I mean to designate the writing of a certain perceived quality or official stature that *literary* has come to connote, I prefer the term *aesthetic.*

CHAPTER ONE

Female Culture
The Repetition of Difference

Feminists share with all critics, and perhaps with all writers, the struggle to untie the knot of intricate and apparently inextricable strands of thought whose entanglement paradoxically first prepares and then precludes writing. Initially, it always seems urgent to say everything at once, a state of mental (con)fusion often aggravated by the simultaneous and contradictory convictions that there exist both a single "right" beginning and progression and multiple possibilities for introducing and ordering the same argument. To the extent that critics also continue to hold some perception of ourselves as representative readers, our discomfort may be further heightened by the textual practice that helped to produce it in the first place, for critics are of necessity *re*readers, a definition that at once reflects both our identity with and our difference from those for whom we profess to write.

My current endeavor to reread and rewrite a series of texts whose very existence as a body of work depends upon Marie Cardinal's prior commitment to repeated rereadings and rewritings of her own novels and essays suggests that feminists may encounter this common critical dilemma in a particularly acute and complex form (though, of course, I am fully aware that this too must be a widely shared belief). Still, as feminist critics, we do need to be especially aware and wary of reading habits distinctly different from those of many of the women whose lives we claim literature can help to alter. Similarly, the linear and logical patterns of thought that have been the customary prerequisite for writing may in our case prove not only elusive but distinctly unsuitable for fulfilling our stated purpose of understanding and translating the specific realities of female lives. Yet, Cardinal's representative practice also suggests the possibility of a curious reversal; the inscription within feminism of a problematic typical of the critical process in general appears to transform rereading and rewriting into techniques particularly suited to the exploration of the textual forms of women's lives and culture. The title of Cardinal's seventh book, *Autrement dit,* appropriately names the strategy by which women writers say it *again* in order to say it *differently.*

A Model for Female Culture

Among the many and varied images that function throughout Marie Cardinal's work as internal duplications of general structural patterns, that of a plant indigenous to the otherwise barren Brazilian *sertão* enjoys an unusual degree of visibility. Not only does the description recur with noticeable frequency, but subsequent versions make specific reference to previous ones: "Journey to the country of roots. I have already had occasion to describe this tree of the Brazilian sertão which burrows so deep in search of water that only thick clumps of it remain visible on the surface. These clumps are the very tips of its branches for, in reality, the colossal tree stands over six meters high" (PR 99; cf. MD 198–99, VD 158).

The plant, whose surface appearance of fragile and isolated brush hides an interconnected network of common roots that plunge deep into the earth to support and nourish what is in fact a single immense tree, always serves as an analogy for some aspect of women's struggle with their cultural heritage.[1] Cardinal uses variant contexts to stress the ambivalence that women experience as they seek alternately or simultaneously to free themselves from cultural ties that imprison them and to rediscover or create new ones that give them strength. Of particular importance here is the general connection that Cardinal establishes between formal and thematic repetition, clearly conceived as the interaction of both identity and difference, and a specifically female relationship to culture. The plant that she describes might also serve as an apt metaphor for contemporary written feminism, whose intercultural conflicts conceal a common core that both nourishes diversity and marks it as essentially "superficial" (on the surface, insignificant).

On a broader narrative scale, the scene to which Cardinal returns most often, the story of a harvest recounted at length in five different works and mentioned, often significantly, in all, further clarifies her crucial link between repetition and women's culture. The harvest episodes offer a preliminary illustration of a broadly connotative contexture that characterizes Cardinal's understanding of recurrence. Read as a whole, Cardinal's multiple narratives of the grape harvest in Algeria identify the dominant culture as oppressive, but they also encode the parallel appearance of a specifically female world that both develops on the margins of male culture and begins to infringe on its rights and challenge its norms.

The harvest always combines the related activities of work and celebration, as the backbreaking daily labor culminates in a final night of festival; both domains are traditionally reserved for men. In what might be regarded as the paradigmatic core of Cardinal's harvest scene, the young narrator of *Les Mots pour le dire* (153–59) recalls throwing trinkets from her colonialist family's balcony to the native dancers below in a ritualistic demonstration of the generosity of her class. But the narrator's guilt at her secret desire to join the male dancers extends beyond the betrayal of her family and her social class to include a developing awareness of the cultural restrictions specific to her gender, for she remembers the event in the context of a conversation in which her mother introduces her to menstruation as an enforced retreat to an all-female (and an all-European) world.

In *La Clé sur la porte* (153–63) the double threat of male sexuality and cultural mixing becomes explicit. The narrator now recalls flirting with the youngest of the dancers, only to watch in horror as he suddenly exposes his genitals in the course of a convulsion whose sexually provocative nature, however unintentional, provides the only explanation for his ensuing death. Although Cardinal's overt commentary associates these events only with the injustice of colonialism, the insistent contextual emphasis that she places on the male-female relationship and, in particular, on the threat of male sexuality encourages us to decode colonialism as a metaphor for women's ambivalent cultural position. Cardinal suggests that women in general, on the model of her female characters, are trapped between contradictory and conflicting commitments to a dominant culture of oppressors and a muted culture of the oppressed; moreover, the specific oppression of gender extends beyond the boundaries of race and class to result simultaneously in women's cultural isolation.

Two other versions of the harvest address this problem through the technique of reversal. *La Mule de Corbillard* offers a variant unique in Cardinal's work: for years the totally autonomous female hero harvests her own vineyards without any assistance. This is Cardinal's only book to describe the actual daily routine of the harvest in an attentive detail in keeping with the pleasure that the narrator derives from her competent performance of a task explicitly characterized not just as the work of men but of non-European men in particular. In *Ecoutez la mer* (152–59) Cardinal pursues a parallel substitution for the harvest festival. Here the child who dances to his death in *La Clé sur la porte* gradually draws the young female narrator into the dance. As she gains confidence, she begins to dance alone, becoming "a dance of love" (158) for the land and the people of Algeria; importantly, girls and women progressively join the group of men gathered around her. Read in juxtaposition, the substitution of the girl for the boy has provoked a clear alteration in worldview. Shared love has replaced sexual fear and aggression; the joy of life has taken the place of the horrors of sudden death; hierarchical divisions based on gender and race have given way to an integrated community.

The different contexts of the harvest passage within *Ecoutez la mer,* where it is internally recurrent, reinforce this sense of the emergence of a more clearly female-centered culture. Maria's first recollections of the dance are interspersed with passages describing her and Karl in the act of making love; even though her confidence in his love initially helps Maria to recover the memory of her childhood, here the male child dances alone and he lies unconscious as the sequence concludes (52–53). Only at the end of the novel, when the reintegration of her past and present selves allows Maria to emerge from the near-suicidal depression provoked by Karl's abandonment, does the female child dance into life and love (156–59). Significantly, it is precisely this version of the harvest scene that Cardinal chooses to repeat as an integral block in *Autrement dit* (149–55). Although its new context at first appears to reintroduce sexual discord—Cardinal claims to have written *Ecoutez la mer* to arouse her husband's jealousy—in fact, his love responds to and confirms her rebirth as writer: "I'm in love with the woman who wrote these pages" (MD 168).

Taken together, Cardinal's harvest passages suggest her determination to explore the implications for women of three intertwined associations of the concept *culture:* the cultivation of the soil or, ironically, the exclusion from culture; social and intellectual formation or the integration into the dominant culture; intellectual and artistic activity or the creation of an alternate culture. Lest I seem to have sacrificed logic to rhetorical balance, I will explain more fully the intersections of this model. The original sense of *culture* (from the Latin *colere,* to till, cultivate) marks a primitive and privileged harmony of nature and culture that contrasts sharply with the opposition to nature that explicitly defines the figurative meanings of *culture.* Thus, in Cardinal's work, the cultivation of the land is denied to women *as women* in the name of their integration into a class culture that is based, in particular, on the rigid definition of gender roles. A newly formulated female culture restores the lost harmony with nature and allows women to reintegrate the land from which Cardinal's narrators always remain in conscious exile. Etymologically, *culture* derives from the Indo-European root *kwel-,* to revolve, and in her most recent reflection on the sense of the harvest, Cardinal explicitly connects it to the very particular meaning that she attaches to the notion of repetition: "There are cycles. There are repetitions that are not stammerings. Everything is always the same and nothing is ever the same. Progression takes place in renewed beginnings. Progression toward what? why? how? There is no security" (PR 105).

The Female Literary Tradition

The observation that writers repeat themselves, that they tend to show a decided preference for particular kinds of characters, plots, or narrative structures, constitutes, of course, an obvious critical redundancy in and of itself, a repetition that is perhaps a "stammering" (from the Indo-European root *stam-,* to push, force). As Cardinal notes, "writers always produce the same book" (Interview, *Parispoche*). Still, if her immediate qualification—"But the writing and the viewpoint differ"—has scarcely any claim to originality either, the notion of recurrence nonetheless occupies a central position in recent and current discussions within feminist theory and feminist literary criticism. Many of those works within the Anglophone feminist tradition whose stature already approaches the canonic argue for a specificity of femaleness based on the repetition and the repetitiveness of women's lives. Feminist historians, such as Nancy Cott, Carroll Smith-Rosenberg, and Gerda Lerner, have identified and described a "female culture," a specifically female sphere of activities and values that developed in the nineteenth century out of women's shared physiological and societal experience.

Within this theoretical framework, feminist literary critics have posited a distinctive female literary tradition as one particularly visible and significant manifestation of women's cultural specificity. Moreover, these critics have quickly extended the concept of a female culture beyond its original historical and experiential boundaries. Thus, if Sandra Gilbert and Susan Gubar initially focused on the female literary tradition in nineteenth-century England and America (*Madwoman*), their recent *Norton Anthology of Literature by Women: The Tradition in English*, a work whose very existence marks the general acceptance of this concept within literary criticism, examines the female tradition from the Middle Ages to the present. Gilbert and Gubar's use of a wide range of parallel terms—*female culture* appears alternatively as *female imagination, female consciousness, female creativity*, and *female community*—signals its vastly increased sphere of reference.

On the other hand, the linguistic boundaries of the female literary tradition have proved more resilient and certainly more problematic. Although one of the very earliest works to examine women's literary "undercurrent," Ellen Moers's *Literary Women*, includes women writing in French and English, Moers's study is based on a theory of direct influence between and among women who read and reacted to the works of their precursors and contemporaries. Moreover, Moers's undisputed historical importance should not obscure the now evident fact that she did not understand language to be of significance in the expression of meaning. The simple assertion in Gilbert and Gubar's *Norton Anthology* that all the texts included are "of course" in the English language similarly reflects the consistent determination of Anglo-American criticism to limit the female literary tradition to the study of content: the recurrent "patterns, themes, problems, and images" (Showalter, *Lit.* 11) whose common focus on experience specific to women directly links them to the female culture at their origin. Significantly, the restriction of the female literary tradition in Anglophone criticism to works written in English has not resulted, as one would have expected, in the detailed analysis of women's linguistic peculiarities but has rather produced the illusion of a linguistically unified body of work whose transparency appears to have erased language as an issue requiring attentive study.[2]

Here originates the well-known discomfort of Anglo-American feminist critics faced with their Francophone counterparts whose parallel investigations of a female culture and a female literary tradition often fuse in the hypothesis of an *écriture féminine* or an *écriture de femme*, a specifically female written discourse. Many provocative attempts to understand and to bridge this complex disagreement about women and language have appeared recently—notably, Toril Moi demonstrates how both complete commitment to *écriture féminine,* on the one hand, and its total rejection, on the other, severely limit feminist thought and action. More provocatively, Gilbert and Gubar reconceptualize *écriture féminine* as the fantasy of an original mother tongue visible throughout the Anglo-American female tradition (*No Man's* 236). In an opposite but parallel reversal, Margaret Homans discovers in the very Anglophone writers who most confidently assert the representability of female experience an underlying anxiety about the adequacy of language ("Her Very").[3]

These recent studies typify the fascination that *écriture féminine* continues to hold for Anglo-American critics. Whether they seek to understand, dismiss, borrow, or redefine the concept, they consistently limit French feminist thought on women's literary activity to this single idea. Without denying either the general importance or the particular originality of a linguistic theory to which I will often need to return, I want to look briefly at another kind of Francophone feminist criticism that has quietly appeared in print while many of us continued to assert that nothing that could properly be identified as feminist *literary* criticism was being written in France. Indeed, even Claudine Herrmann's *Voleuses de langue,* usually cited as the exception that proves the rule, has begun to lose its status as an anomaly within the Francophone tradition; one recent reference uses Herrmann's subsequent academic career in the United States to justify the reinsertion of even this early work within an Anglo-American context (Moi 178). And yet recent studies by Michel Mercier (*Le Roman féminin*) and Béatrice Didier (*L'Ecriture-Femme*) posit a female literary tradition in terms very similar to those of their American predecessors; indeed, for anyone familiar with Anglo-American feminist literary criticism, the fact that Mercier and Didier clearly do not share such familiarity may initially seem responsible for the virtual absence of a theoretical framework that appears to characterize their work. Still, the fact that they independently reach many of the same conclusions about recurrent themes in women's literature strongly supports the notion of a female literary tradition and convincingly extends it for the first time beyond the barriers of language. Mercier's and Didier's inclusion of non-Francophone writers in their own studies, without recourse to a hypothesis of direct influence, also reiterates internally the commonality revealed by an external comparison with the findings of Showalter and others.

But the focus on *écriture féminine* as a thematics or content, which Mercier and Didier share with Anglo-American critics, in fact leads us astray precisely to the extent that it raises the expectation of a common theoretical framework. Two contemporary works by Suzanne Lamy (*d'elles*) and Irma Garcia (*Promenade femmelière*) help to clarify what is particular to Francophone explorations of women's writing; their common perspective also emphasizes the frequent theoretical fusions found in the work of French (Garcia) and Québecois (Lamy) feminists. In contrast to most Anglophone critics, for whom the notions of a female literary tradition and a female culture are always interdependent and at times indistinguishable, Lamy and Garcia approach the female literary tradition as an autonomous entity that can be explored in isolation from the lives of women writers and, indeed, from women's lives in general. Women's writing is a cultural phenomenon in and of itself. Lamy attributes the women's texts of her *écriture au féminin* to a contemporary crisis of values, and Garcia's *écriture féminine* begins with modernism, defined historically as "a societal change that directly imposed a different connection to writing" (13). Consequently, a particular relationship to writing characterizes female specificity and determines rather than illustrates a specifically female relationship to culture. Similarly, the recurrent in women's writing does not so much reflect women's shared experience as constitute it; writing creates rather than manifests female solidarity. Lamy's and Garcia's reconceptualization of the problematic of women's culture and women's writing allows them to extend their analyses beyond the consideration of representative female experience, that is, of thematic content, to focus their attention on language and form.

Interestingly, both Lamy and Garcia identify repetition as a specifically female form. From the role that memory plays in women's writing, Garcia derives the characteristic pattern of the individual text and its expansion into the intertexuality that defines the female literary tradition: "But, by a mirror effect, writing takes on the form of memory as recalls, returns, echos, repetitions, redundancies are inscribed in the syntax and the structure of the writing. . . . woman constantly retraces her steps, advancing prudently, inperceptibly. This is why, as a result, her works echo each other, answer each other, call out to each other, prolonging each other beyond individualities" (1:225). For Lamy too, litany, defined as "every form based on repetition" (62), "circulates from one piece of writing to another, creeps into the majority of texts written by women" (63).

At this point of intersection where Francophone and Anglophone feminist critics begin to repeat themselves and, more importantly, each other, Marie Cardinal's work stands out as exemplary. I propose, therefore, to reverse the critical direction described here by Garcia and Lamy and generally characteristic of studies of the female literary tradition. Rather than read multiple individual texts in search of the common themes and patterns that ultimately allow the identification of a female tradition, I examine the recurring forms and motifs and the process of recurrence itself within the work of a single writer. I am convinced that such a practice will in the particular case of Cardinal also reveal a great deal about written feminism in general, far more perhaps than studies aimed at defining a common tradition have revealed to date about individual writers.

Multicultural Dialogue

The progress(ion) of Cardinal's own work also "takes place in renewed beginnings" (PR 105). In the hope of "advancing prudently," if "imperceptibly," I too want to retrace my own steps to reexamine Cardinal's understanding of culture on the basis of a 1986 essay, her introduction to *La Médée d'Euripide*, in which she addresses the issue explicitly. Although in many ways Cardinal outlines a theory of culture that clearly resembles that of the Anglophone feminists whose work Elaine Showalter usefully synthesizes in "Feminist Criticism in the Wilderness," here, too, identity remains inextricably intertwined with difference ("Everything is always the same and nothing is ever the same"). The desire to repeat Cardinal's own words, which this paragraph already illustrates, informs my discussion throughout this section, in part, no doubt, because of the relative rarity in her work of the direct expression of general ideas. On the other hand, the practice of citation also enacts and reflects what I have described as a feminist practice of rereading and rewriting.

Feminist historians such as Gerda Lerner logically position culture within history itself, fully in keeping with their professional identity as historians of women's culture. For similar reasons, their desire to transform the content, meaning, and methodology of historical inquiry does not call history itself into question, either as discipline or as a potentially accurate record of past events. Although Cardinal too critiques history from within, stressing in particular the persistent exclusion of women that belies its methodological claims to comprehensiveness and objectivity (ME 36–37), she also defines history and culture as autonomous forces that oppose each other as enemy and ally: "the adversary of women and, more generally, of all those who are exploited . . . is not Culture but History" (ME 36). For Cardinal, history functions as an institution that arranges facts to support dominant ideology; culture, in contrast, responds freely to the impetus provided by the works of individuals:

> History, Culture.
> Those two again!
> For if the same goes for History as for Culture, namely that both of them devour everything in sight, still they don't resemble each other. History swallows what those in power make her swallow and she follows the path they make her take. As for Culture, she is nourished by individuals and she is free. . . .
> History absorbs facts, Culture absorbs works. (ME 45)

Both the fact of the distinction that Cardinal makes as well as the form in which she makes it—the capital letters that simultaneously personify history and culture as dynamic forces and fix them as absolutes—also help us situate her thought in relation to anthropological theories of female culture such as that outlined by Edwin Ardener and adopted by Showalter. The model of a muted female culture partially contained within a dominant (male) culture invites, despite Showalter's frequent protestations, two important objections: first, that its notion of a "wild zone" outside dominant culture remains strongly reminiscent of the Victorian notion of "separate spheres"; and second, that by defining culture on the basis of gender, it obscures the differences of race, class, religion, and ethnic identity that separate women. Although Showalter explicitly states that women can be expected to function within several muted groups at once, her own focus on female culture alone and, more importantly, the visual model of muted and dominant culture, figured by two intersecting circles, suggest a fundamentally dualistic view of cultural interaction that Lerner makes explicit: "women live a duality" (qtd. in Showalter 199).

If such a theoretical formulation, now prevalent in all areas of Anglophone feminist thought, implicitly acknowledges the tensions and the contradictions inherent in women's cultural position, it also assumes an equality of value and an enriching exchange between the two cultures that strongly conflicts with Cardinal's personal experience of biculturalism. Her self-definition as "Arab-French, French-Arab" (Muller) leads not to the recognition of identity that such a verbal reflection might suggest but rather to a repetitious experience of alienation, a "division" within her own self (PR 56) that provokes a constant state of "disequilibrium," verging on "neurosis" (PR 20). The chiasmic refrain of her biculturalism in fact reflects the imprisonment that results from this "war between two cultures" (PR 20): "Double culture, double freedom, one might think, but it's just the opposite. Freedom cannot be lived in two different fashions" (PR 111).

Within Cardinal's thematics, the French-Arab bicultural war that Algeria literally incarnates stands in opposition to the multiculturalism of the Mediterranean: "The Mediterranean is overpopulated and active. Different Cultures have intersected there since the beginning of time" (ME 14). Cardinal's constant characterization of both the Mediterranean in general and Algeria in particular as female (far beyond what their grammatical identity as feminine nouns requires) suggests a deliberate effort to write the cultural difference of gender into the text. Margaret Homans ("Her Very") and Rachel DuPlessis both argue that marginality in at least two areas provides the most suggestive origin for women writers, precisely because it offers them a context within which they can reveal the specificity of gender oppression.[4]

Cardinal's refusal to "live a duality" helps clarify her linguistic preference for cultural coordination (History *and* women, Culture *and* women) over the subordination (the History or Culture *of* women) that implies either (or both) separation and a too easy alliance. The difference between the two formulas, reinforced by Cardinal's insistent capitalization, reveals her refusal to qualify, to en-gender, history or culture, in order to respect both their unity and their plurality. For Cardinal, history relates the past of humanity as a whole; those experiences that have been omitted from the official record nonetheless constitute an integral part of human history: "the missing pieces of the historical puzzle" (ME 38). But a unified history also implies solidarity—hence Cardinal's insistence, in the passage quoted above, on a certain commonality of oppression—and, therefore, difference. The integrity of my initial citation can be restored by the reinsertion of the parenthetical contention—"the adversary of women and, more generally, of all those who are exploited (for the cause of women is the cause of people; Feminism was and must remain a humanism) is not Culture but History" (ME 36)—by which Cardinal too restores integrity. (Parentheses here point not to digression or subordination but to an underlying, that is, an essential, observation).

Moreover, plurality does not result only from the association of different groups of people; it also characterizes the internal organization of any particular group. Thus women cannot hope to reenter human history or to alter human culture simply by proposing an alternative image of female experience, since it has been precisely in terms of just such a single, uniform, endlessly repetitive image of this experience that official history and culture have always represented and restrained women. Only the multiplication and the pluralization of heterogeneous images, only the repetition of difference, can provide an accurate description of women's reality and destabilize the reductionary model that has been imposed on our experience: "How did the image of she who is called Woman enter Culture? When? Why? Chase this image and replace it not by another unique image, but by other images, lots of other images" (ME 33). Cardinal considers such a substitution of pluralism for singularity to have been the most important outcome of feminist activism of the sixties: "We stirred things up, the image of woman grew fuzzy; in its place were outlined the gazes and voices of women. These gazes and voices, imprecise but new and strong, entered dailiness, Culture" (ME 32).

If I appear to be repeating Cardinal apparently repeating herself, I do so deliberately to emphasize how she articulates the intersections of the same and the different, the singular and the plural. The "fuzzy" and the "imprecise," the blurred outlines of this new portrait of women, result from a dynamic conception of the image that records both multiplicity and metamorphosis at a speed just rapid enough to allow the simultaneous perception of resemblance and of diversity—of gender and of women. I have, of course, just described the filmic image of early cinema that Cardinal herself uses to introduce *Une Vie pour deux:* "it's a Chaplin film that produces laughter and tears, that flickers, and whose single jerky image is composed of a thousand still, fugitive, unconnected images" (9). The tree of the Brazilian *sertão* with which I began this chapter reiterates within the natural world this same structure of identity and difference.

Oddly enough, up to the very moment of writing this paragraph, I had always been baffled by Cardinal's assertion in *Au Pays de mes racines* that her imagination depends as much on the visual image as on the verbal: "My mind progresses through juxtaposed illustrations. My thought is a comic strip" (182). But, in fact, her visual images, whose repetitiveness compensates for their rarity, have a special significance— and are especially significant—in her work. As with the two examples above, they identify her particular understanding of the complexity of gender; more importantly, they name the essentially spatial—and therefore visual—pattern of repetitions by which her texts represent the difference of individual women, the identity of female experience, and the dynamic mobility of their interaction.

If women figure so prominently among those "individuals" from whom "Culture" seeks "nourishment," why then does female cultural activity nonetheless remain largely unheard or misunderstood? Cardinal attributes this to history's elaboration of an official language of "truth," a scientific and technical language that eliminates subjectivity and ambiguity—and, consequently, women themselves: "It is obvious that . . . we cannot [*nous ne pouvons pas*] use this language and that, as a result, we cannot be heard by historians" (ME 39). This position on language and culture clashes sharply with that of Showalter, who asserts that "all language is the language of the dominant order, and women, if they speak at all, must speak through it" (200). Cardinal, in contrast, clearly does not equate the language of the dominant order with language itself; in her view, women's inability to use such language renders them only incomprehensible, not mute. Moreover, this first *nous ne pouvons pas* ("we cannot"), which initially appears to denote an impossibility ("we are unable to"), must in fact be read as a refusal ("we must not allow ourselves to"), for Cardinal goes on to propose that we borrow "their" language to show the historians of the official, in the only terms that they can understand, the misogyny that determines and falsifies their thought as a whole. As the general context and the introduction at this point of the specific example of Elizabeth Badinter's *L'Un est l'autre* reveal, however, such a language suits only a particular kind of discourse. In this sense, Cardinal does not so much call upon women to adopt official scientific language as their means of expression as to produce the works of feminist history and theory that have been far more prevalent in the United States and England than in France. Her own desire to respect the commitment that she asks others to make presumably explains her recourse here to a (relatively) more traditional essay form, a (relatively) more straightforward narrative, and a (relatively) more abstract language than she uses elsewhere.

Re-En-Gendering Theory and Practice

Like cultural expression's apparent accessibility to both women and men, interest in repetition initially seems to unite not just feminist critics but literary critics as a whole. Yet, even as Peter Brooks describes repetition as "so basic to our experience of literary texts that one is simultaneously tempted to say all and to say nothing on the subject" (99), his stipulation that an element must occur at least three times to be perceived by readers as repetition introduces the paradoxical possibility that the act of repetition itself will pass unseen. Certainly, the critical reception of Cardinal's work raises this specter as it suggests that repetition poses particular and particularly curious problems for women writers. Since the 1975 success of *Les Mots pour le dire*, scarcely any review of Cardinal's subsequent publications has failed to characterize the later work as a slightly altered version of the earlier novel. When such rapprochements go beyond mere assertion, their justification produces only vague references to vaguely similar situations, such as the presence of childhood memories, a focus on the maternal role, or a common setting in Algeria.

Despite such apparently clear signs of critical interest in textual echo in Cardinal's work, not only have the parallels actually cited not resulted in any concrete analysis, and often not even in the comparative judgments that we might think virtually unavoidable, but they have somehow succeeded in totally blinding reviewers to the pervasive presence in Cardinal's work of literal repetition, the word-for-word quotation of extensive passages from other texts. Lest it seem that I am unfairly imposing the standards of the scholarly essay on the book review, let me note that the obsessive interest that reviewers themselves show for a particular kind of repetition in Cardinal's work unfolds in a literary climate in which the practice of autocitation has long been recognized as a common and important technique in the contemporary texts of the predominantly male practitioners of the French New Novel. And precisely therein, I would suggest, lies the explanation for the selective critical blindness toward this aspect of Cardinal's work. Because critics do not view the repetition that they locate in women's texts as a problem—and, even less, as a solution—of a specifically or even distinctly literary nature, its use by female writers as an aesthetic strategy, however blatant, goes entirely unnoticed.

In Cardinal's case, reviewers have used the conviction that her work is straightforwardly autobiographical (the fact of their assertion is not immediately relevant, though its predictability and simplicity are hard to ignore) both to treat everything that she writes as an alternative version of the same story and to define repetition as being temporarily devoid of literary interest. Similarly, in a larger context, critics have long maintained a highly selective awareness of the practice of repetition in women's writings; viewed as an inevitable reflection of the repetitiveness attributed simultaneously to women's lives and to the female creativity those lives are presumed to delimit, it functions as a single paradoxical gesture to bring female art into being and to deny its very existence. We can recognize here the persistence of two of the main strategies that Joanna Russ identifies in her catalog of traditional prohibitions to women's literature, a combination of "The Double Standard of Content—She wrote it but look what she wrote about" and "False Categorizing—She wrote it, but she isn't really an artist, and it isn't really art" (chaps. 5–6).

Such contradictions may help to explain why conventional critical and cultural belief in the homogeneity of women's writings could not lead to and cannot be confused with the contemporary feminist theory of a specifically female literary tradition. At the same time, their undeniable similarity offers an important message of caution. Attention to the multiple and important ways in which the forms and content of women's writings comment on the reality of women's lives need not preclude careful attention to their simultaneous functioning as specifically textual ways of making meaning; furthermore, it *should not do so* to the extent that we are interested in determining the specificity of male or female contributions to a common culture. As is clearly indicated by the use to which repetition has been put, defining a single concept or form as the simultaneous marker of gender and literature can result only in either the global exclusion of one sex from cultural production or the institution of two totally autonomous cultural traditions.

If women writers' (ab)use of repetition—the very writing practice that in theoretical studies determines the literary character of a text—is turned back on them to become the definitive sign of their exile from the domain of literature, the paradox doesn't stop there. This curious inversion extends further to embrace the distinctive reading practice that unites literary critics beyond all methodological differences. For the a priori assumption that women writers individually and collectively always tell the same repetitive story theoretically dispenses with any actual need to reread, even as it makes women's texts the privileged illustration of the general process of rereading.[5] Thus, on several occasions I have heard a group of readers discuss Marie Cardinal's work at length on the basis of each individual's knowledge of a different single text. Any work by Cardinal can be substituted for any other; similarly, Duras can be substituted for Cardinal.

Perhaps the suggestive link that repetition establishes between women's texts and general literary practices of writing and reading can provide us with a thread to unravel such false syllogisms and to find our way out of this logical labyrinth. In her study of modernist women's writing, in which she explicitly identifies the textually recurrent with the female specific, Irma Garcia makes their mutual visibility dependent on readers' willingness to reread: "These passages, which we have set apart as quotations, may escape notice in the course of a linear reading; but they stand out, they catch the eye during a rereading, the decisive moment at which to perceive and to follow the traces of the feminine" (286).[6] These "echoes that . . . are going to show up in the reappearance of the same groups of sentences, in the repetition of entire paragraphs" (233), correspond to Marie Cardinal's quotation of passages from her own previous works, the most original of the different forms of repetition that she uses. With one exception, such passages appear unannounced and unaccompanied by quotation marks or any other sign that would distinguish them from the surrounding text; indeed, concern for contextual coherence sometimes appears to motivate such minor alterations as the ellipsis of a phrase or the substitution of a word. Yet, the juxtaposition of the two texts identifies them beyond any doubt as integral repetitions.

Thus, an interest in teaching us how to read, similar to Garcia's, may have motivated Cardinal's sudden decision in 1980 to announce and identify the textual activity that she had been content to practice for the preceding ten years: "In each of my manuscripts I repeat a passage from an earlier manuscript. . . . This time certain lines of *Les Mots pour le dire* force themselves upon me" (PR 194). Few readers of Cardinal will have forgotten the extraordinary chapter in question, in which the novel's narrator finally confronts the memory of her mother's "dirty trick" (*saloperie*). In the course of a conversation designed to prepare her pubescent daughter not so much for the physical reality of menstruation as for the sexual vulnerability that it institutes (and institutionalizes), the mother relates her determined attempts to provoke the spontaneous abortion of an unwanted child whom she finally identifies as her listening daughter. But even as Cardinal focuses our attention in *Au Pays de mes racines* (1980) on the return of certain sections of this episode, the curious incompleteness of her avowal thoroughly undermines the apparent directness of her admission and the seeming transparency of the procedure. She entirely neglects to mention that the passage she quotes from *Les Mots pour le dire* (1975) already constitutes a repetition of the final pages of *La Clé sur la porte* (1972). This omission confirms Cardinal's desire to emphasize an important reading and writing strategy rather than to provide a key for the privileged interpretation of her own work, or lament our inability to discover it on our own.

In particular, this first (named) of the five extended examples of identical repetition in Cardinal's work allows further exploration of the relationship between literature and life whose considerable significance to discussions of women's writings has already emerged. Although the apparent ambivalence with which Cardinal "reveals" her practice of autocitation suggests the need to approach similar comments with considerable caution, one particular description of her methods of composition recurs with unusual consistency in interviews and essays.[7] When asked to discuss the creative process, Cardinal tends to respond in terms that indicate that she makes a clear-cut and absolute distinction within her own work between the two categories of autobiography and fiction. She characterizes books of the first group not only by their relationship to her own lived experience—she insists, for example, that *Au Pays de mes racines, Autrement dit,* and *La Clé sur la porte* "are entirely my life" (Breen 13)—but, far more significantly, by their relationship to books of the second group. The ease of writing that Cardinal associates with autobiography contrasts sharply with the long periods of writer's block that often accompany her production of fiction. At such moments the autobiographical works not only provide a "refuge" from the novels but in fact act as a "springboard" for their writing.

Given this simultaneity of composition, the occasional appearance of parallel passages in paired works suddenly seems more predictable than surprising. From this perspective, the conclusion of *La Clé sur la porte,* the "springboard book" for *Les Mots pour le dire,* would simply constitute a first draft or an early version of what gradually evolves into the central episode of the later work. And yet, upon closer reflection, Cardinal's apparent willingness to identify certain of her books as straightforwardly autobiographical raises far more questions than it answers. For her use of the designation to stress the intimate connection between these works and her novels immediately erases the clarity of the distinction. This seems particularly puzzling in light of the resentment that Cardinal has often expressed toward reviewers and critics, less at their determination to classify her novels as autobiographical than at the subsequent use of this judgment as a justification for totally ignoring the issue of their aesthetic merit.[8] Even as she acknowledges the desire to challenge conventional boundaries of genre that subverts the very distinctions she herself appears to make, she refuses to accept any reduction of her status from writer to witness: "I don't like books to have a clearly defined genre; I like them to be novel, poetry, essay, research, history, and philosophy all at the same time. What I want is for people to recognize that I write, even if I don't write books that are typically female, 'women's novels.' I don't want people to say that I testify. You don't need to be a writer to testify. And I *am* a writer" (AD 87).

Cardinal perceptively outlines here the double bind that women artists face: the choice between the critical marginalization inherent in their designation as writers of "women's novels" and their total exclusion from the domain of literature as producers of autobiography or social documentary. In both cases, of course, women are presumed to draw only upon their own limited experience, further reduced by its enclosure within the bonds of gender. At times, Cardinal also shares the solutions that have traditionally been women's only resource, the frustrating and necessarily unconvincing combination of the denial of the particular—"I don't like myself enough to invite anyone to come meet me, Marie Cardinal" (AD 61)—and the assertion of the general—"As if all novels weren't autobiographical!" (AD 85).[9]

In a much more radical gesture, Cardinal uses the textual practice of repetition to explore the relationship between autobiography and fiction and to undermine it systematically. Cardinal's work offers the unusual opportunity to confront fictionalized and nonfictionalized accounts of the same event without recourse to external documentation.

On the one hand, integral repetition initially seems to confirm conventional beliefs about women's writing by imposing the unexpected conclusion that fiction and autobiography are indeed indistinguishable for Cardinal. Thus, when she is faced in *Au Pays de mes racines* with the task of describing a childhood memory that resurfaces with particular force during a visit to the place where the event actually occurred, she borrows her description of the mother's *saloperie* from *Les Mots pour le dire,* the very novel on whose fictional status she has most often insisted. Since the connection between autobiography and fiction figures that between life and literature, this deliberate merging of the two has extremely important implications for understanding the benefits that women may derive from the act of reading, an issue to which I will return.

On the other hand, however, the specific nature of the fusion that Cardinal operates constitutes an important challenge to the critical practice that uses the presumed autobiographical origin of women's fiction to deny its literary interest. For Cardinal's dependence on a fictional source in the composition of her memoirs also undermines the common assertion that women writers seek inspiration in experiential rather than textual sources. Moreover, the repetitions that circulate throughout Cardinal's work as a whole ultimately succeed in making any such distinction meaningless. Thus, in *Autrement dit,* Cardinal at times totally assumes the identity of the fictional narrator of *Les Mots pour le dire* who, in turn, modifies her role as mother in exact accordance with the description that Cardinal provides of her own behavior in *La Clé sur la porte.* The narrator of the novel *Une Vie pour deux* experiences the same period of conformity to the conventional role of wife and mother that leads the narrator of *Les Mots pour le dire* into madness and to which Cardinal attributes in *Autrement dit* her own personal desire to write.

Clearly, Cardinal's second revelation about the presence of repetition in her work shares the same problematic status as the first, for in fact she rarely limits her textual recurrences to the pairings that she announces. Moreover, in the cases where she does, her exercises in inspiration so disrupt chronology that the traditional priority of autobiography over fiction cannot possibly be asserted. Since, for example, *Les Mots pour le dire* was already in progress at the time of the composition of *La Clé sur la porte,* we can never know which version of the abortion passage might be the "original" and which the "variant." The possession of actual personal data only confuses matters further. In the supposedly autobiographical *La Clé* where Cardinal herself invites us to equate author and narrator, she does not give her children their real names; on the other hand, the parents of the apparently fictional narrator of *Le Passé empiété* are named for Cardinal's own.

As a result, my determined attempts to locate biographical information about Cardinal in the several sources in which it should logically appear have finally convinced me that whether or not the missing references are indicative of sexism, as I once thought, they also form part of her own determined effort to alter our usual thinking about fiction and reality.[10] Autocitation, moreover, functions in a very similar manner. Not only does repetition automatically disorient readers who find themselves referred elsewhere, but my own experience suggests that they will seldom be able to situate the parallel passage(s) immediately, that initially they may not attribute their sense of *déjà vu* to Cardinal's own work at all nor even identify it as a *déjà lu* derived from a textual rather than an experiential source. This disruption of the reading process further supports the fusion of life and literature in Cardinal's work.[11]

Beyond the connections among different texts and between textuality and reality, Cardinal's repetitions also allow her to explore the relationships between and among people. If the substitution of a fictional for a real memory makes *Au Pays de mes racines* exemplary in the first instance, the substitution of another's memory for one's own makes *La Clé sur la porte* equally so in the second. Although, as we know, Cardinal identifies this text as autobiographical, here she attributes the abortion passage to another young woman and transforms herself into a somewhat detached, if sympathetic, confidant. This strategy reflects the degree to which Cardinal's aversion to the autobiographical label stems from her sense of writing as an important source of solidarity and of collective identity for the female community. She locates her particular talent as a writer not in the ability to express her own self but to discover within it "what I have in common with others" (Breen 13), a concern for commonality that remains importantly gender specific: "In my books I think my readers encounter a woman who lives in France today and who at heart resembles all women. That's what I am" (AD 61).

In this perspective, repetition becomes the proof of repeatability. By writing the essential drama of her own past into Moussia's life in *La Clé sur la porte*, Cardinal transforms a strikingly unique and particular experience into a representative female situation and turns an almost inevitable source of isolation and alienation into one of female bonding. As repetition forces us to reread, we do indeed recognize the abortion passage as the representation of a biological and social condition that is both specific and common to women. The mother's efforts to introduce her daughter to the restrictions that culture and nature simultaneously impose on the female life and body perpetuate "the loss of the daughter to the mother, the mother to the daughter" that Adrienne Rich characterizes as "the essential female tragedy" (*Woman* 240).

This act of textual repetition further emphasizes the fundamental nature of textuality itself. Cardinal's practice of autocitation confirms Antoine Compagnon's insightful observation that writing cannot be disassociated from reading, its complementary form: "Quotation repeats; it makes reading resound in writing: this is because reading and writing are in fact one and the same" (27). Cardinal's repetitions thus constitute a perpetual *mise en abyme* of the primary process by which the personal and the individual are alternately encoded and decoded as the common and the cultural. Both the length at which and the exactness with which Cardinal quotes identify her beyond any doubt as her own (re)reader; appropriately, then, she first casts herself in *La Clé sur la porte* in the metaphorical role of listener. At the same time, the complexity of the subtle alterations that Cardinal introduces between two parallel passages (such that they continue to appear qualitatively identical even as their juxtaposition reveals a quantitatively significant number of differences) equates quoting with careful (re)writing. Consequently, Cardinal's account of Moussia's confidences is followed by Moussia's transposition of her own experience into prose poetry. By the combination of method and content, this *venue à l'écriture* marks the woman writer's simultaneous participation in dominant and female literary culture.

That Cardinal associates her textual repetitions with such a feminist practice of reading and writing is evident in the act of integral quotation that concludes *La Clé sur la porte:* "Moussia has just brought me a poem that she wrote, a kind of ballad of the unloved fetus. I recopy it here" (219). Not only does this narrative substitution define female writing as always already in a state of repetition (were we still tempted to view the abortion passages in their chronological order of appearance), but it emphasizes once again the interchangeability of reading and writing. Repetition now becomes the sign of a creative collaboration in which one woman completes the text that another has begun and in which women alternatively read and write their experience into existence. For Irma Garcia, *l'écriture féminine* as a whole constitutes "an act of solidarity with other women" that produces a single, vast "text that is made up of all previous texts" (117).

In this same perspective, one of the more curious (because apparently unintentional) examples of repetition occurs throughout *Autrement dit* where Cardinal's clear preoccupation with the subject of female literacy causes her to return repeatedly to the subject. She now interprets women's writing as inherently collaborative: the individual writer simultaneously brings a common female world into existence and serves as an example that other women can follow. Cardinal's desire to "write for" those women who live within "the essential world of women" but who "don't know how to express what they have understood" (66) has a double value. Not only do these women represent her ideal readers—"I am touched by these women. I would like them to be able to read my books and I confess that I think of them when I write" (65)—but they also implicitly collaborate in the production of work designed to speak their silence: "It's for them that I want to write; I want to give them words that will serve as weapons" (81). By the associations that Cardinal establishes between female knowledge, women's literature, and the revolutionary potential of female reading and writing, she restores a full range of meaning to the concept of literacy (*literate:* 1. Able to read and write. 2. Knowledgeable. 3. Someone who can read and write). In its double etymology, moreover, originates the complementarity of the two activities (from Latin *lit(t)eratus,* acquainted with writings; from *litterae,* writing).

In retrospect, it appears that Cardinal's repetitions may adopt a characteristically female form that can reinscribe the writing of women within the history of literature and of literary theory from which the very exemplariness of their practice initially seemed to exclude them. Antoine Compagnon, who analyzes in *La Seconde main* the multiple forms of quotation as a privileged strategy of textual recurrence, includes autocitation among the "perversions," the "challenges" to "the system" as a whole that "disrupt" its functioning (362). To the extent that "perversion" designates, in particular, a deviant practice of a specifically *sexual* nature, Compagnon seems already to have female difference in mind: the "native" disposition of women to depart from what is considered "proper, right, or good" that in the context of Western literature can only define a male norm. In confirmation of this preliminary linguistic intuition, Compagnon goes on to equate autocitation with the more explicit (and the more explicitly female) perversion of "prostitution" (369). What apparently leads women astray (from Latin *pervertere*, to turn the wrong way) is the desire for *public* exposure (from Latin *prostituere*, to expose publicly). The act of autocitation challenges the "propriety" of female modesty. By repeating herself, Cardinal dares to claim that the female text is in fact citable, that it incorporates what Compagnon identifies as the fundamental power of discourse: the faculty to be repeated and retained (106).

Not surprisingly, then, Compagnon further links the repetitive act with "narcissism" (395); women's admiration for their own selves (for their textual "bodies") has always been seen as excessive. To the extent, moreover, that the literal reproduction characteristic of the exact copy undermines the "normal" structure of quotation by "coupling" two systems that were presumed to be independent and autonomous (370) (the female prostitute, of course, solicits heterosexual intercourse), autocitation incorporates normative male repetition within its own female value system. As if in anticipation, Compagnon consistently chooses metaphors that recall the social and biological reality of women to describe quotation in general. The quoter, for example, "kneads the dough" (31); submits to the need to cite "like a woman about to give birth" (36); or "cuts out," "bastes," and "overcastes" in a metaphorical series that compares quoting to the work of the "dressmaker" (19).

Writing Female Reality: Theoretical Context(s)

This intriguing feminization of critical discourse, of the male "language of history," finds an unexpected analogue in Cardinal's own understanding of cultural expression. While I repeat, in an etymological sense, by turning back to Cardinal's notion of culture, I want one final time to repeat—to quote—Cardinal at considerable length:

> I had to wait until I was over forty to understand that I can produce Culture, that Culture ceaselessly generates her form, like childhood or adolescence; she never grows up, she is immortal... Culture is not meant to be suffered; she is meant to be digested, known, understood, and, especially, made. Her existence is inevitable. She never stops advancing; she feeds on the new, mixes the new with the old to supply a product that we call modern, and continues her perpetual digestion of people's works (of all the works of all the people, without the least exception, without

distinguishing between the works of men and of women); the more works we provide her with, the more she feeds on them, she is in perpetual gestation, she is inexhaustible... (ME 32)

The curiosity—and the subversiveness—of Cardinal's description of culture lies in its self-reflexivity. She does not settle for an explanation of the ways in which culture does or could work to the benefit of women; rather, she personifies culture as a whole, as female. Moreover, the real irony of such a clearly radical inversion of the norm lies in its near-perfect conformity to traditional images of women. In the course of her own narrative, Culture transforms herself from the incarnation of ideal femininity—eternally youthful, endlessly adaptable, easily manipulable—into her complementary opposite: the monstrous mother who replaces creation with destruction, male superiority with egalitarianism, altruism with narcissism, and fertility with sterility.

The female vocabulary that weaves together this radically new vision of a feminized culture—*generates, gestation, digests, digestion*—transmutes verbs into nouns to define culture as process as well as product. The two essential female roles that are named—nourishment and (pro)creation—explain women's parallel entry into "dailiness" and "Culture." Cardinal's use of "work" to signify simultaneously traditional female labor and women's aesthetic activity redefines the terms in which both have been conceived. Their new fusion retrospectively reveals the actual dichotomy that has always existed between "culture" and "literature," most clearly voiced in recent years by undergraduates demanding more "culture courses," a category in which they manifestly do not place literature courses. The desire to read political theory or analyze economic statistics does not motivate these students; they object to a literature—and to a reading of literature—that exists in apparent isolation from the daily lives of real people. And so does Cardinal, for whom female culture and its aesthetic expression are coexistent: "For decades now women have been writing, painting, singing, embroidering, or cooking the History of the emotions and the desires they live" (ME 38).

Cardinal's feminization of culture and pluralization of women's *oeuvre* initially seem to conflict with traditional feminist views. Few works have been as influential within feminist literary criticism as Virginia Woolf's *Room of One's Own;* and few arguments have been repeated as often as that which determines both the content and the structure of Woolf's germinal essay: female reality, the actual conditions of women's lives, constitute the primary obstacle to their aesthetic productivity. In particular, the multiple tasks of domestic life and the priority that women learn to grant to the needs of others result in a fragmentation of female time and energy that proves antithetical to the concentration and the creativity that all intellectual activity requires. Or maybe not. Of course, this same essay also offers an eloquent rebuttal to its own argument, not simply by the fact of its existence, but by Woolf's systematic transformation of fragmentation, of interruptibility, into a brilliant narrative strategy.

In a recent interview with Hélène Pednault, Marie Cardinal makes such a re-vision of the intersections of female life and literature explicit: "Women are accustomed to dividing themselves—or to multiplying themselves. . . . It doesn't bother me. I would even say that it helps me. Household tasks especially. When I can't manage to find a word or a sentence, when I can't settle on the tone of a paragraph, when I'm having difficulty in short with what I'm writing... well then, I get up and vacuum, or I do a load of wash, or I peel vegetables. During this time, things sort themselves out in my head... quite often, without realizing it, I find what I was looking for" (ME 119). Cardinal's concurrence with Pednault's description of this process as "a very feminine technique" (ME 119) acknowledges only factual accuracy and not biological privilege, for she regrets men's unfamiliarity with a method that they would find equally beneficial. Nor does Cardinal seek to romanticize a domestic situation that for many women has meant little more than servitude. "Interaction with the material world is enriching" only when freely chosen and limited to one part of a generally varied life; otherwise, "it's forced labor" (ME 119).

Cardinal does suggest, however, that acts of feminist reinterpretation such as her own and Woolf's could provide a model and a methodology for transforming the potential constraints and drudgery of women's traditional household labor into a context conducive to productive artistic creation. The narrator of *Une Vie pour deux*, who wonders whether she could manage to think at all at present "without having a vacuum cleaner in hand, or a load of laundry, or a sinkful of dishes, or a sewing project" (25), recalls that as an adolescent she cried while performing such domestic tasks precisely because they kept her from the intellectual activities that she loved. Interestingly, Simone conceives of her solution—the systematic training of the mind until the most imaginative of mental activities and the most mechanical of physical chores become interdependent and inseparable—not as an act of revolt but as one of total submission: "It had never occurred to me to rebel; I was totally submissive. So I had to find a ploy of some kind" (VD 25). Still, if Simone's decision to transform a paralyzing external conflict into a productive internal paradox stems entirely from her inability to rebel openly, it nonetheless results in a radically subversive notion of "women's work."

Cardinal posits this contradiction between appearance and reality, this creative tension between conformity and subversion, this female ability to unite apparently contradictory activities, as common to all women (AD 22). Her own determination to write "the discourse of knitting" (Pednault) responds to another of her recurrent literary motifs, her recollection of her maternal grandmother's favorite saying: "If only knitting could talk...!" (AD 162; VD 25). Cardinal inherits from her ancestor the secret knowledge that, like Simone, women in general are never less bound by the constraints of traditional female life, never more distant from home and family, than when they appear most fully engaged in daily household tasks. But to the extent that knitting does *not* speak, that women do not voice aloud the reality of their domestic life, they remain imprisoned in a silent and silenced material world— "gagged by their knitting, their vacuum cleaners, their stews, their laundry, their canaries, their bouquets, their ironing, and their darning"— and the very objects that could provide the primary means of women's self-expression continue to be defined as "secondary things, all of them" (AD 162), denied the textual existence that Cardinal and I have just given them. To reclaim the primacy of the material objects that literally objectify women and their world, we must proceed with an equal literalness to materialize female matter(s) anew.

Cardinal's proposal that women "open the so-called secondary things" (AD 162) that surround them takes the form of a linguistic and textual revolution: "For those who are against this evolution, which in reality will be a revolution, I see only one method to use: from now on prevent women from learning to read and write, distance them by all possible means from words. Leave them no form of self-expression other than the vocabulary of housework, cleaning, food. And still... It's too late; they will once again find the way to exist thanks to cook, cut, ferment, give birth, blood, tripes, rot, filth, water, air, meat, fish, egg, sweat, fever, vomit, song. And it will all remain to be done..." (AD 163).

In this context, the consistent focus of Cardinal's own texts on "the daily, the banal, the material" (PR 95) identifies them as specifically female, a model for her belief that women can and will use the vocabulary of their own domestic sphere, their own female vernacular, to read and write their way into existence. (I cannot resist pointing out that the notion of a female vernacular has a linguistic density of particularly rich metaphoric potential. What else but female speech could denote at one and the same time the standard language of a group, the substandard language of that same group, and the specialized idiom of particular members of that group? One is hardly surprised to learn that the word derives from the Latin *vernaculus,* domestic, which descends in turn from *verna.* This latter, *The American Heritage Dictionary* tells us, means "native slave"—but surely that's a feminine ending?) It is also worth noting here that Cardinal's explicit designation of female writing as a learned cultural activity contrasts sharply with the implicit understanding of *écriture féminine* as an automatic bodily function that often surfaces in the texts of such Francophone writers as Hélène Cixous and Chantal Chawaf. Cixous' complex and poetic texts, full of clever wordplay and subtle allusions to her own vast literary and philosophical heritage, in fact address an elite minority, while Cardinal potentially provides all literate women (hence her concern with literacy) with the means to name and share their own experience.

In achieving the relatively rare phenomenon in modern feminist literature of preserving women's traditional work as an unambiguously positive value, Cardinal goes beyond her own experience—"Before becoming a writer, I was the woman I was supposed to be... a mother, a wife, a housekeeper" (AD 59)—to transform the traditional woman into the writer. This effort echoes and responds to the frequent speculation of daughters in Cardinal's texts about the unrealized artistic potential of their own mothers, a motif that recurs in the work of many twentieth-century women writers. In *Les Mots pour le dire,* for example, the narrator interprets her mother's life as one of creative frustration as a result of the inactivity that her epoch and her social class impose on women: "She was unaware that she should have lived for a certain aesthetic construction that would have been distinctively hers and which will never be defined. Would she have been a potter? An architect? A sculptress? A surgeon? Or a gardener?" (322). At the same time, however, the diversity of the aesthetic outlets that the daughter proposes reminds us of the important fact that Cardinal views female life and female art as coextensive. Even this mother transforms her daily flower arranging into a form of artistic expression—"my mother erected plant cathedrals" (234)—and her desire to develop the same skill in her daughter identifies female education with the transmission of an artistic heritage.[12] When the mother reads aloud to her sick daughter, the entire family applauds her as "a true artist" (221) in a gesture that simultaneously reveals the constraints of the traditional female life and the determination with which women subvert them from within.

In noting that the imagery that women use to describe the act of writing (e.g., knitting, embroidery, weaving, kneading, nourishing) reflects the constant influence of their traditional domestic role, Irma Garcia reminds us of (what should be) the obvious fact that "how women have lived influences how they write." But she goes on to make an even more important point about her own critical approach that is equally valid for feminist criticism in general and for Cardinal's work in particular: "It's not a question of returning to out-of-date values, . . . but rather of showing how the woman manages to transport her values into the domain of writing and how she succeeds in redefining and transforming them" (2:23). In Cardinal's case, as we will see, the introduction of female values into the domain of writing redefines and transforms the latter at least as much as the former. Similarly, to adapt to my own context a point that Margaret Homans has made elsewhere, to note that women's activities and values have been largely determined by their domestic labor states a historical fact and a social reality; it does not identify a freely chosen nor a desirable condition and certainly not a biologically determined necessity. Neither I, nor Cardinal, nor Garcia are "arguing that women *should* write (or do anything else)" as knitters, kneaders, or nourishers, but only that they did and do.[13]

Cardinal's "knitting discourse" identifies not only the content of female texts but the very process of their writing. In fact, in describing the labor that the completion of a manuscript represents, Cardinal establishes a double parallel with female handicraft and the cultivation of the soil, thus intertwining the natural, social, and aesthetic dimensions of culture in a way that we have seen before: "row by row, the long knitted work became a real sweater that can keep one warm. Furrow by furrow, hard labor resulted in a field where the wheat shoots up in little green arrows" (AD 75). In this way Cardinal restores the female text to its original definition as an artisanal activity: *text*, "woven thing," from the

Latin *texere,* to weave, fabricate. Moreover, this connection to *fabricate,* "to construct by putting together finished parts," names the contexture of written feminism and both identifies within this context Cardinal's practice of autocitation as a form of crafts(wo)manship (*faber,* artisan; *fabrica,* workshop) and reminds us that "fabrications" or "fictions" (*fictio,* a making, fashioning) did not begin as falsehoods but, like Cardinal's fusion of autobiography and novel, as carefully crafted constructions. Using the same imagery as Cardinal, Garcia equates writing in general with female craft: "Writing is also this artisanal activity that is patiently learned, the page representing a loom where words are knit together stitch by stitch" (1:110; cf. Barthes, *Pleasure* 64).

The female artisan similarly informs Jane Marcus's recent attempt to define a feminist aesthetic in direct opposition to Lawrence Lipking's "poetics of abandonment." (I consider Marcus's critical act one of considerable importance and perhaps even courage in the face of the curious eagerness with which many feminist critics have embraced in Lipking a theory that not only celebrates female victimization but in the process ignores fifteen years of feminist scholarship.) Marcus imagines "another aesthetic, call it Penelope's, which grew out of a female culture." Based on her own weaving, Penelope's poetics celebrates the intimate connections between art and daily life and between art and the labor that produces it: "This model of art, with repetition and dailiness at the heart of it, with the teaching of other women the patient craft of one's cultural heritage as the object of it, is a female poetic which women live and accept" (84).[14]

Such a poetics ("with repetition and dailiness at the heart of it") locates the origin of repetitive female narration in the material base of female experience. In this context, the repetition that characterizes Cardinal's writing turns her textual activity as a whole into a metaphor for women's traditional tasks; or rather, it redefines the act of writing as a traditional female task in and of itself. Although the narrator of *Une Vie pour deux* is fully conscious that household work opens the path to "invention," "dream," and "freedom" (25), only when she begins to write does she realize that the daily labor of her domestic past metaphorically recounts the history of a storyteller: "As far back as she can remember, she rediscovers little cocoons in her life within which she used to tell herself stories. . . . it happened while she was apparently busy with something else—she was embroidering, she was sewing, she was fixing a meal—usually a rhythmical task. It required both a cadence and an interest in what she was handling: fabric, colored yarn, wool, vegetables, meat... Then she would escape, she would create" (VD 251–52).

Cardinal thus interweaves two forms of female representation that other women writers tend to portray as only parallel. In what may be the most recent example of this theoretical (dis)articulation, Bettina Aptheker characteristically argues that "women give expression to [a distinctly female] consciousness in their everyday lives by producing specific cultures" that are, on the one hand, "constructed in the artifacts of daily life" (notably quilting, needlework, tapestry, and weaving) and, on the other, "represented in stories, songs, poems" (12–13). Cardinal's fully realized fusion of artifact and story allows her to expand a traditionally realistic framework that can otherwise lead feminist theorists to retain, both in time and importance, a priority of life over text that has always been readily granted to women artists. Although Suzanne Juhasz, for example, initially introduces Kate Millett's writing as exemplary of a particular kind of formal experimentation, her subsequent analysis gradually reverses the terms of the equation until she finally argues that Millett's style "develops from the concept of dailiness as a structuring principle for women's lives" (222). In this context, Juhasz's insistence on the "autobiographical nature" of female fictional texts is, of course, perfectly consistent. By refusing to subordinate women's discursive strategies to the lives they simultaneously copy and create, Cardinal, however, more radically empowers female art, now enabled not only to reflect and to represent but also to *alter* the patterns of female reality.

In similar ways, suggestive of the theoretical importance of women's textual practice, Marguerite Duras and Anne Hébert, to cite only two examples, simultaneously write female reality into the structure of the narrative and the construction of textual artifacts. Duras radically alters conventional beliefs about the very nature and meaning of "The War" that her title names by refracting the concept of war through women's experience of waiting. The abstractions of war and death—"War is a generality, so are the inevitabilities of war, including death" (8)—find concrete form in such daily female tasks as the preparation and consumption of food by which death is first denied (in Robert's absence) and then defeated (after his return). The internal repetition that structures the title text identifies the organizing principle of the volume as a whole. Textual episodes, whose sequence deliberately defies linear chronology ("These texts ought to have come straight after the diary transcribed in *The War*" [115]) and openly challenges the generic boundaries and the presumed hierarchy between what is and isn't presented as "Literature," allow meaning to surface only in and through the obsessively repetitive processes of individual memory and the life patterns they recall and reflect.

In *Kamouraska* Hébert encodes within the description of Elisabeth's needlepoint the restraints that such traditional domestic tasks are meant to impose on the female life: "'Petit point is done in two stages, along the bias of the canvas backing. Vertically: from left to right, moving down. Horizontally: from right to left, moving up. Work with three strands of yarn, follow the grid'" (125). But, as in the case of Cardinal, the image escapes the imprisoning quotation marks that identify it as a culture text that women are forced to repeat, as Elisabeth rewrites the female metaphor to reflect her violent plan of liberation:

> Above all don't let anyone touch my needlepoint frame! I couldn't bear a certain petit point work [*au petit point*]. On a yellow background a bright red rose, unfinished! No, no, I can't bear that! May the scarlet wool, the long needles, the patient designing of the flower of blood come to life. The project dreamed and meditated stitch by stitch [*à petits points*], night after night, under the lamp. The murder imagined and set in motion at one's leisure. Pull the yarn. The little silver scissors hung at my waist. The needle you thread, the yarn wet with saliva that enters the eye. The crime that passes through the door of the willing heart. (42)

The textual (dis)order of these two descriptions clearly indicates the nonlinear structure of the novel as a whole. If female reality is once again both "constructed in" an artifact of daily life and "represented in" the story, needlework and narrative now escape the static boundaries of formal parallelism to engage in a complex, dynamic, and mutually interactive textual process.

Writing Female Reality: Textual Practice(s)

Cardinal's determination to "write the discourse of knitting" finds its most explicit form to date in *Le Passé empiété* (The backstitch). By making an embroiderer her central narrative voice and embroidery the structural as well as the thematic focus of her novel, Cardinal simultaneously complements the art historian Rozsika Parker's efforts to trace the parallel histories of embroidery and femininity through the novel, "women's other major art form" (118), and overcomes Parker's residual concern that "embroiderers employed the needle, not the pen—they left no records of their attitudes toward their subject matter" (102).[15] The paradox of women's conformity of behavior and subversiveness of thought, which Cardinal now transposes from knitting to embroidery, also structures Parker's analysis. Women artists, limited to an aesthetic practice equated with a feminine ideal of submissiveness and selflessness, "have nevertheless sewn a subversive stitch—managed to make meanings of their own in the very medium intended to inculcate self-effacement" (215). Cardinal's contemporary use of the novel to alter related cultural notions of embroidery and of femaleness encompasses a complex reevaluation not only of the female artist herself but of both the traditional and the feminist critical context within which she currently creates. I want to look at *Le Passé empiété* in some detail for this reason and for one other: the connections between Cardinal's text and Parker's *Subversive Stitch: Embroidery and the Making of the Feminine,* to which my discussion here is deeply indebted, illustrate the important role that the intersecting of different disciplines plays within the contexture of feminism.

The narrator's search for self in *Le Passé empiété,* patterned on the linguistic mode of psychoanalysis, initially embraces the traditional definition of embroidery as a female art form: "The word 'woman' surfaces, just as the word 'embroidery' did a moment ago, and the two combine naturally to form a couple" (36). But if Cardinal accepts embroidery as an act whose repetitiveness establishes continuity and connections within and among women's lives, she simultaneously rejects its customary reduction to an act of mere repetition, to the skillful execution of the designs of others. Even as a child, Cardinal's narrator openly revolts against the incarnation in the sampler of a standard of excellence based on the perfect regularity of both the imitation and the stitch. She races through her required figures, producing "a red scribble bearing a vague resemblance to letters and numbers" (32)—surely a metaphor for women's subversive writing—to arrive at the border where she is free to create whatever shapes her imagination dictates and to alter the required stitches until she invents "a technique of my own that I constantly improved" (34).

Cardinal also challenges the long-standing notion of embroidery as a domestic pastime. Although even as a child the embroiderer refuses to complete the seams and hems that would turn her artistic creations into usable household goods, only her later career fully reveals the profound irony in her proud family's view of her embroidery as "the proof that I would someday be a homemaker" (34). In a simultaneous inversion and repetition of the cultural model of Penelope (reminding us that the male absence for which her needlework offers compensation also provides creative freedom), Cardinal's embroiderer openly chases her husband and all that his denigration of her "ladies' fancy-work" represents (42). An activity whose original merit lies in its ability to produce a product for others while still attending to their needs becomes in Cardinal's novel a demanding career whose success depends precisely upon the rejection of others. A female art that the child artist still defines as marginal (freedom lies at the border) becomes for the adult artist the central priority of her life. By elevating embroidery from craft to art and from an amateur to a professional activity, Cardinal also transforms it from an endeavor long synonymous with femininity itself into one totally incompatible with traditional definitions of women as altruistic and submissive. Thus she simultaneously celebrates female culture as experienced by women themselves and exposes the socio-aesthetic assumptions and prohibitions that continue to imprison women artists.

Chief among these obstacles to female creation has been the existence of an artistic tradition specifically and uniquely en-gendered as male. Much recent Anglophone feminist criticism has focused on the strategies developed by women writers to challenge and undermine the equating of literary activity with biological manhood, of textual generation with actual paternity (see Gilbert and Gubar, *Madwoman*). In this context, Cardinal's focus on embroidery has particularly clear subversive potential. In opposition to the traditional dichotomy of the needle and the pen, relegating women and men to separate creative domains and defining the boundary between craft and art, Cardinal not only reestablishes embroidery as a valid artistic medium but restores its semantic unity. Far from being distinct from and subordinate to verbal artistry, she reminds us that embroidery rightfully functions as a metaphor for literature itself.[16] To embroider, *The American Heritage Dictionary* tells us, is not only "to ornament (fabric) with needlework" but also "to embellish (a narrative, for example) with fictitious details or exaggerations."

Of course, the implicit association of women and imaginative flights of fantasy may initially seem of ambiguous value. Recalling Freud's hypothesis that hysteria originates in the daydreams "to which needlework and similar occupations render women especially prone," Dianne Hunter draws the logical conclusion: "That is, people left to embroidery are bound to embroider fantasies" (94). On the other hand, Cardinal's insistence on the link between literary activity and women's traditional domestic tasks also intersects interestingly with modern narrative theory. Walter Benjamin uses the image of the woman embroiderer to figure the profoundly artisanal nature of early storytelling (107–8); and, at the opposite end of the narrative spectrum, Alain Robbe-Grillet finally makes sense of Flaubert's odd claim to identity with Emma Bovary by reading the description of embroidery that he attributes to her as "the metaphor of the work of a modern novelist" (*Miroir* 213).[17]

Cardinal also uses the particular qualities of embroidery as an art form and the specific stitch that her embroiderer prefers to represent metaphorically the woman artist's relationship to the cultural and artistic past that she inherits. Dictionaries and encyclopedias consistently define embroidery by the characteristic that distinguishes it from lace making: its superimposition on a preexisting background. As such, embroidery offers a particularly apt metaphor for the situation of the female artist who creates against the backdrop of the dominant culture. Moreover, the analogy also describes Cardinal's practice of autocitation and so again equates her textual repetition with her desire to represent a female culture. On the other hand, in contrast to the embroiderer's own aesthetic that focuses on the stitch itself, the muted culture of the female artist, Cardinal characteristically insists that women see beyond their own situation to the full complexity of their cultural context.

Although knitting books describe the *passé empiété* as a highly decorative stitch whose beauty depends on its "perfect regularity," Cardinal singles it out for exclusive use because of the liberty and variety that it allows. Notably, only the consistency of the background material limits its freedom. If Cardinal first defines the backstitch straightforwardly in terms clearly analogous to the repetitive structure of her work as a whole—"you encroach on the past in order to propel yourself into the future" (249)—her depiction of the difficult struggle engaged with a fabric of irregular and treacherous weave—"I don't see how to appropriate it, I don't see how to prevent it from controlling my rhythms"

(311)—reveals her parallel dependence on the figurative meaning of *empiéter* (to appropriate a share of the position occupied by another, to assume rights one doesn't have) that identifies women's challenge to dominant culture. Embroidery embodies the palimpsestic nature of female artistic and cultural forms, the superimposition of the muted on the dominant, the female on the male, the subversive on the conformist: "Once the difficulties of the background have been captured, then assimilated, and finally warded off . . . I organize my volumes as I please by embroidering over my first work, sometimes repeatedly. In this way I obtain forms and volumes in which the memory remains—a kind of echo, barely perceptible, but indispensable in my view—of the first conquest, of the first encounter with the material" (250).

This image of the material density of female art, which, like Cardinal's formal repetitions, figures the constant dialogue that women maintain among their own past, present, and future selves and with the dominant literary and cultural tradition, also functions more specifically as a metaphor for intertextuality. In opposition to a current tendency, particularly prevalent in France among male theoreticians (e.g., Derrida and Deleuze), to view intertextuality as a quilting process in which one work is composed of fragments of others, Roger Fowler joins Cardinal in conceptualizing intertextuality as "metaphorically like a palimpsest, a re-used parchment with the half-erased traces of the previous text showing through the lines of new writing" (124; cf. Gilbert and Gubar, *Madwoman* 73). I am well aware that some feminist critics also find writing, and particularly that of women, formally analogous to the female arts of quilting and patchwork. Elaine Showalter, for example, speculates that "piecing" is "a kind of female bricolage" that women writers of the nineteenth century carried over into their "assemblage of literary materials" ("Women's"). Moreover, certain contemporary novels, particularly the work of African-American and working-class women—Pat Barker's *Union Street,* Joan Chases's *During the Reign of the Queen of Sheba,* Gloria Naylor's *Women of Brewster Place*—juxtapose the lives of different women on the pattern of the quilt. I do not wish to set up a hierarchy of female art as textual metaphor, particularly since Cardinal's own repetitions often recall the process of quilting as well; moreover, I have used a similar analogy to characterize feminism itself. Still, the doubly palimpsestic nature of her embroidery metaphor—multiple repetitions upon an already existent background—does serve usefully to connect female texts and female lives, on the one hand, and literary and cultural traditions, both muted and dominant, on the other, by emphasizing the individual writer's dependence on the multiple influences that inform the life and work of all human beings within a given culture. (*Culture* and *palimpsest* share a common etymology that ties both to the notion of repetition [from the Greek *palin*, again; from the Indo-European *kevel-*, to revolve].)

To be perfectly frank, Showalter's insistence that she identifies a "specifically American" female tradition of piecing, patchwork, and quilting ("Piecing") appears once again to reflect a questionable assumption of American cultural primacy and superiority that denigrates—implicitly, at the very least—the foreign (i.e., the French, given the current context of feminism). But perhaps this is not cultural imperialism but a statement of fact? Perhaps, but Showalter provides no context and no evidence for her assertion, although comparative analyses serve textual colonialists well, as I have already suggested. Why is it, one wonders, that an art that "crossed racial, regional, and class boundaries" (224) was stopped cold at the national borders?[18] In any event, virtually everything that Showalter says about quilting directly corresponds to what Parker has said about embroidery; there does then seem to be considerable commonality within the tradition of female art, whatever the specific form that it takes.

However general its cultural background, *Le Passé empiété* also encodes a significant shift in Cardinal's theory of art toward the female and the feminist. The embroiderer is originally committed to abstraction; although specifically designed to foster the self-expression that embroidery otherwise thwarts, abstract art does not readily allow the representation of gender. Indeed, initially Cardinal's embroiderer explicitly rejects any such possibility: "I have a taste for the hidden, the mysterious, the foreign. That's what I embroider, and that has nothing to do with my gender . . ." (257). The early use of this technique to portray a male life, an attempt that ends in failure, no doubt represents metaphorically the degree to which male reality is and will remain an abstraction for her. In contrast, once the narrator begins to embroider the story of Clytemnestra, she immediately finds herself drawn toward figuration. Once again Cardinal challenges traditional conceptions of female art. Because of the use of patterns, embroidery has usually been seen as devoid of significant content and its subject matter has been ignored in favor of its technical execution.

Cardinal reverses this hierarchy by making representation accessible and central; moreover, her shift to realism defines a specifically feminist theory of art. (One for which, by the way, Elaine Showalter deserves a great deal of credit.) Her first realistic work represents Clytemnestra's nude body, a venture that initially seems "indecent" and that will prove so disturbing that the embroiderer can only progress by returning in places to what she calls "the modesty of abstraction, the convenience of a theoretical expression" (319–20). In a reversal of positions too often dichotomized as French and Anglo-American, Cardinal reminds us that women's realistic depiction of their own bodies and their own lives is a daring and potentially revolutionary art practice that can revalorize the culturally devalued and represent the previously unacceptable.

Even more importantly, realism transforms embroidery from a decorative into a political art form and substitutes a representative worldview for individual self-expression. Thus the embroiderer's initial attempt to depict the priority of the specific over the general (of the individual over the gender specific) is necessarily unsuccessful: "My goal was . . . to embroider her in such a way that someone looking at the embroidery could say: 'It's Clytemnestra,' even before thinking: 'It's a woman'... I failed" (321–22). Cardinal's inability to personalize Clytemnestra (other than by the expression of her eyes) reinforces the commonality of women and the continuity of female lives that Clytemnestra and the embroiderer jointly represent and that ultimately identifies a theory of artistic realism as particularly suited to the representation of female experience.

Parker has noted feminism's ambivalent relationship to traditional female art forms. Feminists have often attacked embroidery as the embodiment of the conventions and constraints of imposed femininity. At other times, in a total reversal, they have sought to revalorize female craft on the basis of its intimate connections to women's lives and domestic labor. But, in either case, the feminist position essentially reiterates the dominant cultural norm that denies the aesthetic value of women's art. Judy Chicago, whose work represents the most recent effort of a feminist artist to continue a female tradition, seems similarly caught in contradiction, if not in precisely the same contradictions. Her intentions in *The Dinner Party* and *The Birth Project* seem to echo within the domain of the visual arts those of Cardinal in the novel. Chicago attempts both to revise and to reclaim women's culture and experience, and certainly she seeks to grant female craft the status of high art. But, curiously, it turns out to be precisely the conventional split between art and craft that blinds Chicago to the specificity—and ultimately to the value—of a female aesthetic.

Chicago always refers to the female artists who are supposedly her collaborators only as "needleworkers" or "stitchers"; and she insistently voices her frustration at their focus on "perfect stitching" (the center, of course, of embroidery's aesthetic) rather than on the "background," the overall visual image. This metaphoric (and literal) concern with dominant cultural values presumably explains as well the incredible arrogance with which Chicago dismisses the embroiderers' visual ability ("a lot of needleworkers just can't 'see'"), seeks to reduce them once again to subservient imitators ("And I never understood why so many needleworkers imagined that they could design their own pieces when most of them couldn't even draw"), and laments their ignorance of conventional aesthetic codes ("Additionally, most needleworkers have not been exposed to the contemporary language of art, and their designs are often extremely naive") ("Birth" 226–27). Even more incredibly, Chicago's claims to superiority are made with so little self-awareness that the true irony of the situation appears to escape her totally: *she* is the one, the *only* one, who is totally incapable of realizing her own projects—she doesn't know how to embroider. In this context, Chicago's near-total insensitivity to the intersections of women's lives and women's art is perhaps not surprising; thus she expresses distress that the fragmented life of one embroiderer produces a "broken rhythm" in her stitching. Where Chicago sees only breakdown, one suspects that Cardinal—and Woolf—would have found a newly patterned rhythm, a female voice speaking her own discourse of embroidery.

(Re)Writing Female Culture

If the repetitiveness of women's writing simultaneously originates in and reflects the material conditions of female reality, then textual repetition can also provide a uniquely appropriate technique for the (re)constitution and the (re)creation of female culture in women's writing. I bracket repetition here both to affirm the historical and actual existence of gender-specific experience and to note that in the case of women such experience has often been denied textual expression. Repetition, as the constant interaction of identity and difference, always denies origin and originates at one and the same time; in the words of Maurice Blanchot: "What matters is not to speak but to repeat and, in this repetition, to speak each time for the first time" (qtd. in Compagnon 7). Cardinal accompanies her call to women to use the language of their own domestic world to "open" the material objects that compose it with a complementary proposal to "plug up," to fill in, the textual gaps of women's experience: "we will then be able to invent words to fill in the spaces that have been left empty in our language by vast domains of the unexpressed and the essential—all, as if by chance, female domains" (AD 87).

Leaving to my next chapter the specifically linguistic questions that Cardinal's words clearly raise, I want first to explore the structural and the thematic functioning of her textual "fillers" (curiously, but appropriately, the word unites the essential and the nonessential). The word *reprise* has comparable semantic significance. In French, the term not only combines the repetition and the retaliation for past injury of the English words *reprise* and *reprisal* (of common etymology), but it further identifies the traditional female task of darning. A job far less elegant and aesthetically pleasing than embroidery, darning, even when done skillfully, has the same palimpsestic quality; moreover, its metaphoric potential may be even greater, for where embroidery embellishes, darning, even as it mends, leaves a visible scar of the tears that rend the fabric of the dominate culture when it seeks to exclude and to silence the experience of women. ("To rend" appears to encode the semantics of female oppression: to tear apart a thing's components violently; to remove forcibly; to penetrate as if by tearing; to breach the relationship between persons.) Cardinal's repetitions now weave across the holes of human history (his-story) and culture (*cul*-ture?) to fill in the missing pieces of her-story and reclaim a voice in our-story.

What I propose is that Cardinal's repetitions in and of themselves serve to identify a model of women's culture, of female reality. In an appropriately repetitive way, an act of contexture, of weaving or assembling parts, reveals contexture, an arrangement of interconnecting parts; (re)reading rereads and rewrites prior acts of rereading and rewriting. In this case, my critical gesture metaphorically relates (after all) to the female act of patchwork. We see scraps of fabric reappear in Cardinal's work, different pieces cut in different shapes but taken from the same piece of cloth. (A prior act of patching means that in its original state the female cloth already consists of multicolored patches that respect the diversity of women's lives; but these have been sewn together to reflect the commonality of female experience as well.)[19] Although removing the fragments from their present context to piece them together differently can reveal a coherent image of a specifically female world, women's culture remains within the boundaries of the dominant culture: the pieces of fabric in their visible, textual form are immersed in a larger narrative cloth. As we have seen, many anthropologists of women's culture insist that women always function simultaneously within both dominant and muted culture (Ardener; Showalter, "Feminist"); and Cardinal's work, as we also know, defines the female life in terms of a constant tension between simultaneous conformity and subversion. Or, to put it another way that Cardinal might prefer, Culture indiscriminately incorporates the experience of all human beings without distinction (of gender or of anything else),[20] but the control of language and power by some to the exclusion of others has allowed History (Narrative) to institute discriminatory practices of inclusion and exclusion, of expression and silence, that simultaneously resegregate human experience (by gender, among other things.)

To the extent that women's experience has been literally or effectively silenced, Cardinal's choice not simply to express it but to *repeat* it has the important result of emphasizing a reality that has long been denied cultural and textual validation. She reverses the very process that establishes and confirms the dominance of a given textual tradition and cultural consciousness—Louis Mink notes that the stories we want to hear repeatedly fashion the common vision of a community ("History" 554)—to shape an alternative tradition and culture. I believe Cardinal's strategy here to be usefully metaphorical, whether or not it is intentionally so. She represents within her own work the larger pattern of textual repetition and echo that underlies Lamy's and Garcia's conception of *écriture féminine* and founds Anglophone theories of a female literary tradition or a female poetics. Thus, Cardinal also repeats and, by virtue of this emphasis, helps to make visible the intercultural intersections of feminist theory, the contexture of written feminism.

I want first to look at a thematic network of repetitions in Cardinal's work that when viewed as an isolated whole presents a unified picture of her idea of female reality. Although these are not in most cases literal autocitations (and so allow us to omit temporarily the specific question of repetitive language), neither do they simply reflect a broad pattern of recurrent interests—one that allows us, for example, to associate Virginia Woolf with the expression of subjective consciousness; Proust with problems of memory and metaphor; Colette with affectionate descriptions of cats and gardens—that one could presumably identify for any writer. If I were to speak about Cardinal on that level of generality,

I would note her interest in women's lives, in psychoanalysis, in Algeria. Rather, the passages that interest me here are sufficiently specific and repeated in terms that are sufficiently similar that they call attention to themselves when they recur, almost as if they were underlined or italicized. Indeed, Antoine Compagnon suggests that quotation, rewriting, always reproduces a prior underlining, a rereading (29). In most cases, the episodes in question appear in three or more texts; in the few examples where they recur only once, they have a particularity that makes them instantly memorable, that identifies them as stories to be (re)told. On the other hand, I have not been able to find a way to cite any of them in my own text, since their narrative importance is such that the length of the passage, in at least one of its versions, prohibits their being quoted in their entirety.

To be sure that we nonetheless have at least some common empirical base for further interpretation, let me first provide a simple enumeration of the repeated passages, listed—after the first five examples, which include all incidences of literal autocitation—in totally random order:

1. a man and a woman make love, intercut with certain memories of her Algerian childhood, notably the sensual pleasures of swimming in the Mediterranean and watching the Arab workers dance on the final night of the harvest (EM, AD, MD);

2. a mother reveals to her adolescent daughter her efforts to abort her (CP, MD, PR);

3. a young girl accompanies her mother on her yearly pilgrimage to the tomb of a beloved first daughter who died in infancy (MD, CP, PR);

4. a woman experiences a crisis of madness, characterized in particular by her terror at being the object of others' gazes and by the temptation of suicide (AD, VD); this passage is linked to a general narrative of female madness, with similar causes, symptoms, and consequences (EM, S, MD);

5. the intangible presence of jasmine's haunting perfume gradually permeates the city of Algiers to announce the end of spring (AD, VD);

6. a girl uses colored pencils to pretend that she is performing surgery on her dolls in a context of autoeroticism that implies sexual curiosity about the female body (MD, GD);

7. a fire destroys a husband's apartment, emblematic of a superficial life-style that has imprisoned him in its conventions and separated him from his wife (CP, VD);

8. fathers and husbands, who are always unfaithful, leave their wives and children; usually, the wife refuses to divorce (all);

9. a woman experiences the birth of her child as a battle both with the fetus and with her own body as unity becomes division (S, VD, GD);

10. a young woman loses her virginity—by choice, with a man whom she does not love, often in revolt against conventional values, and, for that reason at the very least, usually with pleasure (VD, MD, PE, AD, S);

11. a traditional mother joins a feminist demonstration in order to watch over her daughter and unexpectedly discovers the commonality of the female condition and her solidarity with other women (VD, CP);

12. middle-aged women gradually create a new identity for themselves as artists, usually as writers (all except S and EM);

13. a woman remembers her childhood and adolescence in the south, usually in Algeria; the specific thematics of these passages includes, most notably, love for the land and the sea (both identified as mother); joyful contacts with the Arabs who work for her family (e.g., trips to and from school with Barded's children, watering the gardens with Youssef, listening to Daïba tell stories); allusions to the horrors of the Algerian war; hatred for the restricted life that vacations in France impose (all except PE and GD);

14. a mother and a daughter struggle for mutual love and understanding: the specific thematics of this relationship includes the mother's daily efforts to force the child to follow the norms of conventional femininity or, alternatively, her near-total indulgence and devotion that leave the child almost completely free of guidance or restrictions on her behavior (CP, MD, PE, GD);

15. a wife, whose husband or lover is unfaithful, encounters, in reality or in hallucination, the woman who is her rival (EM, MC, S, MD); and

16. a young girl is confirmed during the Festival of May, associated with her awakening sexuality and with a repressive church doctrine on virginity and chastity (MD, VD, AD, PR).

Cardinal provides us in these passages with a microcosm of the physiological, psychological, cultural, and societal experience of women: a virtual paradigm of female culture.[21] The description of jasmine, which initially seems to clash with the characteristic focus of these repetitions on human activity, in fact identifies both the structural and the thematic rhythm of Cardinal's self-citations. Citation itself (derived from the Latin *citare*, to set in motion) introduces dynamism into the text. Repetition produces the same effect of simultaneous presence and absence as jasmine's elusive perfume; it surrounds us even as it escapes us, creating a curiously exciting sensation of textual energy and instability. The fleeting instant at which spring and summer overlap in a dynamic stasis reproduces the tension of difference and identity that coexists at the moment of repetition to announce the plurality of meaning and the possibility of change. At the same time, jasmine also announces the structure of most of the situations that Cardinal finds specific to women, the concomitant conformity to and subversion of traditional and/or normative female behavior.

The almost exclusively female community that Cardinal creates is internally repetitive. As a metaphor, it identifies and emphasizes the major purpose served by her textual repetitions as a whole and reflects the relationship between female and dominant cultures. But the complementary feelings of identity with other women and of difference from the societal and cultural norm, which follow from gender-specific experience, also offer a literally accurate description of the reality that many women live. The fact that men and women lead separate lives results in dyadic communities in which women have almost exclusive responsibility for childcare; they also provide the primary financial support for the family unit, although the husband's promising career always provides the initial justification for his departure and the superficial explanation for his prolonged absence. Yet, at the same time that women accept the inevitability of separation that clearly reflects a traditional split between the private domestic world of women and the public professional world of men, they refuse divorce. Female culture remains tied to a dominant culture, one that the division within the heterosexual couple exposes as male-defined and male-specific rather than representative of humanity as a whole. The characteristically female objection to divorce suggests, however, that women do not view the division that gender introduces into culture and society as either necessary or definitive.

Still, as long as gender *does* continue to define experience, it will also knit tight bonds between and among women, regardless of their diversity. The "other woman" reappears in Cardinal's work as a unifying metaphor for the individual differences that separate women (the *other* woman) and for the gender commonality that unites women (the other *woman*). In every instance of confrontation, identity overcomes difference and gradually transforms a female rival into a female ally; that this process is most often imaginary merely serves to claim an important psychological reality without denying the actual societal conditions that leave it most often unrealized. For if Cardinal's repetitions consistently relegate the heterosexual couple and the father/daughter dyad to the background to make connections among women the center of attention, female love remains deeply ambivalent and contradictory, as Cardinal's primary focus on the mother/daughter relationship makes particularly clear. In reproducing the same model of conflictual twinship that we have just seen in another set of repetitions, these two women, linked by a common bloodline and heritage but separated by age and experience, confirm such a pattern as characteristic of women's relationships in general.

The interconnections among different moments of repetition are particularly important to an understanding of the mother/daughter passages. In ways that I will explore more fully in a moment, what initially seem to be acts of neglect and cruelty on the part of an individual mother gradually fit into a larger pattern of societal restrictions on women; the emergence of this background does not serve, by any means, to justify harmful maternal behavior, but it does help both to explain it and to generalize from it, so that we can better understand the common oppression of women. Cardinal's analysis recalls Adrienne Rich's argument in *Of Woman Born:* within Western culture, the experience of mothering has been largely defined and controlled by the institution of motherhood. In this context, it is particularly significant that the female character who comes to a simultaneous understanding of femaleness (of the commonality of women's sociohistorical situation) and of feminism (of the possibility that female solidarity could bring about social change) has been isolated precisely by her identity and her role as a conventional mother (see repetition 11 above).

The focus on the mother-daughter relationship offers the additional advantage of allowing women to reexamine and reintegrate their childhood memories. Irma Garcia argues that a textual fascination with childhood as a time of freedom and happiness, of both autonomy and harmonious interaction with the world, provides the primary thematic repetition of *écriture féminine* (1:114). The fact that Cardinal essentially respects this pattern, despite the many painful experiences that she also incorporates into childhood, suggests a certain confirmation of its importance for women. Moreover, the maternal metaphors that she uses to characterize her native land and her beloved Mediterranean (*mer, mère*) reconstruct through the natural world a love and a supportive intimacy that result more directly from the mother-daughter relationship in the writing of other women.

This repetitive network also reiterates the complexity and the contradictions of women's cultural position. Whereas the separation of the couple explicitly identifies the gender specificity of human experience and articulates its effects on the individual and the familial level, the split between Algeria and France repeats the division on a societal and cultural scale and reestablishes important connections between women and other oppressed groups. In this series of repetitions, France and Algeria function as metaphors for distinctive and strongly contrasting worldviews. A French world founded on reason, order, normative social behavior, hierarchy, and exclusivity opposes an Arab culture based on intuition, spontaneity, freedom, sensitivity to the natural world, democracy, and heterogeneity. That such distinctions are surely false, in their rigidity at the very least, is, I think, fully intentional; Cardinal means for us to recognize the cultural stereotypes that serve precisely to introduce and to perpetuate unnecessary divisions within a common humanity. In addition, she deliberately emphasizes the reversibility of cultural values that allows the same terms to define cultural superiority, when claimed from within, and cultural inferiority, when proclaimed from without. Thus she attributes positive values to the Arab culture with which she identifies and negative ones to the French culture where she remains an outsider, but she depicts both in terms that leave their alternative interpretation readable. While Cardinal would surely not pretend that the specific circumstances that characterize her and her female narrators transcend gender, race, or class, I think that one can fairly argue that her predilection for a metaphorical as well as a literal multiculturalism provides at least a structural model through which experience other than that of white middle-class women might be articulated.[22]

Another series of repetitions serves once again to remind us that Cardinal's primary interest does lie in the specificity of *female* experience. A significant part of what constitutes that specificity results from women's particular physiology, in large part because it has functioned so significantly in determining their societal roles and their cultural value. Appropriately, then, Cardinal inventories the physiological realities of the female body within an explicitly social context. Thus, women's reproductive capacity finds expression in a complexly connective network that includes not only the experience of giving birth but the threat of pregnancy, the anguish of abortion, and the pain of a child's death. Female madness, the direct result of the objectification of the female body, expresses itself in physical symptoms such as uncontrollable vaginal bleeding that both reproduce and protest women's imprisonment in their own anatomy. In other cases, women use their physiology in a more successful subversion of their socially and biologically normative roles and reclaim control over their own bodies. The mother who is about to give birth, for example, lives a privileged and private moment with her child; she deliberately delays awakening the father. Similarly, women experience their sexuality—even when it takes places in a specifically heterosexual context, as in the case of the loss of virginity—as a curiously private and autonomous act in which they make love to their own bodies. Reinforced by the young girl's experimentation with her dolls and the sensuality of the union with the mother-sea, such autoeroticism can be interpreted to mirror sexual attraction between women as well.

A final repetition in some sense encompasses all the others: women's rebirth into writing provides them with the means to claim their own female specificity and to recreate textual and cultural reality as a whole. Cardinal reemphasizes this relationship between the specific and the general, between identity and difference, by an internal mirroring effect that must already be clear. Within the series of generally repetitive passages that paint a microcosmic picture of female culture, the five examples of literal repetition already tell the same story in and of themselves; they recount the metaphorical identification of structure, the constitution of a female community, the centrality of the mother/daughter relationship, the return to childhood, the conflict of cultures, female madness, and female physiology. Thus Cardinal repeats within her own work the relationship between that work and the texts of other women. Although the many books (notably those of Lamy, Moers, Showalter, Didier, Gilbert and Gubar, DuPlessis, Pratt, Stewart, Spacks, Garcia, Jelinek) and articles that have been devoted in recent years to an exploration of the recurrent themes of modern women writers inevitably discover rather diverse sources of commonality, they consistently converge on the same thematic network that emerges from Cardinal's work: a wide range of specific female experience (both societal and physiological), the failure of the heterosexual couple, the reclaiming of female sexuality, the return to childhood, the coming to writing, female madness and the search for self, and the mother-daughter relationship.

(Re)Contextualizing Female Culture

If these endless series of different repetitions of the same are beginning to sound like a litany of clichés, perhaps this is neither surprising nor undesirable. Stereotypes embody generalized repetition and repetitious generalities; they reflect in simplified, accessible form the beliefs of a culture.[23] For female reality, defined from a female perspective, to rival the banality of male-defined images of women; for the complexity of women's experience to have been incorporated into the body of *idées reçues* rather than remain an idea to be excluded or silenced—frankly, that strikes me as progress.

Of course, repetition need not be repetitious. Cardinal's autocitations force a rereading that uncovers the difference that context makes; far from reiterating a single message, repetition actively pluralizes meaning (see Compagnon 38). I have suggested that Cardinal's work provides a context for the exploration of feminism, conceived as contextual in and of itself. Certainly the visibility that she confers on context has clear feminist significance. It guarantees that her repetitions never take the form of simple decals, superimposed on a new but unchanged background; existing social structures must be radically altered for significant change to occur in women's lives.[24] Aptheker includes just such "a continual analysis and reworking of context" among the female-specific values that arise as dailiness structures women's ways of thinking (74). Appropriately, the relationship between *Les Mots pour le dire* and its total textual repetition in *Le Passé empiété* demonstrates how changes in context can further understanding and solidarity among women; how, that is, they can promote feminism.

The unnamed first-person narrators of both novels tell an identical story of their parents' marriage and divorce. In both cases, the father marries a much younger and much wealthier woman without informing her that gassing during the war has left him with contagious tuberculosis; as a result, he fatally infects his own infant daughter. In *Les Mots pour le dire*, the narrator learns these details of her parents' past during the conversation in which her mother reveals her later effort to abort her younger daughter. Consequently, all associations of cruelty and murder center on the mother; and the daughter identifies not with the sister whose martyrdom has transformed her into an untouchable rival who monopolizes all their mother's love but with the image of her own death. Although the narrator of *Les Mots pour le dire* notes in passing that she no longer regards her mother's act as a *saloperie*—"I know why this woman did it. I understand her" (171)—we cannot entirely shift our own perspective until *Le Passé empiété* invites us to reread the same story in a new context.

Indeed, the mother has now become "this woman." The second narrator has a clear understanding of women's social and cultural situation, including an awareness that gender has important consequences for the seemingly private acts of individual women, even those of one's own mother. The daughter now grasps the degree to which her mother has been a victim of societal restrictions on women, consistently denied the education, knowledge, legal recourse, and financial independence that would allow her to function as an autonomous adult. More importantly, she realizes that her mother's divorce and the independent raising of her two remaining children in fact constitute a radical revolt against those constraints and unexpectedly transform her into a worthy model for her daughter.

The narrator of *Le Passé empiété* can identify with the mother because of her own gender experience as well; as a result of the near-fatal accident of her children, she not only understands maternal grief but the extraordinary emphasis that Western culture places on maternal guilt. Indeed, the latter is so powerful and so pervasive that no mother can fully escape its grip. Thus the narrator of *La Clé sur la porte* raises her children in a climate of total freedom and openness that contrasts sharply and intentionally with the restrictive rules and the lack of affection that characterized her own childhood (reminiscent of that related in *Les Mots pour le dire*). *Les Grands Désordres* provides yet a new context for the exploration of motherhood; now the female narrator torments herself over the possibility that the indulgence and the lack of supervision and guidance that characterized her mothering (reminiscent of that described in *La Clé sur la porte*) might have been responsible for her daughter's present addiction to heroin.

The repeated appearances of the mother figure in Cardinal's work identify her most explicitly and most clearly articulated feminist concern. Although the constant changes in both content and context reveal a desire to explore the complexity of maternal experience and to create an understanding that includes the multiple perspectives of both mother and daughter, a common conclusion unifies Cardinal's vision: her female characters finally reject the assumption of maternal guilt that allows society to transform the mother into a scapegoat. In the 1986 essay that accompanies her new translation of Euripides' *Medea*, Cardinal traces for the first time her own brief version of a feminist history of women's condition. She focuses on the nineteenth-century evolution of *la maman*—"this monster who took the place of the mother"—that led to the institutionalization of women as "walking womb[s]" and to the parallel development of a maternal ethic of self-sacrifice (33). Cardinal's identification of motherhood as the source of women's oppression connects her to Simone de Beauvoir and thus situates her thought within an essentially Anglophone feminist tradition that most directly derives from *The Second Sex*. Cardinal's *maman,* for example, clearly recalls the "Supermom" of Betty Friedan's *Feminine Mystique;* and the distinction that she makes between maternal experience and the institutionalization of motherhood reproduces the structural framework of Rich's *Of Woman Born.*

I do not mean to imply that Beauvoirian feminism has lost all influence in France; Elizabeth Badinter, the single feminist theoretician cited by Cardinal, is best known for her critique of the maternal instinct (*L'Amour en plus*). I do mean to point out an important difference. In the United States, such texts as Rich's *Of Woman Born,* Carol Gilligan's *In a Different Voice,* and Nancy Chodorow's *Reproduction of Mothering* frequently provide not simply background or support but the structuring framework for feminist literary criticism. In France, however, feminist theory produced within the general framework of the social sciences rarely intersects with the theory and the practice of women's writing. Indeed, the two groups of texts are informed by fundamentally different premises, for the theoretical and poetic texts of *écriture féminine* (those, for example, of Hélène Cixous and Luce Irigaray) seek to revalorize the maternal as the origin not of women's oppression but of their specificity and thus their commonality. In many ways, Cardinal's alternative maternal discourse, focused on the harmonious union with the land and the sea of Algeria, uses similar techniques to similar purposes, in ways that I will explore more fully in the next chapter.

At times, when Cardinal's use of repetition forces us into a feminist practice of rereading, we rediscover familiar texts in totally unexpected ways. Thus, a particular text provides not only a new context for the specific passage that it repeats, but it also recontextualizes all other repetitions of the same passage. *Les Grands Désordres,* for example, encourages us to return to *La Clé sur la porte* to look more carefully at the quality of the mothering that the narrator provides. Since the focus of the earlier text on the mother's efforts to reconstruct the family in a different manner has always been quite explicit, retracing our steps is unlikely to alter whatever opinion we have already reached about the potentially beneficial or harmful effects of this experiment. And yet, the hint that Cardinal provides—*cherchez la mère*—nevertheless provokes an illuminating rereading of *La Clé sur la porte.*

Throughout this text, the narrator attributes the resistance that consistently undermines her attempts to forge an atmosphere of communication and trust between herself and the adolescents who frequent her home to the fact that at some level they still view her as an adult, a parent, a figure of authority. This explanation strikes us, I think, as vaguely dissatisfying, in large part because the adolescent behavior that it seeks to explain is so decidedly one-sided, involving only a challenge to authority with no signs of the ambivalence or the remnants of respect that we might expect from those barely beyond childhood. But once we realize that the narrator is not, of course, just a parent or an adult but specifically a mother and a woman, everything falls into place differently.

First of all, an awareness of the importance of gender to the behavior of the mother clarifies in turn that of the adolescents; we can suddenly perceive a difference in attitude between boys and girls that reveals that all serious threats to the narrator's efforts to establish an open and egalitarian community come from male adolescents alone. At the same time, we now have a context that allows us to read the feminist text that escapes the understanding of Cardinal's non-(consciously)-feminist narrator. We understand why her proclamations about reforming the family and challenging hierarchical structures have never rung quite true. The narrator considers herself to have abandoned an authority that her own text reveals she never had; she thinks she is creating a radically different notion of parental-child interaction that her own text exposes as largely a repetition of the stereotypical behavior of traditional women and mothers. Cardinal's own text thus serves to illustrate how a feminist methodology of rereading from a woman's perspective can reveal the significance of gender and both make its story readable and teach us how to read it.

Read from within the context reiterated by a double pattern of repetitions (the abortion memory and the cemetery visit), the general societal focus of *La Clé sur la porte* can also suggest not a lack of attention to gender but, on the contrary, an understanding that gender marks an intersection between the experiences specific to one individual and those common to the members of a particular society. In *La Clé*, Cardinal already inscribes her personal experience into the context of gender by attributing her own abortion memory to another mother and daughter. But the organization of *La Clé* around the critique of the traditional family also provides a larger framework for understanding female experience. In context, Moussia's story figures as only the last in a long series of examples of the pain that parents commonly inflict upon their children, regardless of gender, within current societal structures. Cardinal's memory of accompanying her mother to her sister's grave is similarly recontextualized. In *Les Mots pour le dire*, this passage marks the culmination of a sequence of parallel anecdotes that together reveal the dangerous emotional instability of the mother; in *La Clé*, however, her behavior is reduced to yet another illustration of the general destructiveness of the traditional family. The very structure of citation here reiterates such broad thematic interest; by virtue of the fact of repetition, an event loses its uniqueness and begins to exist in multiple versions. At the same time, such repetition usefully orients the helpless rage and unproductive hate of individual suffering toward collective action and the potential transformation of social and political institutions.

The third appearance of the abortion episode, in the autobiographical text *Au Pays de mes racines*, again establishes a key connection between the personal and the cultural that occurs precisely at the point of their intersection with gender. Cardinal's return to the very spot where her mother first revealed her attempts to abort her daughter places an interesting emphasis on context in and of itself. When the narrator of *Les Mots pour le dire* attempts to relate the event, its actual setting troubles her so profoundly that she initially substitutes the cozy living room of the family's country home for the noisy streets of Algiers: "In fact, it didn't happen like that. We weren't at the farm, in the living room, across from an open fire. Her entire monologue, all the information, revelations, and directives that she gave me about the condition of women, the family, morality, money—she poured all that out to me in the street" (MD 160). In *Au Pays de mes racines,* the blockage recurs and this time displaces the memory from its original context within the text itself (in a metaphorical repetition of the general [con]textual instability that results from autocitation): "Why did I have to wait until today to write down my emotional reaction the first day, immediately upon arrival, when I saw the Central Post Office?" (193).

Cardinal's understanding that her mother reveals less a personal anecdote of their private lives than a theory of gender and of class consciousness properly situates her revelation in the busy Mediterranean street that constitutes a virtual microcosm of humanity (see MD 162). Moreover, as *Au Pays de mes racines* makes clear, the site of Cardinal's personal tragedy coincides with that of the cultural tragedy of Algeria: "There, during the Algerian war, ... the crowd was slaughtered at pointblank range. ... There, in the same place, forty years ago, my mother broke my spirit..." (194). The explicit substitution of one mother for another that takes place at that moment—"I hung on to what I could, to the city, the sky, the sea. ... they became my mother and I loved them as I would have liked to love her" (198)—fuses the mother who kills with the mother who is killed, marking a locus at which gender openly mediates between the personal and the cultural.

Recontextualization also allows repetition to act as a form of erasure, of what Cardinal calls *usure,* an erosion or wearing away: "Once again I find myself embarked on my childhood, my adolescence! I will rehash them until they are eroded. In order to find communication at the end of this erosion. In order to take off my uniform, now ragged but still in one piece, of a bourgeois-Christian-Mediterranean woman. ... In order to think for myself and not as I was taught to think" (CP 206). Four texts later, this particular form of Cardinal's repetitions achieves its purpose, allowing her to abandon the painful personal exploration of her own upbringing: "I have considered it from all possible and imaginable points of view and I reject it in any/every case" (PR 26).

Cardinal is not, of course, refusing traditional female culture in these passages but rather the imposition on women of the gender and class consciousness of the dominant society that turns their lives into an endless cycle of sterile repetition designed to reproduce the very norms that constrain and marginalize them to begin with. Indeed, this compulsory role playing acts precisely to prevent communication between and among women by emphasizing the priority of other social ties over those of gender. In *Au Pays de mes racines,* Cardinal selects a comparable example from the lives of Arab women: "Nothing will occur to modify these female lives that will remain identical in every respect to those of their elders. . . . Their years will have no meaning, only the immutable repetition of tradition will have meaning. The old women will see to it that absolutely nothing changes. Nothing" (38). Such passages, importantly linked to a particular type of female experience, emphasize by contrast the crucial role that change and innovation always play in Cardinal's textual recurrences and in the female world that they reflect.

This *repetition* of *difference* that Cardinal uses to write the female life into existence, to introduce women's cultural experience into textuality, also serves to distinguish her work from that of such male writers as Robbe-Grillet in which the prominence and the visibility of repetition follow from the express effort to limit novelistic content to literary form itself. (Thus the parodic stereotypes that in Robbe-Grillet's work endlessly reproduce the objectification and the violation of the female body supposedly reflect textual and intertextual repetition, unrelated to the actual status and situation of women themselves.)[25] Nor, of course, does Cardinal's use of autocitation correspond to Robbe-Grillet's attempt to show that writing and not reality engenders texts. Self-quotation functions in Cardinal's work not as an oppositional but as a relational technique that by turning life and literature, autobiography and fiction into indistinguishable mirror images of each other might finally allow textual production in and of itself to have a political impact in the world of the reader and the writer. Linda Hutcheon bases just such a hope on the possibility of redefining (rather than rupturing) the mimetic link between art and life: "To read is to act; to act is both to interpret and to create anew—to be revolutionary, perhaps in political as well as literary terms" (161).

NOTES

1. The epigraph with which James Clifford introduces *The Predicament of Culture* offers an interesting parallel, namely, Paraguayan Indians use imagery very similar to Cardinal's to represent their own relationship to dominant culture: "We hope that the day will come when they realize that we are their roots and that we must grow together like a giant tree with its branches and flowers" (1). Clifford suggests that the diverse "groups marginalized or silenced in the

bourgeois West: 'natives,' women" enter the "ethnographic space" of dominant ideological systems in similar ways (5).

2. Nancy Armstrong's *Desire and Domestic Fiction* offers a highly original reading of the domestic novel in eighteenth- and nineteenth-century England that significantly alters the theoretical framework of other feminist critics and historians. Armstrong makes the development of a female-specific culture and its textual tradition central to any adequate understanding of political history and cultural change in general. The priority she grants to representation over reality informs a parallel discussion of how language can empower women to represent their own sphere and to constitute their own subjectivity.

3. If my own language (my use of Anglophone/Anglo-American and Francophone/French) continues to appear inadequately consistent, this results not only from my desire to respect the apparent requirements of a given context but, more pertinently, to allow other feminist scholars the terms that they prefer.

4. Lionnet, who reads *Les Mots pour le dire* as "a critique of colonialism," argues that the narrator's internalization of "the debilitating sexual and racial stereotypes of [her] colonial past" is central to Cardinal's narrative of female madness (*Life/Lines* 263).

5. Roland Barthes notes that only "rereading" can hope to save the text from "repetition" since "those who fail to reread are obliged to read the same story everywhere" (*S/Z* 22).

6. In a significant example of intercultural agreement, Patrocinio P. Schweikart locates the central motivation of feminist reading—"actually, a rereading"—in "the need to 'connect,' to recuperate, or to formulate—they come to the same thing—the context, the tradition, that would link women writers to one another, to women readers and critics, and to the larger community of women" (48). Cardinal's use of repetition, of internal rereading, does indeed suggest that repetitive reading provides one example of those "reading strategies consonant with the concerns, experiences, and formal devices that constitute [women's] texts" (45) that Schweikart encourages us to seek.

7. In fact, my conversations with Cardinal suggest that she is not so much ambivalent about revealing her textual practice as she is deliberately nonreflective about it and therefore unaware of precisely how it functions. In either case, the result is the same: we cannot take her precisely at her word. Yalom too notes that Cardinal told her in a 1983 interview "how surprised she was to realize only recently, from the observation of one of her readers, that *La Souricière* and *Les Mots pour le dire* related essentially the same story" (117).

8. Philippe Lejeune (*Moi aussi*) notes that this presumed difference in aesthetic value seriously complicates his long-term critical efforts to distinguish the autobiography from the novel. The designation "novel" has come less to identify a work of fiction than a work of "literature"; it acts as "a stamp of literary

quality that calls the book to the attention of readers and of panels of judges who grant literary prizes" (43).

9. Curiously, Cardinal's objections do at least appear to have introduced a certain instability into current critical categorizations. At least two reviewers (Xenakis, Canestrier) call *Au Pays de mes racines,* the openly autobiographical account of Cardinal's return to Algeria in 1980, a "novel."

10. Corddry, a 1983 interviewer of Cardinal, describes her as extremely reticent to provide details about her own life: "why is her questioner so curious about her relationship to her husband, she asks" (C2).

11. An additional example in which the textual interaction of life and literature becomes particularly vertiginous is found in Cardinal's first published novel, *Ecoutez la mer.* It includes a passage in which the description of Maria's and Karl's lovemaking alternates with its erotic analogy, Maria's childhood memories of swimming in the Mediterranean. When Cardinal herself quotes this passage verbatim in *Autrement dit,* she asks us to reread it through the eyes of her own jealous husband, whom she fully expects to treat it as autobiography. In the intervening *Mots pour le dire,* the fictional narrator gives her first novel, of undisclosed content, to her husband to read; afterward, she describes their lovemaking, interspersed with her recollections of childhood swims in the Mediterranean. Here, the successive metamorphoses of a single passage have eliminated genre boundaries, challenged textual autonomy, and fused writing and its referents.

12. In an interesting repetition, the first woman artist to appear in Cardinal's work, Madeleine Couturier (her very name, of course, associates female creativity and traditional domestic work), literally constructs a vast "plant cathedral" out of all-natural materials (MC).

13. This is what Homans actually says: "I am arguing for the recovery of historical experience, not for the existence, much less the perpetuation, of any essential difference between men and women. I am not arguing that women should write (or do anything else) as daughters or as mothers, but only that in the nineteenth century women did nothing, including writing, except as women. Women's exclusive mothering, which has not fundamentally changed since the nineteenth century (certainly our myths of parenthood have not changed), is the result of a social system oppressive to women" (*Bearing* 29).

14. Suzanne Juhasz makes essentially the same point: "In their form, women's lives tend to be like the stories that they tell: they show less a pattern of linear development towards some clear goal than one of repetitive, cumulative, cyclical structure. One thinks of housework or childcare, of domestic life in general. . . . Dailiness matters to most women; and dailiness is by definition never a conclusion, always a process" (223–24). See also Bettina Aptheker, esp. chaps. 1–2.

15. Gilbert and Gubar interpret the sampler, which always includes both the female autograph and a representation of the alphabet, as a reminder that "when women have not used a needle as a pen, they have needed to needle the world with their pens" ("Ceremonies" 34).

16. Janet M. Paterson's work on Anne Hébert informs her suggestion that embroidery (and repetition) may function together to constitute a characteristically female metaphor for the self-reflective text: "Indeed, it is unusual not to discover in an autorepresentative text a reduction of the signifying practice to the scale of certain signs. In *Les Chambres de bois, Kamouraska*, and *Héloïse*, the metaphor of *embroidery* most clearly expresses the notions of creativity and of textual material. Embroidery, often evoked in these novels, gradually assumes a metaphoric function precisely because of this redundancy" (122). The importance of knitting in Virginia Woolf's work, notably in *To the Lighthouse* and *Mrs. Dalloway* (where its association with art recalls *Le Passé empiété*), further suggests an obvious intercultural repetition.

17. Weaving (*le tissage, le tressage*), the only cultural activity whose discovery Freud attributed to women (though in his view it originated in women's efforts to weave together their pubic hair in imitation of the penis they lack; see Lamy 78), also connects them to textual activity (text, from *texere*, to weave). In this context, too, contemporary theory "repeats" Freud to new ends. Roland Barthes, for example, equates *text, fabric*, and *braid; l'écriture* itself is formed by the interaction of semiotic codes, "these woven or weaving voices" (*S/Z* 166).

18. For an alternative view, see Aptheker, whose affirmation that "quilting in a variety of forms is evidenced in many places throughout the world" allows her to take into account the specific socioeconomic conditions in which "quilting was introduced into the United States" (68).

19. I discovered with delight that Françoise Lionnet's reading of Cardinal leads to the identification of a similar process, described in surprisingly similar terms: "This problematic would point to a notion of the female text as *métissage*, that is, the weaving of different strands of raw material and threads of various cultures into one piece of fabric; female texuality as *métissage*" (*Life/Lines* 277). Moreover, *métissage* subsequently appears as metaphor for Lionnet's own reading practice in *Autobiographical Voices* (3–18, 29). Similarly, Aptheker's discussion of how "stories are pieced together like a quilt" in specific women's texts reiterates "the significance of the quilting process as a way of thinking" (67) that the structure of her own text repeatedly illustrates.

20. Clifford Geertz describes culture as just such a contextual container: "Culture is not a power, something to which social events, behavior, institutions or processes can be causally attributed; it is a context, something within which they can be intelligibly—that is—thickly described" (14).

21. Within Cardinal's work as a whole, her pluralistic incarnations of a fe-

male life—her shifting focus on mother or daughter, on housewife or artist, on girl or woman—reveal repetition's capacity to multiply perspective, to portray female culture with the completeness and the complexity of a cubist painting. In a 1987 interview, Cardinal herself offers precisely this interpretation of her textual repetitions: "I think that those who write always write the same book. First you have the daughter in conflict with the mother; then the daughter becomes a mother. Finally, the wife-mother faces men, her children. When you write, you dig a hole, you make it deeper or else wider. You write only one vast book" (Déméron 71).

22. Lionnet's reading of *Les Mots pour le dire* supports this view (see note 4 above), as does the very structure of her analysis, which presents the work of Cardinal and Marie-Thérèse Humbert as comparable, despite clear differences of race and class.

23. Antoine Compagnon asks: "But what are stereotypes and clichés if not in fact quotations?" (29).

24. In *Au Pays de mes racines,* Cardinal describes the loss of self that results from her false transplantation to France in terms of a decal: "In countries that resemble mine, . . . once in a while, the fleeting impression that I exist, that I'm there, whole, as I was in my childhood. . . . Frenzied desire to rediscover the person I was, who I must still be. It's been too long since I lost connivance with a space, complicity with a natural rhythm, perfect understanding of the signs of color, odor, noise. Here, I'm losing myself. I'm fraying away, I'm being diluted, I'm a decal" (48–49).

25. Alice Jardine also notes that the feminist reader clearly perceives that it is precisely in "those texts chosen as exemplary by the theorists of the-process-beyond-representation that some of the cruelest presentations of women's bodies and destinies remain" (*Gynesis* 140).

CHAPTER TWO

Female Discourse
The Difference of Repetition

"From the beginning," notes Diane Crowder, "the modern feminist movement has confronted the problem of language" (126). Since "the problem of language," however, inevitably refuses to remain stable as the manageable object of feminist discourse but always insists on throwing itself forward into that very discourse (from the Greek *problema,* thing thrown forward), modern feminists have expressed our confrontations with the problem of language in widely diverse terms. We have, for example, variously queried the relationships between *parole* and *écriture,* between the gender of the text and the sex of the writer, between the expression of sexism and sexual expression; we have further pondered language's ability to construct reality or to reflect it, to coextend with our experience or to stand apart from it, to serve us or to fail us. The issue for the moment is less one of a divergence of arguments than of a difference in expression that makes it difficult to identify an essentially similar argument. In these circumstances, we may just as well allow Crowder to speak momentarily for us all, Cardinal included, although I am going to let Cardinal speak for herself as well. Crowder proposes that feminists have responded to the problem of language in terms of "three basic positions":

> *Crowder:* "The first focuses upon women's silence. Women have been systematically excluded from public discourse, and language reflects that exclusion. Women have been quite literally 'seen' as objects of male discourse, but never 'heard' as subjects of a female discourse" (126).
> *Cardinal:* "History has excluded us, it denies us language, it speaks for us: History, not women, tells our lifestories" (ME 37).

"I am interested in the History of women because I am a woman, but especially because it is the History of silence" (ME 46).

> *Crowder:* "A second view is that a woman's speech characterized by specialized vocabulary and syntactic forms has developed" (126).
>
> *Cardinal:* "Leave them no means of self-expression other than the vocabulary of housework, cleaning, food. . . . they will once again find the way to exist" (AD 163). "How can we speak our sexuality, the experience of gestation, women's sense of time and duration? We will have to invent. Language will be feminized, it will open up, it will be embellished and enriched" (AD 89).

> *Crowder:* "The third view holds that women have been forced to accept the appropriation of language by men, but have no inherent alienation from it. They have only to seize language and turn it to their own uses" (126).
>
> *Cardinal:* "Let's use their language, let's adopt their arguments—not to speak *for* them (we don't want to mythicize them) but to show them, texts and documents at hand, just how misogynistic they are" (ME 39).

I am not attempting to turn an Anglophone monologue into an intercultural dialogue, for Crowder has already done that on her own; she connects her linguistic framework to the one outlined in the founding manifesto of *Questions féministes*,[1] and it provides the context for her reading of Hélène Cixous and Monique Wittig. More importantly, Crowder and Cardinal do not appear to be in dialogue: their voices echo rather than answer each other. Since Crowder views her three positions as mutually exclusive—held either by different people at the same time or by the same person at different times—Cardinal's concurrence on all three points does, however, reintroduce a potentially greater complexity into feminist responses to "the problem of language." (Crowder, of course, is well aware of "the risk of oversimplification" that inevitably accompanies any attempt to classify.) Cardinal indeed articulates all three positions contemporaneously, as evidenced most recently in her 1987 novel, *Les Grands Désordres*. Throughout this text, Elsa paradoxically remains, at all times and at one and the same time, the silent object of a male-authored narrative; the author of a text characterized by her own "rhythm," "vocabulary," and "linguistic idiosyncracies" (151); and the skillful manipulator of a male language that she has appropriated for purposes to which its original practitioners explicitly object. Without yet entering in detail into the narrative complexities of a novel to which I will return in the next chapter, I want to introduce *Les Grands Désordres* as an introduction to Cardinal's current understanding of "the problem of language."

(Re)Contextualizing "the Problem of Language"

To finance her study of psychology, Elsa takes a position as secretary to Professor Greffier, a physicist whose specialty is the field of thermodynamics. But through a process that involves a new understanding of language, of gender, and of their interrelationship, a job viewed as a temporary necessity quickly evolves into a permanent need. Originally, Elsa believes that her sex automatically excludes her from any real participation in Greffier's work: "In my eyes, his field of specialization was a male field to which I had no access because I was a woman. It was as stupid as that: 'Women understand nothing at all about mechanics'" (200). But the importance here of traditional assumptions about gender lies far less in this initial exclusion that Elsa accepts without question than in a second, far more significant exclusion that the first simultaneously allows her to deny: "Words forced the doors of this universe to open to me. By the same occasion, I discovered that the fact that I was a woman had an important effect on my work and my convictions" (200). Not only is language accessible to women, but it provides access to that which gender renders otherwise inaccessible and, thus, to the significance of gender itself.

Without Greffier's knowledge, Elsa copies from his work certain passages and definitions that attract her and pastes them to the walls of her own office at home. As Cardinal reproduces Elsa's intertexual constructions within the text of *Les Grands Désordres,* we too begin to live in a world that is literally created and structured by language:

> Words erected a shelter around me. A tent made from a fabric of strange texture but which was strong, very strong, ever stronger. Words, certain words, intermingled, reunited, then moved apart, only to find each other again further on and take off once more. Atomized words whose freed particles zigzagged, obstinately following mad, unpredictable paths, along which, rather than losing their meaning, they were enriched by other

meanings. Instead of incoherence, this explosion of words created a luminous coherence: the dazzling universe of knowledge. (205)

In a passage that represents what Nancy K. Miller calls "the internal female signature" ("Arachnologies" 234), Cardinal's "luminous" metaphors figure the functioning of both her own writing and written feminism in general. She describes a feminist methodology of rereading in which, as Irma Garcia suggests, "to reread is also to join together" (*relire, c'est aussi relier;* 1:16). As in Cardinal's exemplary practice of autocitation, intertexuality, the juxtaposition of fragments of already existing texts, generates new meaning and coherence through the interplay, the echoing and the repetition, of language itself. Similarly, feminist scholarship's rapprochement of widely divergent texts sets in motion surprising similarities of meaning and expression whose coalescence into a common set of assumptions about women and gender produces the new knowledge that is feminism.[2]

Within the specific context of contemporary feminist literary criticism, Cardinal also distinguishes herself by not focusing exclusively on the written text and on women. The connections that Anglophone critics (e.g., Showalter, Gilbert and Gubar) (re)create through the identification of thematic and formal similarities and that Francophone critics (e.g., Garcia, Lamy) (re)construct through (inter)textual resemblance, Cardinal very explicitly locates within language itself. Thus, she makes visible the actual process by which women "seize language and turn it to their own uses." If language has, in fact, been appropriated by men, then the copying of male texts in which Elsa initially engages logically constitutes women's only means of access to language. But this linguistic *vol,* by which women both "steal" language and "fly away" with it, fully confirms "the subversive value of women's writing" (Garcia 2:141).[3]

Appropriately, Cardinal encodes her subversion of male language and writing within the linguistic play of her own words. Greffier's very name names the male as the rightful heir of language. Both the original French meaning and the etymology of *le greffe* (from the Latin *graphium,* stylet) identify a *stylet pour écrire,* a stiletto used as a writing tool. Moreover, in modern French usage, *le greffier* refers to the clerk of the court who keeps in his office (*le greffe*) the official records of legal proceedings; the writer has become the "guardian" of writing, the person (to paraphrase—*to steal*—from the dictionary) legally responsible for managing the property of someone considered by law to be incompetent to manage *her* own affairs. It seems remarkably apt that an instrument of writing denied to women should take the form of a weapon; but in the war of words that Cardinal wages, language itself begins to turn on men, for *le greffe* also identifies a very different type of stiletto used for making eyelet holes in a particular kind of embroidery. The dagger of destruction wielded by men becomes a tool of creation in the hands of women. One likes to think too that eyelet embroidery, its "small holes edged with fine embroidery stitches as part of a design," might represent Greffier's transformed text, not destroyed but embellished by the visible absence of the passages that Elsa removes as part of *her* design.

In any event, Cardinal's subversion of the male text does involve its submergence under her own most characteristic writing practice, so that the text that initially names men's linguistic privilege turns out in retrospect to illustrate women's writing. Not only is the masculine noun *le greffe* undermined from within by a semantic shift in gender that fuses the pen and the needle, but the word itself is doubly (en)gendered. *La greffe* refers to the textual "grafts" that Elsa cuts out of Greffier's work to transplant into a new text of her own making; Cardinal's literal quotation of these grafted passages in the midst of Elsa's narrative further associates the theft/flight of male language with her general practice of autocitation.[4]

This analogy between female writing and surgical procedure introduces women into the realm of science where their usurpation of the role of practitioner effects additional subversive operations. In a textual revolution appropriately figured as an atomic explosion, Cardinal transforms physics into a metaphor for the functioning of women's language: "Atomized words whose freed particules zigzagged, obstinately following mad, unpredictable paths, along which, rather than losing their meaning, they were enriched by other meanings. Instead of incoherence, this explosion of words created a luminous coherence: the dazzling universe of knowledge" (204–5). At the risk of turning a rereading into an overreading (but Miller suggests that uncovering the "female signature" requires just such a practice [288]), this text seems to undermine scientific knowledge and the discourse of science. The splitting of the atom ought to produce permanent rather than temporary chaos; certainly the rules of both physics and semantics outlaw the (re)union of fission and fusion that takes place here. Physics defines particles by the irrelevance of their motion and structure to any particular problem; here their activity multiplies meaning and leads directly to a new knowledge and coherence. Both of these, moreover, are modified by adjectives whose etymology identifies this knowledge and coherence as specifically and originally female. Greffier insists on renaming Elsa: "I understood that by baptizing me 'Luce,' he was appropriating my entire person. I was Luce only for him" (201). But the appropriation, in fact, backfires, for "Luce" (from the Latin, *lux, lucis;* French *lumière* [light]) refuses to be "quite literally 'seen' as [the] object of male discourse" (Crowder 126). Not only does she steal Greffier's knowledge and words, but she alone has the real power to en-gender and to name, indeed, to give her *own* name to a new linguistic coherence that is *lumineuse* (full of light) and a new universe of knowledge that is *éblouissant* (dazzling with intense light).

The juxtaposition of Elsa's own narrative with the quotations that she copies reinforces the difference (made visible by their presence on facing pages) between her self-reflexive, metaphorical, repetitive, pluralistic text about language and the rational, objective, linear, authoritarian discourse of science. But, at the same time, linguistic contamination ("the alteration of a form through misunderstood association with another") explodes science's claim to reproduce an undistorted empirical reality and exposes it as both discourse and discourse of a particular kind. Elsa's predilection for copying definitions, moreover, goes even further to define science as a language, a vocabulary, the raw material for someone else's discourse. Just prior to the passage on the power of words, the female and male texts begin to intersect, to repeat each other, as Elsa rewrites science, using the vocabulary that it provides as a textual generator:

> ZERO: point of departure. Nothingness.
> *Absolute Zero:* ($-273.15°$ C), the lowest temperature attainable at which the kinetic energy of molecules is virtually nonexistent.

> Absolute zero... this zero which isn't one and which is nonetheless absolute. I dreamed about what -273.16 might be like when the cells are paralyzed by the cold, or -273.14, just before immobility when there is still a glimmer of hope... Life, death. (204)

The subjectivity and the speculation that Elsa reintroduces into the objectivity of scientific definition supports her application of the laws of thermodynamics to the behavior of human beings, of a "non-life" science to human life.

In general, Elsa's reorganization of knowledge around the semantic pluralism of language, the ability of words to refer to different things at the same time, incites her to link the fields of psychology and thermodynamics: "Words led me to establish a parallel between the nervous mechanisms of the human body and the mechanisms of any given machine. I discovered that the laws of thermodynamics could be applied word for word to the human machine" (205). Thus language not only opens up male domains to women; once they are inside, it continues to "force doors open" by challenging the traditional fragmentation of knowledge into separate disciplines. By the (ab)use of this very procedure to fragment disciplinary discourse itself into isolated quotations that destroy an illusionary coherence grounded only in submission to the rules and the authority of the discipline,[5] Cardinal uncovers a vast new network of interdisciplinary connections that redefine knowledge as inclusive, synthesizing, and supportive.

In an odd way, Greffier's total rejection, in the name of science, of Elsa's theory of the interdisciplinary nature of knowledge may implicitly define it as a feminist epistemology; in any event, he appears to equate the objectivity and the integrity of physics with the objectification and the substitutability of women: "I'm a man of science and I don't give a damn about individuals. You should know, you've reproached me often enough for not distinguishing between one woman and another" (249). Certainly he recognizes that intertextuality underlies interdisciplinary connections, for he focuses his attack primarily on language itself: "It's possible to make any word mean anything at all. You have a poetic attitude toward facts that is totally unscientific" (247). Greffier's insistent retreat at this point into a world of equations and empirical proof indirectly reveals his fear, appropriate on the part of a scientist whose very own words lie at the origin of Elsa's theories, that science too might be, at least in part, an arbitrary linguistic construction.

Feminist scholarship has not always successfully honored its own commitment to the necessarily interdisciplinary nature of knowledge. Within the social sciences, the boundaries of a particular discipline have tended to delimit a feminist critique that has consequently challenged disciplinary bias less on the basis of where it draws the line than in terms of general methodological values—objectivity, hierarchy, or authority—that conflict with feminist ideology. Thus feminist critiques of sociology, psychology, and economics, for example, may be conducted very similarly and seek essentially the same changes, but they are unlikely to intersect directly or to propose a radical restructuring of their respective disciplinary boundaries.[6]

Feminist literary criticism, on the other hand, has been increasingly informed by feminist scholarship in the social sciences. Nancy Chodorow's psychoanalytic model of female development has grounded the interpretation of women's friendships in literature; Ardener's anthropological model of muted and dominant culture has revealed the coexistence of two different levels of narrative in women's writing; historical knowledge of women's socioeconomic position in ancient Greece has recontexualized a reading of classical tragedy (Lefkowitz and Fant); and so on. But here too interdisciplinary scholarship primarily illuminates the conditions in which women write and the content of what they write, leaving writing itself, a particular use of language, to be cited as the difference of literary texts but to be in fact treated, in the absence of analysis, as if it were identical to historical narrative or political commentary. Cardinal's fusion of the intertextual and the interdisciplinary, her suggestion that we let the intersections of words identify similarities of thought and application, might allow an approach that would respect and illuminate linguistic and textual difference and provide feminist scholarship with an interdisciplinary vocabulary of great density and richness that would more successfully break down traditional boundaries.

Evelyn Fox Keller's critique of scientific discourse has revealed that the parallel attitudes toward knowledge and women that we glimpse in Greffier in fact constitute a persistent and characteristic pattern within science. Keller's work differs from other feminist critiques of science, because her own academic training allows her to speak from within science rather than from the more usual and somewhat more detached position of the philosopher of science. Moreover, she differs as well from most other feminist scientists in that she speaks as a still-practicing (though, admittedly, less and less often) physicist rather than as a former biologist. Yet, despite such differences of situation and perspective, Keller also tends to focus her critique on those sciences whose clear application to human life appear to make them more immediately accessible to an analysis of gender.

Interestingly, Cardinal's dissection of the discourse of thermodynamics reconfirms the promise of Keller's linguistic approach by extending it to an area of science that has remained virtually untouched by a feminist critique. Gilbert and Gubar's analysis of linguistic occultation as the essential strategy used by male modernists to protect their privileged literary domain from the encroachments of women writers (*No Man's* 252–54) surely identifies a practice more clearly and more consistently characteristic of science than of any other field. Greffier hires Elsa to perform a task that, irrelevant for him, is in fact replete with subversive potential: "My job was . . . to clean up [*mettre au propre*] certain articles that he wrote for popular scientific journals" (200–201). If the attribution to women of a language both proper and "common" is a traditional one (*No Man's* 252–54), it is hardly innocent or inconsequential when used to rewrite the discourse of science. (Nor, of course, is the use of the novel form, also associated with women, for the same purpose.) The language of *Les Grands Désordres* at times reveals a certain willful banality that offers textual confirmation for Elsa's assertion that language allows women to accede *as women* to knowledge produced by men. Moreover, the words that attract Elsa's attention in scientific discourse (e.g., *heating, cooling, order, disorder, energy, entropy*), like those on which Keller concentrates in the languages of other sciences, both organize themselves into the paired oppositions that inevitably recall the structure of gender and suggest a semantic link to human sexuality that becomes explicit as Cardinal's text rewrites them into a love story.

Antoine Compagnon uses the same analogy as Cardinal between quotation and grafting to stress the delicacy and the uncertainty of the first operation: even once the passage being cited has been successfully transplanted to a new context, the risk of rejection continues to pose a serious threat (29). The coherent world of reason, order, and knowledge that scientific language has constructed around Elsa protects her only "until Laure's story occurs, until the heroine intervenes. . . . My world was annihilated" (207). Elsa discovers (in circumstances that need not yet concern us) that although male language is fully accessible to women, to the point that they can even rewrite it from their own perspective and so revise the male story that it encodes, it nonetheless cannot serve to tell a female story; women's *own* story remains inaccessible. The narrative structure of *Les Grands Désordres* stresses this from the beginning, for Elsa has not initially been able to tell *her* own story either; her text is being ghosted by a male *nègre*.

It is hard to decide whether the term is more revealing in English or in French. The ghostwriter, the still-creative spirit of a dead person, replaces the woman who has been "killed into [male] fiction" (Gilbert and Gubar, *Madwoman* 14–15); the *nègre* adopts the female persona of oppression and subservience—he steals the woman's identity along with her story. Just after Elsa reads her ghostwriter's manuscript (the first part of *Les Grands Désordres*), she retreats into a period of near madness characterized by the refusal to speak or to eat; having lost her voice, she attempts to actualize this metaphorical death of the self. But leaving aside for the moment the intricate question of the gender of the narrative in *Les Grands Désordres,* I want to focus at this point on the specific question of women's relationship to language. As we know, Cardinal tends to (re)produce texts in repetitive pairs, in which some form of nonfictional (and at least partially autobiographical) writing acts as a springboard for the simultaneous writing of fiction. In the present case, *La Médée d'Euripide* (1986) (consisting of Cardinal's translation of Euripides' *Medea,* accompanied by a prefatory essay and an interview in which she explores the circumstances of the translation) constitutes the companion text to *Les Grands Désordres.*

Cardinal explicitly equates the translator with the ghostwriter, whose profession she herself practiced for some seventeen years. The two share not only the same relationship to a prior text written by another (for Cardinal's work as a ghostwriter always involved the reworking of an already existent text, on the model of Elsa and Greffier), but they also share the same relationship to writing itself, one that determines their specific choice of textual activity: "When I read a text, the writing, the literary construction, interests me more than the subject matter. My life centers around a fascination with writing" (112–13).[7] It seems increasingly ironic that Cardinal should be accused of "writing badly," on the clear, if unspoken, assumption that for both popular and feminist writers (all the more so then for a popular feminist writer), the message *is* the medium. Certainly a passion for writing hardly guarantees that one will write "well" (whatever that means), but Cardinal will at least not write "badly" on the grounds outlined here, for what absorbs her—writing, a textual contexture, a particular arrangement of written words—is precisely what is *not* the message.

And yet, she is hardly indifferent to content. For both the ghostwriter and the translator, reading and writing are totally integrated activities; and Cardinal knows textual meaning by heart before she writes a word: "I used to read their manuscripts ten or twenty times until I knew them as well as they did and sometimes better. . . . I did the same thing with Medea. I read, reread, rereread, rerereread, until every detail of every line was in my head" (117). Moreover, Cardinal repeatedly asserts her absolute fidelity to the text that she translated and to all those that she ghosted. At the same time, as we all know, *what* one says cannot be separated from *how* one says it. And, once again, Cardinal appears to concur: "I think that a genuine art of translation is creative. It involves totally immersing yourself in a text and reconstructing it differently" (116–17).

I do not think that Cardinal means to be perversely paradoxical, but neither do I think that the apparent paradox can be resolved by reintroducing a distinction between two kinds of writing that Cardinal temporarily confuses. Writing a text of one's own and rewriting the text of another certainly constitute potentially different and separable activities, but their fusion in Cardinal's work is deliberate and permanent. Her signature act of autocitation casts her in the role of the translator or the ghostwriter of her *own* work and requires us to pay close attention to the particular conceptions of language and writing that they put into practice. To define writing as the rewriting of another text significantly alters the relationship between content and form. If we write our own text, language and meaning will be coextensive; meaning comes to exist only as we give it form, and we come to believe that what we mean to say could not be expressed in any other way. We make the opposite assumption when we rewrite another text; we now act on the belief that the same thing can be said in many different ways. In this second case, therefore, we accord language an importance and an independence that we deny it in the first. Once we posit signification—or, at least, the signifying process—as stable, we are free to celebrate not only the semantic pluralism of language but its formal pluralism as well. Since we do not challenge the internal coherence of the sign (we have not severed the relationship between the signifier and the signified; we have simply rendered it nonproblematic), we can focus on the relationships between and among signifiers without any need to deny meaning at the same time; indeed, with every possibility of restating meaning over and over.

This linguistic positioning should not be confused with the naive view, often attributed to Anglophone feminists, that meaning exists prior to and apart from its expression in language; Cardinal explicitly rewrites texts, not "reality." On the other hand, neither do we have a repetition of the politically controversial position, sometimes associated with Francophone feminists, that language permanently defers and displaces meaning; Cardinal's texts signify—repeatedly. What we do have, then, is a position that by focusing simultaneously on the signified *and* the signifier, rather than on either the relationship *within* the sign or *between* the sign and its referent, can accommodate at one and the same time the twentieth-century belief that meaning is always temporary and subjective, always constructed in and through language, and the feminist belief that language has the capacity to say things that matter and to bring about change.

In a third and final shift, Elsa emerges from her silence to (re)claim her linguistic rights. For the first time, she provides her ghostwriter with her own written version of events rather than allowing him to transcribe her oral account; she thus assumes responsibility for the construction of meaning in language. At precisely the same time, she becomes aware of the semantic pluralism that could allow someone else to relate her story differently; she literally duplicates her own text to prevent the ghostwriter from rewriting it: "I made a copy. I'm a bit wary of you just the same" (198). More importantly, Elsa comes to writing through what we have good reason at present to identify as a characteristically female form of repetition, through a version of Cardinal's favorite practice of autocitation that now serves as textual generator.[8] On its first appearance, the originary sentence of a text entitled "Portrait of Professor Greffier" ("He was there on his divan" [170]) leads into an inventory of the room. The second time ("He was there on his dark leather divan" [170]), it produces a description of the couch itself. The third time ("He was there on his divan, I could see the claw marks" [171]), the text turns away from its male object toward its female subject to explore the narrator's point of view. Thus, each time an additional element is added, the text strays further from its main clause in pursuit of the new. Only when the original version reappears ("He was there on his divan" [172]) can Elsa finally take off from the initial word to describe Greffier himself. The completion of this project leads to a fifth and final repetition that introduces the difference ("He was there on his divan, dethroned, pitiful" [177]) that simultaneously frees Elsa from Greffier and her own text. That the topic of Elsa's first written text should be "Greffier"—that is, metaphorically speaking, writing itself—identifies Cardinal's autocitations as autoreferential as well as autogenerative, three dimensions of repetition to which we now need to (re)turn our attention.

Self-referential Strategies

Cardinal's springboard theory, in which writing becomes its own instigation and reflection, points toward a mirroring effect common in contemporary Francophone experimental writing. But the particular conjunction in Cardinal's work of autoreflexive structure and the merging of life and text may also identify, as I have already suggested, a specifically female form of a general practice. Michel Mercier, for example, notes the frequency with which "composition in 'abyme'" appears in the "mirror-work" of women writers where it sets up the same "nebulous boundary between novel and autobiography" (18–19) that is visible throughout Cardinal's texts. Similarly, the simultaneity of reading and writing required by repetition produces what Irma Garcia characterizes as "the act of creation distinctive of the woman, who continually watches her writing being written" (1:50).[9] In any event, Cardinal's practice of autocitation requires in and of itself a certain degree of textual self-consciousness. And indeed, two consecutive series of identical passages confirm the fact that autocitation consistently occurs at the moment when writing surfaces as the overt subject matter of the text. Or rather, repetition itself functions to transform apparently unrelated topics into metaphors for the act of writing.

Simone, the narrator of *Une Vie pour deux,* experiences a moment of severe panic after asking her husband Jean-François to read the notebooks in which she has been secretly writing "L'Histoire de Mary MacLaughlin," the story of an unknown woman whose corpse he discovered on the beach (249–50). Simone's sense of vulnerability provokes a radical decomposition of the self to which death seems the only solution. But even as she explores different possibilities for suicide, her imagination establishes a series of connections that more accurately identify the transformation under way as the rebirth of the self as writer: "She imagined her dead body, the body of a suicide, exposed to view. To Jean-François's view. Like Mary's body, like the pages in his hands. No, not death" (249). Simone's allegorical hallucination, in which women's writing is identified with the female body (a metaphor to which I will return) and critical judgment with the male gaze, illuminates the self-reflexive structure of the novel as a whole. Whereas Jean-François obsessively associates the female body with death after his encounter with Mary MacLaughlin, Simone's act of textual transposition not only restores her to life but simultaneously grants significance and importance to what Simone imagines as the most conventional of female lives.

The description of Simone's anxiety also constitutes an integral repetition of a passage in *Autrement dit* (50–51) in which Cardinal recalls the experience with madness that had emerged previously as the essential subject matter of *Les Mots pour le dire*. Thus, textual juxtaposition identifies Cardinal's recurrent expressions of mental and emotional anguish as clear and explicit metaphors for the situation of the woman writer. In particular, the compelling invitation to reread that repetition issues us reveals the important degree to which *Les Mots pour le dire* also recounts the autoreferential story of female silence and expression. At each recurrence of her neurotic symptoms, the narrator finds herself "incapable of speech, of self-expression" (50), and her triumph over madness gradually takes shape as a coming to writing, the single endeavor that she undertakes, significantly, without either informing her psychoanalyst or seeking his approval. Not surprisingly, each of Cardinal's future experiences with writer's block will mark the temporary return of the neurotic state that she associates with female aphasia. Her use here of lexical repetition, as in the following examples, establishes an interesting connection between two different series of textual recurrence: "Admit that I'm sending you on a lovely trip in your little golden submarine. . . . What a superb storm I'm offering you!" (CP 220); "That creates a beautiful storm to smash little submarines to pieces!" (MD 169); "Submarine. To be an armoured, blind submarine. . . . Dead" (AD 50; VD 249). By describing the temptation of suicide that accompanies female neurosis in the same language as the abortion attempts, Cardinal insists on the capacity of female writing to transform death into the birth of a new self.

Cardinal's incorporation into *Une Vie pour deux* of a passage from *Autrement dit* leads directly and immediately into a second example of the same procedure. This repetition of repetition, the use of *mise en abyme* as a *mise en évidence*, appropriately follows the identification of the importance of the act of writing for women with a further explanation of its specific nature. In *Autrement dit*, Leclerc identifies in Cardinal a complementarity between what she calls the "vague" and the "ruled": "Annie often points out that everything in me is a mixture of vagueness and rules. . . . it's true that I need rules. For rules give me a starting point from which to wander [*divaguer*] and I can't live if I don't wander" (22). Cardinal's reflections on this paradoxical description lead her to associate her sense of self with Garcia Lorca's definition of "rootless and floating jasmine" (23). (Once again Cardinal introduces her own replications into an a priori state of textual repetition.) If jasmine's "rule" makes it dependent on the particular needs and requirements of its botanical family, "jasmine is above all a heavy perfume that penetrates everywhere" (23). Cardinal describes its delicately intrusive passage through the springtime air of Algiers; the perfume's Baudelairian powers of evocation awaken a kind of collective consciousness of life's fundamental cycles that she translates by direct quotation: "You smell it and you think: 'spring is almost over,' . . . 'soon there will be grapes,' . . . 'I'll make love tonight,' 'my stomach feels empty,' 'my daughter's almost twenty,' 'now how long has it been since my father died?'" (23).

In *Une Vie pour deux,* the passage recurs as a specific illustration of the act of writing just after Simone recognizes her vocation as writer. Jasmine's qualities now characterize the insidious force of the desire to write—"No obstacle . . . can halt its perfidious progression" (250)—and reflect the evocative power of language—"Ossicles of letters that join together to exhume the skeletons of phantasms and give them the flesh of words" (251). In this context, Cardinal's use of quoted platitudes confirms her commitment to writing as a collaborative enterprise devoted to the expression of common experience. Moreover, the juxtaposition of the two passages establishes an important link between a particular sense of female identity and the specificity of female writing. Cardinal's evocation of the "gardens of my head" leads to the recognition of the plurality of the female self (an issue that I will explore more fully in the next chapter): "How many billions of *fibers* make up the *fabric* of my life? How many lives do I have?" (AD 24, my emphasis). The parallel description of the "gardens of Simone's head" translates this multiplicity and continuity into female writing: "Fluids, currents, emanations, waves, in the *fibers* of sentences. Ideas, notion, thoughts, in the *fabric* of paragraphs" (VD 251, my emphasis). The insistence here on the vocabulary of weaving reiterates the connection between women's writing and both craft and traditional female tasks that we have already encountered in Cardinal's work.

This persistence of repetition after literal quotation has ceased also continues, of course, to reveal the artful insinuation characteristic of jasmine. Or rather, to right the analogy—and to reemphasize a point introduced earlier—jasmine not only illustrates the general practice of women's writing but functions in particular as a metaphor for the act of repetition itself, which reveals the same disturbing power of evocation, the same subversive combination of simultaneous presence and absence. Thus repetition itself, provides the answer to Cardinal's observation that "Simone doesn't know the rules of this freedom" (VD 251); the very fact of recurrence imposes the rule within which the endless possibilities for variation allow limitless freedom.

Autrement dit's digressive and parenthetical structure supports the essay's theme of the *vague* (in French the word connotes the freedom of the imprecise and the formless) and the *réglé* (the ruled) and explicitly connects it to the act of repetition. In a clear example of internal duplication, similar to that which occurs in *Les Grands Désordres,* Cardinal introduces two successive narrative sequences by the repetition of the same sentence. The double story of the submission of her last manuscript simultaneously encodes textual control and freedom:

> The time comes when the manuscript is finished. . . . (68)

> . . . Story that I have been trying to write for several pages, but in vain, because writing is free, it carries me far away. . . . Story that insinuated itself as a parenthesis. . . .
> The vague and the ruled.
> Where was I?
> It began by "The time comes when the manuscript is finished..." (74–75)

The context of this structural duplication, the clearly unfinished state of the text at precisely the time "when the manuscript is finished," emphasizes the capacity of repetition to defy the conventional norms of literature, to transform texts published independently into a body of work, an authentic oeuvre. This is the principal explanation that Cardinal herself provides for autocitation: "In each of my manuscripts I repeat a passage from an earlier manuscript. To form a chain, to show that I will never write but a single book that will be made up of all of my books" (PR 194). Thus the vague and the ruled of Cardinal's repetitions illustrate once again the constant and necessary tension between the desire to conform and the desire to subvert, between the need for rules and the need to break them, that she and Leclerc now posit as common to the lives women lead and to the texts they produce. Women's simultaneous and paradoxical immersion in the very cultural and literary system that they seek to oppose accounts for the dual action of creation and destruction, of ordering and resistance, that defines the process of writing for women today: "We must write. Trace day after day our own text. . . . Subvert day after day the other text that hinders us" (AD 222). In a promising link between Francophone and Anglophone feminist concerns, Leclerc here defines the same textual practice that Elizabeth Abel also identifies as the most recent object of feminist criticism: "Aware that women writers inevitably engage a literary history and system of conventions shaped primarily by men, feminist critics now often strive to elucidate the acts of revision, appropriation, and subversion that constitute a female text" (Abel 174).

Interestingly, the signifier *vague* in French encodes internal repetition in and of itself, for its meaning changes with its gender. Moreover, the imprecision denoted by *le vague* (vagueness) and the rhythm connoted by *la vague* (wave) situate both the vague and the ruled within *vague* alone. This unification of gender and meaning within a single signifier provides unexpected support for Cardinal's desire "that men too might be allowed to be vague" (AD 44). But the repetitions become even more curious and complex when we recall that the masculine form of *vague* also identifies the vagus nerve that sends motor impulses to the muscles of the vocal cords and the abdominal and thoracic cavities. Given the irresistible phonetic association with "vagina," this literal connection between speech and body now seems to encode within Cardinal's *le vague* the specificity of female writing. Furthermore, the *réglé* repeats the same pattern, for the female menstrual cycle, *les règles* in French, also constitutes a near perfect metaphor for Cardinal's dynamic paradox. Women's monthly release of blood has both the regularity of immutable order and the violence of the uncontrollable; moreover, female bleeding both confirms normal femaleness and subverts, if only temporarily, the female's biological destiny of gestation.

Certainly Cardinal's own pattern of subversion and conformity has been closely linked to her bodily rhythms. In events acknowledged as autobiographical, the narrator of *Les Mots pour le dire,* driven into the silence of madness by her rigorous indoctrination into socially approved female behavior, bleeds continuously; once the recovery of self-expression enables her to resist oppression, she ceases to menstruate. Importantly, Cardinal believes that the menstrual cycle falls within the scope of women's power to order their own lives, and in *Autrement dit* she associates the recent interruption of her own periods with her choice to make writing the center of her life: "*les règles,*" concludes Leclerc, "are of no use in writing a book" (AD 36). The metaphorical tie that Cardinal establishes between the woman writer and the disappearance of rules reminds us that grammatical obedience and respect for good (i.e., normative, conventional) writing potentially imprisons us within a dominant discourse and an existing social order that silence women. Cardinal's identity as writer depends precisely upon her ability to free herself from the grammatical rules she has learned so well that they, like female *règles,* have come to seem natural: "It's true that I knew how to construct correct sentences and that I understood grammar. . . . That's what writing was in my view: correct verbal transcription in accordance with rigid grammatical rules" (MD 254–55; cf. *Eté* 5–6).

La vague also informs Cardinal's work, which includes numerous descriptions of the movement of the sea and lyrical reflections on the concept of rhythm; that the two often appear in conjunction is hardly surprising, given the insistence with which the association appears in dictionaries, based on a standard etymology of "recurring motion." In *Au Pays de mes racines,* for example, Cardinal attributes her understanding of rhythm to the Mediterranean, which teaches "that one can always start over, that it's always the same and always different" (164–67). Moreover, Emile Benveniste provides in "distinctive form" an alternative origin for rhythm that has particular significance for the complex meaning that Cardinal attaches to her repetitions. As both recurrent and unique, rhythm simultaneously connotes repetition and identity. In addition, the association and the difference that Benveniste establishes between rhythm and its synonym, form, reiterate the dynamism of the *vague* and the *réglé:* "form in the instant at which it is assumed by the moving, the mobile, the fluid, . . . improvised, momentary, modifiable form . . . resulting from an arrangement that is always subject to change" (1:333).[10]

This context illuminates the frequency with which rhythm appears as theme and form in women's writing (often associated with the flux of the sea and the flowing of menstrual blood);[11] one thinks immediately of Hélène Cixous, and both Lamy (75) and Garcia (1:118) make it the principal focus of their descriptions of *écriture féminine.* Interestingly for the interaction of the *vague* and the *réglé* specific to Cardinal, the waves of the Mediterranean are rhythmical, and irregularly so. Since the Mediterranean has no tides, it escapes from the imposed periodicity of natural order to which Cardinal so strongly objects in relation to the regulation of women's bodily rhythms: "We are subject to physiological and aesthetic norms that we didn't determine (the 28-day rule is the most obvious of these arbitrary laws: very few women have periods every 28 days; so we say that we're early or late—in relation to what?)" (ME 38).

Marcel Mauss's characterization of rhythm as a social phenomenon suggests an additional connection to women's writing through the collective and collaborative tendencies of female creativity. For Mauss, rhythm results necessarily but inevitably from group interaction: "Then language becomes naturally rhythmical because rhythm is the only way to establish a true chorus of different vocal endeavors" (254). In a similar sense, the broad semantic range of the term *rhythm* must play a significant role in the prominence that Cardinal grants it within her carefully constructed lexicon. Rhythm's multiple applications—which encompass speech, music, writing, dance, painting, and sculpture—give it an unusual extension within the realm of art; moreover, its further connections to physical activity and natural phenomena confirm its interdisciplinary richness, the freedom of its regular recurrences, that make it particularly suitable to characterize Cardinal's commitment to the identity and the difference of women's lives and texts.

Irma Garcia already uncovers a concern with the *vague* in the work of George Sand, who inaugurates female modernism (1:13): "[Writing] requires words that define and I can't find any that express vagueness" (qtd. in Garcia 1:43). Cardinal shares this discomfort with the power of language to define and imprison that Garcia extends to all modernist women writers, and her exploration of the *vague* includes a strongly and specifically linguistic dimension: "Speech is an act. Words are objects. Invisible, impalpable, cars wandering in the train of sentences. Men have sealed them hermetically; they have imprisoned women in them. Women must open them up if they wish to exist. This labor that we must undertake is colossal, dangerous, revolutionary. I know what words I am writing. I'm not afraid of the noun nor of its qualifiers. I even maintain that we must open up 'labor' and 'revolution' in order to rediscover the desire and the play of which they have been amputated" (AD 53). Let me add one further sentence to establish clearly that Cardinal's metaphors of vagueness, subversion, and opening constitute identical synonyms: "we must open, open, be subversive, be vague" (Pednault 18).

The excavation of female reality that we explored in the preceding chapter, the opening of the material objects characteristic of women's private domestic world, also relates to Cardinal's understanding of language. The dominant discourse of a culture comes complete not only with correct grammatical rules and appropriate syntactical forms but with a limited vocabulary of words that have been assigned fixed and conventional meanings. Fluency, then, is not necessarily freedom, as the narrator of *Les Mots pour le dire* discovers: "I had written books with words that were objects; I used to arrange them in an order that I found coherent, appropriate and aesthetic. I hadn't realized that they contained living matter" (285). Such linguistic objects objectify not "life" but a system of "values" by which "the entire universe was labeled, arranged, definitively classified" (286). Thus, the linguistic convention that readily concedes the arbitrary nature of the relationship between a word and its meaning in fact conceals an ideological necessity. While it may seem that Cardinal seeks here to disrupt this bond between signifier and signified, in favor of some more direct and authentic link between the sign and its referent, we need to reserve judgment until we have looked more closely at how and to what purpose Cardinal opens words.

Ecriture Féminine

Shari Benstock concludes a discussion of women modernists by emphasizing that "no critique of these women's lives and works that does not pay particular attention to their interest in and experiment with language can hope to account, even partially, for their contributions as women writers" ("From" 20–21). At the same time, one of the persistent criticisms that Anglophone feminists address to those of the Francophone theoreticians who assert that the specificity of *écriture féminine* extends beyond content to language itself, beyond signification to the signifying process, is the failure to prove their point, or at least to illustrate it convincingly. Showalter, for example, dismisses the claims of the early modernists to whom Benstock's remark directly refers: "It is another thing altogether to talk about female style when you mean female content. And it is the hardest of all to prove that there are inherent sexual qualities to prose apart from its content" (*Lit.* 258). Christiane Makward remains equally unconvinced by contemporary French efforts: "feminine writing at its best only differs from other modern poetic texts in the—considerably vast yet clearly distinguishable—area of subject matter" (96).

Cardinal may seem to provide a curious context in which to explore this conflict, given the paradoxical claims that have been made upon her work. In articles that appeared at approximately the same time, Linda Gillman situates Cardinal within the "explicitly word-centered orientation" of the *écriture féminine* group (12–13) while Marguerite LeClézio characterizes Cardinal's "linear, traditional, descriptive" style as precisely what distinguishes her work from that of these very same writers (384). Similarly, Suzanne Lamy devotes one of four chapters to *Autrement dit* as a privileged example of specifically female discourse, while Irma Garcia's two-volume study of *écriture féminine,* heavily dependent on lengthy quotation from a variety of contemporary women writers, cites Cardinal only once. In what marks at least an internal assumption of the balance (or the paradox), Cardinal's work serves as the primary illustration of Marina Yaguello's analysis of *Les Mots et les femmes,* but Yaguello also views female discourse as, at most, a variant of a language common to men and women. The very complexity that this divergence of views reflects—a complexity common to Cardinal's textual practice and to the general question of gender-specific language use—determines the unusual interest of her work; few writers can claim such a broad spectrum of representativeness.

Perhaps we should begin with what for once Cardinal herself identifies as a point of origin: "At sixteen, in the heart of the Casbah, not very far from the cathedral, my first stupifying encounter with a word: in the alley of the bordels, on every closed door was written 'onette house,' 'o net House,' 'Honète house,' 'onnette house,' 'honête house'... Honnête—What exactly does that mean?" (PR 62–63). The pattern visible here in which the opening of a signifier by phonetic and material transformation leads to the literal interrogation of its signified and potentially its referent appears repeatedly throughout Cardinal's work. Her loss of linguistic innocence also focuses on a word that already illustrates her belief that "at the present time all words have two meanings, two sexes, depending on whether they are used by a man or a woman" (AD 88); for, of course, the specific sense of honest [honnête] as "virtuous" or "chaste" that lies at the origin of Cardinal's confusion applies only to women. Moreover, her phonetic play inevitably recalls the actual social situation of the women behind these doors: *honni,* disgraced, spurned.

At the same time, the apparent contradiction between prostitution and (female) chastity exposes the real contradiction within *honnête* itself: the word denies the truth and fairness with which its standard definition aligns it, not only by determining and limiting meaning on the basis of gender, but by excluding male virtue from the presumed taint of prostitution. Cardinal thus brings into view the deception and fraud inherent in the manner in which dictionaries most readily delimit the notion of honesty; this practice of defining by negation or opposition underlies Western culture's commitment to dichotomous thinking, of which the male-female duality provides, as here, the primary illustration. In this context, as Cardinal shows, a division between *human* and *female* in fact equates the generic exclusively with the male, for the contradiction between honesty and female chastity totally obscures the fact that a bordel need not be a place of deception or fraud. Indeed, some would argue that it treats sexual relations between men and women with unusual frankness and even introduces some degree of equity by transforming the female body into a purchasable commodity. Finally, the particular context of this passage once again connects the condition of women to the general cultural problem of colonialism. The Casbah constitutes a "foreign" place at the very center of the European city into which "we plunged, our hearts racing, with the unconscious impression of committing rape" (PR 62). This curious "we" that identifies Cardinal with both rapist and victim reflects the ambivalence of women's cultural position.

The opening of words can also create bonds of female solidarity, as the narrator of *Les Mots pour le dire* discovers when she realizes that she has come to her mother's grave to say, at last, "I love you": "'I' (me, mad, sane, child, woman) 'love' (attachment, union, but also warmth, a kiss, and joy still possible, happiness yet hoped for) 'you' (my mother, the beautiful, the expert, the proud, the demented, the suicide victim)" (341). Cardinal illustrates the importance of her linguistic innovation by deliberately selecting the most banal of phrases, one that virtually everyone would profess to understand, yet one whose meaning is in fact both impossible to determine with precision and infinitely variable. Cardinal opens the pronouns that traditionally mark individuation and individuality, particularly in the case of mother and daughter, to learn that within them lies the commonality of femaleness that continues to unite the most estranged of women. "I" and "you" join in "she" to accomplish the pronominal revolution that Didier associates with women's writing: "a challenging of the distinction between the 'I' and the 'she' and perhaps the 'you' as well" (34).

The verbal structure that here provides a framework for lexical expansion reinforces the stability and the dynamism of female love. In addition, Cardinal opens the verb as well to introduce sexuality and pleasure into the bond of female affection figured by the mother-daughter relationship. Once again, context plays an important role. The daughter's linguistic union with the mother follows immediately upon her recollection from childhood of their quests for shells along the beach; the "treasure" that her mother leads her to seek turns out to be the gift of language itself: "You knew all their names, just as you knew the names of the stars" (339–40). The narrator's self-initiated act of writing had previously reduced her dependence on her psychoanalyst; this passage appropriately ends it.

Sandra Gilbert and Susan Gubar have argued for the existence of a long tradition of women's writing organized around "fantasies about female linguistic power" (No Man's ch. 5). To some extent their choice of the word *fantasy* seems confusing, even contradictory, since they surmise that the female complex (in every sense of the term) of common images and themes that they uncover derives from women's knowledge of the primary role played by the mother in language acquisition, a linguistic and social reality consecrated in the cultural designation of native language as a "mother tongue," a *langue maternelle:* "It seems clear that women's imaginary languages, unlike men's, are for the most part founded on a celebration of the primacy both of the mother tongue and the tongue of the mother" (262). Although Gilbert and Gubar (finally) acknowledge that "much recent French feminist theory about '*écriture féminine*' may be contextualized in terms of a tradition of female linguistic fantasy" (210), they continue to characterize the words of Cixous and Irigaray on the subject as "immoderately mystical" (230). Elsewhere, their objection to Francophone theory has focused less on the theory itself than on its underlying assumption that "the feminine" cannot be inscribed in common (i.e., male) language, from which women thus remain irremediably alienated ("Sexual"; cf. No Man's 229). Since Cixous, whose name has been most closely allied with such a notion of *écriture féminine,* also depicts women's coming to writing as the search for a *langue maternelle* (see Conley 82), intercultural disagreement appears to originate in the characteristically Anglophone belief that sexual linguistics for women will be social and actual, founded in experiential reality (in which case, I repeat, where does the fantasy come in?) rather than metaphorical and metaphysical (cf. Gilbert and Gubar, Madwoman 86).

Cardinal's own "fantasies about the possession of a mother tongue" (*No Man's* 236; fantasy, from the Greek *phantazein*, to make visible) visibly embrace both the literal *and* the metaphorical, an expansion accomplished in part by the repetition of the maternal figure. As we have seen above, the narrator of *Les Mots pour le dire* inherits language from her mother, a gift that she in some sense repays by telling her mother's story in the appropriately titled "Words to Say It." In *Autrement dit,* Cardinal reveals an event that she suppressed in the text of *Les Mots pour le dire*—for fear that it might throw the book off course—that in fact confirms the identification of female language with a maternal tongue. The announcement of her mother's death comes while Cardinal is reading proofs and provokes an explicitly linguistic breakdown: "Letters exploded, words capsized, sentences stretched out like serpentine sirens, paragraphs turned into immense deserts that I couldn't manage to get across" (AD 195). Moreover, this loss of linguistic power revives a childhood memory of language acquisition—an inability to pronounce the sound represented by the letters *gn*—that specifically empowers the mother: "I was ashamed of myself: what if my mother heard about it? Every *gn* I encountered made me break out in a sweat: I had to apply myself; my mother must not discover this flaw" (197).

But Cardinal, as we know, has a second mother, herself a double figure, repeated in Algeria, openly claimed as a *mother*land, and in the Mediterranean sea (*la mer*), the homophonic mother (*la mère*).[12] This mother too is associated with language acquisition, for as a child Cardinal speaks fluent Arabic, explicitly identified as a native language (and, importantly, as the language of the natives): "the language of my country" (PR 85). The woman's loss of this maternal tongue and its replacement by French, the foreign language of a foreign country, repeat Francophone assumptions about women's alienation from dominant discourse. The fact too that Cardinal knows Arabic only as a *spoken* language establishes the same ties between women's writing and voice and rhythm that are so prevalent in Cixous' own *écriture féminine*. For if women can no longer express themselves in their maternal language and cannot yet use their paternal language to express themselves, their writing can nonetheless imitate the one and undermine the other by a metaphorical and rhythmical discourse that celebrates the mother (*la mer/mère*).

Out of the dozens of exemplary passages in Cardinal's work, I cite part of one from *Au Pays de mes racines:*

Beach. Sun. Mediterranean. This sand. This shore. These dunes. . . . The delight of the swim is *inscribed* in my body as soon as I see the sea, its color, its waves. . . . *I know how she will penetrate me* and how I will play with her.

Duration doesn't exist. . . . [Time] flows uninterruptedly, smoothly, and I flow with it, interminable, identical. The child, the adult, just alike, *inscribed* in the Rhythm, indispensable.

. . . I am Moussia. The Rhythm needs my existence, otherwise it wouldn't exist itself. I secrete it, it secretes me. . . .

Inscribe periods and crosses . . . *Inscribe* the roundness of the target . . . *Inscribe* the rectangular trail . . . on this terrain where everything is erased, which will never be a witness, only a mobility with which I can merge.

. . . Didn't these beaches teach me *that one can always start over, that it's always the same and always different?* (164–67, my emphasis)

Not only does this passage repetitively connect the Mediterranean with a rhythmical female writing and end with an explicit description of the characteristic pattern of Cardinal's autocitations, but it also inscribes the sea as a maternal lover, an association that appears frequently in the writings of Cixous and Irigaray as well. Indeed, Cixous presents the exchange between female lovers as a metaphor for the poetic process, for the female text as spoken dialogue (see Conley 118). Cardinal, who consistently fuses the female land and sea of Algeria, logically extends the analogy: "What I never stop writing throughout all my novels is how my land taught me love and to make love, and how I do love and do make, used to make, and will make love with her" (PR 170).[13]

I want to return for a moment to the human mother of *Les Mots pour le dire* (the Anglophone mother, in our present theoretical context) who is specifically empowered to name. Gilbert and Gubar suggest that women's desire for linguistic control has been "most practically expressed through strategies of unnaming and renaming, strategies that directly address the problem of woman's patronymically defined identity in western culture" (*No Man's* 237). In this context, Cardinal empowers herself to write by imagining a maternal alternative to patriarchal naming. Elsewhere in *Les Mots pour le dire*, we learn that the mother always names her daughter's dolls—metaphorically, she establishes a matronymical lineage. Moreover, the daughter herself inherits the right to (re)name her own mother. Her observation that no name appears on her mother's tomb leads into several paragraphs of alliterative textual play on the letter *s* that finally (re)generates the maternal name: "With my index finger I kept on tracing huge serpents in the sand, S's that became entangled. Soso . . ." (340). (Notably, the mother's name is also encoded in the linguistic breakdown that accompanies the announcement of her death: "sentences stretched out like serpentine sirens" [AD 195]). Since the sand in which the narrator writes her mother's name has in the meantime provoked an association that allows her to retrieve the memory of her mother's linguistic power, women's ability to name encloses itself in an autonomous cycle of repetition.

Toril Moi, in a discussion of the focus of Anglo-American feminists on "the question of naming" (158), sides with the French feminists who reject labels and names as a reflection of phallogocentric rationality: "To impose names is, then, not only an act of power, . . . it also reveals a desire to regulate and organize reality according to well-defined categories. If this is sometimes a valuable counterstrategy for feminists, we must nevertheless be wary of an obsession with nouns" (160). Moi's assumption that language, "primarily constructed as a series of names or nouns," seeks to "fix" meaning seems clearly belied by Cardinal's exploration, quoted above, of the nouns embedded in "I love you." In fact, Cardinal opens not only words but also the syntactic structure whose function is by definition to contain, to enclose. Her parentheses subversively open up to linguistic material that is totally dependent on that which surrounds it, so that continuity is established rather than disrupted.[14]

Textual Parthenogenesis

The desire to open language also functions importantly in Cardinal's practice of autocitation. Textual juxtaposition reveals the presence of almost imperceptible changes—the substitution of one word for another, the reversal of two words or two phrases, an ellipsis or addition of a word, a slight alteration in paragraphing—that mark the difference between parallel passages. Interestingly, Garcia's description of internal repetition in a text by Gertrude Stein characterizes Cardinal's own practice with extraordinary exactness: "the repetition of syntagmatic blocks . . . reinserted in a more concentrated syntactical structure. . . . Certain nuances like the substitution of two signifers for a single signified . . . or the use of periphrasis . . . don't throw the central idea off course" (1:238). Let me substitute two examples from Cardinal for those I have just omitted from Stein; although both of the following come from a single set of parallel passages, the identical sections are far too long to allow integral quotation (all emphasis is mine):

In this place *where everything emphasized* annihilation, insignificance, and ignorance, there blew a happy little sea breeze that was lively and gay, that smelled good, that made you feel like dancing and loving. (CP 47)

In this place *which forced everyone to think about* annihilation, *about* ignorance *of our fate,* there blew a happy little sea breeze that was lively and gay, that smelled good, that made you feel like dancing and loving. (MD 230)

She often stopped and *pointed out* to me the vulgarity of the distinction that *had presided at the edification* of the different funeral monuments. Thus I quickly learned that *artificial flowers, little porcelain angels with big bottoms* and marble books *on* whose pages were incrusted *locket* photos of *dead women in make-up with crimped hair* and of *healthy-looking dead men with plastered-down hair* —all these things that I found magnificent were only good enough for "grocers grown rich." (CP 48)

She often stopped and *emphasized* for me the vulgarity of the distinction that *had lead to the construction* of the different funeral monuments *that we encountered.* Thus I quickly learned that *little porcelain angels with big bottoms* and marble books *in* whose false pages were incrusted *color* photos of *dead men with plastered-down hair* and of *dead women in make-up*—all these things that I found magnificent were only good enough for "grocers grown rich." (MD 230)

In general, the identity and difference that simultaneously characterize Cardinal's autocitations far more often involve lexical substitution than structural transformation; they are largely the result of a broadly defined practice of synonymy by virtue of which the signified is repeated as the signifier varies.[15] This technique no doubt reflects Cardinal's effort on the level of theme to illustrate both the diversity and the commonality of female life, to use the multiple signifiers of *women* to signify *Woman*. Interestingly, Marina Yaguello notes that the word *woman* "breaks all the records of synonymy" in dictionaries of analogy and synonyms, despite the fact that this plurality of designation is essentially pejorative and predominantly focused on the female as sexual object (158). I cite at random a section of the corpus that Yaguello has identified to contrast it with one of Cardinal's curiously similar enumerations: "Mother, housekeeper, shrew, miss, matron, slut, mistress, muse, madonna, stuck-up thing, cruel stepmother, Arab woman, Japanese woman, better half, shopgirl, sausage eater, apple eater, granny, kid, bird, whore, woman in charge, housewife, socialite" (152), and so on.[16]

A similar *tour de force* (but rather more impressive since no longer the result of compilation) appears in *Une Vie pour deux;* I quote only a part of a full-page passage: "Warm swellings of women's breasts, high, low, apple-shaped, pear-shaped, close together, far apart, heavy, fat, small, mauve, black pink, red, brown. Women's bathtub-bellies, cradle-bellies, holy-water-bassin-bellies, brioche-bellies, bowl-like-bellies, shell-like-bellies. Women's hair, manes, curls, ringlets, caps, helmets, black, blond, auburn, shining, fine. Women's lips, cracked, distended, split, pulpous, damp, shiny, red, pale, thin, sensitive . . ." (56). Yaguello attributes the general linguistic phenomenon of *woman*'s synonymy to the paradoxical consequences of "euphemism or the fear of words" by virtue of which the desire not to name or to name only negatively in fact results in lexical profusion (158). Cardinal's practice, on the other hand, restores semantic richness to female signs; she uses language not to deny, conceal, or limit but to affirm, reveal, and explore fully the complex diversity of femaleness. Once its integrity has been restored, synonymy's insistence on the variety of language specifically resists the reduction to the same that the compilers of dictionary entries on *woman* have paradoxically achieved.

Lest a single procedure prove insufficient to free femaleness from fixed and imposed meaning, Cardinal combines synonymy with two additional textual practices that affirm the plurality of language. Connotation and enumeration further undermine textual unity and closure; signification becomes infinitely expansive and multidirectional. Barthes, who identifies these three techniques as parallel paths to polysemy,[17] argues that they develop "a correlation that is immanent in the text" and should not be confused with "the association of ideas" (S/Z 8).[18] Certainly, in the passage above, Cardinal begins to repeat the same linguistic forms (notably, the hyphenated terms that at once assert femaleness and enrich it, that situate the female body at the generative center of a verbal universe) and to associate words solely by their phonetic resemblance (the accumulation of words beginning with the same letter, for example). Such linguistic mutability clearly subverts normal referentiality and continually re-creates the sign *woman* within the fluidity of the signifying process. Yet, if Cardinal effects predominantly material rather than thematic transformations, the work that she undertakes on the level of the signifier nonetheless remains in contact with the referential world through its consistently (en)gendered context.

Thus Cardinal challenges the culturally imposed norm of "the Beauty of the Woman" not by (or not *only* by) analytic logic or narrative example but by a linguistic explosion whose affirmation of multiplicity and variety denies the unity of the sign, whose autogenerativity refuses the right of the sign to define, and whose synonymous repetition subverts the identity of the sign. Again, I cite only one paragraph of a four-page text (VD 103–6): "Uniforms. Identical hairdos, outfits, words, behavior. Imposed by the most beautiful, required by the strongest; copied a thousand times, xeroxed, photocopied, reproduced, plagiarized, imitated, mass-produced on the assembly line. Ready to wear, ready to eat/be eaten, ready to love/be loved, ready to please. Exemplary fodder offered up on our screens, our walls. Asses, Hearts, Beauty, patented, stamped 'Ready to Use'" (104–5). Elsewhere, Cardinal uses the material transformation of the signifier, the visual and phonetic (over)exposure of the phallic *I*, to undermine male discourse:

> Immaturity.
> Irresponsibility.
> Ineptitude.
> Impotence.
> All these *i*'s and these *in*'s stamp out virility. *I-i-i-i-* to deny potency, aptitude, responsibility, maturity. *Hi, hi, hi, hi,* that's

the laugh of women, children, and jokers in comic texts. *Hein, hein, hein, hein,* threatens the master or the policeman. *Ouin, ouin, ouin,* whines the dunce or the hussy.

. . . With a vehemence that was frightening, Jean-François demanded his right to indolence, insouciance, instability, indifference.

Insufferable.

Intolerable.

Incapable.

Inferior. (VD 181)

In essence, I am suggesting that Cardinal both does and does not engage in linguistic practices characteristic of Anglophone and Francophone feminist writing. Anglophone feminists are able to equate textual activity with political action because they assume a direct substitutability between the signified and the referent, between fictional realism and the reality of women's lives, but they do so at the risk of reducing language to a transparent (indeed, an invisible) instrument of mediation. Francophone feminists, on the other hand, can transform writing itself into a subversive activity because they divorce the linguistic sign from the referential world and privilege the work of the signifier within the signifying process, but they do so at the risk of reducing relationships of power and oppression to the (invisible) status of linguistic phenomena. One option might lie in the combination of these two approaches, but since they depend upon totally incompatible assumptions about language and reality, presumably their coexistence within the same work would require some system of alternation, as does at times appear to be the case for Cardinal.[19] But if we bypass the signified (not by erasing meaning from view, but by stabilizing, by equating it once and for all with gender), we can then connect the play of the signifier itself to the description and the transformation of the referential world and so create a newly coherent system that allows simultaneous attention to language, meaning, and reality. This appears to be one of the key ways in which the sign functions in Cardinal's work.

Cardinal's frequent use of repetition and enumeration, as in the examples above, grants enormous visibility to the word and transforms it from one of many links in a syntactical chain into an autonomous unit of value. Similarly, her common recourse to spatial fragmentation of the paragraph or the page, to capital letters, and to sentence fragments also serves to isolate and to emphasize the independent word. Garcia posits such self-imposition of what she calls "the word-object" as characteristic of *l'écriture féminine* in general, where it signals the literal renaissance of language: "Once the word has been endowed with this value, everything can begin again, everything can be rewritten from a new perspective. . . . The word is literally swollen, impregnated; it's the seed that fertilizes writing" (2:122).

In Cardinal's case, lexical association clearly acts as a method of autogeneration or of textual "parthenogenesis," to use Suzanne Lamy's wonderfully appropriate term (31). One of the most interesting examples occurs in *Une Vie pour deux* where words engender words by graphic and phonetic association and where repetition simultaneously encodes identity and difference within every word: "There where the *plan*ets *plan*e dizzingly, where the *waves wave* liquids, where *rays ra*diate through space, where *particules part*ition and petrify matter, I took part in the elaboration of life. I lived the second at which the cell divides in two, still both itself and already another" (60, my emphasis).[20] This passage in which Simone recalls the experience of giving birth explicitly links biological reproduction and textual production (each set of paired words illustrates the division of the linguistic cell), so that the woman's procreative powers become the sign of her artistic creativity rather than, as has traditionally been the case, the compensation for its absence. Garcia makes "just such a comparison between giving birth and writing" (1:49) the organizing pivot of *écriture féminine* as a whole: "from time immemorial, women have liked to compare their works to a childbirth" (1:61).

In her recurrent comments on the gradual transformation of psychoanalysis into a permanently new way of thinking, Cardinal focuses on the altered understanding of the word that functions importantly in the process: "To put it another way, the word comes to life; that's the beginning. Later you get in the habit of associating, of establishing relationships between moments, memories, thoughts that you would never have thought to connect before. It's the words that act as the vehicle; they lead toward brother-words, twin-words, synonym-words, mirror-words, enemy-words. These words, in fact become keywords" (AD 62). Even as she celebrates language as the catalyst of thought and appears to grant the signifier a mediating role between the signified and the referent, Cardinal also illustrates the common practice that Garcia identifies as "this way of keeping the word as such intact—as an untranslatable, abstract term—that constantly recurs in [women's] texts" (2:125; cf. 123).[21] In an interesting case of self-referentiality recurrent throughout her work, Cardinal's preferred wording introduces concepts as words, always preceding their identification with the expression *the word,* so that the very repetition of this pattern establishes connections that continue to privilege "the anonymity of the word" (Garcia 2:126) beyond (and despite) its specific incarnations.

Garcia is surely right that an insistence on words as such leaves intact a linguistic potential that the gaps and the limitations of the vocabulary actually available to inscribe femaleness otherwise contradict; such openness of language thus frees women writers from the restrictive framework of the sign (signifier/signified). But Cardinal's example also suggests that Garcia tends to confuse absence with surplus, to hear the same thing as no-thing. However closely Cardinal's repetitions, connotations, enumerations, and associations link her writing to Garcia's notion of *écriture féminine,* she does not finally share the latter's assumption that women writers value the word only as an empty signifier, totally detached from any signified (2:125). Cardinal's repeated suggestion that all of her work can be summed up in the two words *writing* [*écriture*] and *women* [*femmes*] identifies the stability—but also the plurality and the freedom—of the linguistic sign that she redefines to meet her needs: signifier (*écriture*)/signified (*femmes*).

Thus, the simultaneous repetition and renewal that characterizes Cardinal's linguistic expansion—particularly visible in the self-referential enumeration above (e.g., synonym-*words,* mirror-*words*)—is precisely what allows a vision of female culture to emerge from Cardinal's individual works. The inversely parallel processes of repetition and synonymy allow her textual universe to open onto a complexly pluralistic reality and to refer to a common core. Moreover, Cardinal's conviction that "speech is an act" and "words are objects" equates linguistic expression with social change and experiential existence; language gains the power to generate new words that in turn produce a new reality: "*La béance. L'ouverte. La nuite. La nuine...* What word will make my cunt exist? What word will express its active and somber inertia? *Une lalgue. Une puitre. Une bueuse. Une hamère* ... to speak the sweetness of its dampness, the depth of its abysses? *Sente. Ravine. Voille. Tronce...* To speak the scarlet path of pleasure, of the child. And *la rengaine du sang? La sanguaine?*" (AD 98). Garcia, who does assume that once women writers have rid themselves of the rigidity of the sign by erasing the signified under abstraction or silence they will then proceed to create language anew, cites precisely this passage from Cardinal as her first example of such linguistic innovation (2:180).[22]

Writing the Body

Cardinal's conclusions about the power of language to function metaphorically ("to associate, to establish relationships") and to give textual birth to the female body ("What word will make my cunt exist?") introduce us to a particularly problematic issue in feminist criticism and theory. We are all familiar with the provocative question that sums up Sandra Gilbert and Susan Gubar's discussion of the traditional connection between creativity and paternity: "If the pen is a metaphorical penis, from what organ can females generate texts?" (*Madwoman* 7). Elaine Showalter, recalling the equally prevalent equation between textual generativity and childbirth, queries in response: "If to write is metaphorically to give birth, from what organ can males generate texts?" ("Feminist" 188). Showalter's irony reflects her evident discomfort with what she calls "biological" models of female specificity even when they function as metaphor; and when feminist writers and critics ("primarily in France") begin to take seriously the possibility that "anatomy is textuality," she finds them alternatively "sibylline," "perplexing," and "cruelly prescriptive" (187–89). I fully agree with Showalter's important conclusion: "Ideas about the body are fundamental to understanding how women conceptualize their situation in society; but there can be no expression of the body which is unmediated by linguistic, social, and literary structures" (89; cf. Suleiman 2; and Lamy 27). But I find her own work representative of Anglophone feminist criticism in general in that the urgency with which she rushes to impose the second clause tends to leave the first inadequately explored. Cardinal's work offers us an opportunity to right the injustice and to adjust the balance.

As we know, Cardinal's texts not only include passages of integral quotation but also reveal broader connective structures of repetition in which she tells the same essential stories, stories that are essentially the same, over and over. One of the most important of these networks situates the specificity and the commonality of women at the center of the female body. This particular episode already surfaces on four different occasions and in four different forms within a single text, *Les Mots pour*

le dire, in which Cardinal records a gradual progression in consciousness from individual female identity to the social and cultural situation
of women. Her frequent descriptions of this novel as the prototypical
story of female life have been amply confirmed by the letters of women
readers whose responsiveness compares in degree and quantity with
that aroused on rare occasions by such works as *The Feminine Mystique*
and *The Second Sex.*

One series of passages in this network centers on the narrator's childhood memories of the problematic act of "peeing" (*faire pipi*). At the
age of ten, for example (121–29), the desire to have "a boy's tail" in
place of her "smooth fruit" torments her during the hot hours of the
siesta and drives her on occasion to fashion a cardboard tube which she
takes into the bathroom, to "try to piss standing up like boys do." The
furtive caresses necessary to adjust the tube between her legs produce "a
tickling somewhere in-between pleasure and pain" until her whole body
is seized by a violent and uncontrollable spasm that ends in "a feeling of
complete happiness that frightened me." Twenty years later the adult
narrator finally acknowledges that behind her childish shame at want-
ing to piss standing up lies her discovery of masturbation and sexual
pleasure. The use of male imitation to explore female sexuality provides
a particularly curious example of women's ability to subvert an act of
conformity from within. Moreover, Cardinal fuses not only the biological and the sexual functioning of the body but its social significance as
well; the little girl's resentment at being excluded from boys' games as a
pisseuse (a girl) serves to "excite" her initially and to identify her "penis
envy" as the desire to share in male freedom and social privilege.

A parallel passage in *Au Pays de mes racines* (49–55) makes this
same point as it also emphasizes, in a pattern that we have seen before,
the specific merits of the female anatomy. Cardinal's childhood passion
for pissing on ants asserts her revolt and autonomy in the face of ento-
mological behavior that exactly conforms to the moral and religious
codes that regulate her own life. This time the little girl scorns the facil-
ity with which a boy aims his "garden hose" in an appreciation of the
concentration and skill that a girl requires to manipulate the "quantity
of fibers and diabolical little muscles" that control her urination. This
memory now allows Cardinal to dismiss Freud's association of women's
inferiority with their lack of a penis. By addressing the issue of how
anatomical specificity, once it is defined as a sign of inferiority, inevitably evolves into a justification of social injustice, I do not think that

Cardinal can be accused (as Francophone feminists often are) of perpetuating a theory of biological difference, either by repetition or by reversal. Rather, the particular context in which she has the little girl interpret male experience as a model on which to base or by which to measure her own exposes clearly and economically the absurdity of turning a gender-specific standard into a human norm and, consequently, of founding any social or cultural model on biological difference. At the same time, Cardinal insists on the right of all individuals, regardless of sex, to experience their bodies as a source of sexual pleasure and physical competence.

In two other *pipi* passages in *Les Mots pour le dire,* the natural functioning of the female body brings not the expected relief but the public shame of social incorrectness. In the elevator on the way to her father's apartment, where timidity prevents her from using the bathroom, the little girl's initial satisfaction turns to horror as her urine overflows the compartment and resounds in the metallic cage below (68). In a second instance, the adult narrator's effort to locate the origin of a hallucination (173–84)—each time she engages in behavior of which she believes her mother would disapprove, a tube appears before her right eye through which another eye, one "coldly severe with a touch of scorn and indifference," stares at her—leads back to two other experiences with urination. At the age of three or four, her express desire to use the toilet on a train vanishes in the face of the fear at being infested with germs that her mother's massive campaign of disinfection paradoxically instills in her. But her reluctance turns to terror as her mother insists on seating her over what she now perceives as an open hole through whose filthy tube she believes that her own urine will suck her to her death. Moreover, this episode screens the more distant memory of a toddler who explodes in a murderous rage when she realizes that her father is filming her as she urinates behind the bush where her nurse has discretely hidden her.

These passages emphasize the many reasons why women cannot simply ignore their bodies, why, as Showalter says, "ideas about the body are fundamental to understanding how women conceptualize their situation in society" ("Feminist" 89). Although one might argue that Cardinal selects a bad example to illustrate social control of the female body, since male urination certainly faces restrictions as well, this choice of an apparently common situation reveals particularly clearly the specific constraints that weigh upon women alone. In point of fact, the higher standards of propriety that women are expected to obey do affect even a little girl's desire to *faire pipi.* Today in France, and certainly in the 1940s of Cardinal's childhood, neither a little boy nor a man need resort to urinating in an elevator or even behind a bush, since public urination is and was socially acceptable for men. Moreover, the fact that they urinate standing up allows even little boys of Cardinal's social class a less traumatic use of public toilets. If I appear to overinterpret the natural consequences of a simple biological fact, and one for which the female anatomy no doubt compensates in other areas, let me recall that the consequences, the advantages or the disadvantages, of human biology are never "natural" within social structures; notably, there is nothing "natural" about the clothing that facilitates male urination and complicates that of females. For Cardinal, the ease of male urination appropriately reflects the generally wider range of social freedom available to men.

Neither do I think that Cardinal means for us to limit the capacity of the female body for betrayal to the literal fact of urination. The uncontrollable flow that "soaks" the little girl in the elevator as it spills onto the floor seems to me a clear metaphor for the accidents of menstruation that most women have known, even without the contextual support provided by the parallel passages in which the adult narrator describes in comparable terms the constant hemorrhaging that often embarrassed her in the early years of her madness (cf. 11). Similarly, the child in the train explicitly identifies the dangerously open hole of the toilet with the equally open passageways of her own body in a clear metaphor for the frightening loss of control that Cardinal associates elsewhere with childbirth (cf. VD 64–68).

The final passage in this series fully clarifies the cultural context that links shame and vulnerability to women's sense of their bodies even as it justifies the societal restrictions on female exposure that underlie all these traumatic experiences of urination. "A tiny little girl barely able to walk" knows that if her father should not see her urinating, it is not because of the act itself but because "my father mustn't see my behind." The camera transforms the father's invasion of his daughter's privacy, the male look that both reduces the female to her nude body and violates that body, into the general cultural situation in which the male confirms his status as subject by defining the female as object and delineates his intellectual activity in opposition to her material passivity.[23] Moreover, the adult narrator's dual association of her hallucination with her father's gaze and her mother's rules reflects the double bind in which the threat of violation and the attempt to parry it imprison women. The code of proper female behavior also turns women into passive victims; the child's spontaneous and healthy anger gives way to shame and submission as her female nurse joins her father in condemning her fury as inappropriate and unacceptable antisocial behavior.

In the fourth and final version of the female body passages in *Les Mots pour le dire*, Cardinal explicitly connects women's sexual vulnerability to their general social situation. The adult narrator has a nightmare (249–301) in which she returns home to find her mother oddly terrified by three *fellagha* who have entered the house. Despite the daughter's desire to join the men whose views on Algerian independence she fully shares, she finds herself inexplicably drawn to her mother and the other women present: "I was tied to their group in some incomprehensible way." Enclosed in a room with European and Algerian women of all ages and physical types, she succumbs to their fear of sexual violence: "There we were . . . all of us with fear in our bellies and terrible stories in our heads, tales of raped and disemboweled women." Finally unable to bear the women's "submission" and "passivity," she attempts to run for help. But the men catch up with her in the stairwell, and the narrator awakens in terror as one of them prepares to slit her throat with a knife that she concomitantly describes as "a harmless weapon." The dream forces the narrator to confront anew the memory from late childhood of being molested in the stairwell of her apartment building. A man of European descent rapes her with his finger, which, in her fear, she perceives as a weapon capable of killing her.

As the narrator of *Les Mots pour le dire* continues to speculate on the meaning of her dream, her attempt to understand "what it means to be a woman" focuses on the specificity of the female body. She surmises that the fact that women are "all hollowed out," their bodies by definition "abandoned to invaders" (305), produces an ancient and secret fear that women first invent and then instinctively pass on: "Fear of our vulnerability, of our absolute inability to close ourselves completely" (306). Cardinal's nightmare thus reflects a world in which female solidarity appears to originate in the fear, shared by all women, of male sexual force. By equating rape with murder, Cardinal definitively removes it from the false but frequent context of human sexuality to define it unambivalently as an act of criminal violence.

In this context, the bonds of gender clearly figure more prominently than those of culture or society. The rapist appears alternatively as an Arab and a European, and women feel equally threatened by men of their own race and class. Moreover, in the nightmare, the visceral bonds that connect the narrator to women prove irresistible and act to eliminate the intellectual and ideological ties that she believes connect her to men. In addition, the impersonal public identity that she accepts as "a Frenchwoman like all the others, a woman to be shot down" (note the shift from culture to gender) now extends to her personal and private self. The denial of any chance to speak, to explain her position and to demonstrate her sincerity, which she has assumed as an unalienable human right, emphasizes women's silencing within culture, articulated as male. At the same time, it stresses the enormous obstacles to social change, for not even the fact that the narrator here shares the men's political views—views, moreover, that specifically favor freedom and justice for the oppressed—enables her to alter in any way their views on women.

Cardinal's use of rape to reveal the specificity of women's bodies transforms female vulnerability from an unalterable anatomical fact into the unnecessary consequence of abusive power relations. In her primary focus on the social consequences of gender, Cardinal emphasizes that women feel threatened less because rape is physically possible than because rape occurs with a banality and a frequency that grant it the status of a socially accepted practice. Two additional passages in this same corporeal network make the point bluntly by stripping the institution of marriage of any aura of romantic love to portray it as the legal, social, and religious condoning of sexual violence against women. In *Au Pays de mes racines*, Cardinal recalls the painful episode that constitutes her "first memory of human copulation" (68). Inexplicably denied participation in the celebration of her thirteen-year-old friend Zorah's wedding to the fifty-year-old man who has paid a handsome price for her virginity, Cardinal watches in horror from her bedroom window as the groom displays the bridal sheet soaked with fresh blood to the joyful acclamation of his guests: "The terror of no longer being a virgin. Nightmares. An open sore, blood. It's by that wound that purity is verified" (71–72).

Cardinal later recalls this incident when the preparation for her first communion, the barely disguised and relentless insistence on female virginity, teaches her that "among the French too marriage could be an act of savagery" (67–68). Cardinal again uses the resemblance that two otherwise distinct and foreign cultures consistently exhibit in their treatment of women to identify and illustrate the gender specificity of social situation. Moreover, the narrator of *Le Passé empiété,* companion text to *Au Pays de mes racines,* relates the brutal wedding-night rape of her own mother; Mimi discovers in her turn the "immense, visceral, ancient, incomprehensible fear" (214) common to women, as she believes that her bridegroom is "trying to kill her. With what weapon, she wondered" (217). Interestingly, just prior to the rape of his bride, the narrator's father recalls his own loss of virginity in an experience that Cardinal imagines as female. Unaware that he has a phimosis, he finds himself after sex inexplicably "covered with blood" (204), to the amusement of the prostitute with him and to his own shame and disgust. But this enforced sharing of female experience fails to produce any empathy in the male; it may rather make the savage deflowering of his wife an inevitable act of revenge in a culture in which female experience is systematically devalued. Yaguello has noted a similar phenomenon in the consistency with which dictionaries treat *woman* and *prostitute* as synonymous and analogous terms (152).

In a perceptive analysis of the ties between female anatomy and creativity, Susan Gubar notes that "one of the primary and most resonant metaphors provided by the female body is blood, and cultural forms of creativity are often experienced as a painful wounding. . . . the woman artist who experiences herself as killed into art may also experience herself as bleeding into print" ("Blank" 296). Cardinal too uses her female body repetitions to explore the obstacle to female creativity that the constant threat of rape represents. We have already seen that in the narrator's nightmare in *Les Mots pour le dire* she metaphorically describes rape as the denial of her right to speak, violently enforced by the knife positioned at her throat. In *Au Pays de mes racines* (85–90), Cardinal recalls a car accident that she and a female friend have in the desert. Her relief to see an Arab man appear out of nowhere expresses itself in verbal profuseness. Only gradually does the man's strange attitude, his persistent gaze directed below her face, restore her sense of self and allow her to realize that she has been conversing fluently for some five minutes in a language that she hasn't spoken in years. But even as she acknowledges the still-intact presence within her of the little girl who spoke Arabic, the man's stare awakens her to the fact that the accident has left her breasts not only exposed but clearly marked by the outline of her friend's mouth in lipstick. Instantly, she is transformed into a frightened young woman who, confronted by a potential rapist, can no longer speak a word of Arabic. Not only does the female's adult definition as sexual prey result in the loss of linguistic prowess—indeed, of language itself, as she stutters and stammers even in French—but it transforms all men, even childhood companions and adult allies in the struggle against cultural oppression and marginality, into enemies. Here, in addition, Cardinal encodes the cultural assumption that the female body is always sexual and that female sexuality, however unintentional, is always deliberately provocative; she suggests as well that society reserves particularly severe sanctions for female friendship, of which the covert accusation of lesbianism figures as the most important.

Near the center of *Autrement dit,* rape suddenly appears as a brutal rupture in the text that will delay its publication for months (123). In a curiously explicit parallel with Gubar's comment quoted above, Cardinal's and Leclerc's last conversation (before Cardinal leaves for Canada, where she expects to complete the manuscript in the course of the summer) centers on what she calls the "blood chapter" and Leclerc's conviction that "You haven't talked about blood enough" (122). A few days later Cardinal awakens to find herself immobilized beneath the body of a potential rapist. The total "scorn" and "indifference" in his eyes that transform her into "an object" (127) repeat the child's experience in *Les Mots pour le dire* with the cold gaze of the camera. And just as the camera identified the male as artist, Cardinal's fear leaves her unable to work, even though she escapes rape by pretending to suffer a heart attack. Moreover, the peculiar idea that occurs to her in the very midst of her simulation—"I thought about my glasses 'if he steals them, I'll no longer be able to write'" (130)—reiterates the connection between the threat of rape and women's creative possibilities. The broader social context here, in which men shout vulgarities and grab at her robe as Cardinal runs barefoot through the streets to the theater that her husband directs, further emphasizes the contrasting consequences of gender.

Although the relative importance of gender and culture do not function explicitly in this passage, the cultural heterogeneity and the colonial history that draw Cardinal to Canada may provoke her new understanding here of rape as a territorial invasion strictly comparable to "everything, in short, that makes men declare war" (136). This comparison illuminates the role that the constant backdrop of colonialism and the Algerian war play in her work. Metaphors for women's simultaneous oppression and demand for independence, they nevertheless cannot emerge from the background, for women have been denied any significant role in the history of this culture. Hence the nightmare in *Les Mots pour le dire* in which rape replaces the sharing of political views, awakening the narrator to the reason why she has always treated the Algerian war as "a sentimental story, a sad family affair. . . . Because I had no role to play in this society into which I was born and in which I went mad" (311; see also Lionnet's work on Cardinal).

As Cardinal's reflections on the vulnerability of the female body evolve into social critique and revolt, she specifically calls for an end to women's learned passivity and collaborative submission (e.g., AD 134, MD 296). In this context, the connection between language and sexuality announces a defensive (and offensive) strategy that responds precisely to her express desire to find the word that will make her cunt exist: "Not even a word to protect it. The words in our vocabulary that designate this precise part of the female body are ugly, vulgar, dirty, crude, grotesque, or technical" (MD 305). The initial passage that we encountered in this network of associations already links the pleasure and the power of sexual and linguistic femaleness. As a favorite place to read, the family bathroom has become "an annex of the library" (MD 124), and the narrator specifically rediscovers herself as "the little girl who used to masturbate among the dictionaries" (128). Female sexuality thus comes into existence in a context of infinite linguistic richness, even though the narrator will not succeed in naming her experience until many years later.

More importantly, the female artist also appears in this context. As the child enumerates her "sins" in an attempt to forestall her inevitable submission to the "worst" of them, her attention focuses on the equally forbidden and equally irresistible pleasures of listening to Daïba tell stories. This association of female art and female sexuality as parallel subversive activities reappears in *Autrement dit* where Cardinal repeats her memories of Daïba. This time she explicitly describes the old Algerian woman as the example who awakens her own desire to use words to communicate, to seduce, and to convince others. In particular, Daïba represents Cardinal's sense of herself as a "storyteller" that originates in her Mediterranean childhood: "You know, Arabs are fantastic storytellers and fantastic listeners as well. They gather on city and village squares to tell stories and to listen to them. They sit down by groups, in a circle, leaving an empty space in the center, as if it were from there, from that hole, that the dream were to take off, and they take turns telling stories. Those who want to tell stories" (71–72). As a model for feminist art, this description presents literature as a communal activity in which the narrator and the auditor, the writer and the reader share equitable and interchangeable roles. The *parole* of the oral narration serves as a metaphor for the particular kind of writing that Cardinal most values, one whose fluidly digressive and associative structure reflects the freedom of the *vague* and whose rhythm and vocabulary provide the expressiveness that the voice, the hands, and the face convey in spoken language (see AD 6–7, 222).[24]

We have already encountered the provocative connection between the vague and the vagina in Cardinal's work, and the image above, the eruption of narrative from this same "hole" that she so often uses to define female specificity suggests that she too, like many Francophone feminists, situates the origin of female writing in women's awareness of their bodies.[25] Interestingly, for Irma Garcia, *l'écriture féminine* not only originates in "all her hollow organs, those receptacles of speech that are the female organs" (2:21), but it is precisely the openness and the open-endedness of the female to which she attributes the characteristic repetitiveness of women's writing: "the necessity of constantly referring, recalling, establishing points of juncture, for all elements interpenetrate, circulate, outlining among themselves the coherence of the round, the circular, the rotundity of women's writing" (2:139).

Cardinal's key word *open* thus fuses in its double meaning female language and female sexuality; open language—accessible to all: unhampered by restrictions, free of prejudice, receptive to new ideas—corresponds to the open body—accessible to all: exposed, without cover, affording unobstructed passage. But their superposition produces a paradoxical inversion, for a writing freed to explore the female body ultimately serves to restore and preserve its integrity: "The best way to prove that we lack words, that French isn't made for women, is to place ourselves level with our bodies, express the unexpressed, and use vocabulary just as it is, directly, without fixing it up. Then it will become obvious and clear that there are things that we can't translate into words. How can we speak our sexuality, the experience of gestation, women's sense of time and duration? We will have to invent. Language will be feminized, it will open up, it will be embellished and enriched. Our sonority will be fertile and welcoming, for our words will serve everyone" (AD 89). Although Cardinal encourages women to produce texts that would be, in Christiane Makward's words, "'bio-graphical,' in the sense that they 'write' the 'body' primarily" (96), she does so in a context in which she explicitly (and repeatedly [see AD 89, 96]) rejects the notion of an *écriture féminine*, a specifically female language or discourse. The linguistic feminization required for the adequate expression of female reality enriches language as a whole.

To the extent that Cardinal implicitly substitutes the vagina for the penis in Gilbert and Gubar's sexiolinguistic equation, she breaks free from the association between creativity and childbirth that Showalter appropriately finds "even more oppressive" (187). Cardinal selects a metaphor that turns all women, and not only mothers, into potential artists. Moreover, by equating the vagina rather than the womb with the penis, she shifts the metaphorical focus of male creativity as well from paternity to sexuality; thus, the parallelism that has always reinforced the traditional division of labor between male production of art and female reproduction of babies now subverts it. Still, given the strong associations in Cardinal's work between sexual and textual pleasure, I am well aware that lesbian readers may object to her vaginal images as signs of cultural heterosexism (implicitly attached, therefore, to women's reproductive capabilities as well). To some extent, I do think that Cardinal deliberately alludes to heterosexuality as a way to unite male and female in a cultural and literary revolution that she ultimately views as human; by including the vagina *and* the penis in textual metaphors, she in fact restores the qualifier *hetero-* to sexuality and textuality. Similarly, Carolyn Heilbrun, in a specific reference to the analogy that Gilbert and Gubar establish between pens and penises and wombs and creativity, stresses the urgency of developing other metaphors and concludes that creativity is "allied with, if not identical to, sexuality" ("Response" 808).

In this light, Cardinal's critique of male writers who refuse to write their homosexuality identifies her heterotextuality as a process common to men and women rather than an analogy for one specific form of sexual attraction. For Cardinal, the writing of Barthes, Deleuze, and Foucault illustrates the internal censorship that lies behind the predilection for neutral, abstract, technical language: "Not only is it [technical language] sexless but it lets nothing through of the bodies of those who use it. I note that Barthes, Deleuze, and Foucault are all homosexuals. I would like to know how they live their homosexuality. . . . Are they so afraid of their bodies that they have lost their voices? What are the real words they are concealing behind those of science?" (AD 93–94). This linguistic assault on those very writers who profess that language and reality are coextensive exposes texts that profess to be nonreferential as duplicitous and alternative forms of silence.

Still, women who define themselves as heterosexual no doubt represent a majority in contemporary society; and, as we have seen, the representation of a female culture and a female poetics necessarily requires a certain concentration on what constitutes for women the traditional and the cultural norm. In this perspective, however, Cardinal's periodic celebrations of the female body in a context of sexual love between women offer important evidence of her strong desire to create a literature and a culture inclusive of all women. Indeed, one of Cardinal's solutions to the vulnerability of the female body originates in the inherent powerfulness of that same body. In *Une Vie pour deux*, for example, the writer and sometime lover for whom Simone is doing research deliberately arranges to have her discover him making love to another woman. As Simone's shock and embarrassment at being treated as a voyeur shift irresistibly to fascination, she experiences herself simultaneously as lover and beloved and discovers in the very openness of female sexuality the beauty and freedom of women's power: "I had never seen the power of the woman. . . . I had never seen the potency of the hollow, the vertiginous abyss to which led the stubborn sentinel of the clitoris, this efficient guide. I hadn't imagined my crack so beautiful. I thought the deep disarmed and its importance beyond it. I had never thought about the depth that is protected by the whole body. . . . Desire to take Angèle into my arms, . . . to appease her mouth, and her breasts, and her *nuine*, by my cool kisses, by my woman's mouth" (VD 92–93). Simone's eventual recovery through the act of writing of this long-repressed memory of her desire for another woman confirms the complementarity of sexuality and texuality; her substitution for the male as lover is followed by her replacement of him as writer. Throughout the long description of Angèle's genitals, Cardinal also uses a vocabulary—"the shining of her lips," "her round and deep interrogation," "greedy mouth" (91–92)— that once again connects female speech to female sexuality.

Cardinal's work obviously supports Showalter's affirmation that "there can be no expression of the body which is unmediated by linguistic, social, and literary structures" (89). One final look at *Les Mots pour le dire* can help us clarify the intricate connections among the female body, *écriture féminine*, and women's social situation that have emerged from a single network of related passages. The narrator recognizes that the discovery she makes during analysis of the specificity of the female body and of female specificity as the body is in fact foreign to the analytic process. Only outside ("in the streets, in stores, at the office, at home") does she come to realize what it means "to have a vagina, to be a woman" (308). Cardinal's long enumeration of the endless responsibilities and repetitive tasks that fill up the days of the average working wife and mother, a list punctuated by the cultural dictums that determine proper female behavior (310), further emphasizes her understanding of femaleness as primarily a fact not of biology or anatomy but of gender roles. Indeed, the narrator explicitly attaches the label "the consciousness of my female specificity" (311) to her description of daily female reality.

The brutal collapse of "the notion of femininity" (308), which the narrator experiences after thirty-seven years of total and unexamined submission to inequality and injustice, plunges her into despair, until a second nightmare allows her to identify more accurately the fear of sexuality that seemed to emerge from the first as the actual fear of men's power. Although her simultaneous discovery of the solution—"Sharing power would be enough" (315)—may at first sight seem both too obvious and too idealistic to be very useful, in fact it represents for Cardinal's narrator a very concrete plan of political involvement. In an implicit acceptance of the full implications of the feminist assertion that "the personal is political," she recognizes that her desire to play a role in society must begin at home with the *difference* of *repetition*, with the transformation of "a family, a microcosm, the ferment of a society" (315). Within Cardinal's work as a whole, this commitment to revolution in the private sphere translates, as we know, into the textual reconstitution and the linguistic exploration of female culture.

NOTES

1. I quote Crowder: "These three views seem to correspond to what the editors of *Questions féministes* have outlined as three stages in feminist consciousness: 'femininity' which accepts women's exclusion from the world of social discourse; 'feminitude' which valorizes difference and the creation of women's language; and 'feminism,' a reappropriation of all forms of discourse to eliminate the ghettoization of women" (126).

2. Irma Garcia, whose analysis of *écriture féminine* constitutes a "patch-

work" (1:14) of quotations from other women writers, describes her methodology in terms that essentially repeat those of Cardinal: "The textual fragments, the existing pieces that make up quotes are going to gather, merge, interpenetrate, until they outline 'this circular memory' that Roland Barthes talks about: 'And that's exactly what the inter-text is: the impossibility of living outside of the infinite text'" (1:16).

3. Hélène Cixous first theorized such a relationship between women and language: "*Flying/stealing* is woman's gesture; flying in/stealing language; making it fly/causing its theft. We have all learned the art of flying/stealing with its many techniques during the centuries in which *flying/stealing* has been the only way we could possess" (*La Jeune* 178). Claudine Herrmann also examines this relationship in *Les Voleuses de langue*.

4. Out of a theoretical framework that draws upon the work of Bakhtin, Patricia Yaeger demonstrates similar subversive effects. By incorporating Yeats's poetry into her own prose, Eudora Welty undermines the force and stability of the male signified; she transforms original meaning into signifiers whose free play now makes them available to serve her own purposes.

5. According to Hayden White, every discipline is "constituted by what it *forbids* its practitioners to do" (*Tropics* 126).

6. See, for example, *The Prism of Sex, Men's Studies Modified,* and *A Feminist Perspective in the Academy.*

7. Such assertions figure among Cardinal's most important repetitions, and they inform her own writing practice as well as her reading habits. In the case of *Cet Eté-là* and *Au Pays de mes racines,* for example, *l'écriture,* the need to write, not only has priority over any other subject matter but in fact constitutes the *only* subject matter of both texts. Alain Robbe-Grillet defines the *écrivain* precisely by such a lack of imagination: "His desire to write precedes a something to say. The activity of writing prompts the activity of invention by raising problems, imposing directives, providing constant stimulation. It is in and by the text that the text is produced" ("Discussion" 125).

8. Antoine Compagnon notes that quotation provides an excellent "defense against the blank page" (392).

9. Derrida, who has a predilection for female metaphors, describes the narrative structure that produces the *mise en abyme* as "invaginated." On the value that feminists might attach to such ambivalent images, see Jardine, *Gynesis* 204–7.

10. Chapter 3 includes a detailed analysis of Cardinal's particular exploration of the rhythmical mobility of form.

11. For Irma Garcia, "menstrual blood seems to intervene directly in the rhythm of certain narratives" (2:70). By analogy to a loss of words, for example, menstruation emphasizes the unfinished, the open-ended, quality of women's texts (2:75); by association with lexical enumeration ("a menses of

words joined by coagulation"), the flow of blood establishes a fluid rhythm that suspends linear syntax (2:70–71).

12. Marina Yaguello cites *la mer* as the most convincing evidence for the theory of linguistic evolution that attributes a change in gender to a word's metaphorical function. Neuter in Latin, *la mer* becomes feminine in French, in contrast to other Latin neuters, which become masculine in French, and to the other Romance languages, in which the words for "sea" become masculine. Presumably, then, "metaphysical needs" resulted in the assimilation of *la mer* to *la mère*. In Cardinal's case, however, the alternative explanation that Yaguello finds "every bit as plausible" is just as revealing: "*la mer* simply borrowed its gender from *la terre*. Indeed, *terre* rhymes with *mer*, which is the case neither in Spanish (*tierra*/*mar*), nor in Italian (*terra*/*mare*)" (102).

13. I cite two additional examples:

> A life made up of sensations, emotions, feelings, impressions; an invigorating life, a languorous life, a dolorous life, a sensual life, the life of a pied-noir. A life where your soul and the land are in constant communication. A land of strong odors, a land that burns, a land that chills, a rough land that handles roughly, a tender land that caresses, a land that is, after all, only an adoptive mother, a foreigner to whom one can therefore make love.   (PR 77)

> During the scalding nights of summer, the belly [womb] of the little girl, waiting for a breath of air to doze off, is a basin [pelvis] full of love. I know that it is love's invariable rhythm that rocks the sea and my body. I don't know why I know that, but I know it. And it is perhaps because I am unable to name love that it is so grand, so important, so solemn. Regular, alternating rhythm: the other-me, me-elsewhere, difference-me, me-outside me. The universe and I, I in it, it in I. Both perfect.   (PR 103)

14. I have often wondered whether Cardinal does not play similar games (games similar to those that we, as children, used to play at parties, where the goal was to find the most words *within* a given word), using her own name as textual generator. In *Au Pays de mes racines*, notably, the juxtaposition of title and author reveals the *racine* within her own name ([Mari]e *Car*[d]*in*[al]) or even, with an allowance for the multilingualism of the Mediterranean, a more complex image: *racine di la mar* (*racine de la mer*). Cardinal's first name alone delivers the unified complex of land, sea, mother, love, and rhythm that is so important in her work: Marie (*aimer, mer, mèr*[e]*, amie, ma*[man]*, rime, rame*). Cardinal often gives a version of her own name to her female characters (e.g., Maria in *Ecoutez la mer*, Marie in *La Souricière*, Moussia in *La Clé sur la porte*, Mary in *Une Vie pour deux*); by etymology, the Indo-European root *mari* (a young woman) identifies femaleness itself (moreover, the number of insults ad-

dressed to women that are based on compounds of Marie [Yaguello 162] may confirm the generic value of the name).

15. Such a naming process clearly challenges Moi's assertion that the process of naming ultimately acts to fix meaning.

16. "Mère, ménagère, mégère, miss, matrone, maritorne, maîtresse, muse, madone, mijaurée, marâtre, moukère, mousmé, moitié, midinette, mangeuse d'andouille, mangeuse de pommes, mémé, mistonne, môme, morue, maîtresse femme, maîtresse de maison, mondaine."

17. Garcia cites the frequency of both connotation (1:53; 2:79) and enumeration (1:317) among the definitional characteristics of *écriture féminine*.

18. Similarly, Compagnon asserts that the act of quotation definitively frees words from their referents (67) and simultaneously imposes them as "true" by reconceptualizing the issue of "truth" as one of citational exactness rather than factual accuracy (106).

19. *Une Vie pour deux* provides the best example. Although the internal narrative in particular, "L'Histoire de Mary MacLaughlin," in many ways resembles traditional realistic fiction and clearly reflects a certain belief that the literary text can mimetically encode a female life, this novel also includes, as should be obvious from the frequency with which I have cited it, a number of lyrical passages that use phonetic and semantic association to generate the female body. Coincidentally, Cardinal's dual commitment to experiential realism and linguistic experimentalism here divides along traditional Anglophone/Francophone lines, since Mary is Irish and Simone, the principal narrator, French.

20. "Là où les *planè*tes *plan*ent vertigineusement, où les *onde*s *ond*ulent les liquides, où les *rayons ray*ent les espaces, où les *parti*cules *part*agent et pétrifient la matière. Je participais à l'élaboration de la vie. Je vivais l'instant où la cellule se divise en deux étant à la fois elle-même et une autre."

21. Such passages occur frequently in Cardinal's fiction as well, as we have seen, and are particularly characteristic of the novel *Les Mots pour le dire,* whose title simultaneously names the procedure and enacts it, leaving both the signified (*les mots*) and the referent (*le*) untranslated (see esp. 282–83). Garcia cites passages on *les mots,* similar to Cardinal's, from Nathalie Sarraute, Chantal Chawaf, Hélène Cixous, and Marguerite Duras, among others (2:123–38).

22. Since this is the only occasion on which Garcia uses Cardinal as intertext (despite the fact that the latter's practice consistently exemplifies the former's theory), it seems important to repeat her commentary: "The various proposals for linguistic innovation that seek to name 'this sex which isn't one' seem to feel their way, to try out sound, playing on marine associations to evoke humidity (between *l'algue* [algae] and *l'huître* [oyster], *la langue* [tongue] and *le puits* [well]), feminizing words (*'la nuite'* (morphological redundancy) or *'tronce'*), lingering on transitional words (*'abysses'* connects humidity to the notion of depth as does *'ravine'*), forming collages (*Sang/rengaine* [blood/refrain]—*san-*

gaine)" (2:180). Note, in particular, Garcia's identification of *écriture féminine* with fluidity, redundance, verbal association, and the variform structure of collage.

23. Judith Mayne reads this passage as a paradigm for the current problematic of feminist film theory and criticism.

24. Françoise Colin offers a similar interpretation of the connection between body and language that for her, as for many Francophone feminist theoreticians, informs *écriture féminine* as a whole: "Staying close to the body first means knowing that verbal or written language is not the only language possible and that the privilege it is accorded, especially in our culture, is already in and of itself an act of exclusion. There are gestures, contact, movement; there is drawing, dance, music, song, voice" (qtd. in Yaguello 66; see also Didier 17; Garcia 1:167–74; and Lamy ch. 3). The proximity of voice and body is particularly evident in the work of Hélène Cixous, where the woman not only speaks her body but also speaks *from* her own and/or her mother's body (for an example particularly reminiscent of Cardinal's work, see *Jeune* 173).

25. In *Autrement dit,* Cardinal connects her own writing practice to the rhythms of her body: "For me, writing is yet another way to fight. I write with my body" (201).

CHAPTER THREE

Narrating the Female Self
The Difference of Identity

A women's writing defined as self-referential and autogenerative not only produces and names its own textual practice but, taking itself at once both figuratively and more literally, it generates and refers to the female self. Similarly, the repetition of autocitation simultaneously multiplies female identity and reinscribes it as multiple. Such a process identifies another of Marie Cardinal's most frequently recurrent patterns: the use of a narrative framework in which first- and third-person pronouns appear in juxtaposition. Appropriately, pronominal innovation of this sort often characterizes contemporary women's writing.

Even as Paula A. Treichler, for example, argues that studies of women and language have concentrated on meaning and usage rather than syntax, she quickly adds, "Pronominalization, of course, has been a focus for feminist analysis for some time" (77). Indeed, in *Literary Women,* one of the very earliest examples of feminist criticism, Ellen Moers notes that pronouns bother the woman writer at moments of strong awareness that "I the author is a She" (163). Alice Jardine displaces the difference between female-written and male-written texts of modernity from their content to their process of enunciation, that is, to their choice and usage of personal pronouns ("Opaque" 104). Judith Kegan Gardiner explicitly connects female identity and narrative technique: because the texts of women writers serve the ongoing process of their own self-definition, "novels by women often shift through first, second, and third persons, and into reverse" ("Female" 357).

Importantly, this appears to be an area of clear intercultural interest for Anglophone and Francophone feminist discourse. Irma Garcia, in discussing how "the woman writing . . . fuses in her writing with the woman character," also stresses "the rupture of the third-person pronoun: 'she' who splits in two to make room for the first-person pronoun: 'I'" (1:90). And for Béatrice Didier, pronominal innovation represents one of the most original aspects of *écriture féminine:* "The real achievement of modern women's writing will perhaps turn out to be, assisted yet again by an entire current of thought stemming from both psychoanalysis and existentialism, a different way of inscribing identity in the text. This can be translated very concretely by a revolutionary usage of personal pronouns, a challenging of the distinction between the 'I' and the 'she' . . ." (34).

Yet, the emphasis that Didier's own study places on the "I" to the exclusion of the "she" corresponds to a valorization that is implicit in much current feminist criticism and that becomes explicit in *Living Stories, Telling Lives,* Joanne S. Frye's recent analysis of female first-person narrative. Frye first prefers fiction to autobiography for its greater independence from the actual conditions of women's lives and then further reduces women's possibilities for self-expression by limiting fiction itself to the first-person novel. She argues convincingly that the textual recurrence of "a female pronoun" "repeatedly reminds us of cultural expectations for what it means to be female"; in contrast, "the narrating 'I'" incorporates for Frye a potential for self-definition that makes it "one of the most powerful expressions of a woman's capacity to resist cultural definition" (64–65).[1]

Without seeking to perpetuate exclusive value judgments (particularly in a context in which Cardinal's refusal to choose specifically undermines them), I nonetheless find it important to affirm at once the equally revolutionary potential of the third person, based precisely on the assumption of gender identity that it signals.[2] Cardinal stresses this very point when she identifies "I am a woman" as the most difficult and disturbing assertion that a woman can make today (Pednault 20). Her textual alternations between first-person and third-person voices translate the particular difficulty that her narrative "I" often faces: the need to recognize and to accept the fact that she is also a "she," that the problems she confronts are both specific to and common to women. In her own case as well, the importance that Cardinal attaches to gender makes "she" at once a synonymous and a more accurate designation of the self than "I": "When I write, I always start out with something I know, that I have lived, and then it is transformed, it opens up, it wanders off, the 'I' can become a 'she,' *but 'she' is much more me than is the 'I'"* (AD 28, my emphasis).

In this context, the troubling dilemma of the feminist critic who cannot say "I" without simultaneously turning the woman about whom she writes into a "she"—thus, of necessity, Frye's own textual practice systematically undermines the theory at its origin—seems more appropriate than contradictory. This important fusion of self and other, of individual subjectivity and gender commonality, repeats the constantly shifting interaction of "I" and "she" that Cardinal's own textual practice repeatedly enacts. This union of critic and novelist reminds me of what Carolyn Heilbrun appropriately calls "one of the most appealing characteristics of feminist criticism: in deconstructing literature and life, we ourselves become novelists, making fiction out of the texts, and lives, other women have left us" ("Response" 805).[3]

Gender and Narrative Theory

In the course of the last decade, Cardinal and other feminist writers have increasingly transformed this female dialogue into a chorus that has included male voices as well. In her 1981 introduction to *Critical Inquiry*'s special issue on feminist criticism, "Writing and Sexual Difference," Elizabeth Abel identifies a renewed interest among women writers in the literary conventions of the dominant tradition: "the analysis of female talent grappling with a male tradition translates sexual difference into literary differences of genre, structure, voice, and plot" (174). Although Abel believes that this attention to what, in essence, constitutes issues of *narration* may "belatedly accord the feminist critic a position closer to the mainstream of critical debate" (174)—a possibility immediately confirmed by *Critical Inquiry*'s own willingness to pay attention—she is also aware that this new texuality, denounced as "simply a return to formalism" (174), could be interpreted as a betrayal of feminism's ideological commitment. As if in confirmation, Annette Kolodny's work from this same period reflects a similar tension between feminism and formalism. Not only does Kolodny attribute the unity and the vigor of the first decade of feminist literary criticism to the attention that has been paid to questions of form; she also makes the provocative assertion that "in our heart of hearts, of course, most critics are really structuralists" ("Dancing" 20, 17). Yet Kolodny fully understands the paradoxical fact that our very training in a critical practice informed by "inherently sexist preconceptions" may nonetheless prevent us from reading the unique organizing patterns of female texts ("Lady's" 274). Thus, a feminist perspective on the problems of narration may be less likely to accord us a position *within* the critical mainstream, as Abel predicts, than to offer us an opportunity to reposition ourselves *in relation to* that mainstream.

The place of privilege granted in twentieth-century theoretical discourse to the analysis of narrative has resulted in a body of critical work that demonstrates an overwhelming similarity, even though it has been diversely informed over time by Anglophone stylistics, Russian formalism, American New Criticism, and French structuralism and has been practiced most recently within a newly independent field of narratology. But whether the central issue has been point of view in general (Norman Friedman), first-person voice (Bertil Romberg), semiotic codes (Roland Barthes), diegetic space (Gérard Genette), or the single concept of the narratee (Gerald Prince), studies of narration have focused predominantly on the production of alternative systems of classification and on the clarification and the refinement of critical terminology.[4] The interconnecting concerns with empirical accuracy, theoretical coherence, and methodological objectivity that are apparent here unmask a commitment to the powerful triumvirate of Science, Technology, and Truth that recalls Cardinal's analysis of the gender-exclusive (and exclusionist) language of dominant male culture: "Western societies have given Science priority. They have developed a scientific and technical language—the official language—the language of 'truth' that eliminates subjectivity; it seeks to be unambiguous" (ME 39).

Indeed, such catalogs of fictional forms and lexical distinctions often appear frankly irrelevant to a feminist analysis of narrative. The extent to which they could be used as an interpretive framework for reading women's writing, for example, cannot be separated from their explicit purpose of eliminating any notion of textual difference in the name of an abstract concept of literariness. If this might seem like a path to cultural integration, we should remember that gender difference as a whole, and female specificity in particular, already enjoy an unusual degree of vulnerability, if not downright invisibility, without being viewed from a theoretical perspective that is explicitly informed by the a priori exclusion of such issues from its field of inquiry. As Susan Lanser discovered while conducting research for *The Narrative Act,* "some of the most important elements of point of view—the gender of the narrator, the speaker's basis for authority, the narrator's 'personality' and values, and the relationship between the writer's circumstances and beliefs and the narrative structure of the text—were peripheral to most contemporary theories of point of view" (5).

To the extent, moreover, that literary theory has read specific texts, not in search of a more sophisticated description of the abstract notion of Narrative Form, but in view of a better understanding of the formal qualities of particular narrative structures, there has been a strong tendency to concentrate on a select corpus of literary works. When the analysis marked by such critical privilege does not simply reiterate the traditional canon of Western literature (as in the case, for example, of Balzac, Flaubert, Henry James, Faulkner, or Proust—who individually or collectively inform the vast majority of critical discussions of narrative voice), its inclusion of those works specifically designed to challenge the conventions of narrative form (as in the case, for example, of Dos Passos, Gide [*Les Faux-Monnayeurs*], Sterne, Diderot [*Jacques le fataliste*], Edouard Desjardins [*Les Lauriers sont coupés*], or the experimental fiction of Robert Coover or Alain Robbe-Grillet) necessarily results, albeit indirectly at times, in the reconstitution of traditional literary history. The rare cases that fail to conform to this overwhelming male dominance of both literary text and theoretical context (as in the case, for example, of Virginia Woolf) merely constitute the exceptions that prove the rule—to cite a cliché in a situation that seems to call for one.

Furthermore, the essential dichotomy between realistic and innovative narration, which informs the theory outlined above, reproduces itself in two critical traps, the Scylla and Charybdis of narrative study. On the one hand, a focus on experimental fiction tends to lead the critic to emphasize form to the exclusion of content, resulting in the repetition on the level of the individual work of the abstract classification system of a general theory of narrative. On the other hand, readings of realistic fiction tend to sacrifice form to the study of content, leading to the confusion of narrative structure with plot and to the substitution of plot summary for narrative analysis. Nor is there any reason to believe that a feminist theory of narrative, developed within the same theoretical context(s), would necessarily avoid these pitfalls. On the contrary, certain interests specific to feminist critics—notably, the desire to reacquaint the reading public with little-known women's texts, the conviction that women's writing provides direct access to female experience, and a profound distrust of the linguistic and formal analyses that have historically supported a distinctly male canon and literary tradition—combine to make the second danger, that of plot summary, a persistent threat within feminist criticism. Moreover, one could also argue that the implicit subordination of individual texts that is required by the attempt to determine the general outline of a female culture and/or a female poetics poses the risk of abstraction or overgeneralization as well.

Thus, Lanser's experience, though particularly telling, is no doubt neither unusual nor especially surprising. Having set out to study narrative voice in specific texts by women, she finds her original project so significantly altered by her preparatory journey through prior critical discourse that she in fact writes a theory of point of view in which, by her own acknowledgment, "feminist 'content' appears only infrequently on the surface" (10). Although I do not for a moment question the many significant ways in which Lanser's feminist perspective and reading of women's texts inform the "deep structures" (10) of her discourse and thought, her own example nevertheless confirms that contact with the form and format of male thinking and writing about narration clearly involves a risk of contamination, of co-optation.

The danger may well be increased by yet another consequence of our uneasy relationship to narrative theory in general and to formalism in particular. No doubt we have not yet paid enough attention to the formal aspects of women's writing to be able to determine exactly what a feminist theory of narrative should account for, let alone be in a position to articulate a fully developed theory that could guide our reading practices. The importance, to paraphrase Cardinal, of filling in the empty spaces of these specifically female domains (AD 87) provides particularly strong support for my desire to ground feminist criticism and theory in textual analysis. Cardinal, moreover, promises to provide a particularly interesting test case, given her belief, surely shared by many other contemporary women writers, that the critical reduction of her work to a kind of documentary of female reality involves a deliberate obfuscation of its specifically literary merits.

Let me recall Elaine Showalter's assertion that "no theory, however suggestive, can be a substitute for the close and extensive knowledge of women's texts which constitute our essential subject" ("Feminist" 25); my own counterassertion that the analysis of a given textual practice can generate in and of itself a new theory of the text may find its strongest justification in the field of narrative. Lanser, in refuting the prescriptive tendencies of most critical approaches to point of view, which she interprets as the consequence of isolating narrative perspective from its textual function, stresses that "what is important is how a given device operates in a specific context" (28; cf. 19). Louis Mink goes even further; he argues that the individual text provides not only a locus for the *production* of theory but our primary means of *access* to theory: "Particular narratives express their own conceptual presuppositions. They are in fact our most useful evidence for coming to understand conceptual presuppositions quite different from our own" ("Narrative" 132–33).[5]

Self and Other: Une Vie pour deux

Une Vie pour deux (1978) provides an initial context in which to explore the relationship between feminism and formalism. Cardinal here inscribes female experience within dialectical structures that allow the dynamic interaction of ideology and form. I understand *ideology* as a lived system of concepts, values, and structures that represent a vision of the world. For Cardinal's work, the stress that Raymond Williams places on ideology as a dynamic *process* of producing meanings and ideas is particularly useful (55, 70–71; see also Poovey). As for *dialectical,* I am well aware that this problematic term brings with it a host of prior usages (none of which precisely corresponds to my own), including particularly strong ties to historical Marxism. But it is a word for which Cardinal herself shows an affinity, and I use it for the moment only in the general sense in which she does to identify a process of thought characteristic of the rhythms of the Mediterranean ("middle land," from the Latin *medius* + *terra*); it therefore emphasizes the *inter* in a variety of interrelationships and interactions that allow diversity and multiplicity to coexist.

Let me recall briefly the essential narrative and structural complexities of *Une Vie pour deux.* The novel recounts the vacation spent in Ireland by Simone and Jean-François, a middle-aged couple whose life is disrupted moments after their arrival in Corvagh by Jean-François' discovery of the corpse of Mary MacLaughlin on the beach. In an effort to protect herself against this prototypical "other woman" whom she believes can take her husband away from her even after death, Simone proposes that she and Jean-François together invent the life of Mary. Cardinal organizes *Une Vie pour deux* around the interplay of three stories: the couple's daily life in Corvagh, Simone's memories of the past, and the story of Mary MacLaughlin's life. Structurally, Simone's first-person narrative provides a framework (1–92, 263–86) within which the first-person voice alternates both with a third-person account of certain events, past and present, of Simone's and Jean-François' lives and with successive episodes of the self-contained secondary "novel," *Histoire de Mary MacLaughlin.*

The central form that Cardinal calls into question in *Une Vie pour deux* is that of the Couple, an act that Cardinal acknowledges to be one of extreme subversion: "The desire to change the couple is the desire for revolution" (AD 158). Simone, who originally conceives the summer as her last chance to establish the relationship with Jean-François to which she has dedicated (in fact, sacrificed) her own life, quickly comes to realize that she is trapped in a convention whose fixed stagnation must give way to perpetual change: "I went from 'Us' to us, from what was stagnant to what is in a constant state of evolution" (15). As the title of the novel suggests, Simone has been taught that a Couple represents two people who are in reality only one (58). As such, the couple is the central form in which the fundamental dualism of Western ideology has been embodied. The apparent synthesis contained in the two-in-one concept of the couple in fact represents either a fundamental dichotomy (like Ireland, a country divided against itself) or a false unity based on the privilege of the male *one.*

Cardinal's challenge to the couple—a form explored through the opposition of north and south, mother and child, writer and book, as well as husband and wife—is encoded primarily in the narrative structure of *Une Vie pour deux;* an initial attempt at the impossible "we" gives way to the interaction of "I" and "she." This unusual juxtaposition of first and third persons serves first to make narrative form visible and so to emphasize its importance within Cardinal's work. J. M. Lotman argues that a compositional device becomes distinctive only when contrasted with an alternative system; thus our awareness of point of view as an element of textual structure implies the possibility of switching it in the course of the narrative.

More importantly, however, Cardinal's bivocal form also supports the original impetus behind Lanser's study of the narrative act: the inability of traditional literary theory to account adequately for female textual practice (5–6). Cardinal's narrative technique not only refuses to make the either/or choice between "I" and "she" on which almost all catalogs of point of view, however intricate or complex, are based. But she exceeds Lotman's systemic analysis as well, for it is impossible either to predict or to explain fully the particular moments at which the shifts in narrative technique take place—all attempts to determine a globally operative system break down. Although Cardinal initially seems to be juxtaposing the "I" of Simone's "life" with the "she" of Mary's fictional "story," as traditional pronoun usage would have it, in fact Simone herself quickly realizes a simultaneous identity as author, narrator, and character. Thus, Cardinal's characteristic narrative structure stands as a deliberate affront—in the words of Genette, "a strong transgression," "a kind of narrative pathology" (253)—to traditional literary theory and to the ideology that informs it.

By her insistence that she is both "I" *and* "she," Simone at once replaces dichotomous with dialectical thought (for Marcia Westkott, such a process defines a specifically feminist mode of analysis) and reclaims the multiplicity of conventionally fragmented identity. For Cardinal, as we know (but the passage now bears repeating), all discourse engages the self, regardless of its point of view: "When I write, I always begin with something that I know, that I've lived, and then it is transformed, it opens up, it wanders off; the 'I' might become a 'she,' but 'she' is much more me than 'I' is. 'I' is a mask" (AD 28). Cardinal's sense of continuity, of *vague,* marks an important contrast to the painful dichotomy of Rimbaud's celebrated equivalent: "*Je est un autre.*" Philippe Lejeune interprets Rimbaud's fractured, alienated self as the paradigmatic model at the heart of the notion of the individual in Western culture; by acknowledging openly that the first person always conceals the third, Rimbaud reveals "what is the peculiarity of personhood: the tension between an impossible unity and an intolerable division, and the fundamental split that makes the speaking subject a fugitive" (*Je* 38).

For Cardinal, within the individual as within the couple, if unity is impossible, neither is it desirable; and if division is intolerable, neither is it inevitable. Her internally repetitive "I am a woman" responds in a female chorus to Rimbaud's internally disjunctive "I is an other" and exposes this conception of the self as specifically male. By identifying her "I" as a mask and not as an other, Cardinal suggests that women are characterized by "duplicity" (AD 42), not because they are untrustworthy or artificial, but because their multiplicity results in constant metamorphosis. The particular use of the mask to identify the duplicity of a narrative technique designed to illustrate the plurality and the continuity of female identity makes Helen Fehervary's remarks on the mask motif in Christa Wolf's work of considerable interest here. For Fehervary, the mask conceals the capacity for a pluralization of identities that she calls "the secret of the third person": "The mask is a form of relational being and enables the stripping away of an isolated individual identity" (74). Cardinal's characteristic pronoun usage provides a context that usefully illuminates Fehervary's provocative interpretation of Wolf's reflection on "the difficulty of saying 'I'" as "the desire *not* to say 'I' but to say *more* than 'I'" (74).[6]

In *Une Vie pour deux*, Simone claims the lack of unity and coherence of the "I" as an enrichment; her life, "punctuated by women" (101), becomes the repetition (understood, as always, as the imitation and the transformation) of other female lives, both those of the women she has known and those of the women she herself has been. The real two-in-one model of the title of Cardinal's novel refers not to the false couple that she has formed with Jean-François at the price of her own identity but to the multiplicity of the individual and the collective self. Thus, her understanding of female identity as relational ultimately allows Simone to challenge a dichotomy equally important in Western culture and even more destructive for women than that of the heterosexual couple: the bipolarity of femaleness itself that opposes "good" women to "bad." By identifying every woman whom she encounters as the "other woman," Simone positions herself within a dialectic of "not me" (other) and "me" (woman) that reflects the mutability and the plurality of masked identity; moreover, Simone's attraction to these women, at times to the point of momentary confusion of self and other, reunites the good woman and the bad. Simone simultaneously constructs identities for her "other women" that belie female dualism. Angèle, named for the pure and the passive in womanhood, actively re-creates female sexual pleasure; and Mary, named for the virgin mother, bears an illegitimate child and exposes herself "indecently" in her final courtroom evocation.

Simone's participation in a feminist demonstration, the first haunting obsession that she is able to narrate publicly and so reclaim, teaches her—despite her "panicky fear of women's demonstrations"—to feel solidarity as a woman among women: "Simone recognized herself in their words; she was a woman like that" (191). This evolution in Simone's perception of women from enemy to ally, corresponding to the textual transformation of Mary as rival into Mary as double, allows Simone to confront the reality of her most repressed memory: her strong sexual attraction to another woman (194). Indeed, in each of the stories in which another woman originally poses a threat to the couple that Simone forms with a man, reemplotment turns the story of male infidelity into one of female love. Simone realizes that the life that she has narrated as a "female plot" of abandonment by men must in her case be rewritten as a "feminist plot" of solidarity with women.[7]

Cardinal shares with a number of other contemporary women writers her perception of female identity as fluid and continuous, characterized by the interpenetration of self and other. Within Anglophone feminist theory, Nancy Chodorow's revision of female psychology has been particularly influential, informing, for example, readings of women's texts by Marianne Hirsch, Judith Kegan Gardiner, Elizabeth Abel ("(E)Merging"), and Margaret Homans (Bearing). Chodorow argues that the "feminine personality comes to include a fundamental definition of self in relationship" (169) as a result of the prolonged "sense of oneness and continuity" (109) that characterizes the preoedipal attachment of mother and daughter. American feminists have recently begun to use this notion of the female subject to refute the postmodernist attack on the very concept of the self. Gardiner, for example, argues that the postmodernist critique addresses a specifically male concept of the autonomous, unified, and coherent individual that is basically irrelevant to the conception of the female subject. Moreover, like Cardinal, Gardiner finds the substitution of a self perceived as intrinsically fragmented and self-alienated equally foreign to women whose sense of fusion and collectivity represents the very opposite of division and separation ("Mind Mother" 115).[8]

In this area, Francophone feminists, despite their strong ties to postmodernist thought, tend to side with their Anglophone counterparts, although different conceptions of language and different genre choices also produce somewhat different expressions of a similar notion of the female self. Whereas Anglophone feminists are more likely to exteriorize certain aspects of the self in independent fictional characters and/or to explore the self through the relationships and the resemblances among different characters, Francophone feminists—Hélène Cixous, Luce Irigaray, and Suzanne Lamy, for example—transform the first-person essay into a dialogue or a chorus of female voices. To some extent, the parallel multiplying of character (Simone/Mary) and of voice (I/she) allows Cardinal to explore both possibilities in Une Vie pour deux and identifies a pattern that repeats itself throughout her work.

At the risk of repeating myself, it is equally important to distinguish Cardinal's sense of female identity as multiplicity and mask from similar conceptions, male and female, of identity by alterity; in the process, we can better clarify what is particular to her dialectical worldview. As in Rimbaud, Western theory on the notion of the (male) self, from Descartes to Hegel to Lacan, focuses on individuation through opposition to and domination of an other (see Hartsock); thus is born a dichotomous or dualistic worldview, founded on the principle of division into contradictory and mutually exclusive parts. Much recent feminist theory has simply reversed the terms, focusing on the emergence of the (female) self through a merging or fusion with a similar other; this thought reflects a synthetic worldview, based on the combination of separate elements to form a new and coherent whole.

In keeping with the female hero of *Une Vie pour deux* who attributes to herself the "Mediterranean taste for dialectical play" (79), Cardinal consistently rejects the unity of the two in one as an illusion of the moment (see 74, 81, 86, 97), left over from a conventional and misleading romanticism of the couple, in favor of a mobile relationship between the self and a multiplicity of others. Cardinal's worldview is therefore dialectical in the particular sense that Jean Ricardou once attributed to the term; her dialectics is based on contradiction between multipolar (not bipolar) forces in which the different terms are intermingled (not opposed) and whose continuing interaction is their determining factor (with no possibility of resolution) (*Robbe-Grillet* 131–72). Thus, the final couple that Simone creates with Jean-François expresses a nonhierarchical and mutual exchange: "This harmony that now exists between us, this ability for mutual seduction, this impression that I am him and he is me, seems to me to be the most important element of a human life, the first thing worth protecting" (267).

Those critics concerned with the question of point of view often characterize narrative technique as the literary form most closely allied to the problems of life: "In order really to live, we make up stories about ourselves and others" (Hardy 33); "we give our lives meaning by retrospectively casting them in the form of stories" (White, *Tropics* 90), and so on. Certainly, Simone's experiments with voice in *Une Vie pour deux* directly reflect her need to find a voice of her own, to satisfy her "essential need for self-expression" (141); and she relates in this context several paradigmatic stories of female aphasia (85–93, 141–45). At the same time, point of view is closely tied to the question of literature and to the distinction that we make between literary and referential discourse, as *Le Monde*'s review of *Une Vie pour deux* makes clear. Although Bertrand Poirot-Delpech claims not to be denying women access to the novel, his interpretation of Cardinal's decision to recount Mary's story in the third person as an unfortunate relinquishment of "the right to the first person" does precisely that. He cites the awkwardness of style that he discovers in Mary's story as evidence of Cardinal's "duty" to stick to the autobiographical form that she finds "natural." However naive this unexamined association of voice and genre, Poirot-Delpech's assumption that Cardinal seeks to prove herself a "real" writer of fiction may not be totally implausible (particularly since he too insists once again on denying *Les Mots pour le dire* the status of fiction). Cardinal may use narrative omniscience to claim her right to relate the story of a female life in a context of certainty, stability, and control. As Fehervary points out, the modernist literary battle against the omniscient narrator expresses the gender-specific revolt of the son against the father (68).

On the other hand, Cardinal's arbitrary alternation of the first person with the third simultaneously challenges omniscience's claim to be omniscient, to constitute an absolute worldview. Moreover, linguistic theory suggests that it is precisely the combination of these two narrative techniques that allows Cardinal to escape from the structuralist trap of the system that always speaks itself (see Andrew 115). Emile Benveniste distinguishes between two views of language determined by pronoun usage: "this profound difference between language as a system of signs and language assumed as practice by the individual" (1:254). Because the autoreferentiality of the "I" allows Cardinal to appropriate the entire linguistic system (262), this self-designation also grants her control over the "she" that in turn provides access to the referential world (255–56, 265). Thus, Cardinal can orient herself dialectically between the self and the world and be simultaneously defined and acknowledged as the producer and the product of her own discourse, as a creator not only of fictions but of an authentic self. Monique Wittig, in an interestingly similar application of Benveniste's theory to her own pronoun usage, has suggested that the reappropriation of language as a whole also reconstitutes the female "I" as a total, that is, an ungendered, universal subject (65–67).[9]

The interaction of "I" and "she" in Cardinal's work opens up a new space between "life" and "story" (between parallel versions of *histoire,* of *his life story*, as the semantic richness of the French reveals) that allows women a means to express a view of the world that cannot be encoded within traditional cultural patterns, whether formal or ideological. Cardinal's constant insistence on a distinction between "life" and "story," a difference already reflected in the double structure of her novel in which *Une Vie pour deux* contains *Histoire de Mary Mac-Laughlin*, is linked in particular to the discrepancy between female experience and the literary structures into which it has traditionally been made to fit; consequently, Cardinal both recalls and challenges the formalist belief that all literature is by definition about other literature.

Cardinal consistently uses a stylistic form of the question, often repeated and multiplied in rhetorical series, that resembles R. G. Collingwood's notion of the "constructive imagination" (White, *Tropics* 83); the successful writer of narrative is the one capable of asking the right questions. To a considerable extent, a similar effort defines the feminist theoretician. Interrogation may be the most frequent form of the stylistic particularity that Lamy calls the "female litany," and asking questions without responding (and, often, without response) may in fact identify the specificity of feminist theory.

Early in *Une Vie pour deux*, Simone abruptly interrupts her first-person narration to question the forms in which we traditionally recount our lives: "Where is the frontier between truth and reality? Where is the boundary of fiction? What is a novel?" (15). Just as the contextual incoherence of this passage jars the reader out of the story, Simone's self-consciousness as writer allows her to reflect within her own fiction on the dangers for women of the fiction-writing process itself. In a key passage (55–56), Simone explores the intricate movement between literary form and lived experience. The wrong question ("Do I love Jean-François?") leads the woman as writer ("now that my notebook faces me, as I begin to write the story") to produce the "easy" answer ("Yes, I love him, since I'm afraid to lose him") dictated by our inevitable familiarity with literary clichés: "Our vocabulary contains a number of ready-made sentences that lead to preconceived thinking that is dictated by custom and used to answer embarassing questions." But such a "response for the form" distracts us from the real question, the need to challenge form itself ("What is love?").

Although Simone always calls the ideal life of the couple that she attempts to create with Jean-François their "HISTOIRE" (15, 16), with Mary she seeks a new and more authentic reflection of experience: "Simone projected her own life into Mary's, the essence of her own life, what remained of her life when the stories had been stripped away" (182). That certain critics subsequently find Mary's portion of the novel to be "lifeless" (Baroch) no doubt follows directly from Cardinal's success in giving it a lifelike quality, for, as Hayden White reminds us, if we do not live stories, narrative form nonetheless serves us retrospectively to give our lives meaning (*Tropics* 90). Nancy K. Miller has suggested that the implausibility often attributed to fiction by women results from its refusal to reinscribe life in art in accordance with traditional literary patterns ("Emphasis" 36); and Simone, who will eventually rediscover and reclaim a long-term identity as storyteller, consistently encodes Mary's life and her own in anecdotal forms that challenge the literary norm. Her technique outlines once again Cardinal's persistent dialectics of conformity and subversion, for each of these life stories is immediately recognizable as the paradigmatic literary plot that it simultaneously calls into question.

Thus, although Mary's story announces itself as a traditional detective novel and takes the formal aspect of a serialized romance, it in fact refuses the drama and the suspense on which these two genres depend. Indeed, Simone situates the breakpoints of Mary's story at the moments of lowest dramatic tension. At the same time, the deliberate disappointment of our literary expectations forces us to acknowledge the dialectical relationship between "life" and "story." On the one hand, to encode the ordinariness of Mary's life and the absence of love that characterizes it within the structure of romance foregrounds the discrepancy between female life and the destiny of literary heroines. On the other hand, the encoding also reveals the degree to which the mythology of art allows us to confuse the archetype with the stereotype. Just as Simone comes to realize that the cliché that she and Jean-François are living in fact fully embodies the ideal couple that she had sought to have them incarnate (80), so Mary's banal disgrace at the birth of an illegitimate child or her inevitable discovery that her baby's father has a wife and children elsewhere make it clear that lived melodrama may well be not only uninteresting but undesirable. At the same time, in still another dialectic, the allusion to the detective novel encourages us to reflect on the degree to which Mary's story may also conform to literary patterns, for the trap of gender that determines the ordering of her life makes of Mary's death, however decriminalized it may be, both a crime of passion and a murder.

The dialectical nature of Cardinal's discourse renders visible the movement "back and forth," or "running to and fro," implicit in its etymology (White, "Value" 3). As a mediating enterprise, discourse moves not only between received cultural encodations and the phenomena that elude them but between alternative ways of encoding reality. To further illustrate her understanding of the important differences between female and male systems of thought and value, Cardinal inscribes their opposition in a narrative dialectic that demonstrates the multiple ways in which gender influences ideology (what stories we tell) and form (how we tell them). White argues convincingly that we use story types to make sense of our own life histories. By encoding experiential facts as a particular kind of plot structure, a choice that is always ideologically determined, we endow our lives with culturally sanctioned meanings; thus, in White's system, form and ideology are not merely inseparable but identical (*Tropics* 83).

In this context *Une Vie pour deux* seems to be an exemplary illustration of the practice of narrative theory, for Cardinal's novel has conflict as its central subject and structuring device. W. J. T. Mitchell, in the foreword to the 1980 *Critical Inquiry* collection *On Narrative,* suggests that conflict may be an essential of narrative (viii); and White notes in an essay in the same volume that narrative only becomes interesting when the possibility of conflicting versions of events confers significance on the act of claiming authority for one's own account (19; cf. Lotman 352). In Cardinal's theoretical practice, Simone and Jean-François engage in a narrative struggle for the right to impose (over the sometimes violent resistance of the other) his or her own ordering of the events of Mary's life. This new opposition between "she" and "he" not only reiterates Cardinal's challenge to the couple; the context also affords us an unusual opportunity to see exactly how the choice of point of view can matter.

No doubt the importance of the stakes more than justifies the ferocity of the struggle: Simone fights for the right to speak, for what Lanser calls the "author-ity/ization" essential to the narrative process (83). Simone bases her claim to literary privilege on the connection between author and authority, on the etymological union in narrative of knowing and telling (White, "Value" 1). Simone possesses what has come to be acknowledged in feminist criticism as a crucial tool in the countering of traditional illusions about women's lives: the authority of experience. She can best imagine Mary because they are both women: "She's a woman like me. I can certainly imagine a woman's life" (130; cf. 139, 157). Not only can she generalize from her personal situation, but Simone's mutability allows her to weave her own experience into Mary's until their lives and their stories become interchangeable and, in some sense, reflect a paradigmatic story of a woman's life. This duplication thus reflects the general pattern of Cardinal's repetitions.

To Simone's female authority of lived experience, Jean-François opposes the traditional male authority of intellection. Not, it is important to note, that he knows any more about the actual facts of Mary's life than does Simone. Rather, Jean-François justifies his claim to knowledge through the traditional intellectual metaphor of sight; his right to narrative authority rests on the fact of his having *seen* Mary MacLaughlin: "you never saw her. But *I* saw her" (242). The privilege that the Western model of knowledge grants to vision supports the Rimbaudian conception of self; moreover, the separation that seeing introduces between self and other often encodes the will to dominate.[10] The appropriateness and the importance of Simone's resistance to this authority of the male gaze can hardly be overemphasized in light of the lifelong submission, recounted in *Une Vie pour deux*, to its powers of objectification and alienation, to its right to confer or deny female existence. Indeed, becoming female and becoming the object of the male gaze rigorously coincide: "The three boys were looking at me . . . For the first time in my life I felt double. I was me and I was an other: a girl" (35). The I/she split in consciousness that takes place here confirms the third person as the sign of female identity; similarly, the equation between otherness and femaleness supports Cardinal's subsequent thematics of the "other woman." Simone's claim to narrative authority translates her demand for independent existence, and her triumph comes appropriately through the subversion of the male gaze. Only when Jean-François has finally read the notebooks in which Simone has written her story of Mary's life can he acknowledge the rightness of her version of events: in an important reversal, the male agrees to see women through female eyes (259).[11]

Not only is the authority to speak in question in *Une Vie pour deux*, but Jean-François and Simone enter into conflict because of the fundamental differences in ideology that determine their narrative presuppositions. Their individual attempts to make sense of Mary's life no doubt represent sincere efforts toward coherence, for, as White has noted about all sequences of factual events, the known elements of Mary's life do not contain a story in and of themselves (*Tropics* 84), although, even as we read them, we may begin to make one up: Catholic; rural background; illegitimate child; career as a nurse in New York; death by drowning. Cardinal's dialectic of subversion and order continues to structure the novel as Simone both resists through Jean-François the entrapment of women in stories not of their own making and attempts to write a new text that may more accurately reflect female experience.

Because Simone in fact dominates the narrative process, Jean-François' story contains few specifics; essentially he would write Mary's story as a romance, a fairy tale of happiness and fulfillment in which the fact of her death figures as total anomaly, an unfortunate accident: "As for him, he would have wished that Mary might have lived otherwise, that she might be happy, and then one day, as she walked along the coast with her head full of beautiful dreams, the earth gave way under her, dragging her into the void" (246). In particular, Jean-François resists the very centrality of the female role; his strongest objection to Simone's tragic/realistic emplotment of Mary's life—the two codes are synonymous here—centers on the secondary and generally insensitive roles that she assigns to men. Yet Jean-François himself must ultimately face the impossibility, the narrative incoherence, of his insistence on a husband: "'It can't be resolved,' said Jean-François, 'we might as well give up on this story'" (246). But the narrative becomes perfectly coherent once one accepts with Simone and numerous other women writers that this paradigmatic story of female life, as told by the female, can only end in death: "It can be resolved, provided that Mary's life is a failure. . . . without money and with a child, she can do nothing but fail" (246–47).

What finally allows Simone to commit herself to the writing of Mary's story, to public discourse, is her outrage at Jean-François' complacent acceptance of a cultural order from which the reality of women's lives is absent: "That's how things are. What do you expect people to do?" (272). She understands that without her intervention, Mary's story will not only be falsified, but, given Mary's exemplary "dreadful silence" (276), it will never be told at all. Indeed, in Jean-François' first attempt to recount the simple factual circumstances of his discovery of Mary's body, he relates a tale of male bonding, a comic adventure story in which the only woman present is not Mary but the object of the obligatory sexual joke, in this case a former prostitute transformed into the still-ribald wife of the chief of police (69). In his second and final attempt to relate the facts, Jean-François rigorously conforms to the model established by all preceding witnesses at the inquest: he tells not Mary's story but his own. Moreover, as he struggles desperately and unsuccessfully to speak in English, his inability to express himself, the quite literal impossibility that he tell Mary's story, metaphorically confirms what we and Simone have always known: it is not a story in his language.[12] In what Cixous would surely qualify as poetic justice, the male for once must relegate the story that he insistently defines as "his" to a woman who proceeds to steal it from him. Jean-François' initial and appropriately feminine fears are thus confirmed: "He felt raped and dispossessed. He had the impression that Simone was stealing Mary away from him... or that Mary was stealing Simone?" (129).

In particularly revealing ways, Jean-François and Simone seem to invert their own life experiences and the stories that they tell themselves about the lives of others. Jean-François reveals the false unity at the heart of the dualistic model; despite his literary attachment to the myth of the couple, he has never hesitated to claim his own independence even (in fact, especially) at the expense of Simone's: "I had to choose between you and me. I chose myself" (182). The interaction of the female self between Mary and Simone allows Cardinal to illustrate the dialectical process by which women critique the very reality to which they must conform. Although Simone invents in Mary a woman who refuses marriage and despises in her own motherhood an insurmountable obstacle to female self-realization, Simone has sought with desperation to conform to the societal ideal of the wife and mother. But, progressively, *Une Vie pour deux* offers an admirable illustration of Mink's belief that narrative "is not just a technical problem for writers and critics but a primary and irreducible form of human comprehension" ("Narrative" 132). In the course of telling Mary's story, Simone comes to understand the importance of the narrative process as a means by which human beings represent and structure the world and by which she too can make sense of her life.

Through the claiming of narrative authority, of the right to create the life of Mary MacLaughlin, Simone is gradually able to reclaim for herself the authority of her own experience. Gardiner has suggested that the texts of women writers always function importantly in the ongoing process of their authors' self-definition ("Female Identity" 357). Certainly, whether or not it is an interior duplication of Cardinal's own situation, Simone discovers that her "essential need" (141) to relate Mary's story has her own self-expression at stake, that the writing process represents a quest for her own identity. As she incorporates into Mary's story apparently aberrant episodes of her past, irreconcilable with the wife/mother myth that she has chosen to live, Simone comes to understand that she is as alienated a heroine in her own autobiography as Mary is in Jean-François' romance: "And Simone also thought: I don't know myself. I don't know who I am. My story is not the story I was telling. What have I been living for so long?" (117). Simone discards Rimbaud's model of the self as other to claim the multiplicity and the continuity of the self as mask. For as Simone learns that what she thought was her life was only a story, so she sees that the events that she dismissed as mere stories ("I know they can be told" [95]) figure centrally in the development of her life.

In concluding this analysis, I want to stress an important point. Even though Cardinal encodes Mary's story as the representative "female plot" (Miller, "Writing" 125), Mary's suicide becomes life-*affirming* for Simone. Mary's tragic resignation to the societal restraints imposed on women encourages Simone to free herself from the cultural controls that she too has internalized. Ultimately, it is Jean-François, not Simone, who is unable to move beyond his essential association of the female with death—"I can't stop inventing a life for her" (130); "For Jean-François, Mary was first of all someone who knew death" (157).[13] Thus, in the very course of the judicial inquest into the circumstances of Mary's death, Simone provides her with a final reincarnation as an irrepressible, disrespectful, playful, erotic child/woman whose behavior reflects Simone's new-found freedom from cultural control.

Une Vie pour deux offers further evidence then that repetition in Cardinal can serve not only to write female cultural reality into existence, but also to represent the very real differences that exist among individual female lives. Simone's textual superimposition of her own life on that of Mary allows her to claim the commonality of the lived events of female lives even as she realizes that their narrative emplotment can vary: "[Mary] sacrificed herself. Her destiny has been realized, it's perfect. But it's her destiny, it's not mine" (282). Moreover, Simone's decision to repeat Mary's story—precisely so that women in the future will not have to repeat this representative female life—constitutes an internal duplication of the essential feminist act of (re)reading and (re)writing.

(Re)Writing the Past: Le Passé empiété

Le Passé empiété offers a second version of the woman writer's battle for narrative authority and control and further confirmation of the importance that Cardinal attaches to questions of form. In an interview granted during the period of composition of *Le Passé empiété*, she emphasizes the complex narrative structure of the novel and expresses the concern that her readers may be baffled by an instability of the first-person voice that produces what she calls "a kind of flying trapeze act" (Muller 14). This novel also illustrates Cardinal's growing interest in expanding the specific analysis of female reality to include a broader investigation of issues relating to gender as a whole and in extending the exploration of female culture to that of Western culture in general. She argues that Francophone women's writing, now situated at a stage "after" the discovery of the female body,[14] will move toward "the recognition [*la re-connaissance*] of man" (Stanton): "After I had expressed everything I was feeling as a woman, it seemed to me very important to be a man, to say 'I' in the masculine voice" (Breen 14). Yet, Cardinal also continues to examine the interconnections of female voices, and her now explicit realization that *"Je n'est pas un autre"* ultimately confirms even more decisively than in *Une Vie pour deux* that *"Je suis une autre."*

As Cardinal had foreseen, the publication of *Le Passé empiété* in 1983 left critics deeply puzzled by the novel's apparent heterogeneity of content and structure: they read it as three disparate, disconnected stories. At the risk of seeing those readers unfamiliar with the novel initially leap to the defense of the reviewers, let me provide a brief and schematic outline. *Le Passé empiété* opens with the self-analysis of a guilty mother, tormented by her potential responsibility for the near death of her son and daughter in a motorcycle accident two years earlier. Blaming herself for the purchase of the motorcycle, bought with the income that she earned as a professional embroiderer, the unnamed first-person narrator remains unable to work, despite the full recovery of both children. Turning her attention in part two of the novel from her own offspring to her father, whom she hardly knew, the narrator seeks to recover her past and her art by simultaneously creating her father's life in narrative and in embroidery. In a final shift of perspective from her paternal to her maternal heritage, the narrator lives the third section of the novel in the actualized presence of Clytemnestra as the two women attempt to collaborate on an embroidered reconstruction of the mythic past.

In keeping with the metaphorical equation that Cardinal establishes between embroidery and literature, the narrator devotes her first series of works to "embroidering" the theme of literary ancestry. Several feminist critics have described reparenting as a strategy common to the twentieth-century woman who seeks rebirth as an artist (DuPlessis 94). In contrast to the customary search for the mother, Cardinal's embroiderer initially focuses on her father, of whom she knows almost nothing beyond the defining context of her mother's all-consuming hatred.[15] The embroiderer's desire to reconstitute herself "whole," in the specific hope that it will revitalize her art, once again repeats Cardinal's favorite structural pattern of conformity and subversion as the narrator of *Le Passé empiété* both duplicates and questions common assumptions about literary influence and authority.

For example, the embroiderer's transposition of the man who engendered her into her own original creation not only imitates the male practice of authoring female lives that Sandra Gilbert and Susan Gubar (*Madwoman*) place at the core of the Western literary tradition but simultaneously exposes by its own genetic reversal the curious distortions that can result from the confusion of biological reproduction and textual production. In an explicit rejection of History and the actual facts of her father's own story, Cardinal's narrator asserts: "Isn't my real father the one I invent?" (120). Moreover, in another key inversion of conventional patterns, the narrator transforms her own female life into the controlling model for the male's.[16] Not only does she turn events that she alone has lived into episodes of her father's biography, but she alters the meaning of the standard male life by enclosing it within the context of traditional female values. Thus, her narrative of work, sports, and military action changes the feats of daring, courage, and individual prowess that we expect into a sustained thematic elaboration on male friendship and solidarity. Similarly, her few actual memories of her father, which the narrator retains from occasional childhood visits, consistently situate him within the time and space of everyday domestic life. Cardinal's narrator also transforms her father into her own artistic muse and her own literary precursor: he is a storyteller, a diary keeper, a collector of realistic art objects, a connoisseur of exotic wood; most importantly, he is a constructor, a skilled manual laborer, an artisan.

This final transformation of paternity from a metaphor of authority and legitimacy (Brooks 63) into one of creative parity leads to the embroiderer's unsuccessful attempt to cooperate with her father in a feminist "poetics of affiliation" (DuPlessis 225), marked by the temporary fusion of their narrative voices: "I must be my father in order to express him. I must be him. 'I' is him and me. . . . I'm a twelve-year-old boy..." (80–81). Her eventual admission of defeat may be in part a playful salute to the critical tradition that denies women writers the ability to create convincing male characters (see Taylor 6–13), an irony curiously reinforced by reviewers' insistent preference for this section of the novel over those that focus on women.[17] The daughter's effort to speak as a man who turns out to be the rapist of her mother and the murderer of her sister no doubt constitutes an important attempt to understand a male worldview from within, but it also leads directly to the authentication of her mother's original narrative. Thus, the daughter consecrates her mother as her true literary ancestor, the first creator of the father, and reduces his stature to that of a conventional character in a female-authored text.

Importantly, then, the identification of self and other, which Cardinal's frequent juxtaposition of "I" and "she" proclaims, cannot be reduced either to a literary technique or to an openness to difference particularly characteristic of writers. Cardinal's parallel attempt to fuse the female "I" with the male pronoun, to become her father in order to relate his story, ends in failure precisely at the point at which male-specific experience, readily assimilated as long as it merely differs from the female-specific, attempts to dominate and deny the experience of women. The daughter easily assumes the narration of her father's military career, his exclusively male bonding with his fellow workers, and even his initial sexual exploits.

Indeed, in a remarkable, even shocking passage (so unaccustomed are we to viewing male desire and sexuality from a female perspective), the narrator of *Le Passé empiété* moves from observer to participant in her adolescent father's masturbation: "Take it, it's your hand, a woman's hand, your daughter's hand. It's familiar with the nocturnal paths of the hole, the ravine, the mango. It will lead you to the jewelry box, the glove, the sheath, the cradle, the nest, to where you will find what you are seeking. For once in our lives, let's reach orgasm together. You and I together. Two of a kind. The father similar to the daughter, innocent, pure, free. Let's engender each other, let's give birth to each other. I invent you. I am giving birth to you as you gave birth to me. Let's go" (89). The female narrator openly subverts traditional theories of creativity—and the sexual metaphors that inform them—by claiming the literal and the textual paternity of her father for herself. As the passage moves toward orgasm, we pass from a first person whose impossible attribution marks total identification ("I know that I shall come so hard that for a few seconds I will be pleasure itself"), through the subsequent claiming of this "I" first as female ("the sumptuous sword of orgasm will pierce my loins and my pelvis") and then as male ("my sperm . . . will bang against the doors of the other like a battering ram"), to its final culmination in the fusion of "we" ("when the cream of our come will have coated our hills and our valleys, will have fused together our landscapes, we will stretch out side by side like Siamese twins") (89–90).

The narrator of *Le Passé empiété* cannot, however, take narrative responsibility for her father's rape of her mother on their wedding night nor for his sacrifice of his own daughter to professional success. Moreover, Cardinal uses the realization that she reaches here about gender-specific reality to deny the familiar assumption that the so-called universality and objectivity of art allow it to transcend the particular cultural circumstances of its production, necessarily dependent on gender: "I can't manage to think 'He' any more. Since the wedding night, I just can't manage it. 'I' can't be 'He,' he refuses. 'He' can't be 'She', 'She' can't be 'He.' 'Madame Bovary is me' is impossible, a vain boast!" (PE 233).

Twentieth-century women artists, as Gilbert and Gubar point out, inherit not only a male cultural past but descend for the first time from an established female tradition as well (*No Man's* chap. 3; cf. Showalter, "Feminist" 203). As the narrator of *Le Passé empiété* emerges from her fusion with her father to find herself once again unable to create, she becomes increasingly obsessed with four women of the past: her mother, her sister, and their mythic counterparts, Clytemnestra and Iphigenia: "In essence, they are mirrors in which I see my reflection. What a bore it is! Always the same old story [*Quelle rengaine*]! What a tedious spectacle! Me as mother, me as daughter, me as wife, me as woman, as woman, as woman, as woman!" (258). This quadruple replication of selfhood and womanhood, this repeated insistence that the embroiderer is above all woman identified and identified as a woman, takes a more concentrated form in the single figure of Clytemnestra, who literally reappears to share the narrator's life and apartment on the day on which she fully embraces her newly embroidered fantasies.

The relationship between Clytemnestra and the embroiderer points with precision to some of the crucial ways in which Cardinal's *rengaine* repeats the "same old story" in order to tell it differently. Contemporary women who rewrite ancient myths often act out of a sense of connection to legendary female heroes and a belief in the commonality of female experience that transcends historical and geographical distance (see, for example, Ostriker 210–38 and Wolf, *Cass.* 184, 197). Feminist writers also tend to assign a literal reality to the women of myth that precedes their transformation into literary figures (ME 42; Wolf 273). To my knowledge, however, only Cardinal fully explores the logical consequences of these theoretical positions by restoring Clytemnestra to contemporary textual existence and by explicitly and continually intertwining her life with that of the embroiderer. The lived encounter with her mythical double frees the narrator of *Le Passé empiété* from the societal assumption of maternal guilt that she has automatically internalized. Clytemnestra reflects a mirror image of the woman whose demand for independence and autonomy creates a female destroyer who threatens the very "order of nature, what are called 'the laws of nature'" (20), specifically denounced as a male construct: "That's what I'm guilty of, not of buying a motorcycle, not of embroidering! No, guilty of not needing male protection. I didn't stay in my place, I broke out, I created disaster" (48).

By bringing Clytemnestra back to life, Cardinal represents a reading process that may be particularly typical of women, for whom literary characters have actively substituted for their historical isolation from a supportive female community; Rachel Brownstein, for example, claims a similar "reality" for women's literary models as a whole. Cardinal also indirectly speaks to an interesting critical and textual problem. Gilbert and Gubar's practice, relatively common within feminist criticism, of interpreting independent fictional characters as different facets of the female narrator's or writer's own self (*Madwoman*) has been criticized for its effective elimination of the analysis of women's friendships; indeed, some have suggested that such readings may reflect the homophobic attitudes often implicit in mainstream feminist criticism by substituting an acceptable psychological explanation for what might otherwise be perceived as love between women (Jacobus, Rev. 519–22). Although both the reader and the narrator of *Le Passé empiété* know that Clytemnestra materializes out of the embroiderer's obsession with her, itself a result of emotional turmoil, this relationship is subsequently and consistently explored as a friendship between two women. Moreover, Clytemnestra's initial apparition directly confronts the possibility of erotic attraction that often underlies female interaction in Cardinal's work, although, as here, it usually takes the form of a mutual understanding that is neither openly articulated nor acted upon: "Finally her gaze, a deeply moving gaze, came to rest on me: no gaze had ever expressed so much love, no lover had ever loved me to this degree. I wanted to be taken into her arms and to take her into mine, I wanted to caress her and have her caress me. But I stopped myself, I averted my eyes. I thought: 'She's a woman, what's gotten into you, embroiderer!' In the time it took for this reflexion, I lost her gaze: she lowered her eyelids" (261–62).

From the beginning, the embroiderer openly seeks to engage Clytemnestra in a renewed effort at artistic collaboration. She readily agrees that the embroideries of her father are superficial: "I wasn't capable of entering his life... I couldn't live in his body" (273). But against Clytemnestra's conviction that "the body is the body" (273), she argues for the specificity of the female body that will allow her through an other who is woman to experience at once the identification and the separation necessary to artistic creation. Notably, her inability to imagine a small boy's relationship to his body constitutes the first obstacle to her creation of her father (70); and the one-sidedness of the physical metamorphosis that inaugurates their narrative fusion foreshadows its subsequent failure: "Let my breasts disappear, let my vagina close, let my clitoris lengthen, swell, rise up, become the phallus of the man who created me" (80).

Should we be tempted to read this focus on the gender specificity of the body as either a celebration of biological difference à la Cixous or of the woman transvestite posing her pen as "a metaphorical penis" (Gilbert and Gubar, *Madwoman* 7), it is important to note the crucial cultural reversal that establishes its context.[18] Whereas Cardinal's narrator carefully imposes personal and particular biographical limits on the male narrative, deliberately rejecting History for story, she selects as hero of her female narrative the very embodiment of History and Literature, of the artistic and cultural heritage of the West. Because mythology exists in the public domain, as Alicia Ostriker notes, its introduction into women's texts automatically confers some degree of literary and cultural authority on the woman writer (213). Cardinal, moreover, not only inverts the usual references of the female artist's double inheritance, whereby male predecessors embody the dominant tradition within which female predecessors are lost, absent, or relegated to the margins; but her strategy functions in a specific textual context that links her closely to a female tradition. In embroiderers' efforts to give their own interpretation and emphasis to dominant cultural interests, Rozsika Parker notes the historic popularity of the representation of heroic acts by women with, in addition, a decided preference for those who committed planned acts of violence (98). Grace Stewart centers her study of the female *Kunstlerroman* on the innovations that women writers bring to the generically central relationship between the artist and the mythic tradition.

Much recent feminist scholarship, notably that of Rachel DuPlessis and Ostriker, focuses more specifically on the "revisionary mythopoesis" of twentieth-century women writers. DuPlessis and Ostriker both identify two primary strategies used by women artists to rethink myth. DuPlessis, for example, distinguishes between *narrative displacement,* which gives voice to the silenced woman of the past without challenging either the overall structure or the specific events of the inherited story, and *narrative delegitimation,* which substitutes a new and different story for the old (108). Like most women writers, Cardinal combines the two strategies and, indeed, supports Ostriker's hypothesis that they always operate simultaneously (212).

Cardinal uses a double tactic to respond to the traditional artistic dichotomy that reserves "great" literature, including most genres and certainly tragedy and epic, for the male artist and leaves the domestic novel to the woman writer. Her comments during the composition of *Le Passé empiété* point to both the dilemma and its resolution: "I am neither a poet nor a philosopher unfortunately—or fortunately, I don't know which; my book will therefore not pass by the summits of these arts. Like all my other books, it will pass by the daily, the banal, the material; there lies the source of my strength" (PR 95). In fact, Cardinal simultaneously authors a complex metaphysical work and rewrites epic and tragedy as domestic drama by relocating broad philosophical and political meaning within the private sphere.[19] The passage in which Clytemnestra uses a dinner conversation to characterize Agamemnon and their relationship offers a succinct example. Clearly, one innovation that Cardinal claims in her rewriting of myth is the right to laugh; indeed, it seems probable that her recently expressed desire to write a comic novel—"a kind of grand picaresque novel, something like Don Quichotte but seen by a woman" (Pednault 20)—began to take shape during the composition of *Le Passé empiété*. Her disrespect for the seriousness of our mythic and tragic past often takes the form of a rigorous modernization that serves both to trivialize the supposedly sacred and to historicize the supposedly intemporal—two of the most consistent intentions of "revisionist mythmaking" (Ostriker 212) in women's writing.[20]

Although Clytemnestra herself outlines Agamemnon's "main preoccupations" with all due respect—"He has his worries, his problems. . . . He has to reflect on the subtlety of his diplomacy and the dialectic of his affairs... He must remain a master and either stand up to the other masters or negociate with them, outside" (290)—his own words expose him as a petty domestic tyrant: "Oh shit, Clytemnestra, can't you manage any better? Can't you change butchers? Yours cheats you every time. Granted, the other one's farther and won't deliver, but so what? You don't do a damn thing with your time! You spend all day in the garden. Do you really think that flowers and weeds and lettuce are what maintain a house, a family, a country?" (290). But the counterpart to the devalorization of the male within the domestic world is the valorization of this world itself. Clytemnestra uses the frequent female image of the garden to try to show Agamemnon that his dichotomous and hierarchical view of separate spheres—private and public, natural and cultural—distorts his understanding of the world, including, in particular, the domains of philosophy and politics that he considers uniquely his:

> I think he really doesn't know what a garden is. In my eyes this refusal to see what goes on there weakens him; it limits his understanding. I'm not talking about the beauty of the plants. . . . I'm talking about how they are born, live, and die. I'm talking about this war or that peace. . . . About strength or weakness. About glory and decline. About the will or the refusal to live, because of what he calls a trifle: because of a stone, a ray of sunshine, a shadow. A trifle that isn't a trifle for me. A trifle that

is exactly the same thing as what he calls Politics. This comparison makes him laugh so hard he cries. (290–91)

Importantly, Clytemnestra's version of the political and metaphysical order of the world is the only one articulated in Cardinal's rewriting of the myth. Although Agamemnon's sacrifice of Iphigenia functions significantly in Clytemnestra's revenge, there are no references to the Trojan War or to the Greeks as conquering heroes. Stripped of the context that provides its legendary necessity, justification, and retribution, the father's murder of his daughter stands bare in its stark and inexplicable horror.[21] Moreover, Cardinal exposes the myth that war and heroism excuse violence against women as the specifically male myth that it is by displacing it to the story of the narrator's father. The doctors who must finally reveal to the embroiderer's mother that her infant daughter has died of tuberculosis, contaminated by a man who preferred infecting his own child to admitting the contraction of a wartime disease that he now finds incompatible with his manhood, fall back on the justification that lies at the origin of Western culture: "apparently he's a courageous man. . . . Ah, the war did us a lot of harm... We're not through paying for it... and the heroism of our soldiers... On which front was M. Saintjean gassed? I was the sawbones for the 25th" (241). The mother's spontaneous rejection of this male-gendered and engendered fable as foreign to female reality foreshadows its erasure from Clytemnestra's memory of the past: "She couldn't care less what the 'sawbones' has to say about his war and these endless male stories" (242). At the same time, the refusal to acknowledge any consequence of war other than the avoidable death of an innocent child redefines heroism as cowardice and denounces war as a justification of murder in the name of male virility.

The substitution of the narrator's past for that of her culture transforms the personal life of an individual woman, often limited and controlled by the defining stories of our literary canon, into the very model for their reconceptualization. The demystification of cultural models in Cardinal's work frequently involves such a reversal of the usual direction in which analogy operates, often accompanied by a transposition of simile into metaphor that eliminates the hierarchical separation of the two terms being compared along with the explicit statement of their comparison. Thus, Cardinal tends less to establish parallels between the history of her own family (or that of her fictional narrators) and the events encoded in legend or myth than to present personal auto/biography as legendary or mythical in its own right. The father figure, for example, always remains "a myth, a legend" (PE 49) in her work, because the father exists only in and through the stories that are told about him. The legend of the House of Atreus provides the most consistent background for Cardinal's discussion of her own family—"this catholic House of Atreus that was my own" (PR 56; cf. AD 22). In this light, the curious history of the composition of *Le Passé empiété* confirms her total fusion of the personal and the mythic: when the writing of a text about the father momentarily stalls, Cardinal begins the story of Clytemnestra "just for fun, so I wouldn't 'get out of practice'"; but her subsequent identification with Clytemnestra redefines the original text as the story of her *own* father, a precision that acts in turn to transform an apparent disgression into a logical sequel (PR 93–94). Such a privatization of myth furthers Cardinal's effort to domesticate the public narrative of our literary and cultural heritage. Indeed, the Trojan War, erased from the public record, resurfaces throughout her work in the relentless battle of the sexes that opposes her mother and father.[22]

Cardinal also undermines the rigidity and the normative power of our official textual models by infusing them with the fluidity that she attributes to female identity. On first sight, Clytemnestra's physical appearance alters to resemble, in rapid succession, the embroiderer herself, her mother, and her daughter; this protean capacity for metamorphosis represents the multiplicity of the female self that finally identifies Clytemnestra as simply a woman: "What emanated from Clytemnestra made me feel she was a woman like me, not my superior nor my mistress nor my elder, but my double, my sister, my twin" (PE 260). Similarly, Mimi, the embroiderer's mother, whose wedding night is encoded as the sacrifice of the virgin, first incarnates Iphigenia, until the sacrifice of her own daughter transforms her maternal love into the cruelly relentless pursuit of the Furies ("And so she remained, terrible, magnificent, pure . . . never abandoning her cruel watch" [245]).

The embroiderer, too, successively identifies with all of the women of Mycenae: the child's visits to her father cast her in Iphigenia's role of "a martyr, a sacrificial victim" (109); the daughter who pours champagne in hom(me)age to another father, who might exist outside the mythic one inherited from her mother, imitates Electra "laying out her offerings on the tomb of Agamemnon, her assassinated father" (51); the wife and mother, in revolt against the injustices of women's situation, fuses with

Clytemnestra until she no longer knows "whether she or I committed the murder" (310). Moreover, the embroiderer's initial fear that she might have sacrificed her own daughter to her career implies an ability to internalize, at least temporarily, the situation of Agamemnon as well. Similarly, as a child, the narrator of *Le Passé empiété* totally rejects "the warpath" that her mother seeks to "bequeath" to her at her father's funeral: "on that day, in that place, I even swore that I would love a man and cherish the children he would give me" (255–56). The apparent desire to define not just the female but the human self by a capacity for change and comprehension finds confirmation in yet another version of the same myth that the embroiderer uses to shape the story of her father's past; here, the mother avenges the son whom the father has sacrificed to his financial interests.[23] In general, this coexistence of multiple versions of the same story recalls the original state of all myth, born from a synthesis of many variants (see Bullfinch), and confirms once again the possibility of historical change.

In the presence of a female collaborator, Cardinal no longer limits artistic creation to the act of appropriation figured by *le passé empiété*. By literally restoring Clytemnestra to life, she allows her the chance to author her own story and to collaborate in its reproduction in visual form. In this sense, Clytemnestra offers both a duplicate and an alternative image of the woman artist. Her name, which first attracts the embroiderer (258), links her to the female art of needlework. In one French etymological tradition, "Clytemnestra" derives from the verb *tramer* (Auffret 73), whose double meaning of "to weave" and "to plot" supports the image of needlework as subversive, indeed, destructive of men—Clytemnestra both plots Agamemnon's death and weaves the net that immobilizes him—and again establishes needlework and literary creativity as synonymous activities.

Cardinal uses Clytemnestra primarily to explore the female artist as actress, an image as traditional and as ambivalent as that of the embroiderer.[24] In keeping with the frequent association in female writing of women and the oral tradition (see, for example, Didier 17), the actress represents for Cardinal the potential power of the female voice, authorized to speak aloud and be heard. But the ambiguous status of the actress as creator also requires her transformation from the translator of another's text into the author and narrator of her own. Clytemnestra's initial rejection of the narrator's plan to interpret her story in embroidery—"I've had enough of interpretations" (273)—linguistically encodes the parallel rejection of imposed meaning and of her own passive execution of it.

The necessity that Clytemnestra speak for herself has been previously established by the embroiderer's futile attempt to locate her in the massive documentation that defines her only in terms of her relationships: "As for her: total neglect. She has been lost" (259). Cardinal's narrator here reaches verifiable conclusions, fictional or not. The current editions of both the *Collins* and the *Britannica* encyclopedias do not include any listing under "Clytemnestra." Under "Agamemnon" the *Britannica* assures us that he was "forced to sacrifice" Iphigenia; the only free and responsible agent appears to have been Aegisthus, who gets credit for seducing Clytemnestra and "treacherously" murdering her husband, an act subsequently avenged by Orestes. (The absence of Electra suggests a general determination to deny women any significant role, regardless of whether or not their behavior conforms to cultural norms). The *Americana,* which does have a listing under "Clytemnestra," acknowledges that she took Aegisthus as her lover and "entrusted him with the management of the kingdom"; we would have to assume that this apparent unwillingness or inability to reign in fact motivated her adultery, since there is no mention whatsoever of the sacrifice of Iphigenia. Actually, the *Larousse* comes closest to granting agency to Clytemnestra, since it attributes her liaison to her "irritation" at her daughter's sacrifice and allows that both she and Aegisthus kill Agamemnon.

Thus, Cardinal's Clytemnestra reclaims the one significant act by which she can lay claim to having altered the course of history. In reaction to the embroiderer's conviction that "this woman was surely not a murderer" (261), she affirms her sole responsibility for the planning and execution of Agamemnon's murder and her total lucidity at the moment of action (284, 298). The first story that she relates, the sacrifice of Iphigenia, reinscribes her daughter as well in the narrative of myth and substitutes Clytemnestra's fundamental identity as mother for that of the adulteress favored by standard reference guides.

Subsequently, and somewhat to the narrator's dismay, Clytemnestra refuses "her status as murderous mother" (295) and redefines what seemed to be her primary motivation as only a symptom: "My daughter's death was not a pretext but a revelation" (317). She finally defines herself as *homi*cidal, in the gender-particular sense of the term: "I eliminated the man who had power over me . . . simply because he [was] a man (300). . . . I committed a crime to save my life. I eliminated Agamemnon in order to be free" (305). In this context, Agamemnon's royal rank functions primarily as a metaphor for an order that assigns power on the basis of sex, an arbitrary fact of birth. Because the murder of the male explicitly challenges a conception of power as domination, Cardinal's Clytemnestra flatly rejects the role of queen: "She had no desire to exercise the kind of power that had generated the murderer and she hadn't the slightest idea of what any other kind of power might look like" (316). She also refuses to remarry, for if Clytemnestra does "more than kill [her] husband" (299), marriage nonetheless identifies the specific situation in which most men exercise their power and establishes another bond between Clytemnestra and Iphigenia, one as strong as that of the mother-daughter relationship. In a clear metaphorical equation, Iphigenia is dressed as a bride on the day of her sacrifice (the narrator later wonders whether the same mask might have served in Greek theater for "the bride" and "the daughter"), and, as we already know, Mimi's wedding night is described as the sacrifice of the virgin.

In support of Estella Lauder's observation that the creation of new cultural myths is always a communal process—informed, in the case of women, by distinctive aspects of female experience (6)—Clytemnestra has proved to be of considerable interest to a number of feminist critics, both European and Anglo-American. Predictably, Virginia Woolf inaugurated this period of mythic re-vision: "Do you ask for more solemn instances of the power of the human race to change? Read the *Agamemnon* and see whether, in process of time, your sympathies are not almost entirely with Clytemnestra" ("Mr. Bennett" 194). Readings of the *Oresteia* from a feminist perspective do indeed concentrate their attention on the character of Clytemnestra, and, to some extent, their diversity of interpretation reflects that of feminist criticism itself. Thus, Jean-Pierre Vernant and R. P. Winnington-Ingram offer examples of the tendency to interpret Clytemnestra's revolt against male domination as an instance of role reversal in which she reveals a number of "manly" attributes that justify her desire to replace the male. Other readings, such as those of Froma Zeitlin and A. Betensky, follow another trend in feminist scholarship by making female specificity their primary center of interest; viewed in this light, Clytemnestra's attachment to Iphigenia illustrates the primacy of her maternal role and of the mother-daughter dyad that threatens the stability of the patriarchal institution of marriage.

The same pattern of interpretation is discernible in texts where Clytemnestra serves broader purposes. Although in theory Aeschylus's trilogy no longer determines the central focus of the critical text, the fact that the *Oresteia* in general (and *The Eumenides* in particular) still often serve as a primary reference point has important consequences. Gilbert, for example, uses the *Oresteia* to identify a pattern of alliance between father and daughter that she finds characteristic of modern novels by women ("Life's"). Phyllis Chesler's parallel assumption that "at some level, women are (and believe they are) Electra" characterizes, in her view, many of their psychoanalytically informed readings (Rev.). Carolyn Heilbrun uses the *Oresteia* to illustrate a general argument for basing feminist rereadings on female identification with a male model. Thus, she suggests that we interpret Clytemnestra's murder and its subsequent justification by Apollo and Athena as the "symbolic overthrow of the institution of motherhood" (*Reinventing* 154), defined, in this case, as an oppressive patriarchal invention (similar, no doubt, to that analyzed by Adrienne Rich in *Of Woman Born*). Those interpretations that emphasize Clytemnestra's incarnation of specifically female values—the readings of Cixous (*Jeune Née*) or Irigaray (*Corps-à-corps*), for example—nonetheless continue to concentrate their attention on *The Eumenides,* the final play in Aeschylus's trilogy, in which the consecration of patriarchal law and the institution of marriage mark the final defeat of matriarchy and mother-right.

Curiously, all of these readings erase Clytemnestra from view. Even when the critics' explicit intention lies in the revalorization of the specifically female, the decision to privilege a primary text whose action takes place *after* Clytemnestra's murder ends up repeating the same version of the myth—one from which Clytemnestra, Iphigenia, and finally even Electra are all absent—that we read in standard reference materials. Moreover, allowing one's perspective to be defined (whether positively or negatively) by a work that subordinates individuals to institutions and the personal to the systemic almost inevitably results, at the very least, in the reinscription of the play's patriarchal structures, regardless of the attitude that one takes toward its overt ideological message (the parallel subordination of the mother to the father). Inspiration undeniably presents a difficult problem, however, since, as Séverine Auffret points out, "Until very recently, Clytemnestra had never stepped out of male writing" (42). It is hardly surprising, then, that most work on Clytemnestra limits itself to the reinterpretation of male texts or to the exploration of available mythological documentation in search of variants to the dominant tradition that would reveal a "lost" female hero.

Cardinal's strategy for rewriting Clytemnestra's story differs in interesting ways. Racine's *Iphigenia* serves as Cardinal's male source, to the extent that she claims one. Racine's dramatic version, in contrast to most others, grants not only visibility but centrality to the roles of Iphigenia and Clytemnestra and thus to the mother-daughter relationship. Since the play's action takes place immediately prior to the sacrifice, Clytemnestra's maternity subsumes her entire being. Although she cannot finally protect her daughter, she is by far the strongest, most resourceful, and most active character in the play, prepared to use all possible means to save Iphigenia. Clytemnestra flatly rejects every attempt to justify the sacrifice, and even after the death of her own daughter has been avoided (in deus ex machina by the substitution of another Iphigenia), she refuses to see Agamemnon and to retract anything she has said about him.

If a male text serves as a reference point for Cardinal, she neither repeats nor reinterprets Racine's work. Rather, she picks up where he left off: "I pick her [Clytemnestra] up where I left her thirty-five years earlier, at the moment when, in my textbook, she shouted out Racine's verses and wrung her hands because her daughter was setting out for the funeral pyre" (265). This technique allows Cardinal to attain immediate credibility by inserting her own work on Clytemnestra within a preexistent literary tradition and also leaves her totally free to re-create Clytemnestra's subsequent life from a female perspective. In particular, given the persistent silencing and subordination to men that Clytemnestra experiences in official sources, Cardinal can claim complete originality for the psychological reality that she attributes to Clytemnestra and for the re-creation of her voice. In this context, the characteristic choice of feminist writers to rewrite stories inherited from drama in the form of poetry or, particularly in the case of Clytemnestra, in that of the novel, reflects, on the level of genre, a strong awareness of the need to accord Clytemnestra a private and personal identity to accompany the generalized public persona represented by her theatrical mask. By ignoring *The Eumenides*, which other feminist critics favor despite Clytemnestra's absence, Cardinal also insists on the centrality of the individual woman whose life span determines textual boundaries and who acts in her own right rather than as the representative of an institution.

Séverine Auffret's *Nous, Clytemnestre,* born of the desire "to launch Clytemnestra back into the world" (19), alternates between conventional textual analysis and passages in which the re-creation of Clytemnestra's own lyrical first-person voice allows her, as in *Le Passé empiété,* to participate in her own story. Interestingly, Auffret favors a style of interrogation, used to challenge the forms in which human life has traditionally been encoded, that strongly resembles Cardinal's own textual practice; I cite a single comparative example:

> But who manufactures myth? Who chooses, prunes, amputates, cleans up History? Who decrees what is important and what isn't? Who? (PE 266)

> Where does history begin, where does it settle, where does it take on its definitive version, where and how is it altered, if it is? Where, how, and why does it last the enormity of its duration? (Auffret 22)

Auffret also recalls Cardinal by the equivalence that she establishes between the institution of marriage and the practice of female sacrifice—marriage, for example, also separates mother and daughter (57). This connection allows apparently diverse myths to be reconceptualized as variants of the same story, thus inaugurating a female mythic tradition; in particular, it allows us to recognize in the story of Clytemnestra and Iphigenia the repetition of the originary feminist myth of Demeter and Persephone (54; cf. Heilbrun 156).

Although Wolf selects Cassandra as her focal point for rethinking myth, she too reinterprets Clytemnestra in ways that echo Cardinal. Cassandra understands that Clytemnestra's freedom depends on the murder of Agamemnon ("Either she gets rid of her husband, this empty-headed ninny, and makes a good job of it, or she gives up herself: her life, her sovereignty, her lover" [41]), and she attributes to her adversary the same knowledge that Cardinal does of the systemic flaw represented by conventional notions of power ("I credit her with knowing that she, too, will be stricken with the blindness that comes with power" [12]). Wolf also attaches a similar importance to female friendship; for her, the clearest sign of Aeschylus's misogyny lies in the hatred that he has Cassandra and Clytemnestra display toward each other (176). Moreover, the implicit substitution of Cassandra for Electra serves once again to identify a connective pattern in female myth; Cassandra's fascination with the story of Agamemnon, Iphigenia, and Clytemnestra stems from its paradigmatic quality, for she too incarnates the initially father-identified daughter who will evolve only gradually into an avenger of all the daughters sacrificed by fathers.[25]

In *Le Passé empiété*, Cardinal characterizes the birth of the female artist as hurtful and difficult. The single story that Clytemnestra succeeds in telling on her own, the sacrifice of Iphigenia, once again recalls by its content and its narrative process Gubar's perceptive analysis of the ties between female anatomy and creativity: "one of the primary and most resonant metaphors provided by the female body is blood, and cultural forms of creativity are often experienced as a painful wounding. . . . the woman artist who experiences herself as killed into art may also experience herself as bleeding into print" (296). Cardinal's narrator wants to embroider Clytemnestra in shades of red, associated with the specificity of the female body: "I must have red! . . . Garnet, ruby, madder, wine-red for the menstrual blood, the mother's blood, the queen's blood" (262–63).

Clytemnestra's neck bears the indelible imprint of her historical silencing—"A wound that cut across her throat. . . . Couldn't she talk any more? Did she no longer have a voice?" (260)—and the scar reddens and reopens as she struggles unsuccessfully to speak. Still, her inability to continue alone has important, if temporary, implications for female creativity in and of itself. As the actress and the embroiderer begin to relay each other in the composition of the narrative, the fluidity and often indistinguishable interpenetration of their voices suggest a new model for artistic collaboration, reminiscent of Lamy's description of female conversation as, appropriately, "an embroidery on a background that disappears under the movements and the colors" (30). This process differs significantly from the narrator's earlier attempt at total fusion with her father. In the sections where she speaks in the male "I," she adopts a very direct narrative style that focuses on events rather than description. Since the narrator juxtaposes these passages with others in which she retains her own first-person voice and her typically associative manner of speech, she illustrates a woman's ability to speak like a man rather than a woman and man's ability to create a new, hybrid voice together.

Let me note in this context that two of Cardinal's works present themselves as extended examples of female collaboration. *Au Pays de mes racines* concludes with "Au Pays de Moussia," a text written by

Bénédicte Ronfard, her youngest daughter. The stress that Cardinal places on the act of writing here results in the total reversal of its conventional relationship to reference as she comes to see the textual repetition of her return to Algeria as the motivation for the trip rather than its consequence: "My problem has become the following: how should I organize the days spent there to allow me to type what I've already written and to take notes on what I shall see" (112). Such emphasis supports Cardinal's explicit desire to serve as an example for her daughter's initiation into writing: "I would like her to write her own travel diary as well" (79). But neither the generational repetition of the mother-daughter bond nor the experiential repetition of their shared trip can sufficiently account for the textual repetitions that surface. Ronfard focuses independently on the same themes that preoccupy her mother; moreover, she also exhibits such recognizable stylistic traits, particular to Cardinal, as lexical enumeration. Even more curious is her ability to join—in fact, to replace—her mother as a practitioner of autocitation: Ronfard tells a story about her great-grandmother (230) that Cardinal has related elsewhere in similar terms (AD 105).[26]

Lest we think that such repetition is either an anomaly or somehow attributable to ties of kinship, Annie Leclerc's sequel to the portion of *Autrement dit* that Cardinal writes exhibits precisely the same qualities. Once again the "imperious need to write" that motivates Cardinal specifically provokes Leclerc's "desire that I too might enter this book through a few pages of text" (212). We should note, however, that here collaboration characterizes the book as a whole, based on a series of conversations between Cardinal and Leclerc.[27] Leclerc's written text elaborates on themes introduced elsewhere by Cardinal and exhibits her same digressive and associative style. In addition, Leclerc's text "continues" Cardinal's work.[28] Not only does Leclerc describe Cardinal's fascination with mathematical structures in a textual replication of a passage from *Les Mots pour le dire* (51–52), but she takes on Cardinal's "I" in the process (217–18). Repetition again shows us female community, continuity, and collaboration; in fact, it shows us the creation of a female literary tradition actually in progress.

Clytemnestra, however, cannot finally overcome her fear of creative choice and responsibility, and she reclaims an existence in which her theatrical mask provides her identity and legend dictates her actions: she mouths only the words of others, "like a parrot" (333). The lexical repetition of the word *mask* emphasizes the difference between the fixed features—and identity—imposed by the mask of classical Greek theater and Cardinal's understanding of the capacity for metamorphosis otherwise inherent in the masked identity of women. Thus, it is precisely at the point when Orestes, in his anger, knocks off his mother's mask that she might claim a human complexity: "Clytemnestra could have answered since she no longer had her mask—she could have turned it to her advantage by reaching out to her children, convincing them, defending herself; instead of that, her only thought was to find her mask again" (367–68). Clytemnestra rejects the self-expression that the embroiderer offers, equated with life itself, to repeat Iphigenia's sacrifice of her right to speak, equated with death itself: "My daughter still upsets me deeply. What happened in what she never said? Because only others made her speak. She never expressed any opinion. . . . Millenary silence of obedient women! Where do their words go?" (267–68). Ultimately, Clytemnestra prefers the alternate etymology of her name: "*Klutos:* that of which one hears, famous because talked about" (Auffret 72). In opting to be "killed into art" (Gubar 196)—"For she much preferred remaining the horrible queen of the legend to no longer figuring in the legend at all" (284)—she reminds us that one of the major obstacles to women's ability to see themselves as artists has been their established role as characters in male-authored creations (Gilbert and Gubar, *Madwoman* chap. 1).

Elsewhere in Cardinal's work, the recurrent association of aesthetic frustration, third-person narration, and literal death also clearly makes this point. The two stories that end in suicide, *La Souricière* and the internal "Histoire de Mary MacLaughlin" in *Une Vie pour deux,* stand out in Cardinal's work for the inability of the female hero to find an outlet for her creative talents. Alternatively intrusive and invisible in both the theatrical group directed by her husband and the community of male painters from whom she seeks help, Camille discovers in Goya the power of art and the desire "to do something, to communicate" (S 164). But without any way to become an artist, she finds herself once again "killed into art" (Gubar 196), as a final hallucination before her death transforms her into an image in a Goya painting (219). The financial and temporal constraints that weigh on Mary as a single mother do not permit her to complete the medical studies that would allow her to exercise her creative talents as a diagnostician; unable to become the psychiatrist who might save others from depression, she dies a victim of that very illness.

These two narratives are also the only texts of Cardinal's that are written entirely in the third person; unable to find their own voices, Camille and Mary remain literary characters, textual objects. In *Ecoutez la mer,* in contrast, the first-person narrator finally resists the temptation of suicide after she is abandoned by the male writer whom she loves; although she does not yet assume overt responsibility for the written text, the primacy of Maria's own narrative voice not only recovers the childhood memories that restore her sense of self but implicitly turns the male character into her own artistic creation. Thus, in contrast to *Une Vie pour deux,* Cardinal here rewrites the romance plot to eliminate the traditional ending in which abandonment by men equals death for women. Moreover, in opposition to the consistent narrative voice of the traditional male text that irremediably objectifies female characters, the interaction of "I" and "she" in Cardinal's texts always assures the simultaneous presence of a successful female narrator. Thus, as we know, in telling the stories of Mary and Clytemnestra, both Simone and the embroiderer learn to narrate their own lives as a female story. The narrative framework of *La Souricière* works to the same purpose. The novel is preceded by an exchange of letters between Camille's husband, François, and the fictional novelist Marie. In opposition to François' objection that Camille's "authentic" story would have to be "theirs" (that is, *his*), Marie asserts her right to publish a *woman's* story that, however incomplete from François' point of view, is nonetheless "true": "Why publish this incomplete story? Because it's the exact reflection of a woman, of her experience" (12).

Although the embroiderer's identification with Clytemnestra as rebellious woman and artistic collaborator makes her personally vulnerable to the appealing refuge of cultural conformity, she frees herself from the female ancestor as she has from the male. Paradoxically, Clytemnestra's decision to reintegrate the role of "rotten queen" (284) allows the narrator to repeat successfully the queen's revolt. In contrast to Clytemnestra, who, as actress, as one who repeats texts written by others, defines herself as the traditional female artist and woman, the narrator's redefinition of embroidery as a nonrepetitive art form grants her the creative autonomy necessary to invent and tell her own story. This time, moreover, she explicitly rejects the quest for models as such, in keeping with the sense of her title image: "Once and for all I must refuse to be trapped by the sorcery of models. They should remain in my memory but they must not represent my future" (360).

It is tempting to see in this gesture the explanation for Cardinal's substitution of the term *le passé empiété* for the variant *le passé empiétant* that actually figures in books on embroidery. Cardinal eliminates, along with the present participle, the inevitability of a constant and continuing intrusion of our cultural and literary past in the lives of contemporary women; the past participle, in contrast, defines the twofold feminist act of reclaiming our heritage and freeing ourselves from it. At the same time, however, this also constitutes a striking break from general feminist practice. If women readers have consistently rejected male models, including the structures and plots in which female characters have been imprisoned, their simultaneous efforts to imagine a different textual reality for the latter have been informed by the express desire to discover or invent the literary and cultural heritage that women have always been denied. In this sense, feminist revisions of myth complement rereadings of our "lost" women writers of the past.

Paradoxically, Auffret's (mis)interpretation of *Le Passé empiété* on precisely this point may help us understand the difference of repetition in Cardinal's work. I quote Auffret (who, in the text that I have elided, quotes the same sentence I cite above, italicizing "I must refuse"): "But will the heroine's (the author's?) final willful declaration somehow change the destiny that is reenacted in her as from time immemorial? . . . Can a magic spell be broken by an act of the conscious will? Do models cease to be models just because we want to forget them?" (46). Auffret's publishing association with "des femmes," whose very clear statements of ideology include a commitment to female difference that is sometimes hard to distinguish from traditional notions of the "eternal feminine," does not strike me as insignificant here. Auffret clearly believes in a female "destiny," that is, (in opposition to Cardinal's "conscious will") an involuntary, unconscious femaleness that inevitably repeats itself in and through all women. Cardinal, on the other hand, argues for conscious choice and therefore for the possibility of change.[29]

Since most Anglophone feminists would readily embrace this position for women today, I think that the different conclusions that Cardinal reaches about the value of textual models have much to do with her distinctive combination of the mythic character and the realistic narrator. In her translation of *The Medea*, where contemporary reality remains outside the text proper, Cardinal readily claims her identification with the mythical figure, made to speak as woman and as contemporary.[30] She may also wish to acknowledge a complexity from which the

fundamental optimism of American feminists in particular can sometimes distance us. Not all women choose to reject the security of traditional female roles (a situation of which Simone de Beauvoir's fiction,
persistently denounced by American feminists for its "pessimism," repeatedly reminds us). History, as such, cannot in fact be changed, despite formal shifts in tone and narrative technique; as the embroiderer
tells Clytemnestra: "I can't change your legend, but I can change its
meaning and its significance" (301).

Importantly, the narrator's gradual liberation from Clytemnestra
takes the form of her progressive assumption of artistic authority: "I
gave up trying to identify with her. I interpreted her stories in my own
way and I didn't care whether she approved or not" (335). Clytemnestra's final performance, the reenactment of her own silencing, respects
the cathartic function of Greek tragedy: "I exorcized myself by justify-
ing her murder, . . . in order to stop behaving with others as a guilty
woman and to start acting like any ordinary human being who has a
natural right to selfhood, to self-expression" (347). The narrator's decision to embroider a motorcycle in one corner of her representation of
Clytemnestra's death marks her final understanding of the importance
of modernity, and, although she expects to be accused of surrealism
(358), justifies after the fact both the false note that the story of the
accident initially strikes and its troubling juxtaposition with Greek
myth: "the motorcycle is a sign. I hadn't understood it. If I'm guilty of
anything, it's of failing to understand the importance of modernity, of
remaining a mother of Antiquity" (361). The narrator has mistakenly
attempted to transform herself into a tragic heroine, to give the dimensions of tragedy and myth to an event that was, in fact, only an "accident." Similarly, she has credited the erroneous belief that female creative autonomy constitutes a "tragic flaw."

If the embroiderer's understanding that the common events of wom-
en's lives need not lead to a single, endlessly repetitive emplotment
seems clearly liberating (as in *Une Vie pour deux*), her conception of the
woman artist has become more problematic. From the point at which
she stops listening to Clytemnestra and begins to design her embroideries without the other woman's assistance, she bears a disturbing resemblance to the model of the artist as authoritarian, interpretive, and ap-
propriative, a model against which Clytemnestra attempts to rebel. As
Toril Moi points out in a discussion of feminist literary criticism, "it is
not an unproblematic project to try to speak *for* the other woman, since

this is precisely what the ventriloquism of patriarchy has always done" (67–68). In this context, the embroiderer's determination to let Clytemnestra tell in its entirety the story of her own choosing, even though the end is predetermined and the embroiderer no longer believes that the story has value, plays an important role. Even provoked by Clytemnestra's exasperating silence in the instant before her death, the narrator resists the "desire to pass her my words" (362), the temptation to speak in her place. In allowing the opposing woman artist the same creative autonomy that she claims for herself, she discovers that her own rebirth as an artist depends upon it.[31]

Indeed, since myth poses an obstacle and a threat to the woman artist precisely to the extent that it has become a reified and deterministic plot structure, one could argue that Clytemnestra's assumption of narrative authority has considerable aesthetic importance in and of itself, regardless of the particular story that she tells. Moreover, given the tendency of standard reference works to reduce Clytemnestra's role to that of Aegisthus's victim, at worst, and of his associate, at best, the claim that she makes to the stature of the archetypal evil queen and the insistent display of sexuality with which she provokes Orestes to murder (363) ("'the rotten queen' of the legend" [284] and "the whore of History" [362] are explicitly equated) already constitute a feminist re-vision of her myth.

Although *Le Passé empiété* reveals most of the traits that Grace Stewart identifies as characteristic of the female *Kunstlerroman*—notably, the linking of artistic creation and the mythic tradition, the refusal of the traditional literary image of women as antithetical to that of the artist, the conflict between the self as artist and the self as woman, the motifs of rebirth and reparenting, the search for literary ancestors, the rejection of men, the awareness of the societal denigration of women artists, and the knowledge of how existing myths pattern our lives—the novel may be most remarkable for what it refuses to share: the polarization of female reality and the realm of art, the failure of the artist as artist or woman or both, artistic rebirth resulting in either abortion or the creation of a monster. Stewart herself may provide the explanation for Cardinal's success: "one of the most difficult things for a woman is to assume the role of destroyer. But without destroying—conventions or overused word patterns, for instance—one cannot create" (141–42). Cardinal does not embrace the role of destroyer uncritically—indeed, Clytemnestra's decision to reintegrate her literary image as destroyer determines her destruction as artist and autonomous woman—but she subverts the false dichotomy between destruction and creation.[32] By embroidering over the cultural and artistic background hostile to the woman artist, she outlines, as we have seen, a new future that is paradoxically based on continuing respect for the past and the traditional activities of women that form a crucial part of it.

Realism and Experimentation: Les Grands Désordres

The success with which *Les Grands Désordres* (1987), Cardinal's most recent novel, has managed to unite readers and reviewers in its praise—the best-seller was nominated for the prestigious Prix Goncourt—puts it in the same category as *Les Mots pour le dire* and *La Clé sur la porte*. Indeed, Pierre Démeron explicitly recalls these two earlier works (whose generic status, as we know and as Cardinal never ceases to insist, disrupts any clear distinction between novel and autobiography) in describing her latest novel as yet another "fictional transposition of lived experience" (67). Similarly, Janick Jossin asserts that the emotional power of the novel offers in and of itself irrefutable proof of its factual basis: "Clearly the author knows what she's talking about: you have to have 'lived through it' in order to set out so convincingly such a range of emotion." Moreover, in an exact repetition of the critical reception of *Les Mots pour le dire*, Jossin not only denies the novel's literary merit ("But efficacy chases away literature") but assumes that Cardinal will not care ("Marie Cardinal only wants to communicate an emotion"). Jossin's conclusion, however—"Rereading 'les Grands Désordres', concentrating on its subtleties, would be a disappointing venture, but that's not the best use of this kind of book"—appears to designate an effort that she might have done better to make than to dismiss on the basis of hypothesis. Or, at the very least, she might have reread her own review, for it is, strangely enough, on the success of the novel as novel (and even as experimental novel) that she keeps insisting: "Marie Cardinal opted here for the novel. A risky business. But she knows what she's doing"; and again, "the novel within the novel works perfectly." The immediate rejection of the proposition that Cardinal invents, in particular, a narrative device that "might reek of artifice a mile off" (but "that's not at all the case") confirms Jossin's a priori commitment to reading Cardinal's narration as an accurate record of an authentic experience.

Still, it is not without some trepidation that I am about to argue that *Les Grands Désordres* is not only the most "artificial" of Cardinal's novels but the very epitome of narrative artifice. Although I would maintain that the novel's artfulness begins to clamour for our attention almost immediately, even at first reading, there is no doubt that *Les Grands Désordres* also tells a powerful story of the emotional chaos wrought by drug addiction. But this surface story—or rather, this novel in which the story is structurally superficial—constitutes in and of itself a "crafty expedient," an "artful strategem," that explicitly supports the artifice of the novel precisely to the extent that it cleverly distracts us from it. Cardinal has produced in *Les Grands Désordres* a novel whose primary concern is the novel's own production, the visible structuring of the narrative process. She thus repeats (both returns to and expresses differently) the interest in crafts(wo)manship already evident in *Le Passé empiété* (*artifice,* from Old French; craftsmanship, from Latin *artifex,* art + maker). Although artifice differs from its synonyms (e.g., trick, ruse, feint—all of which denote "means for achieving an end by indirection") in that its creation of a desired effect does "not necessarily" include an "intent to deceive," such a deeply ironical novel suggests to me that Cardinal must surely take some pleasure in the simultaneous (and appropriately bilingual) *deception* (deceiving) and *déception* (disappointment) of the reviewers, particularly since any disappointment at this novel's lack of attention to specifically literary matters of form and technique can only be the result of a blinding determination to be deceived (the consequence, no doubt, as in the case of Jossin, of prior self-deception).

The title of *Les Grands Désordres* accurately reflects the difficulty of providing any coherent outline of its narrative structure, although its content is easy enough to summarize (assuming, that is, that we ignore for the moment the immensely problematic status of names and pronouns in this text). Elsa Labbé, noted psychologist, hires a ghostwriter to tell the story of her daughter Laure's devastating battle against heroin addiction. But Elsa's parallel need to transform this experience into writing and her inability to write it alone announce the gradual transformation of Laure's story into her own. Only a nearly successful suicide attempt finally forces Elsa to begin an examination of her personal and professional past. Because drug addiction destroys her confidence in scientific knowledge and her fundamental belief in an ordered world, she concentrates in particular on her strange collaborative relationship with the professor Greffier, including an exploration of her sexuality and her effort to apply the laws of thermodynamics to human psychological behavior. In the course of the equally odd collaboration that presumably produces the novel we are reading, Elsa and the ghostwriter fall in love.

If this sequence of events seems relatively straightforward, the reintroduction of its narrative framework renders it considerably more complex. We confront "the great disorders" of a continual process of textual metamorphosis, incorporating written and oral narration and first-person and third-person voices, each with multiple referents, that looks something like this:

    a. 9–14: the ghostwriter's first-person narration

FIRST PART

    b. 15–147: "The 143 pages"—the third-person narration of Elsa's and Laure's life (each alternatively determines narrative perspective); one first-person passage attributed to Elsa

SECOND PART

    c. 151–63: the ghostwriter's first-person narration
    d. 163–69: Elsa's first-person narration (a text recorded by Elsa, written by the ghostwriter, read aloud by Elsa to the ghostwriter)
    e. 169–70: the ghostwriter's first-person narration (such texts, which I shall subsequently identify as "Interlude," often include lengthy passages of dialogue between Elsa and the ghostwriter)
    f. 170–78: "The Portrait of Professor Greffier"—text written by Elsa in the first person, revised by the ghostwriter, read by Elsa when alone
    g. 178–82: Interlude
    h. 182–96: Elsa's first-person narration (a text recorded by Elsa, written by the ghostwriter, read aloud by Elsa to the ghostwriter)
    i. 197–99: Interlude
    j. 199–207: "Professor Greffier (continued)"—text written by Elsa in the first person, revised by the ghostwriter, read by Elsa when alone; incorporates lengthy quotation from diverse third-person scientific sources

k. 207: Interlude—one sentence (in parentheses)

l. 207–9: pages added by Elsa to j., above

m. 210–14: "Laure's Studio"—text written by Elsa in the third person

n. 214–19: "Laure's Dreams"—text written by Elsa in the third person

o. 220–23: Interlude

p. 223–33: Elsa reads aloud a first-person text concerning Professor Greffier (it remains unclear whether the ghostwriter has revised Elsa's written text or transcribed her recorded text)

q. 233: Interlude

r. 233–41: continuation of p., above (same ambiguity)

s. 241–42: Interlude

t. 242–52: "Professor Greffier (continued)"—the presence of a title *might* finally identify in p., r., and t. a text written by Elsa; first-person text read by Elsa when alone; includes third-person intertexuality from diverse scientific sources

THIRD PART

u. 255–62: the ghostwriter's first-person narration

v. 263-70: two letters from Elsa to the ghostwriter

w. 270–90: the ghostwriter's first-person narration (includes a long passage of dialogue with Elsa)

Les Grands Désordres clearly incorporates a number of narrative concerns that we have already encountered, now presented in a form that I would characterize (were it not for the reviewers) as more transparent. From the first word (*elle*/she), the text explicitly en-genders its central character, and since we never learn "her" real name, the frequent repetition of *elle* throughout the text insists, by simultaneously emphasizing impersonality and gender specificity, that we are reading a woman's—Everywoman's—narrative. Moreover, the fictional name that the ghostwriter assigns to her—Elsa Labbé—obsessively reiterates the same message: the female pronoun resurfaces in the first two letters (*El*) and in the intitials (*EL*), and the name further identifies femaleness by incorporating the feminine forms of the possessive adjective (*sa*) and the definite article (*la*).[33] The other fictional names by which women are identified in *Les Grands Désordres*—Greffier always refers to Elsa as Luce and the ghostwriter calls her daughter Laure—begin with the letter *L*, which phonetically echoes the female pronoun (*elle*).

But Cardinal insists on maleness too, introduced not by the overt and repeated reference to gender, as in the case of the female, but by the sudden and unexpected revelation of its presence. Whether because we temporarily tend to associate an unidentified first-person pronoun with the author (Lejeune, *Moi* 70) or because we learned in *Le Passé empiété* that "I cannot be He," I think that most readers, and certainly those who have any prior familiarity with Cardinal's work, will initially assume, as I did, that "I" [*je*] is a woman. In fact, although an attentive rereading quickly locates a grammatical revelation of masculinity on the second page (*"Ça m'a étonné"*), I suspect that I am not the only one to have experienced shock upon first reading the explicit identification of gender in the final sentence of the first section of the text: "I was no longer the same man" (14). Indeed, the narrator's self-designation as a man at precisely the point at which, having written the first 143 pages of the woman's story, he is ironically no longer the *same* man, seems to me clearly designed to surprise and unsettle the reader. Although the narrator ultimately has no way of encoding "he" [*il*] in the text, a matter whose significance I will explore in a moment, once his maleness has been announced, the fact that he too has no name allows him to represent every man or all men. To overcome the potentially greater gender neutrality of the first person, even in French, the ghostwriter often insists on the ordinariness of his person and his life. Moreover, Elsa's[34] inability to assign him any particular name, after almost a full year of collaboration, denies his individuality to define him only as the anonymous representative of his sex (whose respective members she simultaneously classifies as interchangeable): "Believe it or not, I forgot your first name. . . . Since I particularly didn't want to hurt you, I looked it up in Dr. Bourget's book; you're not even mentioned in it... I looked it up in the street directory; I found the initial "P." Pierre? Patrick? Philippe? Paul?... I even dissected the official postal calendar. It can't be Pedro or Philibert or Philémon or Pancrace or Pantaléon, I would have remembered..." (263).

Clearly, then, *Les Grands Désordres* once again structures female and male voices, as in *Une Vie pour deux,* in a potential dialectic of opposition and/or collaboration; Cardinal also renews the attempt, first made in *Le Passé empiété,* "to say 'I' in the masculine, to be a man" (Breen 14). But whereas the earlier novel shows us the unsuccessful process by which a woman seeks to speak as a man, to tell a male story from a male perspective, this time the male "I" has been fully assumed, and it seems at present to be with relative ease that *"Je est une autre."* Indeed, as I suggested earlier (see chap. 2), Cardinal initially seems to have chosen to repeat the most traditional of narrative techniques in which the male voice assumes authority not only for his own story but for that of the female as well.

On the other hand, if the male writer actually constructs the text and determines its language, as *nègre* he theoretically acts only as the invisible servant of the person who hires him. He has no identity of his own, as demonstrated less by his namelessness than by the inability of those who employ him to remember his name. The text that he has ghosted for Dr. Bourget (see quotation above) verifies this phantom existence; the substitution of another's signature for his own both erases the physical reality of his work and denies his very existence. As ghostwriter, then, the male relives an experience that has historically been that of the female artist: his creative work is stolen from him and attributed to another.

Moreover, in this case, the writer himself is forced to deny, by definition and in advance, the value of his own creativity, to pretend that the actual crafting of a text, the choice of a language and a structure, are irrelevant; as the ghostwriter repeatedly assures Elsa: "Listen, let's get things straight: I don't write, I translate" (11; cf. 13). By analogy of condition, the term *nègre* identifies those persons, including women, who have been denied the literary expression of their own experience, not only because they cannot write—at least not "well"—but, more importantly, because their lives are deemed insignificant, unworthy of public attention. The ghostwriter thus incarnates the literal selflessness of female altruism; to the extent that he gets paid for allowing himself to be used, he acts as prostitute.

The fact that in *Les Grands Désordres* the male narrator's self-effacement takes place in deference to the story of a woman's life offers interesting possibilities for the subversion of traditional gender roles and of conventional patterns of textual relationship. At their first meeting, the ghostwriter describes himself to Elsa as a chameleon—"I try to get inside the skin of the person who will sign the book, to identify with her" (11)—and, indeed, as the writing of the text proceeds, the narrator finds himself progressively subjugated by the female story. In this, he already repeats Elsa's own behavior (or, at least, that which he attributes to her): "Elsa has an enormous capacity for adaptation, for self-effacement before someone else whom she seeks to understand" (86).

But the obligation to speak as a woman gradually undermines the ghostwriter's own sense of self and threatens his identity. On the one hand, this ability of the male to identify with a female perspective and situation delivers a decidedly hopeful message about the possibility of understanding one another beyond the boundaries of gender specificity; furthermore, it attributes a key role to the text and to textual acts of reading and writing in realizing this otherness. On the other hand, however, the transformation of the narrator's usually nonproblematic fusion with another into a psychological disorientation that verges on the nervous breakdown and that seeks an outlet in various attempts at textual revolt and subversion simultaneously suggests that the process will not be an easy one.

Already, in "Les 143 pages," the single sequence of *Les Grands Désordres* that presumably represents a coherent fragment of what the "finished" manuscript of Elsa's story might look like, the narrator succeeds in reducing his own presence to objective, third-person authorial narration. Moreover, the narrator often allows a single consciousness to determine the field and range of the third-person perspective, and he adapts his point of view and his language to those of Elsa and Laure, in turn. During the three-day period that the two women spend apart (immediately after Elsa has learned that Laure is an addict), the juxtaposition of two narrative sequences—passages that are informed successively by the paradoxical stops and starts of Elsa's desperate and futile activity and by her endless waiting alternate with those that are immobilized and sped up in turn by Laure's cyclical existence of drugged euphoria and her desperate quest for the next fix—reflects a sense of female time and rhythm that Cardinal has identified as one of the significant textual "gaps" women writers will fill (AD: 89, 96–97).[35] Elsa justifies her satisfaction with the ghostwriter's first text by citing his successful reproduction of her own characteristic verbal style: "She told me she was pleased with the text. I had rediscovered her own rhythm and vocabulary; I had understood a great deal about her, about her linguistic idiosyncrasies" (151).

In the most remarkable example of formal and linguistic echo, an "I" attributed to Elsa suddenly speaks out in the midst of "Les 143 pages" (117–21). The personalized female voice subsumes the male narrator and erases the distance and the neutrality of the third-person at precisely the moment when the text focuses on a reality that is not only specifically female but that incorporates two key elements of Cardinal's own distinctive pattern of textual repetitions. The passage in question includes both a description of the paradigmatic experience of the expectant mother, who, at the first movement of the fetus, understands the intensely private and paradoxical unity and duality that define the mother-child relationship, and a celebration of the female body, informed by women's mutual love and attraction. Moreover, the male narrator writes this physiological and anatomical specificity of women in a characteristically female language whose feast of repetitive forms simultaneously introduces linguistic autogenerativity as a complement to biological generation, reflects the commonality of female experience, and reproduces the rhythms of childbirth:

> Laure's body!
> The curiousness of that body, Laure's body! So many months locked in body to body combat . . .
> On my belly, spiteful one! Wet, pinkish, streaked with blood, the down stuck to your head, my Laure! What beauty! What a miracle!
> Laure's body!
> Laure's body when she dives!
> Laure's body when she dances!
> Laure's body when she is seated at her desk!
> Laure's body in front of the mirror, when she is getting ready to go out!
> Laure's body punctured by heroin, . . . (120–21)

Yet, at the very moment at which Elsa professes her admiration for "Les 143 pages," the ghostwriter suddenly finds her "more reserved, more suspicious" (151). Her subsequent suicide attempt suggests that this reaction may stem from a sense that the *nègre* has perhaps been *too* successful; that his parallel appropriation of her identity, her language, and her experience threatens the integrity of her story and the autonomy of her self. Her deliberate staging of her own starvation, with the ghostwriter cast in the role of sole witness, seems to enact an almost ritualistic exchange of identity; as the carefully chosen gifts, which the narrator brings on his daily visits, pile up unopened in her apartment, the dimensions and the density of their material presence increase in direct proportion to Elsa's physical decline and withdrawal into silence. In any event, Elsa accompanies her eventual decision to live by the immediate assumption of a much stronger sense of textual responsibility and a much more active narrative role.

If Elsa initially still records significant portions of her story, she now does so alone, without the presence—or the prompting—of the ghostwriter. Moreover, she immediately begins to write certain episodes herself, and although the ghostwriter assures her that his revisions essentially recopy her original text, "give or take a few commas" (169), she becomes increasingly suspicious that he has altered, and even eliminated, parts of what she has written (180). Her solution, to retain a copy of her own work (198), allows us to assume from that point on that any textual version that we are shown reproduces Elsa's writing accurately and with integrity. The attribution of titles to certain of her textual fragments confers on them a closure and a completeness that already identify them as "literature." During this second period of collaboration, the ghostwriter not only finds his role increasingly limited to the menial and uncreative task of textual transcription but Elsa progressively reduces him to the reader of a text in whose production he no longer plays any significant part.

Importantly, Elsa's demonstration of her literary talents includes two third-person texts whose imitation of the normative techniques of "Les 143 pages" entitles her to claim a professional status as writer equivalent to that of the *nègre*. Moreover, Elsa's revelation that the two new texts constitute an integral and essential part of the ghostwriter's original manuscript, to which she has willfully denied him access ("These are not involuntary omissions. On the contrary, they involve facts that I intentionally censored" [209]), undermines the male text by exposing the superficiality and ellipsis that lie beneath its false aura of coherence. In retrospect, then, Elsa steals "Les 143 pages," since its fusion with the two "missing" episodes creates a new and different whole for which she alone can claim authorship. But these two passages aside, once Elsa becomes actively responsible for her own story, she narrates predominantly in the first person, in recorded and written texts. This evolution from "she" to "I" reflects Elsa's recently recovered sense of self that allows her to claim narrative authority and control over her own experience. Moreover, it also means, of course, that we no longer hear the repetition of the proper name that insisted on her gender identity. To some extent this omission may reflect Elsa's new sense of personhood, of individuality; more importantly, it marks her evolution from the objectified role of literary character to the responsible subjectivity of narrator and writer.

The sense that his "character" is escaping him, that she is replacing him as the author of her own text, no doubt contributes importantly to the ghostwriter's increasing irritation and discomfort. He begins to complain about the quality of Elsa's text and about her adoption of working procedures that severely limit his original role. He tries, for example, to convince Elsa that they should return to the method of "Les 143 pages" in which he takes notes as she speaks; the particular advantage that he cites—the elimination of the repetition characteristic of the female text—specifically re-en-genders their narrative battle: "I've run quickly through the rest of the tapes: it's confused, repetitive" (181). At other points, he objects to her insistence on reading his revised text aloud to him (197) and expresses his shock at the "scandalous" nature of her sexual relationship with Greffier (233).

In another ironic reference to gender, Cardinal clarifies the profound alienation that results when anyone is expected to develop reading habits that directly conflict with her or his gender identity. Women, trained to read as men, have often been forced to deny the female self, particularly in reading texts that describe heterosexual intercourse from a male perspective (see Fetterley and Millet). In Cardinal's reversal of gender roles, she now casts the male as the reader of a female text. Since we are constantly reminded that we are reading *with* the ghostwriter, a female reader of *Les Grands Désordres* has a split consciousness that emphasizes the difference between male and female readings. (Because male texts are filtered through Elsa's eyes as well, the male reader presumably has the identical experience). In particular, Elsa forces the ghostwriter to read texts in which her autoeroticism reduces the interest of her male lover to that of his penis, itself conceived as a "toy" designed for female pleasure. If the woman reader is almost inevitably amused by a sexual objectification that has traditionally worked to her detriment, her sense of revenge is also suitably tempered by her simultaneous identification with the necessary discomfort of her companion male reader. This complexity of response serves usefully to remind us that only a reconceptualization—and not a reversal—of power structures can lead to full humanity for men and women.

In spite of his persistent complaints, the ghostwriter finds himself increasingly caught up—virtually imprisoned, in fact—in Elsa's story:

"Elsa didn't know that I was becoming her shadow, her double, her echo" (178). He plays her recorded texts over and over, for example, even though he knows them by heart (179). Here too the ghostwriter lives an eminently female situation. If he can so easily lose himself in a text that bears no relation whatsoever to his own life, this occurs largely because he has no story of his own. He repeatedly describes himself as "someone ordinary" (242), perfectly content to live the most conventional (that is, significantly, the most nonliterary) of lives: "I have no taste for tragedy, and even less for drama, despite my interest in detective novels" (288). But precisely because he is drawn into a narrative that is totally alien to his character and to his past, his obsession becomes an experience in alienation that seriously threatens the coherence and the stability of his identity. Once Elsa adopts the first-person pronoun for her own use, the ghostwriter has no formal access to textual inscription. The absence of his *il* from Elsa's narrative clearly identifies both the female story and the male exclusion as gender specific. Curiously, the ghostwriter's torment ultimately derives less from his loss of narrative authority than from his inability to force Elsa to transform him into a literary character: "Does Elsa talk about the book? Does she talk about me? Do I exist for her? Am I anything but a ghostwriter?" (271).

The ghostwriter's initial solution—the attempt to abandon the joint project, the desire to end the pretense of collaboration—ironically forces him yet again into an exact imitation of a pattern of behavior that Elsa has previously established. But whereas the autonomous act of writing has subsequently provided the female narrator with a path to salvation, the male discovers, when he attempts to complete a manuscript of his own creation, that he has lost not only a particular text but the very capacity to write. For Writing itself has now become the essential personification of femaleness: "Up to now writing has solved all my problems; I don't see why it shouldn't solve this one too. Come, my lovely, put on your dress of lace letters; let me hear the castanets of my typewriter. No music on earth is more beautiful. You and I have lived through worse things than this. . . . I've been here for two weeks now. Writing refuses to have anything to do with me; she is jealous" (259). One might then interpret the ghostwriter's love for Elsa as a stratagem to recover in the "real" world the control that he has lost in the textual one.

On the other hand, the radical change of direction that appears to resolve *les grands désordres* of Cardinal's novel in the most conventional of happy endings actually functions not to distance us from literary self-consciousness but to identify a still more fundamental narrative battle that confirms the profoundly autoreferential nature of this thoroughly modernist exploration of the relationship between gender and genre, between sexuality and texuality. If the ghostwriter has lost control of Elsa's story, contained within the titled portions of the manuscript that together form a potentially coherent (though still unfinished) sequence, the interludes in which he continues to speak in his own first-person voice constitute another potentially coherent narrative sequence that tells a very different story. These intertwined but independent texts, respectively encoded as female and male, compete with each other for final narrative dominance. Although the triumph of Elsa's story appears increasingly probable in the second part (151–252) of the novel, as the interruptions of the male "I" become progressively less frequent and more brief (reduced at one point to a single, parenthetical sentence that functions only as a transition between two of Elsa's texts [207]), in the third part (255–90), the male first-person voice suddenly reasserts itself to claim both quantity (28½ pages of text to Elsa's 7½) and control (it provides the framework [255–62; 270–90] for her first-person letters [262–70]). Significantly, part 3 contains no completed (i.e., titled) fragments. The male and female battle only over two possible conclusions to a narrative in progress; either ending, should it triumph, would retrospectively assign closure and coherence to one of the two sequences that we have been reading and so identify it as the primary text.

We have known from the beginning of *Les Grands Désordres* that the ghostwriter also has an alternative identity as an independent writer of detective novels that belong to what he characterizes as "a bastard genre"—"I would like to write novels that the critics would not characterize only as detective stories. . . . They're detective novels [*des polars*] without being detective novels" (11). Despite his admitted lack of success, his professional status allows him a comfortable sense of superiority over Elsa precisely in the domain of literary competence: "A mature woman, still beautiful, was conversing about literature... In my view, she didn't know much about it" (12). Thus the ghostwriter's condescending compliment when Elsa first begins to write—"You've made an effort. That's good; I'll show you, it's along the lines of what I write" (170)—is no doubt only partly ironic. Moreover, if the male narrator's expertise as a writer of fiction ought to be irrelevant, since as *nègre* he ghosts "essentially documents—almost exclusively" (11), it rather alerts us immediately to the possibility of a generic diversion of the "true" story of Elsa's life. Indeed, Elsa herself almost appears to invite the transformation of fact into fiction, since she initially considers her experience of writing technical or theoretical texts to have accustomed her to the use of an "academic style" (13) that she judges inappropriate to the narrative of her lived experience.

Interestingly, Elsa's unsuccessful effort to write her own story takes the particular form of an inability to settle on a point of view, and it is precisely a conflict of pronouns that determines her recourse to the ghostwriter: "The 'I' is too private. I find it indecent. And yet, it is a question of me, of relating something that happened to me personally. I juggled with the 'I,' the 'we,' the 'they.' I didn't get anywhere, I couldn't find the right distance... That's why I have called you in" (13). The particular problem that Elsa faces is indeed that which Cardinal's frequent juxtaposition of first- and third-person pronouns and/or of the subjectivity of a female narrator and the objectivity of a female character aims to resolve. As elsewhere in Cardinal's work, Elsa will need to experience the gender specificity of the third person, which serves to identify her story as female, before her "I" will be able to reclaim this female story as also her own; the intervention of the male writer allows Elsa to function alternatively as both character and narrator.

The only two texts that Elsa herself writes in the third person, the two narrative events that she deliberately conceals from her male collaborator, confirm the important use of the female third-person pronoun to identify that which is specifically female and which, precisely for that reason, cannot be contained by the narrative sign of individuality.[36] This context clarifies Elsa's apparently paradoxical refusal to relate in her own voice two events that might seem eminently private and personal: "In writing them down, I realized that they were linked to my own sexuality. I used the third person. The 'I' struck me as a prison to write about that" (209). Female sexuality in fact identifies the commonality of women; indeed, taken literally, it *defines* femaleness. Moreover, the two texts in question focus on a love between women that includes an explicitly erotic dimension; that sexual attraction here takes the near-incestuous form of the symbiotic bond between mother and daughter functions metaphorically to suggest that women's deepest and most fundamental ties are to each other.

On the other hand, if the use of the female third person by a male writer and/or narrator serves more clearly than in perhaps any other case to identify femaleness, both the use of the pronoun and the interpretation of what it means to be a woman then function very differently. Cardinal's first published work, *Ecoutez la mer* (1962), already offers one version of a narrative situation that her most recent novel repeats. In the earlier text, Maria's love affair with Karl, a German writer, initially helps her recover from a nervous breakdown; in particular, Karl's love provides a supportive context in which Maria can recover the joyful memories of her Algerian childhood that allow her to reconstruct an autonomous sense of self. Even though Karl's subsequent abandonment plunges Maria back into madness and leads her dangerously close to suicide, her restored identity finally triumphs. Although Maria essentially narrates her story in the first person, the text also includes some third-person passages whose appearance initially seems arbitrary.

The very first example, however, already describes Maria, Karl, and their relationship in terms of gender stereotypes ("One must always tell Karl he is loved, that he understands, that he knows what to do. One must always show Maria her way and approve her docility" [31]). The most extended example of the technique confirms that the switch to the third person marks those moments at which Maria substitutes a literary model—a happy version of the boy-meets-girl plot, a fairy tale of true love that triumphs over all obstacles—for a reality that includes such incontrovertible facts as a husband in Canada, long-term separation, and Karl's distaste for commitment. This long, lyrical, third-person passage surfaces during a trip to Germany that Maria conceives as a test to determine whether her affair with Karl is to be a "beautiful story" or a "mere adventure" (108). Although all of the textual evidence supports the latter hypothesis, Maria writes into existence what is quite literally a beautiful story, a literary artifice. Not only does the third person mark the inevitable alienation involved in such an attempt, but the visibility that lyrical and symmetrical repetition grant to language exposes Maria's construction as an entirely verbal creation whose parallel structures enclose this passage in an endlessly circular self-reflection that serves precisely to erase the conflicting reality of the textual representation of the referential world.

When Maria comes to acknowledge (during a second breakdown precipitated by Karl's long silence) that she has "invented happiness," that the things in which she believed "didn't exist" (146), she explicitly blames Karl's *words*, now transformed into instruments of torture, for "this invented love" (148). If, in fact, Maria actually constructed the text we are reading, the third-person passages noted above always take the form of a dialogue between male and female voices. Moreover, the power of literature and language that seduces Maria has traditionally been a male privilege, illustrated here by the fact that Karl is not only a professional writer but also one who writes in a foreign language to which Maria has no access. The first-person voice of the female, in contrast, remains closely tied to reality; when Maria reclaims her "I" along with her life, she chooses (redundantly) "to face up to events," "to look at things as they are," and "to determine her future" (146). The final use of the third person to mark the loss of identity that characterizes Maria's breakdown explicitly equates literary and literal alienation; the woman's transformation into a *personnage* (a fictional character) signals the death of the *personne* (the human being). Both in madness and as literary creation, the woman allows herself to be defined by others, to act out stereotypical femininity.

Les Grands Désordres confirms the male writer's will to transform the female "I" into "she," to substitute a static and stereotypical male-defined femaleness for the complex reality of the living woman. Cardinal has structured the novel as a whole around a simple play on words that would immediately reveal a perfectly obvious textual order were it not for "the great *disorders*" that such an unthinkable lexical association simultaneously induces. Yet, in any other context, we would certainly be able to recognize the French word *héroïne* as an exact homonyn (same sound, same spelling, same *gender*), designating both *heroin*, the addictive drug, and *heroine*, the principal female character in a literary work. Moreover, the two words further share a common etymology: *héroïne* (from the Greek *hērōinē*, feminine form of *hērōs*); héroïne (from the Greek *hērōs*, "by analogy between the hero's ardour [*fougue*] and the exuberance caused by the drug").

Even if one ignores what seems to be a strikingly inexact analogy, perhaps based on a misunderstanding of the effects of heroin at the time that the word was first introduced into the French language—the drug in fact produces not *fougue* (a display of fire, spirit, passion) but its polar opposite, a particularly lethargic high (a passive tranquillity that often induces sleep itself)—it is hard to resist speculation about the apparently arbitrary decision to feminize the word. (*Le Grand Robert* specifically tells us that the word derives from *hērōs*, not from *hērōinē*.)[37] Are we to assume that women are somehow associated with passion once it has turned bad, turned toward evil? Certainly the literary and cultural connotations of *hero* and *heroine* are widely disparate. *Hero* suggests leadership and superior courage, individuality and initiative, a commitment to action, to a public life of adventure. *Heroine,* on the other hand, alternatively evokes self-effacing dedication to serving others; quiet conformity to conventional female roles (if not wife and mother, then teacher or nurse); the helplessness of the victim awaiting rescue; in short, passivity, submissiveness, obedience, invisibility. (Ironically, this totally private and internal *fougue* allowed to women might fairly serve as an analogy to the heroin-induced high.)

An appreciation of the global structure of *Les Grands Désordres,* however, does not require even minimal linguistic knowledge, since Cardinal carefully establishes the analogy between literary femaleness and addictive drugs within the text itself.[38] Curiously, Cardinal's narrative associations appear almost deliberately designed to recall the etymological parallelism between heroic *fougue* and drug-induced exuberance. Elsa's desperate effort to understand heroin addiction, to construct some kind of coherent intellectual framework whose explanatory power might extend to disorder itself, leads her to the revelation that "Drugs are a Love story." Addiction begins with "the illusion of the absolute" offered by the ecstasy of the high; it can only end if one encounters the passion whose orgasm provides an adequate substitute: "The absolute and passion, the two main avenues of Love" (264). But if both love and heroin are addictive passions, Elsa's original formulation also explicitly conceives the connection between them in terms of *story*—that is, of narrative structure, of literary plot. Moreover, Elsa, whose access to knowledge operates principally by word association (see chap. 2), concludes the very passage in which she explains this procedure by a similarly suggestive use of language; the perfectly coherent world that she has constructed holds firm "Jusqu'à ce que survienne *l'histoire de Laure.* Jusqu'à ce qu'intervienne *l'héroïne*" (207, my emphasis). Is Laure's story to be that of a heroine? of heroin?

Significantly, from the moment at which Elsa first outlines her *histoire* (after the ghostwriter has already reminded her twice that he is a translator and not a writer), he nonetheless begins at once to substitute his own authorship for hers: "She had come up against the very subject that I had been mulling over for quite some time" (13). His subsequent revelation of the precise nature of this subject confirms that from the beginning he has been writing a very different story from that which

Elsa believes she is telling. The ghostwriter's inspiration lies in the death by overdose of a woman writer with whom he had an affair (153): "I made love with her... I don't know anymore what 'in love' means" (197). It is precisely at this point, when it becomes clear that "Les 143 pages" has been inspired by the male's effort to transform a documentary account of drug addiction into a love story, a confusion further emphasized by his insistence that Laure's adventure is in fact Elsa's own story, that she first accuses him of fiction writing: "You're creating a novel" (152).

Nonetheless, during the initial period of their renewed collaboration, the ghostwriter continues his own novel; I quote at some length to clarify the precise nature of his fictional transposition of reality (of his substitution of a male for a female story):

> *I imagined* what her perdition with Laure must have been like. *I imagined* her determination to keep loving, to love Laure. . . . She must have held on because of love, only because of love, a pure, *mad love [amour fou]*...
> I wanted to love her and *I wanted her to love me*...
>
> The day I took her the transcription of cassettes 4 and 5, I was like a *madman [dément]*. I had just spent a week of *madness [folie] with her*. A week, day and night. A week spent reassuring her, protecting her, settling her into happiness, *inventing her happy*. But it was *my kind of happiness*. Would she want it? (179–80, my emphasis)

The simultaneous realization of Elsa's capacity for love and of another woman as its object immediately gives rise to the ghostwriter's determination to replace this unacceptable story of love between women with a traditional narrative of heterosexual passion. From his perspective, only this conventional version can save the woman from a madness (*"folie avec elle,"* *"un amour fou"*) that he clearly perceives as female; his own status as *dément* seems rather, through an association with the verb *démentir* (to contradict), to name his contradictory (in)version of love. His story, like the one authored by Jean-François in *Une Vie pour deux*, is principally defined by its happy ending, a happiness characterized as male (*"du bonheur à ma manière"*) in which the woman is cast as an *héroïne*, a frightened, manipulable object in need of male protection. Had he not abandoned his addicted lover a few months before her death, her story presumably would also have had a happy ending.

It is hardly surprising, then, that this is the point at which Elsa first raises questions about the accuracy of the ghostwriter's transcription (180) and suggests that he means to turn her into *"une coquecigrue"*: "It's an old word; it used to designate a fantastic bird, something invented" (181). Indeed, the ghostwriter specifically falls in love with "Elsa," with his own fictional creation; and his pronouncement that he is "in need" [*en manque*] in her absence (274) explicitly identifies him as a *héroïnemane*, a man addicted to heroines. But, unfortunately, given his new determination to "live stories" (289), the male writer is decidedly not, as he points out himself, "equal to his imagination": "I'm someone ordinary, mediocre. I'm neither short nor tall, neither fat nor thin, neither handsome nor ugly; I don't even have a mustache. Nor glasses. Until I met Elsa, I had led a life in keeping with my appearance, an easy life, a life that could pass anywhere. It's only with my books that I can't pass anywhere; I can't even pass at all. I must not be equal to my imagination; I translate it badly" (272–73).

Certainly the "translations" that he offers us of his imagination produce remarkably unoriginal plots and unconvincing characters. For example, his five successive fantasies of Elsa's reaction to his declaration of love all repeat, often openly announced, literary stereotypes. In the first, her rejection of him as "young enough to be her son" proves that "conventions count for her" (257); in the second scenario, her psychoanalysis of him quickly reduces Romeo to Don Quichotte (257); in versions three and four, Elsa alternatively incarnates Pythia and the Statue of Liberty (258); and the ghostwriter presumably recognizes his final appeal to the happy ending, in which the two lovers wordlessly melt into one anothers' arms, as sufficiently well known to require no overt identification of any particular model. The writer has no greater success in re-creating himself as a literary character. His role as Lancelot du Polar, the chivalrous knight who swoops the damsel in distress onto his horse and rides off into the sunset, barely convinces him even as fantasy, so clear is it that Elsa does not require rescuing (272). In her presence, moreover, the imaginary Lancelot becomes only a tormenting ideal against which to measure the reality of the ghostwriter's physical awkwardness and predilection for saying precisely the wrong thing (277).

The most revealing example of the ghostwriter's commitment to romantic literary stereotypes appears in the final narrative battle to impose a conclusion on the text as a whole. Elsa produces the original version of the story of Mlle Véla, her catechism professor, in the second of her two letters that also constitutes her final written text. The introduction of this anecdote, immediately after Elsa's speculations on drug addiction as "a Love story," directly contradicts her intervening assertion that she does not know how to put her abstract reflections "into context" and needs her male collaborator, who is "accustomed to fiction" (265); in fact, Elsa proceeds to steal his final remaining talent. The name *Mlle Véla* repeatedly encodes the centrality of femaleness, both in the plural form that asserts the commonality of women (*ll = elles*) and in the singular form that designates their gender specificity (*el = elle*); appropriately, then, the name also appears to be a near anagram of Elsa's own. Mlle Véla's transcendent love for God offers Elsa a model of a totally satisfying love that she explicitly describes as superior to the passion she felt for her husband (267) and curiously similar to her idolatry of Greffier's sexual organ as an autonomous abstraction ("like the magnificat of sex, as if it were the entity of sex" [268]). Moreover, the absolute love incarnated by Mlle Véla allows Elsa to pass beyond conventional distinctions between purity and impurity in order to fuse *orgasm* and *ecstasy;* all passions, equally addictive, "tend toward the absolute," including, in particular, total solitude and total freedom from material reality (269).

What seems most significant in the female story is its explicit rejection of heterosexuality and its implicit celebration of female bonding through a commonly shared conception of love. As Elsa once explains to Laure, "men have never much counted" for her (214), and the first of the two successive passages in which she openly discusses her sexuality encodes heterosexual lovemaking as a totally private experience, in which both her partner and the sexual act itself are irrelevant: "Usually sexuality implies the other. . . . for me, it's lived in solitude. . . . For me, orgasm has nothing to do with sex, even if sex brings it about" (208–9). The second passage suggests a symbiotic love between mother and daughter in which the reflection of the same (of another woman) doubles the experience of solitude without destroying it and to whose understanding the equivalence of orgasm and ecstacy is surely pertinent. (Curiously, *amma,* the Indo-European root of *amour,* designates "various nursery words" of Latin origin, all of which—*amma,* mother; *amita,* aunt; *amica,* friend—repeat an originary story of female love.)

The ghostwriter immediately produces a male version of the story of Mlle Véla that is hardly recognizable; only the femaleness of the "heroine"'s name (including, no doubt, its reference to Elsa's own) retains its original importance. Mlle Véla now leads a double life; at night she works as a prostitute, offering her body "to be consumed" by men (279) in imitation of the communal host. Since, by definition, "it will end badly, a story like that" (270), Mlle Véla will be murdered when one of her clients realizes that she reaches orgasm, that she dares to introduce the sacred into the basest, most profane form of sexuality (and, no doubt, that she defies her role as male-defined sexual object). Although the narrator has no intention of sharing this revision with Elsa, he blurts it out (in a greatly expanded version, moreover) at their reunion dinner, in reaction to what he clearly regards as deliberate provocation. In this context, the story of Mlle Véla obviously functions as a warning.

Elsa has just returned from a visit with Laure: "Laure here and Laure there. Laure does fascinating things. . . . In my view, when a woman is happy and beautiful, it's because of a guy. She's beautiful and happy because Laure's doing well and the book's on her mind" (279). Ironically, what the ghostwriter finds unbearable is precisely the realization that he does *not* have a (male) rival; he reacts against the rejection of heterosexuality that Elsa has already encoded in her story of Mlle Véla. He therefore proceeds to substitute another traditional plot for the romantic tales that he normally imagines for Elsa; the two stories are as interchangeable as the letters of the names of the two "heroines." Any woman who refuses the conventional role of the passive heroine, eagerly awaiting the male lover who will rescue her from solitude and/or a world of women, is a prostitute who deserves to be punished by death; any form of love or eroticism beyond the boundaries of the traditional heterosexual couple, in which the female remains subservient to the male, is a form of prostitution that, again, deserves to be punished by death. Moreover, just as the death of the heroine in such cases marks the end of the book, in the face of Elsa's refusal to behave like a heroine, the ghostwriter symbolically destroys *her* own book (from which he is as totally excluded as from her life): "She's got in hand a book about dope, about the importance of science and knowledge when faced with the problem of dope. A book about love too... And I serve up a story, as big as a mountain, about a prostitute and a fanatic" (281).

How, then, are we to explain what happens next? When Elsa finally lifts her head, she looks at the ghostwriter in the way that he imagines she must gaze at Laure when they are alone (282); shortly, she asserts the desire to cease protecting herself from "just plain love" (283); and at last, after he has declared his love (287–88), the couple takes a romantic walk to the Seine, where they agree to begin "living" their "story" (289). I would suggest that this ending is, quite simply, a final male delusion that fails to take into account the very different conclusion Elsa has already announced (she and Laure will take over her parents' store [284]—once, that is, she has finished her book [286–87]). Elsa's own dénouement, moreover, totally preempts the male's, since the ghostwriter looks up from his declaration of love to discover that Elsa has fled (289).

The male story can only end in literary fantasy, in the endless repetition of different versions of the same plot until it finally comes full circle and begins repeating itself: death by heroin (ex-lover, Laure); death of the heroine (Mlle Véla); death of the writer (the unfinished book); death of the woman "reborn" as heroine (Elsa). Although the ghostwriter, in renaming Elsa, certainly shares Greffier's desire to appropriate her very being, both men en-gender only private narratives in which the roles that Greffier attributes to "*sa*" Luce (201) or the ghostwriter to "his" Elsa have nothing to do with the independent life of the real woman. The ghostwriter's sudden realization that Elle has begun to call herself Elsa (262) (in her phone messages and letters in part 3 of the novel) merely marks the point at which she abandons any hope of transforming him into either a co-collaborator or an accurate reader.

En-Gendering a Feminist Theory of Narrative

In support of my conviction that "the analysis of a given textual practice can generate in and of itself a new theory of the text," I would like to think that this chapter might help us to explore possible critical strategies. In rereading the analysis of *Une Vie pour deux* with which I began my quest for a feminist theory of narrative, I now see that the structure of my commentary imitates that of Cardinal's novel as I ultimately define it; both constitute "an internal duplication of the essential feminist act of (re)reading and (re)writing." I reread material previously published in another form in order to rewrite it for inclusion here. This recontextualization unexpectedly reveals my own struggle to win the right to speak, to gain narrative control and control of the narrative, within the boundaries of traditional theory and criticism.

Despite my initial skepticism about Annette Kolodny's assertion that formalism embodies "inherently sexist preconceptions" ("Lady's" 274), my own dependence on its tools and framework clearly had immediate and persistent consequences. I paused almost at once to define my terms, and I quickly began to define them negatively (I *meant* what I *didn't* mean) and in opposition (*I* didn't mean what *others* meant). I must now wonder to what extent my *pre*-occupation with dichotomy and dualism, rather than Cardinal's text, led me to identify conflict as central to her narrative concerns. Certainly such structures and categories continued to inform my own critical practice; not only do I feel the apparent need to keep repeating Cardinal's difference, but the very process of making such distinctions obviously encourages some tendency on my part toward classification and thus, at least implicitly, toward hierarchism. Even though my analysis also generates new forms, different dichotomies, and altered oppositions—including repeated challenges to formalism's own conventions—my critical practice continues to unfold within the framework of formalism. It is, then, revisionist, at best.

Bettina Aptheker, in describing her own experience of rereading prior work informed by Marxism, expresses an amazement similar to my own at "the contortions through which the theory was adjusted to accommodate women's reality" (9). Adapting her words to my situation, I arrive at the same conclusion: in reading Cardinal's text, I proposed to put women at the center of my thinking about formalism (9). In that event, to continue paraphrasing Aptheker, presumably my work was equally inaccessible to the vast majority of women, including feminists, because it too was constructed from categories of analysis that had no immediate reference to women's actual textual practices. Its matters of concern had also been generated primarily by priorities of the theory as it might be applied to women's texts (or by efforts to reform the theory to accommodate women's texts), rather than by women's writing (10). Aptheker's altered understanding of her own past practice initially results in a simple reversal of the original relationship between theory and text: "I wanted to start with women's experience and form the patterns from it" (11). But she quickly realizes that the decision to "place women at the center of [her] thinking" requires that not only her priorities but the very "structure of [her] thinking had to change" (11). The subsequent decision "to break up old patterns of thinking" leads in its turn to new and far more radical consequences, of which the most important is the transformation of her "ideas about the privileging of theory as the most important or most significant way of knowing" (7–8).

As I continue to reread my analysis of *Une Vie pour deux,* it becomes apparent that my central concern, both textual and theoretical, gradually shifts from formalism to narrative itself. Carol Gilligan's hypothesis that the "different voice" in which women speak reflects "a mode of thinking that is contextual and narrative rather than formal and abstract" (19) now encourages me to believe that the very act of reading Cardinal may have led me to place women at the center of my thinking after all. Moreover, Gilligan's description of this narrative mode of thought as neither formal nor abstract appears to identify a "way of knowing" that could challenge both the privileging of theory in general and my own attempt to privilege formalist theory in particular. Certainly, feminist scholarship has accorded its own place of privilege to the narrative forms of fiction and autobiography that have often been the special province of women writers. Indeed, editing the *Norton Anthology of Literature by Women* led Sandra Gilbert and Susan Gubar to the conclusion that male and female texts reveal only a single significant pattern of difference: women show a consistent preference for more narrative forms (personal conversation, July 1984).

I am, of course, fully aware that the frequent references to Hayden White and Louis Mink that accompany my new critical concern with narrative suggest the persistence of a tendency not only to define theory as male but to allow (male) theory to define the interest(s) of the female text. Still, I think that White's and Mink's recontextualization within the field of history of a discourse originally bound by notions of literarity, the very essence of literature, has a number of encouraging implications for my own analysis. In the first place, even if I allow theory as such to retain its primacy, my choice of a *particular* theory has now been largely determined by the interpretive challenges of a female text and by feminist scholarship's general commitment to the interdisciplinary nature of knowledge. In addition, if I have not yet claimed either my own or Cardinal's right to *produce* theory, I have at least claimed our right to the original *application* of theory.

The analysis that results from this female collaboration is, of course, theoretical in and of itself, for it incorporates attention to issues of gender into critical premises and practices from which they were notably absent. This revision of the thought of White and Mink not only alters its conditions of applicability, but it significantly transforms their theoretical framework as well. Although White and Mink develop an understanding of narrative in function of their desire to redefine the discourse of history as indistinguishable from that of fiction, their theory, once allowed to interact with Cardinal's text, successfully clarifies her very different desire to disrupt literary conventions and to move beyond the boundaries of fiction in order to rewrite the stories and structures of women's real-life narratives. Thus, the very success of this reading of her text validates the initial choice of critical context. For if White's and Mink's original intentions might seem to leave us thoroughly entrenched in formalism, their work in fact proceeds from assumptions about narrative similar to those we encountered in feminist scholarship. Mink too defines narrative in direct opposition to theory and as its privileged alternative: "Narrative form as it is exhibited in both history and fiction is particularly important as a rival to theoretical explanation or understanding" ("Narrative" 129). For Mink, theory explains every occurrence by relating it to "a systematic set of generalizations or laws" (132); theory, then, would appear to be inherently formalist. Only narrative can account for "the connected series of events" that make up a given occurrence at any particular moment. This focus on context as an "intersection," a locus of interrelationships, would seem to support my hypothesis that Mink's approach to narrative can provide a particularly productive framework for reading women's writing.[39]

In this light, I am interested to see that once Cardinal and I let Mink and White add their voices to ours, feminist analysis begins to change in significant ways. In a reversal of traditional priorities, a fictional text now serves to read—rather than allowing itself to be read by—the abstract principles of theoretical discourse. Cardinal's pronominal innovation provides a context in which Emile Benveniste's theory of pronouns reveals a new richness of meaning and applicability. I note too that my critique of reviewers' interpretations of Cardinal's choice of narrative technique is no longer directed at a wrong *reading* of her text but at a reading grounded in the wrong *theoretical* assumptions. My interest in oppositional structures, newly centered on those explicitly encoded as male and female, now means that formalism too makes gender the constant focus of its analysis. This ideological invasion of theoretical abstraction (from Latin *abstractus,* "removed from [concrete reality]") causes subsequent references to male critics to read increasingly like a feminist (re)appropriation of traditional thought. Thus, if White may have initially introduced a concern with etymology into my work, its eventual transformation therein from a decidedly secondary concern into one that had become increasingly central to my understanding of both the textual analysis of women's writing and the generation of feminist theory seems to find its most accurate reflection in Cardinal's gradual reduction of her male narrator to incoherence and finally to silence.

If the vacuum created by the abandonment of traditional narrative theory has not yet been filled by the voices of feminists, my own included, my analysis of *Une Vie pour deux* can provide some further understanding of the specific conditions required for the production of feminist theory: the need to "start with women's experience and form the patterns from it" (Aptheker 11). My reading of Cardinal's novel gradually allows the theoretical suppositions of the text to emerge and to define a new context in which women might read and write. Thus, the analysis of dialectical structures, a notion attributed to Cardinal from the beginning, ceases to function in a supportive role, designed to further an understanding of formalism, and takes on an autonomous identity in her own feminist dialectic of conformity and subversion. Similarly, the initial mutation of conventional forms (*hetero*-textual/sexual, notably, as in the case of the Couple or in that of stylistic patterns of interrogation) becomes, first, a metaphor for the multiplicity of female identity and the plurality of feminist community and, finally, a theoretical paradigm for Cardinal's signature practice of repetition, which creates female culture and, in the process, provides a model for "the essential feminist act of (re)reading and (re)writing."

My analysis of *Le Passé empiété*, the second context within which I seek to generate a feminist theory of narrative, logically succeeds the first and appears once again to adapt its own structure to that of the text it is reading. The most obvious difference between this interpretation and the one that precedes it, the total absence of all references to male theorists and to traditional literary theory, reenacts the final and definitive silencing of the father that takes place in Cardinal's novel. Similarly, her narrator's subsequent rediscovery of her maternal ancestry finds its critical parallel in the feminist scholarship that now flows through my text to fill in the theoretical gaps left open at the end of my analysis of *Une Vie pour deux*.

Although the use of Cardinal's narrative framework as a model for my own does not prevent me from simultaneously seeking a theoretical perspective outside her text, my new dependence on feminist theory nonetheless now puts women at the center of my thinking. Indeed, the inclusion in my own analysis of theoretical work based on prior readings of other women's writing further supports and illustrates my conviction that the analysis of a given textual practice can generate in and of itself a new theory of the text. Moreover, Cardinal's novel does not function as a static object to which feminist theory applies itself. Rather, her text actively identifies critical problems and/or gaps in the theoretical discourse; fiction and theory now engage each other in mutual interaction so that each in turn recontextualizes the other. Thus, the structure of Cardinal's fiction—the quest for a maternal ancestry—appears not only to influence its own critical context—my central focus on a female literary tradition—but also to offer evidence of the latter's validity. Adding Cardinal's voice and my own to those of other feminist readers and writers immediately alters the female tradition, defining an ongoing creative process of cross-cultural collaboration that is of considerable importance. As Shari Benstock notes, feminist critics must be willing to engage each other in constructive dialogue if we are to profit fully from our own theoretical positions and critical perspectives ("Feminist" 148).

In terms of the specific concerns that a feminist theory of narrative might be prepared to address, *Le Passé empiété* confirms the importance of textual practices that we have encountered elsewhere in Cardinal's work—notably, the alternation of different points of view and the engendering of the narrative voice. Cardinal's repeated experiments with alternative emplotments of female lives now appear to justify the attention that Anglophone feminist critics have often devoted to plot; indeed, her work revalorizes what I was initially tempted to dismiss as "plot summary" as a general methodology of reading whose potential respect for both the textual production of many women writers and the textual practice of most women readers identifies it as appropriately feminist. My suspicion that what my academic training in formalism and modernism encouraged me to reject as plot summary might, in fact, be more accurately viewed as an attack on realism itself finds confirmation in Cardinal's narrative fusion of the patterns common to women's reality and to its textual representation.

At the same time, the persistent inability of reviewers to unravel Cardinal's complex narratives, to understand how the different parts of the text combine to create a richly coherent whole, suggests the inadequacy of traditional formalist theory. The tendency of Cardinal's narrative structures to exceed the boundaries of most conventional categories—including, for example, those of linear chronology, unity of tone and action, generic definitions, and the autonomy of the individual work—

means that her writing cannot be understood in theoretical terms at all to the extent that it cannot, in Mink's words, be related to "any systematic set of generalizations or laws." Indeed, only narrative would seem able to account for the interrelated series of events that make up the contexture of any particular text of Cardinal's—a narrative, moreover, whose form might well resemble the "repetitive, cumulative, cyclical structure" of the stories women tell and the "circumstantial, complex, and contextual" style in which they tell them (Juhasz 223).

My final analysis of narrative technique in Cardinal's work differs most significantly from the previous two by restricting its focus entirely to the text of *Les Grands Désordres;* at no time do I make any reference to any theory or criticism, either traditional or feminist, that might exist beyond the boundaries of Cardinal's novel. Placing the female text at the center of my thinking, granting the primary role to the generative source, confirms the hypothesis that women's writing can and will engender its own theoretical paradigms.[40] In particular, Cardinal's self-referential novel repeatedly tells us how it was written and how it should be read. Moreover, its double identity as both a realist and an experimental novel curiously reflects the ambiguities of my own critical position as a feminist *and* a formalist. Susan Lanser, whose description of her training as "deeply formalist" and her perspective as "deeply feminist" reiterates my own, clearly outlines the important consequences: "This uneasy union has led me beyond traditional formalism without diminishing my interest in form. I have come to conceive the notion of form more broadly, to understand form as content and ideology as form, and to recognize relationships between textual and extratextual structures" (7).[41] There seems every reason to believe that Sandra Harding's explanation for why feminist scholarship inevitably transforms the nonfeminist ideas with which it comes into contact also holds true for narrative theory in general and formalism in particular: "it has never been women's experiences that have provided the grounding for any of the theories from which we borrow. It is not women's experiences that have generated the problems these theories attempt to resolve, nor have women's experiences served as the test of the adequacy of these theories" ("Instability" 646). Certainly, Cardinal's writing makes it clear that feminism and formalism need to work together to develop new critical tools that take the significance of gender into account.

One suspects, for example, in light of the conflicting textual evidence offered by Cardinal's work, that assertions such as that of Marilyn

DeKoven that "most published experimental writing so far has been done by men" may well stem not from the "formal conservatism" of most women writers (xx) but from a definition of textual innovation that is in fact based only on a consideration of male texts. (In the face of Cardinal's irony and comic vision, one wonders whether a similar explanation might not underlie the celebrated theory that feminists lack a sense of humor.) Paradoxically, such counterassertions as that of Margaret Higonnet, who maintains that the "idolatry" of the self-generating text is "unacceptable" to the feminist (xiv), appear to result from the very same tendency to identify all experimentation with that done to date by men. The *difference* of *identity,* the probability that women experiment distinctively, should obviously not be confused with their failure to conform to a male norm. Although the textual innovation of the late twentieth century has been by definition both a theory and a practice, it may be primarily in texts by women that it can become an ideology and a form.[42] Thus, the self-generative character of male fiction may indeed tend to serve the predominantly autoreflexive function of exposing the text's nonreferentiality. In writing by women, however, generation retains/regains referential meaning; form, narrative and linguistic generation, reflects feminist ideology, the generation of the female self.

Cardinal's narrative practice points to the multiple and diverse subversions (VD 255) of women's writing as a means toward the achievement of the paradoxical goals of liberation and self-definition (the vague and the ruled) that, according to Kolodny, can lead from literature back to life: "in altering the images and narrative structures through which we compose the stories of our lives, we may hope to alter the very experience of those lives as well" ("Lady's" 258). Form and ideology constantly interact in feminist textual practice: the undermining of conventional narrative order allows the critique of traditional patterns of thought; the generation of new narrative strategies creates potential schemes for the (re)organization of experience. The consequences for textual theory and criticism seem obvious. As troubled as the dialogue may be, feminism and formalism are surely inseparable.

NOTES

1. While the parallel between Didier and Frye might suggest that a preference for first-person narration also crosses cultural boundaries, it may be particularly characteristic of thematic analyses, informed by the expectations of real-

ism that are more typical of Anglo-American feminist criticism. Thus, Elaine Showalter's clear discomfort in *A Literature of Their Own* with writers of the "female aesthetic," who "renounced the demands of the individual narrative self" and produced "oddly impersonal" works, equates a shift from the first to the third person with the denial of self-expression and defines the desire to incorporate the experience of others as the death of the self (240). For Jardine, however, such a position, frequent within the context of Anglo-American empiricism, in fact stems from a confusion of the third person (representing universal statements) with the first person (representing subjectivity). By clinging to the "third person function" of representation, American critics affirm "the self over language," precisely because they fail to emphasize the process of enunciation (*Gynesis* 16).

2. In this light, Cardinal's evident preference for female nouns, which provoke a repetitive series of insistent "elle(s)" in their wake, appears as a complementary strategy for writing gender specificity into the text. As Ellen Moers notes in one of the first studies of the female literary tradition, grammatical gender may have some unexpected benefits for Francophone women writers: "Gender in French—in all Western languages, excepting only English—is free of sexual connotation, purely arbitrary: the female apple, the male tomato [that both of these words are, in fact, female in French, a point of obvious significance given their clear sexual connotations, does not undermine Moers's specific point, although it certainly casts doubts on the quality of her research and reflection]. Or so says the grammatical rule; but not, in my reading at least, the great women writers of France. My notes are full of significant instances where a Mme de Stael, a George Sand, a Simone Weil will, at a moment of heightened sexual self-consciousness, choose a word for its gender, and for the train of adjectives, pronouns, and endings resonant in sexual consequence that follow after her choice" (322–23).

3. Given the complexity of Cardinal's pronoun usage, the presence of an unnamed first-person narrator, although commonly cited by reviewers to identify a narrative voice as the writer's own, never confirms autobiography. Nor, of course, does the presence of a named third-person character guarantee fictionality, particularly since Cardinal often selects some variant of her own name in such instances. Moussia offers a curious example, since in three separate texts, all published after *La Clé sur la porte*, Cardinal identifies it successively as her childhood nickname, her adult nickname, and Russian for Marie (PR, AD, Stanton).

4. See also works by Seymour Chatman, Mieke Bal, and Shlomith Rimmon-Kenan. It is not my intention, however, to attempt to provide a comprehensive bibliography of narrative theory.

5. Lanser too acknowledges that "it is possible that the very choice of a narrative technique can reveal and embody ideology" (18).

6. Fehervary's remarks are based on a reading of *The Quest for Christa T. . .*, but all of Wolf's work reveals a remarkable reflection on identity, encoded in a self-reflective interrogation of narrative technique. *A Model Childhood*, for example, opens as "the dilemma crystallized: to remain speechless or else to live in the third person" (3) and moves through an exploration of the division of the self toward "the final point [that] would be reached when the second and the third person were to meet again in the first or, better still, were to meet with the first person. When it would no longer have to be 'you' and 'she' but a candid, unreserved 'I'" (349). Within Francophone literature, Monique Wittig quite appropriately identifies the subject matter of each of her books as "personal pronouns" ("Mark" 67). *L'Oppoponax* erases gender behind the neutral *on; Les Guerillères* turns the female plural *elles* into a generic third person; and *Le Corps lesbien* both explores the relationship between the first and second persons (*je/tu*) and challenges the unity and coherence of the "I" (*j/e*).

7. I have argued elsewhere ("Patterns of Influence") that Simone de Beauvoir's *Femme rompue* repeats the same story of the female couple. Jane Gallop believes that the question of female identity is always double, since it necessarily incorporates a lesbian awareness of the otherness of other women. We ask "not merely 'who am I?' But 'who is the other woman?'" ("Annie Leclerc" 154).

8. Irma Garcia, however, does explicitly link the inevitable duality and/or plurality of female identity to division and fragmentation; she speaks, for example, of a "broken identity" (1:76), a "rift," a "conflict . . . within the woman who has trouble unifying, recuperating herself" (1:77); a "split that turns the woman into an oppositional being, perpetually confronted with an other" (1:78). Like Gardiner, Jane Flax also argues that "postmodernists tend to confound all possible forms of self with the 'unitary,' mentalist, deeroticized, masterful, and oppositional selves" that are in fact congruent only with recurrent Western definitions of "masculinity" (93). Flax, however, seeks to revalorize D. W. Winnicott's notion of a "core self," in implicit opposition to the model of female subjectivity outlined by Gardiner or Chodorow.

9. This conception of pronominalization not only calls into question, once again, the advisability of privileging, with Frye and others, "the female 'I,'" but it also raises doubts about the very possibility of saying "I" "in the female." On the other hand, the opportunity to re-create gendered identity appears to follow directly upon the assumption of a *human* "I."

10. For a feminist discussion of the visual in Western thought, see Evelyn Fox Keller and Christine Grontkowski, who conclude that vision should not be rejected as an inherently patriarchal mode of knowledge since it also has the potential for connectiveness.

11. Simone describes the woman Jean-François "saw" in her notebooks as "a sorceress capable of changing my gaze and his" (286).

12. The other witnesses alternatively create "*une femme sans histoires* [a

woman without a past]" and the kind of woman who *"fait des histoires* [makes trouble]," confirming the close ties that exist between women's lives and literary plots. The inquest as a whole constitutes a *mise en abyme* of the novel's central concern with narrativity and language. All of the men use the technical language of the dominant culture in which the female story cannot be told: the judge's legal jargon and the doctor's medical vocabulary make them both incomprehensible; Jean-François partially recovers his voice only in mathematical computations of time and distance. The one sentence that he is totally unable to articulate, despite repeated attempts, is, significantly, the oath to speak the truth.

13. Nancy Hartsock (299) joins such feminist theorists as Simone de Beauvoir in arguing that the male experience typically substitutes death for life.

14. The "discovery of the female body" is, of course, the essential subject matter of *Une Vie pour deux.* At this stage, a discovery that is literally still that of the man nonetheless provides women with an occasion for the metaphoric and linguistic exploration and autocelebration of their own bodies.

15. Signe Hammer notes that after the discovery of their mothers in the 1970s, women have finally begun to think about their fathers. The focus of the work published during these two periods would seem to support such an evolution; as in the case of Hammer herself, studies of the mother-daughter relationship (e.g., Arcana, Friday, Chodorow) have recently been supplemented by books devoted to father-daughter interaction (e.g., Leonard, Wakerman, Boose and Flowers, Owen).

16. Elaine Showalter suggests that women writers should adopt precisely such a strategy: "A thorough understanding of what it means, in every respect, to be a woman, could lead the artist to an understanding of what it means to be a man" (*Lit.* 289). In any event, as Showalter notes, male critics already tend to perceive women writers' male characters as "in large part projections of aspects of women themselves" (136).

17. In *L'Express,* for example, Jean-Didier Wolfromm discovers with relief the portrait ("far more interesting") of the father: "One has rarely read, *coming from a woman's pen,* a more beautiful narrative of war and love." Not only does Wolfromm marginalize women writers by the disclaimer of quality that I have italicized, but he is only willing to let them write with the understanding that they will not attempt to tell their own stories. For him, "the central part of the novel could stand all alone," but unfortunately, "the author can't forget herself for a second." Gérard-Humbert Goury of *Le Magazine littéraire* also finds the central section of the novel "very beautiful and powerful"; as for the rest, "it's not easy to get into." The reviewer for *Nouvelle F* thinks the novel "admirable," but only "up to page 256," after which it becomes "indigestible"; here too we have a "novel to read for the portrait of the father." The reviewers of *Le Passé empiété* as a whole not only appear oblivious to any relationship between the

middle section of the novel (whose presumed "maleness" defines it qualitatively as "the central part") and those that precede and follow, but they also remain curiously unaware that part 2 ends with the definitive rejection of the father.

18. As we have seen, Cardinal unquestionably attaches considerable importance to the female body, particularly as a source of imagery. As Estella Lauder points out, however, "patterns of female sexual imagery in works by women need not mean that all women think through their bodies, or that women are more closely connected with nature than are men, or anything at all about Woman. . . . They are . . . manifestations of female experience (in this case of living in a female body)" (10). On the one hand, Cardinal's focus in *Le Passé empiété* on anatomy and sexuality, the only undeniable sources of gender specificity, stems no doubt from her effort to understand where and how male and female experience might differ. On the other hand, the female anatomy not only informs textual patterns of imagery, dominated by the linguistic repetition of such terms as *empty, hollow,* and *gap,* but it also identifies the organization of the novel as a whole, the "hole" that exists at the very center of the mythic structures we have inherited.

19. Early in *Le Passé empiété,* the narrator's rejection of "'serious' terms: God, the Essential, Death, Time" to identify embroidery as "the origin and the cause of everything" (36) already introduces a traditional female task into the category of metaphysics.

20. DuPlessis notes, for example, that women writers understand myths as prototypical rather than archetypal forms (107). The substitution of the prototype for the archetype redefines reality as historically specific and alterable rather than eternal and unchanging and replaces universal paradigms with optional models. Cardinal's belief that laughter constitutes "a formidable weapon" (PE 303) leads her to the deliberate confusion of myth with popular culture. Thus, the embroiderer proposes to figure Aegisthus as "an American football player" (302), and her portrayal of Electra and Orestes as typical adolescents obsessed with guitars and motorcyles both identifies them with her own children and brings to life the posters of James Dean and Marilyn Monroe, the very symbols of popular culture, that hang in Clytemnestra's bedroom (325–30; cf. ME 122: "James Dean, or Marilyn, or Joan of Arc, etc. are myths. They no longer have lives, they have stories"). Cardinal also uses a comic form of generic self-reflection to undermine the seriousness of ancient tragedy and to expose cultural models as "only" literature; thus, Orestes and Electra are introduced as "young actors from whom a great deal is apparently expected" (359).

21. Cardinal also omits most other traditional references—Aegisthus, for example, has no mythic past, and Clytemnestra does not rule Mycenae, since Agamemnon has never left. The legendary curse on the House of Atreus and the very notion of destiny disappear with the mythic structure that supports them,

further emphasizing Agamemnon's personal responsibility. Ultimately, Cardinal chooses to repeat the single event—the murder of Iphigenia—that is most often omitted from accounts of the Trojan War and even of Agamemnon's murder.

22. The rewriting of women's lives as mythical also responds—subversively—to what Cardinal sees as a historical and textual fact: "For three thousand years dreams and symbols from the imaginary world of historians have invaded women's reality so that today this reality has merged with the mythical universe of historians. They are inextricable. We are mythical beings just like the goddesses, gods, and heroes of mythology. We are legends, dreams, men's dreams" (ME 37). In openly reclaiming this assigned status and redefining it from a feminist perspective, Cardinal's twofold transformation of Clytemnestra into a contemporary woman and of the embroiderer into a mythical character transgresses the conventional boundaries of reality and of the novel form. Furthermore, the incarnation of Agamemnon in the narrator's father uses imitation to turn men's own practice against them.

23. In a pattern that repeats the displacement of the thematics of war and heroism, Cassandra appears only in this inner story, where she fulfills her customary role as the father's mistress. Although she also continues to be defined in terms of voice, this Cassandra is remarkable for her persistent silence, broken only by the "howl" with which she marks the moment of Théodore's (Agamemnon's) death.

24. Claudine Herrmann, for example, defines the role of the actress as prototypic of the culturally accepted relationship of women to language (16).

25. See also Nancy Bogen's *Klytaimnestra Who Stayed at Home*. For a poetic re-vision of the story of Clytemnestra, see Judith Kazantzis, who juxtaposes in "The Queen Clytemnestra" the public myth of the cruel queen with the private reality of the (twice) wounded mother; here Clytemnestra's pain and loss center as much on Electra as on Iphigenia. Curiously, feminist revisionists have so far repeated the elimination of Chreseia, the third daughter who alone remains faithful to her mother, from official versions of the myth. Auffret, however, cites an Italian revision by Dacia Maraini (*I Sogni di Clitemnestra*) that would finally appear to challenge the authority of *The Eumenides*. Athena has become a feminist psychoanalyst with whom Clytemnestra is in treatment.

26. Since Ronfard states openly—and convincingly—that she has never read any of her mother's texts, such a repetition cannot be attributed, even inadvertently, to actual quotation (personal conversation, 23 Nov. 1987).

27. *Autrement dit* is, in fact, one of the two key texts (with *Les Parleuses*, by Marguerite Duras and Xavière Gautier) from which Lamy develops her theory of the difference of female dialogue (37–51).

28. Appropriately, no origin can in fact ever be presumed for the mutual textual repetitions that affect Leclerc and Cardinal—and which they effect. Le-

clerc's *Parole de femme,* for example, constitutes one of the primary textual practices around which a theory of *écriture féminine* has been constructed.

29. Auffret, by the way, although she approves of the resemblance established between Clytemnestra and the embroiderer's mother ("A way for a woman to understand, repeat, and continue the myth" [45]), follows most reviewers in seriously misrepresenting the resemblance between the embroiderer and her father: "Just like Giraudoux's Electra, Marie Cardinal's heroine . . . labors to restore the image of the father" (45–46). Moreover, by moving directly from this assertion to her insistence on the unconscious influence of models, Auffret ignores the lengthy exploration in *Le Passé empiété* of the most significant of a triple pattern of resemblance, that between the narrator and Clytemnestra.

30. In the preface to her translation, Cardinal describes a textual trajectory that explicitly seeks to connect the past and the present, the literary and the real: "It's been twelve years now that I've been trying to progress by telling the Histories/Stories of women: the women of today and the women of the beginning. Clytemnestra is one of the heroines of my last novel. And now Medea" (41). Interestingly, the fact that Cardinal has so far devoted her attention to the two most prominent *mothers* of the Western mythic tradition not only supports her central interest in the institution of motherhood but, more specifically, repeats the dynamics of her own maternal discourse: the mother who destroys (Medea/ the human mother) complements the mother who is destroyed (Clytemnestra/ Algeria). Similarly, Cardinal's conceptualization of women's *Histoire du silence* as a metaphoric *viol* (46) connects our textual "bodies" to our real ones in support of Cardinal's equally important discourse and thematics of rape.

31. In fact, her very life depends upon it: "I must let the queen finish out her life; my own survival is at stake" (354). Adrienne Rich, who believes that a radical feminist critique of literature should read the work "first of all as a clue to how we live," attaches the same importance to revisionary readings that Cardinal does: "Re-vision—the act of looking back, of seeing with fresh eyes, of entering an old text from a new critical direction—is for women more than a chapter in cultural history; it is an act of survival" ("When We Dead" 35). Rich also asserts that we need to break tradition's hold over us rather than to pass it on. The quotation from Cardinal continues: "I must pull her out of my head by the roots; may she die, may she croak" (354).

32. Stewart herself may fail to destroy a theory that has served men to deny women access to art. In her catalog of traditional obstacles to female creativity, Joanna Russ also quotes Otto Rank, who makes his original point to clearly different purposes: "to create it is necessary to destroy. Women cannot destroy" (14).

33. Given the insistent visibility here of lexical form, I find it tempting to

speculate that Labbé, interpreted as an abbreviation for *l'abécédaire,* an alphabet book, might designate the linguistic primacy of women, the female origin of language. In this light, I am grateful to Françoise Lionnet for pointing out that Elsa's name also echoes that of Louise Labé (Labbé in its original sixteenth-century spelling), one of the earliest professional women writers in France. On the other hand, by substitution for another designation of religious rank—cardinal—*l'abbé* might also write the author into one of the few texts from which some version of her own name is absent.

34. For the sake of convenience, I will subsequently use the name Elsa without quotation marks, but we should remember that it is only the name of the female hero of the internal novel that the ghostwriter is composing and not that of the female protagonist of *Les Grands Désordres.* Were it not potentially confusing, I would do better to designate this latter as Elle. To assign her a name of my own choosing, moreover, would be fully in keeping with the practice of the text—perhaps something like the bilingual mirror-name that Cardinal gives in *Une Vie pour deux* to the woman in whom Mary sees reflected the gender specificity of her own situation: MELanie DunaHER.

35. As we have seen elsewhere, Cardinal often connects female rhythms to the menstrual cycle. Thus, if women's official temporality is limited to the regularity of twenty-eight–day periods, falsely imposed by a male need for order and coherence, women's own sense of time can be more accurately identified with "*des règles anarchiques* [menstrual anarchy]," ranging from the total cessation of bleeding to the constant loss of blood (AD 37).

36. That the third-person male narrator switches from "she" to "I" to narrate childbirth and the celebration of the female body in "Les 143 pages" strikes me as consistent rather than contradictory. In this particular narrative situation, the "I" best distinguishes experience that the male cannot claim as his own.

37. The problem does not arise in English, where heroine and heroin are neither homonymic nor homophonic and the etymology of the drug is attributed to "a trademark."

38. I must admit, however, that although the possibility of such double meaning kept recurring throughout even my first reading of the novel, the equation seemed somehow so shocking—as if, I suppose, it made light (because heroines are frivolous, superficial, decorative objects? because *women* are?) of the seriousness of heroin addiction—that I welcomed the reassuring permission that the dictionary grants to think the unthinkable.

39. In *Desire and Domestic Fiction,* Nancy Armstrong selects another productive theoretical base, Foucault's work on the history of sexuality, and refines his thought "to include the issue of gender" (13). Similarly, a number of feminist critics, including Patricia Yaeger and Joanne Frye, have turned to Mikhail Bakhtin in recent years in search of a theoretical framework to inform the reading of women's texts. Given my present understanding of my own revision of White

and Mink, I am amused to recall that in one early draft of this work I retained the problematic term *dialectic,* in explicit preference to *dialogic,* on the grounds that Bakhtin's exclusion of gender from a theory of language devoted to hearing different voices made me wary of his own voice.

40. Not only does my critical practice repeatedly model itself after the narrative structure of the text I am reading, but the sequence of my analyses curiously recalls the three stages that have often served to define the historical development of feminism: the exclusion of women writers from the domain of (male) theory (*Une Vie pour deux*), the creation by feminist writers of an alternative theoretical framework (*Le Passé empiété*), and feminism's reappropriation of all forms of discourse to make women's writing central (*Les Grands Désordres*) (see chap. 2, n.1).

41. DuPlessis's *Writing beyond the Ending* puts Lanser's theoretical hints into practice. Her interpretation of narration as a version of ideology informs a series of brilliant textual analyses. Gilbert and Gubar should also be singled out for the consistent attention that they devote to form and content simultaneously in all of their work, individual and collective.

42. Gilbert and Gubar mean something similar, I think, when they propose that literary conventions serve women to define their own lives. Thus, Gilbert and Gubar characterize the distinction between male and female uses of the same images as one between that which is metaphysical and metaphorical and that which is social and actual (*Madwoman* 86).

CHAPTER FOUR

Feminism and Psychoanalysis
The Identity of Difference

What one truly understands clearly articulates
itself, and the words to say it come easily.
Boileau, *L'Art poétique*

I don't know how or why the lines from Boileau that appear to
have inspired the title of Marie Cardinal's *Mots pour le dire*
came to serve as epigraph in the English translation, but their absence
from all French editions of the novel, beginning with the original, makes
perfect sense. Boileau expresses a seventeenth-century belief in the pre-
eminence of a universal faculty of Reason that has very little to do with
Cardinal's effort to speak the two equally unspeakable stories of madness and psychoanalysis. Nor does Boileau's confident assumption initially appear any less foreign to an understanding of the central issue,
an issue to which Cardinal's work is central, of the relationship between
feminism and freudianism.[1] And yet, on second thought, if we scratch
the surface of this epigraph (from the Indo-European *gerebh-*, to
scratch), its seemingly appropriate claim to begin a new book, rather
than to repeat a prior one, in fact reveals a text "written on" others that
we have seen before (Greek *epigraphos*, written on, from *epigraphein*,
to write on). For that matter, to choose an epigram as epigraph already
marks the process, since the etymology of the second is written on that
of the first.

To the extent that Boileau's words state the priority, in time and importance, of thought over its linguistic expression, they encode what has
seemed to be one recurrent distinction between Anglophone and Francophone feminism, and in this role they rightfully surface only at our

entry into the English-language edition. In this light, a certain repetitious tendency among critics to describe Cardinal's portrayal of the analytic process as classically freudian *and* distinctively rational and coherent suggests that the addition to her text of a neoclassical epigraph may after all remain more on the order of a translation than a betrayal. Moreover, I may have repeated the same critical error that I have just noted by attributing too great a clarity and too obvious a reading to Boileau himself. That which "articulates *itself*" might after all refer to the kind of linguistic autogeneration that Cardinal practices; nor would she dispute the fact that "the words to *say* it" (but not to *write* it) come easily at times in an analytic process whose beginning coincides precisely with the removal of all barriers to free expression.

Let us pause a moment to listen to what others have "written on" the palimpsestic text of language, literature, psychoanalysis, and feminism whose multiple layers have begun to e-merge, a process facilitated in particular by the double register that makes such terms as *repetition* and *translation* equally at home in the vocabulary of both freudian and textual analysts. The "claim to an act of repetition," asserts Peter Brooks, appears to be "equally initiatory" of narrative and of the analytic experience (97), founded on Freud's discovery that the analysand "is obliged to *repeat* the repressed material as a contemporary experience"; thus the analyst continually encounters a "compulsion to repeat" and patients find themselves constantly subject to the "perpetual recurrence of the same thing" (qtd. in Brooks 98–99). Moreover, from the identification of psychoanalysis as "a primarily narrative art" (xiv), it follows, Brooks suggests, that one might discover in "the analysand-analyst relation, a possible model of text and reading" (58). Interestingly, Brooks's dual fusion of psychoanalytic and narrative theory and of literary criticism and therapy, itself widely repeated in a number of other contemporary works (e.g., Chambers, Schafer, Skura, Felman), produces a textual practice that becomes strongly relational and repetitive in and of itself: *Reading for the plot* uses a technique of alternating readings that places Freud in dialogue with a series of modern novelists.

The effort of Francophone and Anglophone feminists to establish a working relationship has, from the beginning, focused on psychoanalysis and takes, in one of its early examples, the explicit form of a dialogue, the initial part of which I take the liberty of repeating here:

> *Mary Jacobus:* One question that has been made critical by
> French feminist writing is psychoanalysis, which means

something very different in France from what it might
mean in America.

Sandra Gilbert: I think there is also a sense in which all of this is
a way into Freud. Lacan is a way into Freud. The mediating process that Irigaray performs, for example, is part of
the mediating process that Freud is also performing. It's
like doing a Virginia Reel into the center of things. That's
why I have this feeling about its being a key.

Carolyn Allen: I have always felt resistant to American psychoanalytic criticism which I identified, in sort of naive ways,
as being Freudian and also wrong-headed about women.
It doesn't feel like it's talking about me. I'm trying to read
French feminist writers who are obviously coming out of
a psychoanalytic tradition which is different but related.
("Feminist Readings" 7–8)

It is worth noting that even though we hear only Anglophone feminists speak in this conversational excerpt (and each one only once), a
mediation through dialogue has nonetheless taken place. What begins
as one possible Franco-American distinction that Jacobus asserts to be
"very different" is immediately redefined by Gilbert as simultaneously
the same—"all of this is a way into Freud"—and absolutely central;
yet, the fact that her contradiction emerges from a commentary on "the
mediating process," a phrase whose own centrality and repetition suggests its autoreferentiality, prepares us at the same time for Allen's effectively mediated conclusion that French and American positions are "obviously . . . different but related." The cautious or uncertain speech
patterns favored by all three women (Jacobus: "*something* very different," "what it *might* mean"; Gilbert: "a *sense* in which," "it's *like*
doing," "this *feeling* about"; Allen: "I have always *felt*," "in *sort of*
naive ways," "it doesn't *feel like*"), combined with an unusual degree of
pronominal vagueness (of which Allen's "*It* doesn't feel like *it's* talking
about me" is merely paradigmatic), no doubt allows a transformation
of thought to take place and may even be consciously intended to deflect
the unfair advantage that potentially results from the absence of the
French interlocutor. And yet I, for one, find that this language serves
predominantly to reinforce the curious impression emanating from this
text that it produces its meaning unconsciously, that it reproduces the
unconscious textually; as such, this dialogue among Anglophone feminists, all of whom eventually express deep skepticism about Franco-

phone interest in psychoanalysis, does indeed suggest that freudian thought can perform some astonishing mediating processes.[2]

In another text on the same subject that appeared at approximately the same time as the special edition of *Yale French Studies* from which I quote above, Jane Gallop and Carolyn Burke structure their voices in a similar alternation to discuss once again "Psychoanalysis and Feminism in France"; we can be sure that their decision to enter into dialogue represents a deliberate choice, since one section of Gallop's contribution was originally published elsewhere as an independent and single-authored text. Moreover, we now have an explicit example of the same phenomenon that is implicit in the successive interventions of Jacobus, Gilbert, and Allen: Anglophone voices, speaking less to each other than to the missing voices of Francophone psychoanalytic feminists (present only through textual references), turn out, somewhat unexpectedly, to be in agreement as they end up repeating one another.

Gallop's book on the same issue, *The Daughter's Seduction: Feminism and Psychoanalysis*, deliberately repeats Juliet Mitchell's *Psychoanalysis and Feminism: Freud, Reich, Laing, and Women* (but differently, of course, as reflected in the multiple mirror images that name the two works; we see title and subtitle, discipline and ideology, and filial relationships all change places). Gallop's book enters into global dialogue with Mitchell's and structures each chapter around the encounter of at least two texts representative of contemporary feminist theory and of Lacanian psychoanalysis. In the course of *Reading Women,* whose title names a process again dependent on the interrelationships of psychoanalytic, narrative, and feminist theory, Mary Jacobus replaces the traditional linear pattern of reading one text *after* another with a spatial configuration of reading *between* texts that appear to invite such a bilingual exchange of *correspondance*/correspondence.

The simultaneous appearance of repetition and dialogue (of repetition *as* dialogue) at the intersection of psychoanalysis and feminism does not by any means constitute a specifically Anglophone phenomenon. Indeed, as Gilbert notes above, Luce Irigaray's intricate writing of her own text on those of Freud and Lacan (*Speculum, Ce sexe*) initially awakened American feminists to the importance and the potential difference of psychoanalytic theory within the context of Francophone feminism. In perhaps the broadest of repetitive dialogues, Freud's case study of Dora (the only study devoted to the case of a woman) has become the centerpiece for rethinking the interaction of narration, feminism, and psychoanalysis in the United States and in France. For example, in forms representative of the cultural differences between feminist writings, Hélène Cixous has rewritten Dora's and Freud's voices into a lyrical drama in her *Portrait de Dora,* and in a collection of essays entitled *In Dora's Case,* Dora (and Freud) are the focus of Anglophone textual analysis.

Once again, Cardinal provides a promising context in which to explore further the complex intersections of Anglophone and Francophone feminist writing on psychoanalysis. Still best known in France as the author of *Les Mots pour le dire,* Cardinal first entered into direct dialogue with Anglophone feminists on the campuses of American universities during the 1983 lecture tour that marked the publication of *The Words to Say It,* the first of her works to appear in English translation. Moreover, as we will see, Cardinal's consistent connections to issues of repetition attain here an unusual degree of palimpsestic denseness, for not only do the psychoanalytic plot and framework of *Les Mots pour le dire* reappear in a number of Cardinal's other works, but the three existent versions in which this novel alone reproduces itself— a film adaptation offers a visual mediation between the original text and its translation—reflect one another in decidedly curious ways that serve particularly well to illustrate repetition's paradoxical identity as always one of difference.

"Classical" Freudian Analysis

The attribution of the 1976 Prix Littré to *Les Mots pour le dire,* a prize that doctors accord annually to the best medical arts book published in France, consecrated the novel's critical reception as the factual relation of Cardinal's own experience with psychoanalysis. Although some reviewers acknowledged the originality within the history of analytic literature of a therapeutic account related by and from the perspective of the patient rather than the physician, Cardinal's story was generally read as a classically—and classical—freudian analysis. Indeed, the determination to force the novel into conformity with this model appears to lie behind a curious confusion of analysand and analyst that virtually erases what initially seemed to be Cardinal's one clear claim to difference.

In a characteristic reversal whose paradoxical perversity remains particularly visible, the reviewer for *Le Nouvel Observateur* first objects to the "strange idea" of writing the story of an analysis that excludes the viewpoint of the analyst; subsequently, Norbert Bensaid indirectly manages to restore order: his description of Cardinal's account as "too clear, too confident" reintroduces the missing "coherent construction" that the analyst might have provided, even as it continues to lament the analysand's presumptive claim to autonomy. Similar characterizations of Cardinal's narration as "too linear" (Rev. of MD, *Esprit*) or "too intentional and hyper-rational" (Chapsal 45) reiterate the same ambivalent objection. Since the reviewers, by their own account, have no comparative models that would allow them to label a patient's perspective as "too" or "hyper" anything, they apparently continue to read in the only terms to which they are accustomed by rediscovering the analyst's account in that of the analysand. In this context, their negative commentary serves the necessary function of denouncing the usurpation that is presumed to have taken place, but not, significantly, at the cost of disrupting the traditional structure of psychoanalytic narrative.

Since reviewers have the luxury of writing an impressionistic and evaluative prose that largely omits the textual analysis that would presumably justify their conclusions, let us explore more closely the possibility of reading *Les Mots pour le dire* as a classical experience of freudian analysis. Since Cardinal refers in an explicitly autobiographical text to a personal experience with "the most freudian of analyses possible" (AD 10), I will momentarily accept the identification of the unnamed first-person narrator of *Les Mots pour le dire* with Cardinal herself and temporarily credit the assumption that the novel narrates verifiable events of her own life; she thus offers us a case study of her seven-year analysis. Daniel Lagache, in his historical and theoretical overview of psychoanalysis, insists that "an abstract exposition cannot replace the case study and still less analysis itself" (84), a view fully consistent with Freud's own careful documentation and publication of his case studies.

Both the initial conditions established by Cardinal's analyst and the therapeutic procedure that he outlines correspond to a practice that has remained standard since Freud first described it (*Technique*). Cardinal's doctor schedules triweekly sessions for which she must assume full financial responsibility, insists that she stop all medication, and warns her that "an analysis threatens to disrupt your life" (35). The only "remedy" that the doctor offers corresponds to what Freud calls "the fundamental rule of psychoanalysis," which requires the analysand to associate freely, to attempt to articulate mental content beyond censorship or conscious control on the assumption that nothing is irrelevant to the analytic process: "Talk, say everything that crosses your mind, try not to select, try not to think, try not to arrange your sentences. Everything is important, every word" (85). The behavior of Cardinal's doctor remains rigorously faithful to the rules initially established by Freud: he sits behind the patient, out of the range of her normal field of vision; and his sole activity consists of attentive listening. He does not, for example, take notes, nor does he attempt to provide any direction during the long periods of silence in which Cardinal professes that she has nothing to say.

In fact, initially Cardinal's doctor does not intervene at all in her monologues, except to announce the end of the session; later, he occasionally singles out a particular word as a focus for the additional generation of ideas: "Such and such a word, what does it make you think of?" (119). Since Cardinal specifically associates her confidence in her doctor with his ability to choose the significant word, this procedure appears to correspond to what Freud defines as the analyst's primary objective: the dual effort to attach the analysand to both treatment and doctor. Moreover, since Cardinal confirms that the word selected often constitutes "the key that opened a door" (119), we can assume that she was on the verge of identifying its importance on her own, an imminence that Freud regards as a precondition for the analyst's direct intervention. In all other cases, including the interpretation of her dreams, the doctor's active role can be deduced only from Cardinal's own skillful manipulation of interpretive strategies that she has presumably developed in the course of the analytic experience.

Cardinal's occasional statements of confidence and admiration for her doctor (119) appear to confirm that transference, judged by Freud to be essential to a successful analysis, has taken place. If Cardinal's emotions do not quite seem to equal what Freud describes as "intense feelings of affection" (*Gen. Intro.* 448), the intensity of her anger during a period of negative transference is certainly clear enough. Moreover, its expression confirms the fact of the initially positive transference and includes a specific acknowledgement, parallel to Freud's own, of the therapeutic centrality of the transferential relationship: "I went to the cul-de-sac and I insulted the little doctor. I flung in his face everything I had heard about psychoanalysis. . . . I called to my rescue the vocabulary of psychoanalysis, those words he had asked me to set aside at the beginning of our sessions. I juggled with the libido and the ego and schizophrenia and complexes and Oedipus and repression and psychosis and neurosis and paranoia and phantasm, and I always kept transference for last. Because it hurt me to have surrendered to him so completely, to have had such confidence in him, to have loved him so much!" (193–94).

In general, Cardinal often makes a not uncommon distinction between psychoanalysis as therapy and as theory: "As someone who has been through analysis, who was saved by psychoanalysis, . . . I don't understand a word of what specialists of psychoanalysis say. . . . I think there's a great difference between those whom psychoanalysis has cured of a neurosis that prevented them from living and those who know everything about psychoanalytic theory" (AD 10).[3] Yet, Cardinal's rapid enumeration of freudian terminology in the passage cited above suggests a familiarity with psychoanalytic theory as well, whose influence can indeed also be perceived in *Les Mots pour le dire*. In Freud's view, the intellectual framework of psychoanalysis rests upon the theory of the unconscious, of sexuality, and of the Oedipus complex: "The assumption that there are unconscious mental processes, the recognition of the theory of resistance and repression, the appreciation of the importance of sexuality and of the Oedipus complex—these constitute the principal subject matter of psycho-analysis and the foundations of its theory. No one who cannot accept them *all* should count himself a psycho-analyst" (Freud's emphasis, qtd. in Lerman 166).

Cardinal's analysis quickly comes to focus on childhood repression, and on two occasions she regains access to previously unconscious material (182–86, 246–49). The literalness of the repetition provoked by this "return of the repressed" fully corresponds to freudian theory; for example, Cardinal endures a painful dislocation of time and identity during her regression to the stage of a fifteen-month–old child: "I was four, I was thirty-four. . . . I was no longer any age, I was no longer a person. . . . A terrible headache, an intense pain at the base of the skull. . . . My head is bursting! It's toppling, it's toppling. . . . I'm a baby, a tiny little girl barely able to walk" (182–83). In the supportive context of analysis, however, Cardinal characteristically learns that what the infantile ego must repress to assure its survival retains little emotional force in the consciousness of an adult (Freud, *Gen. Introd.*).

Much of the material that proves to be of greatest significance in Cardinal's analysis deals directly or indirectly with issues of sexuality. For example, the first memory whose repetition and reinterpretation result in important analytic progress centers on the recognition and the acceptance of childhood masturbation. Moreover, although Cardinal herself never specifically relates this experience to freudian theoretical models, her memory of urinating through a paper tube in explicit imitation of boys clearly invites reference to concepts of penis envy or a castration complex. These same issues appear to resurface in the adult nightmare of the phallic serpent whose resolution leads to the termination of Cardinal's analysis (313). Other episodes focus more broadly on corporeal functions, notably on what freudian theory might well regard as an obsession with excrement (see chap. 2).

Cardinal's analysis can also be read in terms of a fairly traditional freudian family romance. We might, for example, interpret her father-absent childhood as responsible for an unresolved oedipal crisis that can finally be brought to a successful completion by virtue of its repetition in the analyst-analysand relationship. The absence of paternal intervention would explain the unhealthy symbiosis of the mother-child dyad and the obsessive attachment to the mother from which Cardinal cannot fully free herself until the latter's death. Clearly, the mother imposes her own sexual repression on the daughter so that Cardinal is only able to achieve a "normal" genital expression of feminine sexuality—"Now I was discovering my vagina" (307)—once she recovers the memory of childhood masturbation whose repression coincided with that of her masculinity (see Lerman 110–11). Although the mother's relentless efforts to indoctrinate her daughter into socially normative femininity appear to result in the tyranny rather than in the deficiency of Cardinal's superego, the fact that her mental breakdown is directly and specifically related to the problematic constitution of the superego nonetheless remains entirely consistent with Freud's theories of female psychological development (Lerman 110).

To some extent, reading *Les Mots pour le dire* within the boundaries of classical freudian psychoanalysis already situates Cardinal rather ambivalently within the contexts of Anglophone and Francophone feminism. If, for example, her insistence on therapy over theory coincides with a characteristically American transformation of freudianism into a specialized medical practice (Turkle), she also attributes a very limited and distinctly noninterventionist role to her analyst, which strongly conflicts with the belief of Anglophone feminists that psychoanalysis actively seeks the patient's adaptation to societal norms. On the other hand, Cardinal's central focus on individual psychology and her belief in the possibility of a therapeutic cure also place her in fundamental contradiction with Francophone feminists who seek to reemphasize the radical undermining of the self and the individual that they consider inherent in freudian theory of the unconscious and the libido.

Feminist Subversion(s) and Revision(s)

In any event, an interpretation of Cardinal's analysis as traditionally freudian cannot withstand any but the most superficial of overviews; here, as elsewhere, her dialectic of conformity and subversion functions to challenge the most basic assumptions of the ideology that she initially appears to respect. Metaphorically, Cardinal returns to the beginnings of freudian thought to rewrite its evolution differently or, rather, to rediscover and reclaim the originary female story on which the subsequent his-story of psychoanalysis has been written. Female madness, feminism, and psychoanalysis have always intersected, since Freud developed his theory and practice on the basis of clinical experience with hysterical women (this last phrase is, of course, redundant; hysteria's own linguistic origins predefine it as a female disease) (Bernheimer 15–29). Moreover, credit for the invention of both the "talking cure" as a whole and for the method of free association that provides its principal directive rightfully belong to two female patients, Anna O. (Bertha Pappenheim) and Elizabeth von R. (Hunter 88–89), the first of whom went on to transform her hysteria into feminist activism, a pattern that Lucien Israël views as paradigmatic (Hunter 113).

Cardinal's repeated assertions that Les Mots pour le dire is a novel about female life explicitly reclaim both gender and genre in the face of an obstinate critical determination to reduce the book to "a psychoanalytic document": "personally, I had absolutely no desire to talk about psychoanalysis, . . . I hadn't written a book about psychoanalysis. I had written the story of a woman in which psychoanalysis is very important, even crucial. In my mind, that was my book: one moment in a woman's life, a novel" (AD 27). The reviewers' almost desperate insistence on openly denying the fictional status of Les Mots pour le dire (that is, when they are not ignoring it) identifies what appears to be a simple clarification—one, moreover, that critics might have used to dismiss Cardinal's work as "only a novel"—as somehow profoundly threatening. The novel form presumably subverts the effort of psychoanalysis to present its discourse as one of scientific knowledge that speaks "the truth"—about women in particular. In Cardinal's revision, a woman now reveals "the fiction" of psychoanalysis, as a further reversal of traditional priorities subordinates psychoanalysis (in which women have always been subordinate) to women in its turn. In one sense, then, Cardinal simply recalls and confirms Freud's own troubled suspicion that his case studies read a great deal like novels (Bernheimer 10).

But Cardinal's self-definition as novelist also grants her a narrative authority and a linguistic control whose intradiegetic repetition results in her narrator's usurpation of the analyst's role. As Lacan has reminded us, psychoanalysis presents itself above all else as the theory and the practice of language. Therapy depends on the establishment of a dialogue and on the gradual construction of meaning through the development of a lexicon of significant words. Not suprisingly, then, it is predominantly our general familiarity with a particular terminology (freudian slip, oedipal complex, id, ego, superego, the unconscious, penis envy, castration complex)—a familiarity, moreover, that derives much more clearly from the ability to recognize words than to define concepts—that marks psychoanalysis's infiltration of popular culture. Given such an absolute fusion between thought and language, Nancy Chodorow's retention of freudian terminology seriously undermines her claim that *The Reproduction of Mothering* represents a feminist revision of freudian psychoanalysis.[4] On the other hand, Roy Schafer's repeated insistence in *A New Language for Psychoanalysis* that his development of a new vocabulary calls into question only language and not the essential findings of psychoanalysis itself represents an understandable (if unconvincing) rhetorical precaution, for as Schafer also notes, "to stop using Freud's theoretical language is to alter radically our relations with this most intricate, intimate, pervasive, and consequential set of mental categories" (6).

Cardinal repeats Schafer's revolutionary act, though the subversion is far greater since she is neither male nor a doctor.[5] If the analyst initially instructs the narrator of *Les Mots pour le dire* to invent a new psychoanalytic vocabulary of her own ("find equivalents for the terms of analytic vocabulary"), a directive that is specifically motivated by the need to think differently ("try to ignore what you know about psychoanalysis" [37]), his directive actually serves to predefine her as a knowledgeable authority on traditional freudian thought. The narrator's concomitant confirmation and rejection of her own expertise thus serves from the very beginning of the novel to discredit traditional analytic theory—including, notably, the significance of the unconscious, of sexual dysfunctioning, and of the absent father that we know play a central role in any effort to interpret *Les Mots pour le dire* as a classical freudian analysis: "I believed that what I had learned about psychology and especially about psychoanalysis at the university, my two years of the physiology of the nervous system (at the psycho-technical institute), allowed me to define myself, situate myself, understand myself. . . . I knew that my mother had always unconsciously blamed me for being born. (My birth took place, in fact, in the middle of a divorce.) I knew that because of this my father was a total stranger. I knew that their conflict had created complications in me that affected my sexuality" (57).

The narrator actually uses freudian terminology only on the single occasion, noted above, where it serves to express her anger at her analyst. Thus, she identifies this language as specifically male, redefines it as a vocabulary of insult, and associates it with a rigidly authoritarian theory and practice that of necessity transforms her doctor into "Freud's Punchinello" (194). Critics such as Marilyn Yalom, who insist on reintroducing into their discussions of *Les Mots pour le dire* the freudian lexicon that is so conspicuously absent from the novel not only betray Cardinal's intentions but no doubt seriously limit their own understanding of her work as a result.

The female analysand does indeed develop a vocabulary of her own that the analytic process allows her to impose as the common language of communication; metaphorically, she not only usurps men's linguistic primacy but she substitutes women's common vernacular for their abstract discourse of science. Moreover, even if the analytic cure always depends on the recovery of the power of speech, on the reclaiming of the right to self-expression, Cardinal here redefines that process as female specific and foreign to the therapeutic process. Not speech but writing, not autobiography but fiction, finally allow the narrator of *Les Mots pour le dire* first to limit and then to leave analysis. As we know, she begins to write without consulting her analyst (to whom she otherwise relates everything), and there is no indication that she ever informs him that she has become a writer.[6] This situation is at interesting variance with two equally common alternative patterns in women's fiction in which the doctor either proscribes (Charlotte Perkins Gilman's *Yellow Wallpaper*) or prescribes (Simone de Beauvoir's *Femme rompue*) female writing; the silence of Cardinal's narrator may result precisely from her unwillingness to risk either form of male co-optation.

Cardinal's rigorous association of the analytic situation and the writing process emphasizes the substitution that has taken place. She writes on a regular basis, at specific and predetermined times; and the joy that accompanies each session with her notebooks—"the same joy as if they had been a brand-new handsome lover" (254)—describes the new transference that has taken place onto the text.[7] When she finally seeks her first reader, both her position—"stretched out on her back, with her eyes closed, like at her doctor's" (263)—and her choice of Jean-Pierre—"he who *analyzed* the texts he read so intelligently" (267, my emphasis)—clearly equates the psychoanalytic and the textual analyst. But what the narrator momentarily fears is the definitive sign of her "madness" (267)—the act of writing now appears to indicate that her analysis "has gone to her head" (265) and she reflects for the first and only time that she should have discussed it with her doctor (267)—becomes in fact the proof of her cure. Jean-Pierre, who has long treated her as "someone sick" (267), now confirms her healthy new identity as a writer (268).

Cardinal's critique of traditional psychoanalysis explicitly focuses our attention on the importance of gender in understanding a therapeutic interaction that has historically represented in microcosmic form the relationship between men and women in general. A hierarchical and dualistic confrontation traditionally opposes the analyst's male realm of science, authority, health, order, and reason to the analysand's female realm of ignorance, illness, disorder, emotion, self-obsession, and lack of conscious control. In this context, the very fact of novelization transforms the male doctor—whose comparative silence in therapy itself has always been radically overcompensated by his right to publish, to reclaim publicly his narrative control over the female patient's life—into a character in a woman's story. Cardinal's decision not to quote her analyst's words in *Les Mots pour le dire* (except for occasional isolated phrases) no doubt accurately represents, at least in quantitative terms, their respective verbal contributions to the analysis itself; but within the context of fiction, the absence of a voice identifies his role as decidedly secondary. Moreover, the narrator's descriptions of her doctor are not precisely flattering. In particular, the consistent repetition of the adjective *petit* (little, short) serves as a visual metaphor for his literal and his metaphorical subordination to the woman; a far from complete list includes the following examples: "the little dark-haired man" (8); "the little man" (119); "his pretty little suit" (120); "the little doctor" (173, 187, 189, 193, 198); "this mute little puppet" (179); "I was tall, taller than the doctor" (185); "confounded little fellow" (343).

In an interestingly parallel situation to that of Cardinal, Philippe Lejeune has expressed the shock that he experienced upon discovering that a fabrication lies at the heart of Serge Doubrovsky's *Fils* (1977). Lejeune had determinedly read the novel as an account of the writer's own analysis, on the (clearly questionable) grounds that the credibility of the story and the apparent identification of character and author far outweigh the improbabilities of the narrative situation and the highly visible exploration of techniques borrowed from experimental fiction (*Moi* 62). Lejeune only abandons his autobiographical illusion when confronted with Doubrovsky's revelation in a subsequent essay that despite the factual reality in *Fils* of the central dream, he had never reported this particular dream to his analyst nor had the specific problems that it raised ever played more than a secondary role in the actual therapeutic situation ("Initiative" 113). Lejeune interprets this subversion of the truth as the analysand's clear usurpation of the analyst's role and authority: "If the dreams are 'true,' their insertion into the analysis is 'false' and the role of the analyst in their exploitation is invented. Doubrovsky therefore took the place of his analyst in order to continue . . . his analysis on his own" (*Moi* 67).

If such discrepancy between fact and fiction does indeed imply "the murder of the analyst" (*Moi* 67), then Cardinal's own successful assassination attempt predates that of Doubrovsky by several years. In *Autrement dit*—a text whose relationship to *Les Mots pour le dire* also provides a preexistent model for Doubrovsky's decision to write his own textual commentary on *Fils*—Cardinal uses precisely the same kind of revelation to reaffirm the fictional nature of her own psychoanalysis; I quote the passage at some length since we will need to refer to it shortly in a second context as well:

> I looked at this story as a writer, not as a witness. Consequently some parts of my analysis have disappeared and others have been expanded. For example, I didn't write a single word about the beatings my mother used to inflict on me at the drop of a hat. Yet they were often the topic of my analytic sessions since I'm afraid

of blows even today. . . . The subject was important then, but as a writer, it bored me to tears. . . . On the other hand, the story of my mother's confession of her failed abortion attempt didn't play much of a role in my analysis. Since I had a very clear memory of the incident and had already drawn every possible conclusion before entering therapy, I didn't need to delve into it much with the doctor. But it grew incredibly as I wrote about it; it took on a tremendous role. (27–28)

Cardinal does not simply take the place of her analyst at a particular point and continue an analysis begun by him; from the very beginning, she totally suppresses his major contribution and restructures the therapeutic experience as a whole around her own analysis. Moreover, since the latter has already taken place when she enters therapy, the analyst does not even serve as example for a procedure or technique that the analysand subsequently adopts; on the contrary, the model for this fictional cure, which reviewers find so convincing that they insist on its factual reality, has been provided by a woman—and a sick one at that.

The unwillingness to acknowledge that the father/analyst has been killed and his position usurped, when the murder (now an originary act) has been carried out by the daughter rather than the son, can hardly be interpreted as innocent. Both Lejeune's and Doubrovsky's commentaries on *Fils* make specific reference to Cardinal's *Mots pour le dire*, introduced as a *contrasting* example.[8] The assumption that women repeat (men, in this case)—Cardinal is once again presumed to relate her analysis in the most "classical" of fashions (Lejeune, *Moi* 62; cf. Doubrovsky 97)—apparently frees men from any obligation to read what women (but not what other men) have to say about their own texts. Yet, if the willingness to make the effort in one case but not in the other cannot be ignored, an extra effort is not really even necessary in the case of the woman. Doubrovsky's novel remains, in the absence of its metacommentary, a sort of narcissistic private joke; as Lejeune notes, "all the voluptuousness" of the murder is reserved for Doubrovsky alone, since readers cannot possibly discover it without the author's extradiegetic assistance (67). Cardinal, however, respects the integrity of her text and her responsibility to her readers by clearly announcing the general fact of fabrication, if not its specific focus, within *Les Mots pour le dire:* "I promised myself that one day I would write the story of my analysis; I would turn it into a novel" (293).

As the female usurps the traditional functions of the male, a parallel gender reversal feminizes the doctor's position. Before we even enter the text, the very fact of the dedication predefines the analyst out of the male task of writing and into the female role of muse. (The etymology of the term from the Greek *Mousa,* muse, of unknown origin, so closely resembles the name Moussia—Cardinal's nickname and one of her favorite diegetic pseudonyms—that one almost suspects the doctor is announced [denounced?] as Cardinal's textual double at the very instant of his apparition.) The particular form of the dedication—"To the doctor who helped me to be born"—further emphasizes the analyst's repeated relegation to various incarnations of the female assistant, of which the midwife is merely the most frequent and the most clearly gender specific. In general, the male acts in the female role of the good listener; his only active verbal function consists of asking the leading question that allows the woman patient to continue to dominate the narrative and to maintain the illusion of a dialogue.

In only one important way does the doctor resist gender transformation and retain a traditionally male attitude. Despite the narrator's deliberate and repeated attempts to transform the analytic situation into an authentic conversation, the analyst refuses to engage in any interactive exchange. Yet, such efforts specifically take place outside the boundaries of therapy itself, at times when the narrator addresses the doctor not as a patient but as a fellow human being. For example, when the narrator encourages the doctor to get rid of the horrible gargoyle that decorates his office—"It was the first time I had addressed him other than as a patient"—he steadfastly maintains his silence: "He made no response" (129–30; cf. 307, 343). This failure of communication most clearly identifies the traditional analytic situation, even one altered by the reversal of roles and the reattribution of authority, as fundamentally nonfeminist. If Cardinal reclaims both language and the right to self-expression in *Les Mots pour le dire, Autrement dit* suggests that there may be another and better way for women to achieve the same result. As the interplay of the two titles suggests, the second work is conceived less as a sequel to the first than as its repetition: an opportunity to say the same thing differently.

The juxtaposition of the parallel descriptions with which each of the two texts opens immediately reveals both the return to the same place and the difference that it makes:

> The little dead-end street [*La ruelle en impasse*] was *badly paved,*
> full of holes and bumps, bordered by narrow sidewalks in ruins.
> It plunged like a chapped finger between one or two-story private
> houses, *squeezed up against each other.* At the end, it bumped
> into two gates invaded by some petty greenery. (MD 7, my
> emphasis)

> Annie Leclerc lives in *a passageway* [*un passage*] in the XIIIth
> arrondissement of Paris. *A passageway paved any old way,* with
> houses intimately *squeezed up against each other* on one
> side. . . . In *this little street* that slowly climbs . . . Annie's house
> is double; the façade hides another building just like it. Between
> the two lie a courtyard on the ground floor and a footbridge [*une
> passerelle*] on the first floor. (AD 8, my emphasis)

Inside, in Annie's office, Cardinal's immediate claim to "an old sofa"
leads to an explicit announcement of the comparison that is already
implicit in the description itself: "because of the little street, the sofa,
and the spoken word—especially the spoken word—these times could
have been psychoanalytic sessions" (9).

But whereas the context in which the initial psychoanalysis takes
place identifies it from the beginning as an *impasse,* we are told no fewer
than three times that the second experience resituates itself in and as a
passage (if *passerelle* simply signifies "footbridge," the rich play of the
signifier—*passer + elle*—names the female specificity of transitional
movement). Although the individual, restored to emotional health, can
retrace her steps after analysis (the final description in *Les Mots pour le
dire* reverses the direction of the first to transform the dead end into an
exit [343]), traditional analysis nonetheless proves to be an impasse for
the woman who seeks to understand her femaleness and the female condition in general, in large part precisely because of the impass(e)iveness
of the analytic interlocutor. The passage, on the other hand, that connects the two women in *Autrement dit* not only allows for free and continuous movement but also identifies the procedure—the *exchange* of
words *between* two persons—that leads to such progression. This
doubleness of meaning, further emphasized by Annie's "double" house,
supports a reconceptualization of psychoanalysis as a dialogue between
female doubles. Hannah Lerman defines feminist therapeutic interac-

tion in similar terms as one in which the therapist maintains an egalitarian stance toward the woman patient rather than the authoritarian stance of the expert (179).[9]

Cardinal's and Leclerc's voices are both clearly present; in fact, significant portions of *Autrement dit,* representing the integral transcription of the two women's recorded conversations, retain the textual structure of direct discourse. Moreover, the text deliberately transforms what might have been an interview into a dialogue as Cardinal and Leclerc alternatively question each other about their lives and their work. In retrospect, the specific nature of *Les Mots pour le dire* as a written text exposes the absence of dialogue that characterizes the relationship between the fictional narrator and her silent analyst. In direct contrast, the privileged position that *Autrement dit* accords to "spoken pages" honors those qualities of speech that distinguish it from writing, of which the most important is precisely the dynamic mobility that eliminates the threat of textual impasse: "The spoken word is fluidity, a passageway, a current" (6). But *passage* has yet a fourth meaning that *Autrement dit* also respects by including textual segments that Cardinal has written. Indeed, the equality of the female interaction is such that Leclerc will also contribute a written passage; she will, in fact, have the last word.

In an explicit reminder that this female friendship originated in the metaphorical re-presentation of the relationship between analysand and analyst, Leclerc recalls an anecdote that Cardinal told to illustrate "madness, alienation (you use these terms interchangeably), to explain them to me who always seemed so distant from them." Leclerc's instantaneous recognition of herself in Cardinal's "ravaged face, the faraway gaze shattered by distress" (220) immediately and definitively erases the "alienation" between the "mad" and the "sane" whose retention in the distance and the hierarchy that characterize the traditional analytic relationship inevitably leads to a therapeutical impasse:

> In the course of the analysis, the analyst remains behind the patient, doesn't he. . . . Why behind? Who is this man who must not, who cannot, see the other? The analyst will hear every word of what can be said, but that face, that gaze, when in the absolute nakedness of nightmare the voice is mute, the sound cut off, the body broken, ruined, crushed; that gaze, that gaze alone, he will never see. . . .

Your face, your gaze, you surrendered them to me full-face, but already they were no longer yours: it was us, there where we had been together, there where we are together, all of us more or less, and those of us who are little girls, young women, women more than the others. (221)

From another perspective, the specular relations between analyst and analysand offer an entirely accurate metaphor of those between men and women. The analyst can in fact *see* the woman, and the invisibility of her face merely represents the objectifying and voyeuristic nature of his gaze; he looks at a female body, not at an individual woman. The woman, on the other hand, is metaphorically blinded; the man who deliberately positions himself outside her visual range denies her the right to claim subjectivity for herself, to reverse the subject-object relations of the visual act. In *Les Mots pour le dire* (as in many other accounts of madness by women), the narrator's initial symptoms include near blindness; such visual disorders clearly represent problems with selfhood—the "eye" weakens as the "I" disintegrates. Two passages that specifically address the issues of gender and vision should serve to remove any remaining illusions that Cardinal offers an unambivalently (or even an essentially) positive portrayal of the male/analyst.

The first example establishes a connection between the analyst and the narrator's father that functions simultaneously to justify my interpretation of the doctor as the general representative of specifically male behavior and attitudes and to challenge both the fact of the analytic transference and the assumption that it reenacts the relationship with the father. The identification of the analyst's role—and therefore of the transferential repetition—as paternal has been traditional since Freud and informs such conventional readings of *Les Mots pour le dire* as that of Yalom (65).[10] In point of fact, the two moments at which the narrator establishes a specific parallel between her doctor and her father constitute the only two textual examples of openly negative transference and thus of rejection of the analytic procedure in general.

In the first case, the narrator finally tells her analyst about the hallucination that frequently torments her: a tube attaches itself to her right eye through which another eye, positioned at the opposite end of the tube, stares at her intently, with "a cold severity with nuances of scorn and indifference" (178). When the doctor asks her what the word *tube* makes her think of, in order to induce an associative process that will eventually uncover the unconscious memory that lies behind the hallu-cination, she initially explodes in anger: "This little puppet exasperated me with his impassivity and his knowing tranquillity" (179). The most curious cluster of lexical associations clearly precedes that which actu-ally allows the return of the repressed: impassivity, impasse, cul-de-sac, tube. The impasse, resulting from male impassiveness, leads, via the synonym with which Cardinal often replaces it—*cul-de-sac* names both a dead end and a tube open only at one end—to the hallucinatory eye that, like the analyst's gaze, simultaneously denies the woman the sub-jectivity of her own vision and defines her as the object of the male gaze. Moreover, the hallucination masks a little girl's memory of her rage at the discovery that her father is filming her from behind (the analyst's position, of course) as she urinates. The association of the eye of the father with that of the camera elevates the voyeuristic male gaze that violates the female body to the stature of a cultural phenomenon.[11]

Laura Mulvey notes that in a world in which visual pleasure and power have been split between active/male and passive/female, "women are simultaneously looked at and displayed, with their appearance coded for strong visual and erotic impact so that they can be said to connote *to-be-looked-at-ness*" (11). This association informs and illu-minates the episode that immediately follows the memory of the impas-sive male camera, whose power imposes (im)passivity on the rebellious female object as well, for the narrator's father shames her into silence by redefining her appropriate madness ("formidable anger and rage") as an aberrant madness ("Insane, insane, insane") (184).

Although the narrator professes her gratitude to the analyst for freeing her from the terrorism of the paternal eye, the curiously ambiv-alent form that her adulation takes undermines this superficial meaning; the doctor in fact reenacts the father's public exposure of the female body. Cardinal portrays the analyst, complete with spangled top hat and whip, as the sideshow impresario of a "fantastic parade" who sum-mons the general public to contemplate the "spectacle" of the female body: "Come closer, closer! Spread her legs apart. . . . Beautiful! Beau-tiful enough to take your breath away! Beautiful enough for *Playboy* and for *Dim* stocking ads. . . . The doctor would have lifted his whip, its gentle braided laniard would have licked my loins, and forward! . . . Hop! Hop! A pirouette here, a somersault there! And once again hop! hop! jeté battu, pas de chat, chassé-croisé, pirouette. And on with it. Ass on top!" (187–89). This description, whose ironic self-deprecation recalls the very similar portrayal of the female striptease and circus freak in Sylvia Plath's "Lady Lazarus," indirectly reveals Cardinal's very clear understanding that the power of the male gaze to reduce women to a dehumanized, fragmented spectacle informs popular culture as a whole.

Feminist Analysis and Female Stories

During the preliminary conversation with the doctor that precedes the beginning of the analysis as such, the narrator of *Les Mots pour le dire* describes her illness in terms that illustrate the extraordinary resemblance between madness and socially approved female behavior that Phyllis Chesler has studied at length. The first doctors consulted attribute the narrator's initial attacks of anxiety to her biological femaleness and immediately propose the standard societal solution to the presumed problems of female sexuality. When marriage proves an aggravation rather than a cure, gynecologists then propose to alter the normal functioning of her sexuality by surgical intervention; one specialist encourages her to "get rid of" her uterus as quickly as possible (MD 14). Her alternative choice of hospitalization in her uncle's private clinic leads to her virtual imprisonment in a room on the top floor; excessive medication aims to restore this literal "madwoman in the attic" to the passive obedience that simulates conventional femininity. The narrator's primary symptom of severe agoraphobia emphasizes the traditional restriction of all women to the private and domestic sphere; she increasingly spends the better part of her time huddled up next to or on the very female bidet. Her family alternatively treats her as a capricious child and an insensitive shrew who deliberately seeks their dishonor and inconvenience; and indeed the narrator accepts total responsibility for her illness, attributing it to personal inadequacy, her "bad nature," and the very female flaw of "ugliness" (47).

More importantly, however, Cardinal explicitly identifies the analysis as well as the illness as female. This gender-specific narrative, written in *les mots pour* la *dire,* can be expected to operate subversively almost by definition. Lerman dismisses freudian psychoanalysis as "not clinically useful for women" because of Freud's originary failure to deal significantly with central women's issues such as menstruation, childbirth, female sexuality, or mothering (180). In a more recent example, Elaine Showalter notes that a comparison of Mary Barnes's and J. Berke's parallel accounts of her illness and treatment highlight the blindness of the male psychiatrist to the explicit sex-role issues that are raised in the female patient's narrative (*Female Malady* 232). Within the revisionary framework proposed by Lerman, the therapeutic interaction in *Les Mots pour le dire* not only fails to meet feminist criteria (by virtue, for example, of the doctor's nonegalitarian authoritarian stance), but non-sexist ones as well, dependent upon "the therapist listening to and validating the woman's experience and having knowledge about the psychology of women" (179).

In Cardinal's novel, the therapeutic process in its entirety follows directly from the analyst's original rejection of specifically female experience. Initially, the narrator insistently talks about the constant vaginal bleeding that makes menstruation, raised to near-mythic proportions in order to emphasize female specificity, the defining experience of her life. In her preferred narrative structure, the endless flow of blood allows her to relate her own life as the collective story of women: "I liked to make it the center and the cause of my illness. . . . What woman would not be panic-stricken to see her sap flow like that?" (10). Her agoraphobia and her alienation from others stem directly from the unacceptable stains that she leaves everywhere that she goes; metaphorically, the narrator's illness results from a gynephobic society that defines the sign of the woman's presence as repellent. The doctor reenacts precisely the same rejection; his expression of personal (i.e., male) indifference immediately imposes silence on female reality: "That doesn't interest me. Talk to me about something else" (42).

In direct contrast, the reaction of Annie Leclerc demonstrates that the female analyst/reader fully understands the primacy of this story of women that the male would relegate to an insignificant digression: "What struck me first in *Les Mots pour le dire* is the blood. Blood, blood, blood... I was right to be struck by that because that's what struck you too. You evoke your childhood, your life as a woman, your life after analysis, and I learn a great deal about blood, blood that is a woman's blood" (AD 26). In *Autrement dit*, women's bleeding, identified as a source of female commonality and community and as an explicit metaphor for women's writing, reclaims narrative centrality. Even so, Leclerc has only one objection: "You haven't talked about the blood enough" (122).

By the time the narrator of *Les Mots pour le dire* next dares to speak openly of female experience, she has learned to reverse the terms. The dichotomy between therapy and femaleness remains in place, but it now leads the woman to reject psychoanalysis rather than her own story: "for the first time, this discovery left me perplexed. I felt it was foreign to psychoanalytic therapy. . . . I would have to leave" (307). But, in fact, *rape*—the gender-specific reality whose significance appears to be foreign to the analytic process—precisely identifies the damage that the therapist ([the]rapist) inflicts by denying the significance of female experience. Indeed, Cardinal's richly subversive narrative names freudian analysis as the rape of women in the opening paragraph of *Les Mots pour le dire*. The description of "the dead-end street" that "plunged like a finger" (7) already repeats the memory of the narrator's childhood rape—"the intense fear of this finger that groped about in me" (300)—whose subsequent return in the form of a dream leads the narrator out of the analytic impasse.

The rape metaphor explicitly equates freudian therapy with the gynecological interventions of the narrator's previous medical treatments as well; there too she lies with her eyes closed, the blind object of the scientific male gaze (of the speculum): "while expert searches, indiscrete explorations, learned fondling were carried out at the very center of my self. *Raped*" (13, my emphasis). Similarly, the association established between the father and the analyst, between male voyeurism and the camera, whose metaphorical status as not only the eye but the penis and the gun dates from Freud himself, repeats once again the threat of sexual violence that defines women's particular situation in a paternalistic society.

Significantly, the passage in *Autrement dit* that immediately follows Leclerc's protestation that Cardinal "hasn't talked about blood enough" reintroduces the narrative of rape. The reappearance, after the sexual assault, of her former symptoms of madness leads Cardinal to question the reality of her psychoanalytic "cure."[12] Because female neurosis returns as the direct consequence of traditional gender relations, Cardinal can now dismiss freudian analysis as an inadequate framework in which to understand the situation of women: "My fear wasn't diffuse as it had been at the time of my illness; it was entirely localized on the story of the man on all-fours above me" (133). Importantly, this time the woman organizes her own cure. Her "analysis" of the societal conditions that oppress women allows her to convert insanity back into anger, to reclaim a specifically and appropriately feminist "madness": "That was what had made me ill, had pierced my mind: the repression of revolt, the annulment of refusal, the ignoring of revulsion, the mockery of disgust, the invasion of territory, the scorning of integrity. Everything, in short, that leads men to declare war. Everything that we women endure, passive and ashamed, while war rumbles incredibly in us! . . . Rape is unbearable, rape is a crime, rape leads to madness!" (136).

The centrality that Cardinal "falsely" accords to abortion in *Les Mots pour le dire* confirms her intention to rewrite analysis as a female story and a female text. In substituting abortion for child abuse, Cardinal explicitly re-en-genders an otherwise potentially gender-free narrative: "I realized while writing this story that it was worth all the beatings in the world; it was even more powerful, it marked more clearly the rejection of the *little girl*" (AD 28, my emphasis). As we know, the switch from first to third person in Cardinal's work consistently identifies the transformation of the personal and the individual into the gender-specific and the common. Within the psychoanalytic framework of Cardinal's novel, one is tempted to read her insistence on abortion as an ironic commentary on Freud's original clinical contact with hysterical women. If the abortion attempt is largely responsible for her madness, as the narrator of *Les Mots pour le dire* suggests, then she is indeed hysterical (from Greek *husterikos,* suffering in the womb). In that case, the medical specialists who recommend hysterectomy appropriately repeat the Greek assumption that female neurosis originates in uterine disturbances.

The disinterest that the analyst initially expresses in the narrative of the female body inevitably blinds him to all subsequent manifestations of the female story. In essence, there are two kinds of unconsciousness at work in *Les Mots pour le dire.* Until the very end of the text, when the narrator arrives at "the consciousness of [her] female specificity" (311), she remains unaware of the central role that the fact of her femaleness and the societal condition of women play in her life, her identity, and her illness. In this context, the freudian unconscious acts only as a metaphor for the narrator's lack of a feminist consciousness; as in the paradigmatic case of Anna O., Cardinal reinterprets psychoanalysis as a specifically feminist methodology, a process of consciousness raising that leads to feminism.[13] This global subversion of freudianism constantly repeats itself, since we too must learn to become conscious of the specifically female narrative—the story of the mother—that underlies key analytic moments.

Feminist discussion of *Les Mots pour le dire* has tended to react to the daughter's apparent hostility to the mother with hostility of its own in the face of what is seen as a nonfeminist portrayal of women's most significant relationship. In a specifically psychoanalytic framework, Yalom wonders "to what extent [the] essentially phallocratic nature" of the freudian transference "may have stimulated the patient's antipathy for her mother" (52). It seems rather that Yalom's own insistence on decoding Cardinal's novel within a "classic Freudian" framework falsifies her understanding of both sets of textual relationships: analyst-analysand and mother-daughter.[14] If Freud indeed almost always presented the analytic relationship in terms of the father (and the son) and adopted a patriarchal model of the superego, he did so, as Roy Schafer points out, only by the willful neglect of the maternal authority that the analysand *also* always defies. The fundamental problem, then, is one of narrative perspective; in Schafer's words: "Not ever looking at things in more than one way is easily the most powerful resistance of all" (258). The editors of *The (M)other Tongue* establish a similar link between psychoanalytic and narrative theory in terms that are particularly useful for (re)reading *Les Mots pour le dire:* "It is possible, and perhaps inevitable, that mother-based and father-based stories coexist in the same narrative (as they do in Freud's theories), the emphasis shifting as one co-opts or is set in opposition to the other" (9–10).

Simply by changing her narrative framework, Cardinal already significantly alters the "patriarchal model of the superego." Whatever transference takes place in *Les Mots pour le dire* clearly operates through the identification of the mother and the analyst, as Cardinal's summary of the process explicitly announces: "I brought him my discoveries with gratitude. Just as in the past I used to bring my mother pebbles, hoping that in her hands they would turn into jewels. My mother rejected my imaginary treasures, whereas the doctor listened to my stories, without reacting but with great attentiveness, thus helping me to come to my own understanding of the exact worth of my reports" (189–90). Early in the initial analytic session, moreover, the narrator describes herself as "a satisfied child in her cradle" who, in the presence of the doctor, feels "protected by her mother's gaze" (42–43); significantly, this is the moment at which tears, an equally female liquid of bonding, replace the narrator's symptomatic blood.

In keeping with the restructuring of psychoanalytic thought within both Francophone and Anglophone feminism, Cardinal also explicitly shifts the oedipal emphasis of traditional freudianism, whose repetition in any male-female transferential interaction necessarily remains implicit, to refocus on the preoedipal relationship between mother and daughter. Early in the analysis, the narrator talks extensively about her father precisely because of his insignificance: "to tell the truth, I risked nothing in talking about him" (118). Only the shift to the mother finally removes resistance and not only sets the analysis in motion but determines its subsequent direction: "I began to talk about my mother and I didn't stop until the end of the analysis" (86).

The central incident of *Les Mots pour le dire* and of the mother-daughter relationship, the narrative of the attempted abortion, encodes within itself two key moments of specifically female bonding. In the first place, however painful and shocking the context (and perhaps precisely because it is both), the failure of the actual abortion attempt confirms with particular clarity the inherent symbiotic fusion of mother and daughter; in the mother's words: "when a child has grabbed hold, there's nothing you can do to uncouple it" (165). The mother logically shifts, almost immediately and without transition, from the memory of her failed abortion to that of the birth, a "charming memory" (166) that initiates a rare attempt on her part to embrace her daughter.

Moreover, the mother's narrative repetition of the abortion attempt takes place in a context of female specificity that establishes female community. Although the narrator overtly situates her mother's explanation of menstruation and female reproductive capacities within the framework of "an initiation session" into her "caste" (142), what in fact shocks the narrator—and so identifies the real story in question—is to hear her mother profess a solidarity with other women that precisely and appropriately extends beyond the class boundaries she otherwise upholds so rigidly. Her female "we" explicitly seeks to embrace a friend of her daughter whom she has just dismissed as an unsuitable companion: "'we don't much like to talk about it.' This 'we' that linked them, Huguette Meunier and my mother, it was unthinkable!" (141). The narrator immediately confirms her correct reading of the message that her mother conveys by abruptly asking "the idiotic question"—do Muslim women also menstruate?—that forces her mother to reemphasize the strength of the bonds of gender by announcing their priority over those of culture as well as of class (143). As a result, the commonality of women is established in direct opposition to the heterosexual community that forbids intercultural relationships between men and women.

In noting the key importance of narrative to life, literature, and psychoanalysis, the editors of *The (M)other Tongue* emphasize the difference of feminist models: "The stories we tell ourselves about who we are or hope to be play a primary role in creating and sustaining our identities. . . . It makes a difference, we maintain, where one stands as reader as well as writer, and whether one constructs or responds to a mother-based or father-based fiction. On the whole, oedipally organized narrative (as well as interpretation) that is based on the determining role of the father and of patriarchal discourse tells a different story from preoedipal narrative, which locates the source of movement and conflict in the figure of the mother" (9–10). Appropriately, Cardinal's change in parental viewpoint alters not only the content of the stories that she tells but also the forms in which they are told. Once the narrator of *Les Mots pour le dire* emerges from the weeks of silence into which her attempt to construct a father-based fiction leads her, her emphasis on psychoanalytic interaction (the constant reminders of the doctor's presence, if not of his words) gives way to a sustained narrative reconstruction of the story of mother and daughter that reproduces *within* the analytic text the simultaneous reinvention of an identity as woman and as writer that will finally allow the narrator to leave analysis. Sandra Gilbert and Carol Gilligan, from within their respective contexts of female writing and women's psychology, have identified narrativity itself, a commitment to a continuous story line, as one trait that appears to distinguish the thought patterns of women from those of men (see chap. 3).

In this microcosmic narrative of female reality (internally identified by the inclusion within the series of episodes of one of Cardinal's signature passages of autocitation), she transforms psychoanalysis from a way into patriarchy into a way out of it. In the first "chapter" (212–17) of this story, the mother imitates the cry of the ragman by whom the daughter is terrorized, in an attempt to force her to eat a soup that she despises. The mother thus enacts in a particularly cruel fashion the traditional maternal responsibility for initiating daughters into obedience and proper social behavior. At the same time, however, her male impersonation indirectly exposes the androcentric power structure that underlies and actually determines female behavior; in psychoanalytic terms, the paternal superego substitutes forced feeding for preoedipal nourishing.

The mother's "theft" of the male voice also points to a woman's ability to reclaim language and to write her own story into the dominant culture that becomes the explicit focus of the second episode (217–21). Cardinal now constructs the maternal model of the artist as the multi-voiced female narrator. In reading stories to her sick daughter, the mother uses her talent as a ventriloquist to claim female community; gender identity allows her transformation into a narrator from whom language, age, and social class otherwise separate her: "My mother lent her her voice. This transformation of my mother, as if she had put a whore's mask over her face, a poor woman's disguise on her body, gave birth in me to an extremely keen curiosity" (220).

In the third anecdote (221–29), the narrator reestablishes her characteristic internal pattern of repetition by offering two successive illustrations of her mother's fear of communists; within a general and overt narrative of class conflict, Cardinal once again embeds a key story of gender relations. In the first incident, the confrontation already opposes women and men; a crowd of male demonstrators defiantly faces the female community of mother, daughter, and nanny. A triple repetition situates the mother-daughter dyad at the center of female solidarity; not only does the narrator's nanny clearly function as a substitute mother, but the women escape from France, encoded as male, to return to the safety of Algeria, the motherland.

When the incident is repeated, however, not only the female country but the female home risks invasion. The generalized nature of the threat is encoded in the paradigmatic story of the sexual vulnerability of the female body. As the horrified daughter lies awake in bed in a barricaded household, her terror transforms a perfectly innocuous event into a metaphoric rape: "About fifty centimeters above my head, there was a deep, round hole in the wall whose purpose was unknown to me. Suddenly I thought that it would be unbearable if the *cock*chafer [the English is particularly appropriate here] dove into it. Yet that's just what happened eventually. I was paralyzed by fear, nailed to my bed, incapable of the slightest movement!" (228). As the young girl's screams bring the only male in the household to her rescue, her fear characteristically turns to "shame" (228). Here, the recontextualization of sexual vulnerability as a fact of gender—of social inequity, of unequal power relations—indirectly subverts the limited focus of traditional psychoanalysis on the biological and anatomical destiny of women.

The fourth episode (229–34) repeats the autocitational passage in which the narrator and her mother visit the tomb of the elder sister/

daughter who died in infancy. The permanent symbiosis of the mother-daughter dyad that takes place through death clarifies both Cardinal's feminist interpretation of the preoedipal relationship and the central narrative role that the abortion attempt plays in its articulation: "little by little, her dead baby had once again germinated within her and would live there forever. She would be pregnant with her until her death. At that time I imagined that they would be born together into infinity, cradling each other, floating, happy, frolicking in the Harmony. . . . They would laugh; they would fall asleep, satiated by the mutual and constant love they would give to each other" (233). The narrator's association of death with maternal love—"At those moments I would have liked to be the tombstone and, by extension, to be dead. Then perhaps she would love me as much" (234)—confirms her intuition (described in the second episode) that she momentarily replaces her dead sister as the object of maternal love during—and only during—periods of illness (219).

Through a tragic paradox, only in death can the mother retain her primary bond with the daughter and protect her from the threat of murder by the father. The mother thus attempts to abort her second daughter (and not, notably, the intervening son) to save both of them from her sister's fate, the metaphorical death with which life in androcentric society threatens female selfhood. In Cardinal's rewriting of freudian theory, Thanatos, the death wish that identifies an instinct to self-destruction in men, acknowledges women's desire for self-realization. At the same time, Cardinal implicitly alters our understanding of Eros, of the life instincts as well; for women, the heterosexual relationship is self-destructive rather than self-preservative and threatens love between mother and daughter in particular.

"The return of the Harmony" (238) that suddenly resurfaces in the tragic version of the mother-daughter relationship confirms its status as a metaphor of the preoedipal bond. In the concluding episode of the maternal narrative, the narrator recalls the luminous evenings on which her mother taught her to see and to name the constellations: "she put me in touch with the cosmos" (238). The mother's story of the celestial bodies, which bestows on the daughter the gifts of knowledge and narrative as well as those of sight and language, unfolds under conditions of close physical and emotional bonding that subsequently raise women's primary relationship to the stature of a feminist worldview: "Is it because of these moments that throughout my entire life up to the present my reflections have always led me to my condition: a particle of the universe? Is it because of the harmony of these long-ago nights that I only accept my existence to the degree that I experience it as cosmic? Is it because of the harmony that then existed between her and me that I am happy only when I feel I participate in a totality?" (239). Cardinal once again directly subverts traditional psychoanalytic thought; pre-oedipal narrative here substitutes a female story of continuity and collectivity, in which identity is constructed through and with others, for the conventional oedipal narrative of conflict, separation, and individualism. Moreover, the repeated linguistic return of the Harmony identifies the contexture of feminism as a "pleasing interaction of elements in a whole." The word itself joins (from the Latin *harmonia*, means of joining, from *harmos*, joint) emotions, sounds, and texts; and in this latter case, denotes a process—"the collation of parallel passages with a commentary demonstrating their consonance"—that names Cardinal's textual practice and my own.

From Freudianism to Feminism

Identity, psychoanalytic theory tells us, is intricately tied to our entry into the order of language. From a feminist perspective on psychoanalytic linguistics that reintroduces the issue of gender—that pays close attention to societal relationships between men and women as well as to the psychological interaction of male and female—Dianne Hunter stresses in this context the connection between the paternal role in the family and male dominance in general: "The interlocking of linguistic with cultural rules suggests an equation between the organization of language and the systematic organization of patriarchal culture and its sexually differentiated, oedipal subjectivity" (99). If the mother awakens the child's capacity for speech during a period of preoedipal union, only the resolution of the oedipal complex, the recognition of the father's role, leads to subjectivity, to both our psychological sense of ourselves as separate beings and to our linguistic sense of ourselves as grammatical "subjects" (Hunter 99).[15]

Identity, then, is closely tied to pronominal usage, to an understanding that "'I' and 'you' conceptualize and mark separate persons, as 'she' and 'he,' 'mother' and 'father' differentiate genders" (Hunter 99). In this context, we can expect that the emphasis that feminist psychoanalysis has placed on preoedipal symbiosis over oedipal autonomy in the formation of female identity will have visible linguistic consequences. Indeed, such a feminist disruption lies once again at the origins of psychoanalysis; in Bertha Poppenheim's simultaneous invention and subversion of the "talking cure," the linguistic discord that figures among her primary symptoms marks her regression from both the father and the cultural order of language (see Hunter 100). It seems particularly appropriate, however, that a revision of female identity formation should result, as in the case of Cardinal, in a different sense of the grammatical subject, that is, in a revised usage of pronouns.

Cardinal's celebration, cited above, of the mother-daughter bond as a harmonious understanding "between her and me" suggests that her characteristic alternation of first- and third-person pronouns may include a functioning particular to her rethinking of traditional freudian psychoanalysis. Through the narrative repetition of her mother's life, the narrator of *Les Mots pour le dire* comes to identify madness as the key factor in maternal/filial resemblance and heritage.[16] Initially, moreover, in yet another significant repetition of the beginnings of psychoanalysis, the original linguistic inscription of femaleness and insanity in the "hysteria" of the womb reproduce themselves in Cardinal's own language. In French, of course, grammatical gender immediately identifies *la folie* as a female subject, but Cardinal deliberately raises a (supposedly) arbitrary linguistic occurrence to the stature of a conscious textual strategy; she consistently prefers the literal female subject, *la folle,* to the abstract noun. In addition, she systematizes the interchangeable use of *la folle* and *la femme* to the point that *la folle* comes not just to represent a particular madwoman but to define the woman, all women, as mad.[17]

From the perspective of Hunter's psychoanalytic interpretation of pronouns and gender, Cardinal's juxtaposition of multiple voices disrupts traditional notions of separate persons and of gender differences. By recombining the usually oppositional pairs I-you and she-he into the new unit I-she, she defines femaleness not in contrast to maleness but rather in relation to individual personhood. Femaleness thus gains a *self*-definitional autonomy of its own. (Given current and traditional sociocultural values, femaleness can never escape subordinate status when it is paired with maleness, and the duality of the female-male unit inevitably signifies opposition, hierarchy, and dichotomous division).

Nonetheless, within the specific context of *Les Mots pour le dire,* the I-she combination initially appears to encode a painfully divided sense of identity, in keeping with traditional notions of madness as alienation from self and others. But, in fact, before analysis as such has actually begun, the narrator already redefines its stakes by rejecting the notion of insanity as an estrangement between the self and the objective world; for Cardinal, the duality of female madness does not designate either distance or an external relationship: "I had become certain of one thing: the madness was inside my mind; she wasn't elsewhere in my body and she wasn't outside it. I was alone with her. My entire life was only a story between her and me. Given that, my isolation took on new meaning: it might be a passageway, a moulting process. Perhaps I was going to live again? For I suffered a great deal from the alienation in which I had taken refuge. I was split apart, waiting for solutions from others which, when they were given to me, wounded me every time or distanced me still more" (47).

In one reading, this passage demonstrates that the "madwoman" has instinctively understood that it is the external world that defines women (and in which women are defined) as alienated, by virtue of the omnipresent and insidious power structures that distance women from a "human" norm that is actually based solely on the experience and the values of men. Women, then, as Francophone theorists point out, are foreigners (alienation, from Latin *alienus*, alien) within their own culture, Simone de Beauvoir's prototypical *other*. In this context, *isolation*, the *choice* to withdraw from society, appropriately redefines self-*generated* female alienation as a *self*-generating *refuge*, one that protects the woman from the necessarily harmful—because truly alienating—imposition of socially acceptable gender behavior. Because isolation reclaims and re-creates femaleness within the internal, that is, the autonomous, realm of the female self, gender specificity leads not to a stagnant and permanent distancing but to a dynamic and transformational process of female development—"a passageway, a moulting process," in Cardinal's characteristic imagery. The passage, as we know, identifies the mutual exchange between two women that leads us out of the impasse of the traditional male-female analytic interaction. Finally, Cardinal's insistence that gender and identity must be reconceptualized within the context of the female mind, as distinct from her body, challenges both the traditional emphasis of freudian psychoanalysis on the anatomical destiny of women and its original positioning of madness within the reproductive organs of the female body.

Cardinal's reorientation of freudian therapy illuminates traditional reactions to psychoanalysis that she includes *en abyme* within her own text: "I learned that one can only speak of analysis in order to describe its failure. I shocked them with my cure, my new strength. 'You weren't sick, you had ladylike vapours. They give us a pain in the ass, all these chicks with their fake problems! It's all just women's diseases, it's not serious'" (292). However typical this rejection, its insistence on gender designates one possible—and, in some sense, perfectly appropriate—response to Cardinal's rewriting of traditional analytic narrative. Obviously, as the narrator objects, "mental illness was not a female speciality" (292), except, of course, in the specific case of *Les Mots pour le dire*. The consistent focus of critical discomfort on the issue of the cure may stem from some degree of recognition that Cardinal has not respected the terms of the traditional freudian analysis. If, in both cases, feminism is associated with madness, Cardinal claims that which she should logically have rejected; moreover, she turns analysis itself into the justification of her claim.

More difficult to explain is the fact that feminists too appear to be troubled by the success of the analysis. As Suzanne Lamy notes, "in practice, for one Marie Cardinal saved from marasmis, how many Doras are there for whom analysis has been nothing but a jam or uncurdled mayonnaise" (59). But Lamy introduces a significant contextual alteration here; in refocusing our attention on "practice," she turns away from the text and back to reality. When Cardinal herself addresses the issue of the psychoanalytical cure within the framework of women's actual experience, both her own and that of others, she too readily admits that her own personal adventure is exceptional and that traditional therapy will most often lead to failure. Indeed, in an interview following the publication of *Les Mots pour le dire,* Cardinal attributes her current knowledge that "analysis is not a panacea" to the experiences her readers have shared with her (Lodovici 71).

Thus, it is precisely the fictionalization of the analysis, the reconceptualization of freudianism in specifically feminist terms, that alone allows a successful outcome, that, in fact, makes success the most subversive of all possible outcomes. In the case of the narrator's mother, the paradigmatic madwoman of *Les Mots pour le dire*, female madness leads inevitably to death because of what is explicitly identified as a failure of (feminist) analysis. In describing the reverse parallelism of their situations—during the final year of the daughter's successful therapy, her mother "was living her agony"—the narrator makes a freudian slip that reveals her understanding of how she has been saved and of how her mother might have been: "On the draft of my manuscript I made a freudian slip; I wrote 'my mother was living her analysis' instead of 'my mother was living her agony.' Obviously it's not by chance that I confused the two" (317).[18]

Still, one potential danger in reclaiming and revalorizing female madness, even when the equation functions to connect feminism and anger rather than femaleness and insanity, lies in the risk of the textual idealization of what is in reality a debilitating emotional and mental illness. This issue has become newly pertinent as the critical reading of fictional madwomen invades feminist theoretical discourse as a whole in the form of a recurrent preoccupation with psychoanalysis in general and with Freud's work with female patients in particular. Showalter, for example, reads the interest that Francophone feminists have repeatedly expressed in Dora as an "extreme identification with the madwoman" that comes "dangerously close to romanticizing madness as desirable rebellion" (*Female Malady* 4). In the case of Cardinal, a similar critical discomfort has been based solely on the successful outcome of the daughter's story in *Les Mots pour le dire.* Yet, not only is this not the only narrative of madness contained even within that one novel, but this is also a context in which we must once again remember that Cardinal very carefully constructs her texts as an oeuvre, a body of work in which repetition serves to assure coherence and cohesion and to tell the same stories over and over in different ways and with variant endings. *Les Mots pour le dire* cannot be fully understood when read in isolation from *La Souricière,* the earlier novel of female madness that it clearly repeats, though to a different end.

As in the case of the mother in *Les Mots pour le dire,* Camille's battle with madness in *La Souricière* ends in suicide; Cardinal here writes the traditional story of women and madness that provides the context for its subsequent revision in *Les Mots pour le dire.* The doctors who treat Camille diagnose her illness as specifically female—postpartum depression—and immediately transform this "common phenomenon" into the neutral terms of a "classic case of melancholy" (145) whose denial of female specificity guarantees the failure of treatment. Throughout the novel, Camille remains under the control of a series of men, all of whom reenact her original fixation on her father. Their incarnation of the paternal role of the analyst denies her the right to her own voice, resulting in the only example in Cardinal's work of a text written entirely in the third person. At one of her key moments of impasse, Camille's lover is described in terms that specifically recall the potential dangers of psychoanalysis whenever it repeats the inequitable structures of current gender relations: Alain "listened to her and took complete charge of her" (139).

Camille's marriage separates her from her literal mother and from the maternal landscape of the Mediterranean whose nurturing rhythms—rather than their loss—she mistakenly equates with madness: "She takes the real Camille, the woman who dreams and wanders, for a madwoman; she wants to get free of her" (218). Thus, as her estrangement progresses, she sends away her last female companion, the Provençal housekeeper with the revelatory name of Maria who has provided her only stability in the northern wasteland of Paris. In this perspective, two particularly significant passages function as metaphors for the communication with other women that might have saved Camille. The single moment at which she brutally rejects Alain occurs when his advances interrupt her fascination with a woman dancer (160–61). Similarly, Camille's suicide follows directly upon her abandonment of the hallucinatory presence of her husband's lover. In *La Souricière,* as in traditional psychoanalysis, men succeed in separating women from other women and from their own femaleness.

Perhaps it is in part the reality of most women's experience with traditional psychoanalysis that ultimately leads Cardinal in *Les Mots pour le dire* to move beyond her feminist critique and reconceptualization of freudianism and out of the analytic framework altogether; in this sense, the cure, the termination of the narrator's literal therapy, reflects Cardinal's final choice of consciousness over the unconscious, of gender over sex. Appropriately, Cardinal also constructs this narrative around the figure of the mother; for the key nightmare of simulated rape that permits Cardinal's narrator to reconceptualize women's sexual vulnerability as a political rather than a biological issue casts the mother in the dominant role. She draws her daughter, against the latter's will, into the group of highly diverse women whose solidarity results entirely from the shared subordination to which society's narrative of gender roles confines them: "There we were, squeezed tightly together, young women, old women, adolescents, children, mature women, hussies and ugly ducklings, all of us with fear in our bellies and terrible tales in our heads, stories of raped and disemboweled women" (296). Thus, the mother herself implicitly claims responsibility for a revised narrative of gender inequity and of feminist solidarity that aborts her earlier story of sexual determinism and of female helplessness. The women's specifically sexual/textual preoccupation here with narrative as such ("tales," "stories") usefully focuses our attention on the importance of women's writing within the political context of feminism. Not only must women escape from the destructive male (his)stories in which they have been imprisoned to narrate new (her)stories (and therefore h[i]sterias?) of their own, but the intimate connection between male discourse and the reality of their own bodies reveals why women can never totally divorce literature from the referential facts of their own condition; why they can never read with total objectivity or indifference.

Let me recall the etymology of *nightmare* that Cardinal here appears to take literally, to literalize textually. *Nightmare* (like *cauchemar*) derives from the "Middle English *nihtmare,* female incubus: NIGHT + *mare,* incubus"; I quote the exact formulation as it appears in *The American Heritage Dictionary* because of the bizarrely ambivalent shift that seems to have taken place and to which I will return in a moment. The first meaning of *incubus,* an "evil spirit" believed to descend upon and have sexual intercourse with sleeping women, becomes, in its second meaning, simply a nightmare (from the Latin *incubare,* to lie down upon). From this perspective, nightmares become a specifically female terror, one whose reflection of women's consciousness of the reality of male power and sexual force offers a provocative feminist subversion of the freudian analysis of dreams as a reflection of unconscious desires. Moreover, Cardinal's narrative of the sexual vulnerability of all women in the face of the potential rapists that culture's devaluation of women and exploitation of the female body make of all men provides us with the truly generic nightmare. What I find curious in the official linguistic version of these events is the transformation of the incubus, clearly an evil spirit conceived as *male,* into a *female* incubus in the Middle English etymology of *nightmare;* in a truly incredible actualization of the tendency to blame the victim that is so common in stories of rape, we are apparently to believe that even the responsibility for the sexual violation of our own bodies lies, indeed originates, with women themselves.

At *incubus,* moreover, the dictionary incites us to compare *succubus;* interestingly, but hardly surprisingly, the "female demon" who has sexual intercourse with sleeping men produces a secondary meaning that now focuses not on the nightmare of the act itself but on the woman who perpetrates it. Her evolution into *"any* evil spirit" (my emphasis) presumably explains both the initially unspecified gender of the incubus ("evil spirit" appears in the position parallel to "female demon") and the potential for sexual metamorphosis that underlies this appearance of gender neutrality. Since *succubus* derives from the double inferiority of women's position, both social and sexually literal (from Latin *succuber*, prostitute; from Latin *succabare*, to lie under), the result seems to be identical in any case to that already produced by the incubus. Women now escape violation but only by their own prior submission (however disguised by the semblance of initiative and dominance) to the terms of male desire.

Cardinal's exploration of the meaning of women's nightmares identifies a more general strategy at work in *Les Mots pour le dire* where the shift from sex to gender challenges the shift in Freud's own thinking from reality to fantasy that lies at the heart of any critique or defense of his attitude toward women. Juliet Mitchell's desire to retain freudianism within a feminist revision of psychoanalysis leads to a typical accusation that Freud's feminist detractors commit the error that Claudine Herrmann views as definitional of a specifically female understanding of the world and of language: women consistently and insistently take the figurative literally. As Mitchell puts it, those feminists (predominantly Anglophone) who reject psychoanalytic theory can be most accurately identified by their refusal to follow Freud at the specific point at which he reconceptualizes the *reality* of paternal seduction as *fantasy*, thus recasting the *act* of the male as the *desire* of the female. Mitchell therefore views the feminist critique of Freud—characterized by a commitment to "social realism" from which the notions of desire, fantasy, and the unconscious are conspicuously absent—as more "pre-Freudian" than "anti-Freudian" (9).

It seems to me particularly unwise and unfair to judge women's understanding of the key elements of psychoanalytic theory entirely (or even in part) on the basis of their ability to accept (let alone to adopt) an argument that necessarily supports and perpetuates the sociohistorical conditions of actual rape by defining it once again as a twofold female "fantasy": both, and at one and the same time, the fulfillment of women's unconscious desires and a figment of their own imaginations. In any event, although we have seen ample evidence of Cardinal's willingness to rethink female identity from within a psychoanalytic framework that includes a theory of the unconscious and of desire (however differently they may be en-gendered), she too stops short in the face of this particular denial of the real circumstances of women's lives. Indeed, the near-total rejection of freudian theory (including the essential notion of the unconscious) that ensues from her encounter with this obstacle supports my view that the centrality granted it by such freudian feminists as Mitchell proves severely counterproductive to their own ends.

Not only does Cardinal undermine the freudian concept of the dream as the reflection of unconscious desire by en-gendering and literalizing the very notion of a nightmare as the feminist consciousness of the reality of gender relations; but, in a total and explicit reversal of the path that Freud chose to follow, she deliberately moves from fantasy to reality. Behind the nightmare of the rape attempt lies neither unconscious desire nor hallucination but the memory of an actual sexual assault. Similarly, the narrator's literal hallucination of the hostile eye repeats the facts of a very real case of attempted seduction by the father. It hardly seems insignificant that it is at this particular point that the narrator suddenly seeks her mother's confirmation of the reality of the event. In the context that most specifically echoes Freud, Cardinal's revelation that the female analysand speaks truth and not fiction leads her to a parallel (and finally more serious) therapeutic challenge to psychoanalysis. The reliability of women's memories at the very least controls—and perhaps replaces—the impulsions of the unconscious.

At the same time, however, Cardinal's determination to describe accurately the reality of female oppression cannot for a moment be contained within the terms of the freudian concept of the reality principle. If her feminist demands include a fully conscious awareness of "the conditions imposed by the outside world" (LaPlanche and Pontalis 379), they are also explicitly predicated on the revolutionary refusal to adjust to such requirements, even (or especially) at the cost of "sanity" itself. As a result, by the end of *Les Mots pour le dire,* continued allusions to psychoanalytic principles or terminology serve primarily as reference points that allow us to measure the distance that separates feminism from freudianism.

For example, the interpretation of dreams that Freud describes as "the most important instrument at work" in analytic therapy (*Gen. Introd.* 464) provides Cardinal's narrator with material that she finds totally irrelevant to the therapeutic process (307). Yet, the discovery in question—the meaning of the anatomical specificity of women—constitutes the very discovery that would normally be viewed as integral to freudian theory. But Cardinal now reinterprets physiological female-ness—"what it meant to have a vagina, to be a woman" (308)—in terms of culturally defined notions of femininity and culturally approved gender roles: "That's what it means to have a vagina. That's what it means to be a woman: to serve a man and to love children until you reach old age" (310). Logically, then, the conclusion of the novel and of the analysis cannot and do not coincide. The final chapter—"A few days later it was May 68"—consecrates the complex movement of the narrator's "passage" from the psychological to the social and the individual to the collective, from talk to action and sex to gender, and from madness/insanity to madness/anger. In short, in the course of *Les Mots pour le dire*, Cardinal moves definitively from freudianism to feminism.

The Language of Analysis: Translations(s) and Repetition(s)

The preoccupation of psychoanalysis as well as narrative with the terms and the processes of repetition and translation suggests the unusual interest of the English-language edition of *The Words to Say It*. Furthermore, the intercultural dialogue between Anglophone and Francophone feminists has been largely established, as noted earlier, on the basis of available translations from the French. (Indeed, since French and Americans share a common reputation for their lack of foreign language competence, translation alone can both institute and prevent repetition.) In this perspective, the contextual nature of written feminism becomes particularly clear and equally problematic. Since most Francophone feminist theory has been excerpted and translated in anthologies (e.g., *New French Feminisms, French Connections*) and reviews (e.g., *Signs, Feminist Studies*), Anglophone readers are doubly dependent on the translator, whose responsibilities include resituating the passage within its original context and "contextualizing," joining together (from the Latin *contexere*, to join together, weave), two languages and two cultures. Thus, Susan Gubar, for example, identifies with gratitude "those figures who really do crucially important translations (trans-lations)" as the "bridge figures" between Francophone and Anglophone feminism. Yet, as Carolyn Allen's immediate response to Gubar indicates, such dependency may also involve a frustrating and dangerous loss of power and control, since "you can't always tell how much has been lost in translation" ("Feminist Readings" 6).

We can expect this problem to be especially severe when we are deal-
ing with a multilingual movement such as psychoanalysis, to whose primary texts many of us have access only in translation. In the exemplary
case of Freud, Francophone and Anglophone readings have already and
by definition been precontextualized at the moment of their initial encounter by virtue of prior and independent interpretations of the original German text. In this event, Sherry Turkle's thesis that contemporary
psychoanalysis has become "culturally specific" is hardly surprising.[19]
The repeated appropriation of a German Freud into alternative linguistic and cultural frameworks reflects and helps to explain why the compulsion to repeat extends beyond its theoretical or therapeutic importance in freudian thought to affect the nature and the structure of
psychoanalytic narrative itself. Discussion of the repetition compulsion
per se echoes not only within Freud's own writings but throughout the
subsequent psychoanalytic literature as well; moreover, as we have
seen, many textual critics equate repetition with literarity itself.

This theoretical interaction of repetition, narrative, and psychoanalysis brings to light a curious distinction between analyses of repetition in and by women writers (e.g., Lamy, Garcia) and similar ones in
and by men writers (e.g., Brooks, Chambers, Compagnon, Schneider).
The men, and only the men, but the men without exception, use the
notion of repetition to establish an explicit and crucial connection between narrative and psychoanalysis. This may represent a need to repeat
on their part that recalls the question with which J. LaPlanche and J.-B.
Pontalis summarize the conceptual uncertainty of the freudian notion of
repetition that in their eyes requires and explains its continual repetition
within the interpretive discourse that surrounds psychoanalysis: "must
we postulate the existence, alongside the *repetition of needs,* of a *need
for repetition,* the latter being both radically distinct from and more
basic than the former?" (79).

The repetitiveness of *écriture féminine,* grounded in the commonality
of women's experience, indeed appears to reflect the repetition of similar needs; within this context, women writers thus implicitly challenge
precisely any need for such a repetition. Moreover, in the absence of
knowledge of their female precursors that has until recently characterized the situation of women writers, they can at best include that particular need for repetition as one of the needs they repeat. In the case of
men, on the other hand, the need to repeat would seem to result from a
desire to establish and/or to perpetuate an artificial intellectual frame-

work, based not on a shared reality but on the creation and re-creation of a power structure whose existence and continuity depend on the establishment of influence and authority. To connect narrative to psychoanalysis confirms the male lineage and unity of Western thought as a whole; it makes freudian narrative, in which the need to repeat the words of others (of women, in particular) becomes the *right* to repeat them, the model for an authoritarian male (meta)discourse. Hence the strongly psychoanalytic nature of theories of (male) literary influence, as in the exemplary case of Harold Bloom. Most explicitly, Michel Schneider establishes the intellectual operation specific to psychoanalysis—"the communism of ideas," the deliberate practice of plagiarizing one's colleagues and one's patients (129)—as a paradigm for "the communism of words" (13) that defines (male) literature, always produced under the influence of "the love of the masters" (11), of the father (16). Although women are denied access to this closed circuit of male bonding, the fantasy of violation that characterizes the now literal (the)rapist's victim (159) identifies this role as traditionally female.

In relation to *The Words to Say It,* the need for repetition produces a translation that initially appears less notable for what has been lost than for what has been found and repeated, despite (but also because of) its absence from Cardinal's original text. In this light, the preliminary textual intrusion that Boileau's epigraph constitutes—"What one truly understands clearly articulates itself, and the words to say it come easily"—metaphorically summarizes and prepares a vastly more significant male invasion. If, as I noted earlier, Boileau's words sound a distinctly false note as an introduction to Cardinal's novel, they describe with total accuracy the perspective articulated in Bruno Bettelheim's preface and afterword that provide the narrative framework for the American edition of *Les Mots pour le dire.*

Although the originality of Bettelheim's texts theoretically distinguishes them from the translation as such, they reintroduce a psychoanalytic preoccupation with the process of translation that appropriately complements and completes the linguistic transfer. Freud, for example, characterizes analytic interventions as "translations" of the unconscious into the conscious; and Lacan calls psychotherapy the "repatriation of alienated signifiers" (qtd. in Hunter 109). Lacan's terminology proves particularly suitable here, for repatriation, the return to the *father*land, does indeed characterize Bettelheim's intention. Moreover, his version of the analytic intervention masquerades as the (re)translation into consciousness (into *his* conscious mind) of a content presumed to remain unconscious in Cardinal's. In addition, the process specifically revises signification as well; Bettelheim will write the "alienated signifiers," the signifiers of alienation, back into the text from which the woman writer has so carefully removed them.

Bettelheim successfully achieves the transformation of *Les Mots pour le dire,* which the critical response to the novel has already sought to bring about in a variety of ways, into a text that conforms to the standard model of the psychoanalytic narrative. The very manner in which he repeatedly emphasizes the originality of Cardinal's novel awakens the suspicion that he protests too much; in the space of two pages, for example, he makes the same point no fewer than six times:

> Reading this novel permits us to comprehend what is involved in a psychoanalysis as seen from the perspective of the patient. . . . But Freud wrote mainly from the analyst's point of view. . . . Since Freud's day practically all accounts of psychoanalysis have been written by analysts. There are only a few stories of analyses written by patients, and even fewer which are any good. One of the best is H. D.'s *Tribute to Freud,* but in it she speaks mostly about her analyst. . . . Of all accounts of psychoanalysis as experienced by the patient, none can compare with this novel. . . . I am writing this preface, and the afterword at the end of this book, because in my opinion *The Words to Say It* is the best account of psychoanalysis as seen and experienced by the patient. (x–xi)

Nevertheless, we can still take this final assertion at face value, provided we do not confuse a simple description of causality with a statement of motive, for what appears to prepare a tribute to the patient's text in fact serves to justify the subversion and the appropriation of her account.

Already in the preface (and prior to the passage cited above in which Bettelheim seems to respect the patient's narrative authority), he first introduces Cardinal via a repeated analogy with Dante that immediately substitutes the male's "voyage of self-discovery" for the female's. There seems, in any event, to be very little self involved in any such discovery, since Bettelheim portrays Cardinal as totally lost and confused without the direction provided by a male savior: "she needed a compassionate guide who possessed the *requisite* wisdom to *steer her* along the *right* course of self-discovery . . . and who had the *particular skill* of the psychoanalyst" (x, my emphasis). In this context, Bettelheim's acknowledgment that "her analyst had to be mainly a silent guide" (x) serves less to reflect accurately Cardinal's own text than to respect the traditional temporal sequence of the freudian therapeutic exchange; in conformity with the latter, we will be allowed to observe the patient's symptoms before we hear the analyst's interpretation.

To state the issue more clearly, the doctor always has the last word, and Bettelheim devotes his afterword to the "clinical speculations" in which he "could not help engaging" (298). This (re)produces, of course, the very analytic discourse that Cardinal denies to her intradiegetic doctor and that Bettelheim cannot bear to leave unsaid. Like Freud in the case of Dora, he imposes his own narrative, even at the cost of incoherence, on what he perceives to be gaps in the woman's text. Thus, the first two sentences of the afterword totally contradict each other; the assurance that Cardinal's story "speaks for itself" leads directly to the surprising conclusion that "at the end there remain a number of unanswered questions for the layperson and the psychoanalyst alike" (297).

Moreover, the cause to which Bettelheim repeatedly attributes this lack of closure (the virtually identical sentence appears twice in successive paragraphs) explicitly equates narrative failure with mental illness. Bettelheim subjects Cardinal once again to the control of the unconscious, that is, to insanity: "the author seems at the end not to be consciously aware of all that was once involved" (297); and a second time, "we are not enlightened about these and other matters because the author does not consciously know the answers to them" (298). Freud also classified those narrators prone to "leaving gaps unfilled" as hysterical; as a result, the construction of "an intelligible, consistent, and unbroken case history" becomes the goal of analysis (qtd. in Sprengnether 67). But, as the example of Bettelheim makes eminently clear (as does Freud's substitution of "case history" for an initial reference to the patient's "communications"), therapeutic success depends upon the achievement of the analyst rather than upon that of the analysand, upon "the power of *his* voice to create her reality," as Sprengnether puts it in the case of Freud and Dora (70).

Bettelheim's position is unusually contradictory, however, since his endeavor to reestablish the authority and the competence of the analyst also requires the rehabilitation of his textual double. Thus, the afterword paradoxically continues to stress the success of the analysis as such, even as it outlines the inability of the analysand to fully comprehend this very success; implicitly, then, the male analyst reclaims extra-diegetically the role that the woman patient has clearly usurped within Cardinal's text. At the same time, Bettelheim expands to the greatest extent possible the limited textual evidence available of the doctor's actual intervention; for example, he uses the disappearance of Cardinal's somatic bleeding, discussed at considerable length, as a means to valorize the doctor. As for Bettelheim himself, he incarnates virtually the mirror opposite of the psychoanalyst in Cardinal's novel. He never doubts the correctness of his interpretations, and he delivers them as truth. Since he also reads Cardinal's text very badly, however, he illustrates in particular how a reader's preconceptions can falsify a reading; in other words, Bettelheim identifies what has been the historical problem of classical psychoanalysis.

As in the case of the parallel accounts of female madness by Mary Barnes and her therapist J. Berke (Showalter, *Female* 232), Bettelheim's afterword gives us an opportunity to compare the male analyst's and the female analysand's interpretations of the same experience. Like Berke, Bettelheim either cannot or will not read the female-specific story that Cardinal tells in *Les Mots pour le dire*. In fact, he does virtually everything possible to conceal the fact that he is not discussing a man's case history. In particular, he consistently combines potentially gender-neutral nouns (e.g., the patient, the child, the author) with the generic "he"; as a result, Bettelheim denies Cardinal her name, her identity, and her consciousness, not only as novelist, but, more importantly, as the author of her own experience. Although this might seem to represent an effort to raise a woman's story to the level of universal significance, the generic "he" serves in fact to equate the human only with the male—often at the price of some curious non sequiturs. At the end of his preface, for example, immediately after noting the importance of a life-threatening symptom "*strangely* located" in the womb, Bettelheim concludes that reading *Les Mots pour le dire* "restores one's faith in *man*" (xii, my emphasis)—which presumably explains why the location of the symptom might appear "strange"!

Similarly, Bettelheim's constant references to the "many parallel cases" (301) that inform his discussion of Cardinal's illness allow him, first, to assert repeatedly the authority of his own experience and, second, to deny the significance of gender as a whole, an act whose consequences are very different in the case of women than in that of men. As

Carol Gilligan's work has revealed with particular clarity, research in psychology has consistently founded its theoretical principles and models on the study of male experience alone. Subsequently, however, psychologists have not hesitated to assume that they have nonetheless discovered general human truths that can be applied to the very experience—that of women—that was originally eliminated as a prerequisite to their development. Paradoxically, within this vicious circle, it is precisely the denial of the femaleness of experience that allows the parallel erasure of the maleness of experience as well; but what in the first case leads to exclusion *from* the human results in the second case in an exclusive claim *on* the human. Note, for example, what happens to the uncontrollable bleeding of Cardinal's narrator when Bettelheim views it from the perspective of "parallel cases." It is difficult to believe in this particular incidence that "symptom formation" can be made to depend only on "the age of the individual" and on "the past and present details of that person's life experiences" (301) without any reference whatsoever to sex or gender.

If there is anyone, then, who "seems at the end not to be consciously aware of all that was once involved" (297), it is Bettelheim himself whose "unanswered questions" specifically focus on the narrator's hemorrhaging: "We are not told, for example, why the 'Thing' caused the near-continuous flow of menstrual fluid that tortured, incapacitated, disgusted, and shamed her, nor why this symptom stopped as if by magic" (197–98). Leaving aside Bettelheim's own transparent disgust at the thought of female bleeding, surely the answers to such questions are perfectly clear to most readers of *Les Mots pour le dire*—"the layperson and the psychoanalyst alike"—unless, of course, one deliberately chooses to ignore or to misread the significance of gender and/or the difference of art.

Interestingly, Bettelheim claims equal competence as therapist and textual critic—indeed, his assumption of authority in this latter realm pinpoints with particular clarity his determination to usurp from Cardinal all analytic powers. In his opinion, *The Words to Say It* is both "the best account of psychoanalysis as seen and experienced by the patient" (xi) and "as near perfect as a novel can be" (298). Since Bettelheim gives no indication of the criteria that allow him to determine novelistic merit, one is tempted to assume syntactical and semantic synonymy and to equate the excellent novel with the excellent analysis.

In that event, however, the implied reversibility of his terms—that is, the complementary definition of psychoanalysis as a fictional narrative—can hardly be avoided.

In substituting direct expository statement for the more complex means by which Cardinal's novel repeatedly makes precisely the same connections as he does between the narrator's bleeding and her mother's abortion attempt, Bettelheim not only fails to usurp Cardinal's novelistic authority, but as a textual critic his unconsciousness of her work as a whole exposes him as either uninformed or a plagiarizer. For example, his key "revelation" that it is much better for children to have actual knowledge rather than mere suspicion of a maternal death wish already figures prominently in Cardinal's *La Clé sur la porte* (215) (as well as in *Les Mots pour le dire* [170–71]). *Autrement dit,* moreover, undermines Bettelheim's entire endeavor. In what is already a reexamination of *Les Mots pour le dire* in relation to her personal experience with analysis, Cardinal reconfirms that long before beginning therapy she already fully understood the significance of the abortion attempt and its connection to her psychosomatic bleeding. Bettelheim seeks to define these very same issues not only as the primary revelations of the psychoanalysis on which Cardinal's novel has been based but of his own essay as well. Success in this endeavor would prove yet again the superiority of the male analyst, of Bettelheim himself and of his textual double, of Bettelheim the psychoanalyst and the textual critic.[20]

To be fair to Bettelheim, however, we should remember that *La Clé sur la porte* and *Autrement dit* are not the only texts he has not read. He has not read *Les Mots pour le dire* either; he has read only *The Words to Say It*. In light of Cardinal's characteristic act of autocitation, the repetition of the original French text in English translation paradoxically (re)produces a recognizable pattern. In psychoanalytic terms, the compulsion to repeat now appears to have given way to a parallel failure of translation and of transference. Upon an initial reading even (or particularly) by someone who is thoroughly familiar with *Les Mots pour le dire, The Words to Say It* appears to respect Cardinal's practice of translation by "carrying across" (from the Latin *transferre,* to carry across, transfer, translate) the integral text from one language to another. In both cases, then, a practice of synonymy essentially determines lexical difference, and the reappearance of the same kinds of insignificant syntactical variations further reinforces a basic pattern of resemblance. Whereas Cardinal, for example, slightly alters word order or breaks apart a sentence, her translator, Pat Goodheart, at times divides a paragraph or fuses two paragraphs together; just as such changes tend to assure contextual integrity in the passage from one French text to another, interlinguistic movement results from such structural particularities of English and French as the presence or absence of paragraph breaks in the representation of direct discourse. The realization, then, when one turns to a direct comparison of the original text and its translation, that the latter in fact omits significant portions of the former, is all the more startling.

And yet, the translation ends with an explicit announcement of its own betrayal, of its determination to "give over" (to betray: *trans-*, over + *dare*, to give) rather than to "carry across" (to translate: *trans-*, across + *latus*, carried) Cardinal's original text. We are invited to retrace our steps, to repeat our reading of Cardinal and Goodheart simultaneously, by the inescapable—and inexplicable—absence in *The Words to Say It* of the final chapter and sentence of *Les Mots pour le dire:*

XVIII

A few days later it was May 68.

The importance of this conclusion should be judged not by its brevity but by its right to a chapter all its own; in a final stroke of her pen, Cardinal definitively shifts and fixes the framework within which we will remember *Les Mots pour le dire*. She guarantees that we will recall reading far less the story of the private analytic cure of one individual than the political narrative of the social transformation of the situation of women.

Even if we are willing to entertain the possibility that Goodheart drops chapter 18 because she believes that the culture-specific allusion to May '68 will be lost on an American readership (the argument immediately appears unconvincing, however, because the events that took place in France in May 1968 attracted international attention and because a very similar situation in the United States provided ample material from which to choose a suitable substitute), it still indicates either a serious misunderstanding or a willful distortion of Cardinal's text. A renewed attentiveness to additional changes, moreover, brings to light a pattern of omissions that confirms the consistent elimination of the social context of *Les Mots pour le dire* that allows Cardinal to generalize from the particular case of one individual to the gender-specific situation of all women. Even if intentionality remains difficult to prove, the opening up of such textual gaps produces of necessity a new version of the original text in which the possibility that the reader will focus on the psychological, individual, and personal dimensions of the narrative has been strongly reinforced.

Because the passages that Goodheart removes tend to center on the narrator's mother, a major ideological reversal also takes place that serves to justify from within the text the restoration of the power and authority of the father/analyst that Bettelheim's framework establishes from without; repetition once again reverses the movement away from the patriarchal structures that Cardinal had so carefully set in place. One omission, for example, that has unmistakable significance for our understanding of ideology and gender occurs during the initial therapeutic session. By eliminating the passage in which the narrator of *Les Mots pour le dire* compares herself to a contented baby, protected by her mother's look, Goodheart leaves unchallenged the implicit suggestion of a classically freudian transference that operates in the paternal line (WS 32, MD 42–43). A second elimination, in the course of a comparison between France and Algeria, of the narrator's unequivocal statement of preference for Algeria offers a more subtle example of the less-serious division between male-identified and female-identified values that characterizes the English edition of Cardinal's novel (WS 105, MD 83). Once a slight shift in the overall context has taken place, even a missing pronoun can potentially have a discernible effect; the daughter's frustration and discomfort in conversation with her mother does not originally result from a general lack of social ease—"I didn't know how to talk" (WS 116)—but rather from the specific tensions of the mother-daughter relationship—"I didn't know how to talk *to her*" (MD 144, my emphasis).

Perhaps the most significant cut involves the omission of the key passage from *Les Mots pour le dire* in which the narrator speculates on her mother's unrealized creative potential (WS 322, MD 274); Goodheart here eliminates an episode that is clearly essential for an understanding of the situation of women in general and of the societal obstacles they face in particular. Similarly, at the moment when the narrator directly confronts the incarnation of female madness in the person of her own mother, Goodheart erases the simultaneous awareness of the significance of gender and of the responsibility of society that takes the form in the French text of an explicit accusation and analysis of the power of

"ILS," that is, of male-defined and male-dominated societal structures as a whole, to oppress women (WS 284, MD 332). In the absence of this passage, the narrator of *The Words to Say It* remains mired in the interpersonal dynamics of psychological conflict between mother and daughter, with no awareness of the larger context of gender relations that allows her French counterpart to reconceptualize maternal guilt and filial hostility.

The same deemphasis on gender appears to determine the omissions that surround the narrator herself and her experience with madness. The description of her initial anxiety attack denies from the outset the crucial connection between female alienation and societal constraints on women that Cardinal herself immediately sets in motion. By simply eliminating the passage in which the narrator explains the conflict between traditional gender roles and her love of mathematics, Goodheart presents the narrator's madness as an undefined and inexplicable existential crisis. Here too the most apparently minor of omissions turns out to contribute to a curiously consistent effect. Thus, in translating the second of the narrator's two therapeutic translations of specifically unconscious material—the moment, described as "the most important of my psychoanalysis" (MD 249), in which she recovers her violence—Goodheart opens a textual gap that subtly undermines the appropriateness of the little girl's subsequent outrage at male injustice.

These are the circumstances that lead in each case to her brother's deliberate destruction of her favorite toy:

> Suddenly my brother grows irritated, he wants to take away from me a ping-pong paddle that belongs to him *but with which I am playing for the moment*. I don't want to give it back to him. *Therefore* he grabs my monkey. (MD 247, my emphasis)

> Suddenly my brother gets bored, he wants to take a Ping-Pong paddle away from me. It belongs to him. I don't want to give it back. *Then* he grabs my monkey. (WS 209, my emphasis)

The reduction of causality ("therefore") to temporality ("then"), though a mistranslation, may at least serve to soften Goodheart's implicit reattribution of moral right to the male. Initially established by the elimination of the female narrator's claim to consideration, it is then reinforced syntactically by the promotion of male right from subordinate to independent clause. In the context of the paradigmatic male-female relationship between analyst and analysand, such parallel omissions as that of a paragraph in which the woman notes her ability to autoanalyze her dreams (WS 233, MD 275) function in the same way to leave male authority unchallenged.

Although the loss of certain stylistic effects is virtually inevitable in the course of translation, lexical and syntactical repetition need not necessarily figure among them. The fact that Goodheart eliminates with some consistency the last two words in a series of synonyms (e.g., WS 139, MD 169), the second in a sequence of two successive questions (e.g., WS 163, MD 194), or the reiteration of a word (e.g., WS 163, MD 168)—all cases in which the necessity of recurrence indeed relates not to meaning but only to the establishment of the idea and the pattern of repetition in and of itself—stands as a metaphor for her failure to understand Cardinal's compulsion to repeat.

Multicultural Dialogue

Although I began by rejecting the hypothesis that Goodheart omits material out of a concern for a cultural specificity that cannot easily be carried across from one linguistic context to another, once the omissions have occurred, they may subsequently reflect the assumptions of the culture in which they appear. In this light, for example, the elimination of passages that insist too overtly on societal structures and on gender roles produces a text that more closely conforms to an American belief in individualism. In a further effort to understand the multicultural importance of Marie Cardinal within the context of the differences between and within Francophone and Anglophone versions of psychoanalysis and feminism, I would like to reinitiate dialogue, to reconsider *Les Mots pour le dire* from the perspective of two other examples of what we might include within the category *female repetition*.[21] In *Tea with Demons* (1985) and *Le Jeu de l'origine* (1985), Carol Allen and Marie Bellour, an American and a French woman, respectively relate their successful experiences with psychotherapy.

Let me recall, initially, Sherry Turkle's analysis of how psychoanalysis becomes culturally specific, especially since she outlines a process that should be applicable to other domains as well and—to the extent that psychoanalysis represents at one and the same time an institution, a theory, an ideology, and a therapeutic practice—to feminism in particular.[22] Turkle emphasizes three possible factors of transformation (48–

49). First, cultures selectively filter the elements available to them, retaining only some and bracketing others that appear "most threatening or least useful." Thus, Americans prefer to stress early childhood memories over infantile sexuality, and they remain doubtful about the role that the unconscious plays in determining human behavior. Similarly, Anglophone feminists attach particular significance to the effects of early socialization on female development, and they tend to believe that one's consciousness of oppression depends upon altering one's perspective on one's past experience; they often find Francophone explorations of the female unconscious and of an explicitly erotic preoedipal bond between mother and daughter either "mystical" or politically unwise.

Second, psychoanalysis functions, in Turkle's words, as "a screen onto which a culture projects its preoccupations and values" (49). Thus, Americans initially attempted to graft a "new therapeutic optimism" onto a theory that had never seen psychoanalysis as more than a means to understanding—but not to "curing"—the inevitable contradictions and fragmentation of the human self; and finally, they essentially abandoned Freud in favor of the more optimistic versions of his ideas that object relations theory or ego psychology created. In parallel fashion, Anglophone feminists remain strongly committed to the radical transformation of individual lives *and* societal structures, and this belief in the possibility of productive action necessarily draws upon an underlying, if unanalyzed, strong and coherent sense of self. The most common objection to even such an influential and widely admired Francophone feminist as Simone de Beauvoir stems from a reaction of irritation and frustration in the face of what is perceived as her pessimism.

Third, Turkle notes that psychoanalysis is shaped by social institutions. In the United States, the early monopolization of freudian thought by the medical profession led to an emphasis on therapy over theory and to the infusion of psychoanalysis with both pragmatism and the prestige of scientific authority. In France, on the other hand, the early championing of freudian thought by writers and artists transformed a clinical practice into a philosophical discourse. The Anglophone feminist critique of psychoanalysis has consequently been directed against a therapeutic practice in which a powerful male analyst is perceived to equate the mental and emotional well-being of women with their acceptance of traditional gender roles. Francophone feminists, in contrast, challenge psychoanalytic thought through the deconstruction of its theoretical assumptions and principles. In terms of a more general analogy between the cultural transformation of psychoanalysis and that of feminism, we might note in relation to this third point that Anglophone feminists have tended to produce a pragmatic discourse whose carefully documented analysis of the real conditions of women's lives (or of the "realistic" representations of such conditions) seeks to convince others of the necessity of change. Francophone feminists, in contrast, tend to see writing as an autonomous activity and an end in itself; their discourse, as we know, embeds ideological critique in a highly lyrical, playful, and metaphorical prose whose primary appeal remains more specifically aesthetic than political.

At the point at which Allen's descent into madness forces her to seek professional help, her general situation reveals curious parallels with that of the narrator of *Les Mots pour le dire:* both are wives and mothers in their early thirties; more particularly, both have been trained as philosophers. Therapy for both involves an experience with hospitalization and medication as well as analysis; hallucination and recurrent dreams play a key role in the evolution of each woman's madness. Both engage in a private writing practice, related to their experience with analysis, which each keeps hidden from her male doctor. Both have occasion to rethink their early relationship with their mothers; both discover that they have attempted to conform to an externally imposed model of acceptable womanhood that has required the repression of an authentic self for which, in both cases, anger serves as the identifying mark. For both women, the understanding of their individual circumstances connects to some degree to a larger reflection on gender roles and on women's societal condition.

Most significantly, perhaps, Allen and Cardinal attribute central importance to the analytic relationship as such, and both express enormous gratitude to the male doctors with whom they establish what they regard as a truly interactive, if not precisely egalitarian, collaboration. But here there are crucial differences—particularly in the form in which the two women choose to recount their stories. *Tea with Demons* relates a characteristically American experience of psychotherapy rather than of psychoanalysis. Since in this case, too, therapy nonetheless depends entirely on "the power of healing with the spoken word" (Allen 283), the distinction that matters lies not in the nature of the professional interaction between a female patient who speaks and a male doctor who listens but in its metaphorical reflection of the personal relationship between the man and the woman. Allen's doctor is a real interlocutor whose analytic presence and participation merit constant textual prominence. As a result, we are not seriously surprised to see the analysis evolve into friendship, since Dr. Lustig largely functions as a friend from the beginning.

To some extent, then, it might seem that Allen successfully establishes, from within analysis and with a man, the feminist interaction that Cardinal only creates in the course of her subsequent friendship with Annie Leclerc. Yet, the textual importance that Allen allows her doctor also has some potentially troubling consequences that run strongly parallel to those that characterize the American edition of *The Words to Say It;* male authority once again provides the controlling framework for the woman's story. Lustig's name (and title) appear on the front cover of *Tea with Demons* where he receives credit, significantly, not for his contribution to *analysis* but for his joint authorship of the *text* that results from it. Certainly, he has a right to such an acknowledgment of the "invaluable collaborative role" that Allen attributes to him; their joint reconstruction of their therapeutic conversations is based on his clinical notes as well as on her notebooks. But this means, of course, that Allen in some sense betrays the integrity of her story and sacrifices the authenticity and the autonomy that her decision to write originally meant. Indeed, it is the doctor who now proposes that Allen write about her experience as a "final step in [her] process of healing" (279); and, from the beginning, despite her revelation at this point that she has been keeping a journal, she conceives public narration as dependent on male affection and direct assistance: "Perhaps if we become friends, I thought, we might someday work together to write my story" (180).

In this context, although Lustig is right to describe her story as "almost a universal one," one wonders whether this troubling "almost" does not in fact acknowledge the remnants of a female specificity the new text that emerges from their combined narratives definitively erases. Like Bettelheim, Lustig also has the last word; *Tea with Demons* concludes with the "Psychiatrist's Note" in which the male narrator's intercession serves primarily to authenticate the woman's word ("This book is an accurate chronicle" [282]). Moreover, the doctor definitively reduces his female collaborator to a secondary character in his own success story: "This book publicly confirms my cherished belief that competent and compassionate psychiatric treatment of people with mental illness is a reality" (283).

Of course, we might view this collaboration as representative of a not atypical tendency of American feminism to emphasize the commonality of human experience (rather than the specificity of female experience) and to adopt a strategy of integration into dominant society that necessarily attaches greater significance to cooperation between men and women (than, for example, to female friendship). To a large extent, however, any such reading is undermined from within the text itself by a secondary analytic narrative that functions as a central metaphor. Paradoxically, Allen's account of specifically nonfreudian psychotherapy does precisely what Cardinal's account refuses to do. In a manner fully worthy of Freud's own dictates, transference not only plays a central role in this analysis but the entire therapeutic process defines itself as nothing more nor less than the enactment of the transferential relationship. The parallel established on this issue alone between Allen's psychotherapy and that of her best friend, Marion, repeats the only thing that matters. On the other hand, the absence of freudian theory means that the transference does not repeat any other private relationship; it thus stands as a transparently visible illustration of the relations between men and women in male-dominant society.

Allen and Marion become inseparable doubles through the process of sharing a common experience with therapy that functions for each as "the center of her world":

> The two of us were like sisters in search of wholeness, or perhaps closer than sisters even, because we were spiritually attached, seeking refuge from a world whose men—our husbands, but not our therapists—had let us down, alike in concentrating our energy on our therapy, sharing its magic with each other.
>
> She delighted in fantasy as much as I did, especially about our therapists' love for us, and as we talked for hours each day, we played out this theme in all its variations—Dr. Wainwright loved her and would marry her; Dr. Lustig loved me and, though I did not dare to say it out loud, would soon recognize the inevitablity and correctness of our attachment. Our inferior husbands would be replaced by our superior mentors, who would provide us with true guidance in our lives, who with sensitivity and understanding would lead us to the land of milk and honey, where we would settle into a comfortable domesticity, where we would be forever loved, and never alone. (113–14)

For women, of course, such an evasion into a fantasy world has all too often determined the reality of their daily lives. Allen's illusion of male superiority—grounded in female dependence, fear of solitude, and externally defined self-worth—in fact portrays traditional gender relations with painful accuracy.[23] Particularly painful here is a conception of sisterhood that involves women's shared commitment to men rather than any attachment to each other. But such a divorce from reality also defines madness, as Allen, no doubt despite her conscious intentions, also allows us to see. The particular terms in which Marion's fantasies become reality (119) clearly recall—and subvert—Freud's own theoretical position, for Wainwright transforms the analytic situation into a paternal seduction: "He was like a father to me, she told me, so it had begun by her sitting on his lap for comfort" (119). Allen challenges Freud's conviction that such female narratives express desire rather than describe experience and thereby exposes the therapist as literally (the)rapist. Not surprisingly, Marion's analyst prescribes a treatment that reenacts the traditional resolution of the female oedipal complex: "'He wants to have a baby with me,' she said, her face aglow with her recent lovemaking. 'A boy,' she continued" (120).

Importantly, it is precisely this inversion of reality and fantasy that severs Allen's "tenuous connection with the world and with Dr. Lustig as its spokesman" (118), forcing her into actual madness. For Lustig, once he learns Marion's story from Allen, immediately betrays her confidence; he phones his colleague, on the supposition that "one of Dr. Wainwright's sicker patients was slandering his reputation" (121). Typically, men's betrayal of women leads women to betray each other even as it reinforces male bonds of solidarity. That Allen's subsequent loss of confidence in therapy leads directly to a total breakdown usefully exposes traditional analysis as the causal factor in female madness. At the same time, however, it makes her final confidence in Lustig as successful therapist and reliable conarrator all the more troubling.

Two episodes of Allen's text that reveal a curiously close resemblance to similar passages in Cardinal's novel also emphasize the difference of their perspectives. Allen too suffers from a visual hallucination that limits her own sight and transforms her into the terrified object of others' hostile gazes. In Allen's case, however, the explicit association of "I" and "eye"—a metaphor for the dynamics of self and other—informs a characteristically American analysis of the conscious ego; this theory specifically denies the existence of the unconscious to which Cardinal's parallel hallucination allows her access. Consequently, the lyrical linguistic associations that allow the narrator of *Les Mots pour le dire* to explore the poetic logic of madness and the female self are replaced in Allen's realistic account of her own insanity (*Tea with Demons* is announced as "a true story") by a framework of Platonic images that insist on the coherence and the rational order of the mind and the world. Significantly, neither Allen nor Lustig ever interprets any of her dreams (277).

Only very late in her therapy does Allen ever consider the role that might have been played in her illness by her childhood and, in particular, by her anger at a mother perceived as unloving. In this context, she recalls a memory that repeats Cardinal's narrative of the mother's rejection of the "treasures" offered by the daughter of *Les Mots pour le dire*. Allen's mother refuses the flowers that her daughter has innocently gathered from a neighbor's yard; more importantly, the mother's "fear of social censure" also leads her to deny her daughter's right to feel anger: "'You're my good girl, and good girls don't get angry'" (269). Even though Allen's analysis of the psychological effects of such events—the learned repression of anger as the price of love and acceptance but at the cost of any sense of "personal power" (269)—explicitly acknowledges its female specificity (270), she nonetheless totally denies it any explanatory role in her subsequent madness. In general, Allen conceives feminism in terms of individual psychology rather than collective solidarity: "I did not see the women's movement first and foremost as a political force. . . . It called me to consider the issue of my worth" (239). Such an analysis confirms the influential role that Betty Friedan's *Feminine Mystique* still plays in American feminism, as does Allen's final belief in salvation through a career. In more general terms, the rejection of the influence of the past, equated with absolute determinism (165), reflects a fundamentally American optimism in freedom and self-determination.

The comparison between *Les Mots pour le dire* and Marie Bellour's *Jeu de l'origine* highlights different aspects of Cardinal's understanding of the female narrative of psychoanalysis, although here too there are significant parallels between the general circumstances of the two narrators. For example, both Maries share a similar familial and social background that emphasizes, in particular, the mother-daughter relationship; both assert confidence in traditional freudian analysis, especially as an initiation into the power of language that transforms both women into writers; both are sensitive to the importance of the Mediterranean context in which they grew up and whose rhythms continue to affect their minds and their emotions in significant ways; for both, analysis continues for over seven years and focuses on the return of the unconscious and on their liberation from childhood repression. Indeed, at times, Bellour's and Cardinal's textual expression has a closeness that is almost eerie; note, for example, the following passages:

> The Mother. . . . she didn't stop irrigating the analysis until the end. (Bellour 69)
> I began to talk about my mother and I didn't stop until the end of the analysis. (MD 86)

> Soon afterwards I had a dream received as premonitory of the end of the treatment: *On a grassy hill a cavalier is standing . . .* (Bellour 136)
> One night I had a dream that I hadn't had in ages. . . . Into the peace and harmony of this setting penetrated a cavalier . . . (MD 205)

> My mother represented rules, daily harassment. . . . Thus she delivered me up to the gaze: of others, of God. (Bellour 65)
> My mother's eye, which I confused with God's (and unconsciously with the eye of the camera), was there and was watching me, evaluating my gestures, my thoughts, letting nothing get by. (MD 191)

Although the particular events that traumatize Bellour (the early repression of lesbian attachments) differ significantly from those that precipitate the illness of Cardinal's narrator, both write an identical maternal narrative—one, moreover, that often stresses the same significant words and concepts. The two daughters are raised (*dressée*) in a matriarchal world in which mothers assume responsibility for the indoctrination of their daughters into patriarchal assumptions; the latter both fall definitively under the oppressive control of the maternal *règle* at the onset of menstruation (*les règles*). In particular, Cardinal's narrator and Bellour each experience severe sexual repression that instills a fear of the very words that name the body they have been taught to ignore; not surprisingly in this case, the recovery of the memory of childhood masturbation plays a significant role in each analysis.

Importantly, then, despite the fact that Bellour and Cardinal credit freudian analysis with their recovery of mental health, they nonetheless substitute a feminist analysis of gender for Freud's theory of sexual anatomy; notably, Bellour also reanalyzes freudian notions of castration and penis envy in terms of phallic power structures (78, 114). Since Bellour publishes with "des femmes" and, like Cixous and Irigaray, reclaims the mother-daughter relationship in terms of lesbian eroticism, her parallel understanding of the politics of gender suggests that Francophone psychoanalytic feminism no doubt has a greater theoretical complexity (at least potentially) than Anglophone feminists have sometimes acknowledged.

Despite the fact that Bellour's confidence in Freud leads her at times to retain conventional psychoanalytic terminology (although she too seeks to write "outside of technical gibberish" [50]), in other ways her feminist revision of traditional analysis goes even further than Cardinal's. Initially, Bellour deliberately chooses to enter therapy with a male analyst: "a great deal of history is in the hands of men. And this business—one of sorcery, of the police, and of law—it seems normal to me that it be a male business" (26). But Bellour soon discovers that her own (female) story has totally disappeared under the general (male) interpretive narrative of traditional psychoanalysis; she realizes simultaneously that she displays no symptoms whatsoever of transference. Bellour's self-liberation from "a conception of mental life and a technique imperatively tied to the transference onto the therapist" (23) constitutes the most radical of challenges to traditional psychoanalysis.

If Bellour's subsequent engagement in a rigorous process of *auto*analysis claims Freud's own as its model and its justification, such an attempt in fact enacts the most profound usurpation possible of the position and the authority of the father/analyst, of the father of analysts. (One wonders if it is not precisely because of the preponderance of female patients that Freud himself and postfreudian therapists so quickly outlawed autoanalysis and installed the transferential relationship at the heart of a successful therapy). In this context, the pronominal fusion of *Ilje* by which Bellour identifies the unification within the female self of "the analyst self and the analysand self" (150)—no doubt the only possible structure at present that can fully guarantee an egalitarian relationship between analyst and analysand—provocatively recalls, even as it subverts, the original maleness of the analyst. Since Bellour's notebooks constitute the primary source material for her autoanalysis, she also emphasizes the centrality of female narrative in feminist psychoanalysis and successfully extends the analytic wholeness of analyst and analysand from the domain of therapy to that of textuality.

The resemblance between Bellour's and Cardinal's respective texts operates most extensively on the level of form and language. Appropriately, such repetition centers on a similarly autoreflective and autogenerative understanding of repetition itself. Like Cardinal, Bellour conceives of psychoanalysis as an essentially linguistic process, an act of writing in which the patterns of repetition, variation, and association that create the distinctive verbal fabric of the text (13, 15) also identify elements key to the analysand's self-understanding (in a pattern, of course, that exactly repeats that of the literary analysis of texts). Bellour's text produces the same lyrical "litanies" (72) that characterize not only Cardinal's writing but the texts of écriture féminine as a whole; she too clearly practices textual autogenerativity (one, moreover, that is often openly multilingual) in the interest of generating an authentic (a multiple) female self (see, for example, 59, 72, 79, 145–46). Not surprisingly, perhaps, given in particular the Mediterranean context she shares with Cardinal (and that both share with Cixous), Bellour is fascinated by verbal rhythms that imitate the repetitive movement of the sea: "the image of the wave that slowly ebbs and flows on the sand . . . ebbs and flows... the wave, the breeze... the wave, the breeze..." (42).

These three narratives of women and psychotherapy confirm the *identity* of *difference* that Turkle's analysis of the cultural specificity of intellectual movements reveals between feminism and freudianism. Although *Tea for Demons* and *Le Jeu de l'origine* differ significantly, even radically, from each other, each bears a strong resemblance to *Les Mots pour le dire*. By separating the diverse tendencies that are combined in Cardinal, by reinforcing some while excluding others, Allen and Bellour make particular aspects of Cardinal's work more visible to us. At the same time, their respective omissions make equally evident the complexity of Cardinal's work and the possibility of achieving coherence and consistency from *within* multicultural dialogue.

Cardinal echoes at one and the same time a characteristically Anglophone commitment to feminist consciousness raising and a more typically Francophone exploration of the en-gendering of the unconscious. She reenacts the dynamics of transference to challenge, on the one hand, the traditional power structure of the heterosexual couple and the priority of the father-daughter relationship, and to reclaim, on the other hand, women's right to love each other by reuniting the mother and the daughter. Like Allen, Cardinal repeats the realistic narrative of women's actual experience that allows the female text to function as analyst in the lives of its readers. Like Bellour, however, Cardinal also creates an autonomous *écriture* that uses linguistic experimentation to rewrite the text of the female self. Whatever "cure" Cardinal herself may have achieved in psychoanalytic therapy, it does not appear in any event to have freed her from the "compulsion to repeat."[24]

NOTES

1. I have intentionally chosen not to capitalize *freudianism,* despite its derivation from a proper name. Given the particular authority of psychoanalytic discourse, imposing at least a semblance of (gender) equality between feminism and freudianism seems to me of far more importance than respect for grammatical rules.

2. The rest of the conversation merely reinforces what in retrospect appears to be the oddly unconscious and yet premonitory nature of this discussion. Jacobus, who goes on to encourage the others to be "very suspicious" of Cixous' and Irigaray's psychoanalytic discourse, has since produced a series of textual interpretations quite similarly informed by Lacanian thought (*Reading*). Gilbert, who totally rejects the Francophone notion of a female language and raises no objections to Jacobus' dismissal of "Father Ong" as "very conservative," will, a few years later, develop a theory about gender and language that not only bears some resemblance to that of Francophone feminists (and certainly includes a serious reflection on their work) but draws heavily—and sympathetically—on Walter Ong's ideas for its articulation ("Sexual Ling.").

3. The narrator of *Les Grands Désordres* attacks freudian theory from a specifically feminist perspective that recalls, in particular, Anglophone charges of personal and cultural bias: "[Freud] would have done better not to theorize his brilliant discoveries. In theorizing them, he fell into every trap he denounced. With every word written by Freud, one has to undertake the psychoanalysis of Freud. With each one of his words, you have to remember that he was a man, an Austrian Jew, who lived in the 19th century and only treated the middle class" (222).

4. Hannah Lerman makes the same point: "One's use of Freudian language demonstrates, unfortunately, an acceptance of Freudian metaphysics and philosophy and therefore its premises and viewpoint about women even though one tries overtly to repudiate just these aspects of the theory as Chodorow does" (187).

5. It is not my intention to undermine the important challenge to traditional psychoanalysis that Schafer represents; he is the one scientist to have

joined textual critics in the use of narrative theory to reconceptualize psycho-analytic discourse and therapy (*On Narrative*).

6. During a recent appearance on "Les Dossiers de l'écran," when a viewer asked whether Cardinal attributed her cure to *l'écriture* or to *l'analyse*, she asserted, "I owe everything to analysis." Her subsequent justification, however— "I had never written before; I began as early as the second year of analysis"— would seem to support the opposite conclusion better. In her autobiographical account of her madness included in Suzanne Horer and Jeanne Scoquet's *La Création étouffée*, she names her first book—and not her analysis—as "the key that opened the door of my life" (154).

7. Jane Gallop confirms the plausibility of such a process: "My trip into the dictionary seems to have induced certain repetitions, certain acting outs. It seems appropriate to say that I have had a transference onto the dictionary. Now this is neither so silly nor so precious as it might sound. According to Lacan, transference occurs in relation to a 'subject presumed to know'" (*Daughter's* 108).

8. If the existence of verbal play characteristic of the experimental novel can apparently be overlooked in designating a (male) work as autobiographical, the process does not seem to work in reverse. The a priori conviction that Cardinal relates her own story appears to blind both Doubrovsky and Lejeune to the autoreferentiality and the autogenerativity of Cardinal's own linguistic practice: "the new 'novel of analysis' has never heard of the 'new novel.' Whatever in modern writing might prove disturbing to a mass audience has been eliminated: hence the welcome reserved, for example, for a book like Marie Cardinal's *Les Mots pour le dire* in which the words to say 'it' remain reassuring, leaving the habitual order of words untouched" ("Initiative" 95).

9. Elizabeth Abel argues that women's friendships in general show an affinity with the analytic relationship. The difference that clarifies the specific dynamics of female friendship results from the analyst's refusal to identify fully with the analysand. Only in female friendship are the roles interchangeable and indistinguishable ("(E)Merging" 419).

10. If the narrator's initial desire to use analysis to "bring her father back to life" stems from an assumption similar to that of Yalom, that his absence has left "an ugly wound" (77), her search quickly leads her to the opposite conclusion: "He never hurt me, never marked me, never touched me, and perhaps that's why I have never sought to substitute any other father for him" (80). Perhaps Yalom dismisses such narrative assertions as a fabrication of the conscious mind, but Cardinal's textual evidence actually consists in the analysis of two recurrent nightmares; both confirm that the narrator has no independent knowledge of her actual father and no nostalgia for the incompetent father, unable to protect her, whose image she has inherited from her mother (78).

11. Significantly, Michèle Montrelay's description of the adult male's typical

fantasy repeats virtually all the key elements of Cardinal's hallucination: "First, a *central tube* which cannot be closed and satisfying [*sic*] container of an interior. . . . Intestine, pipe, image of cavern. . . . Inside, either it's the void, or else a superfluity that must be jettisoned as soon as possible. A kind of vague and terrifying suction. A permanent state of blurring. On the surface—and isn't that characteristic of male sexuality—there's *an eye*" (qtd. in Jardine, *Gynesis* 70).

12. Daniel Lagache notes that after a successful psychoanalysis relapse becomes possible in specific circumstances "able to reawaken infantile neurosis" (95). Here, the attempted rape of the adult exactly repeats that of the child. In the meantime, however, the "therapeutic" neurosis that transference is designed to substitute for the "clinical" neurosis (Lagache 90) *also* repeats the rape.

13. Catharine MacKinnon has described consciousness raising as a "critical method" specific to feminism (543).

14. In other contexts, however, Yalom also recognizes that women's texts tend to reinscribe into psychoanalysis the mother-daughter story that is absent from Freud's writings (66).

15. Ellie Ragland-Sullivan provides an excellent feminist analysis of Lacanian psychoanalytic theory in the final chapter of her book on Lacan. Ragland-Sullivan and Hunter both focus their critique on the consequences or the interpretation of Lacanian linguistic theory, but they fail to challenge the core assumptions on language acquisition that to me seem most problematic: the division between "unconscious and conscious language" along maternal and paternal lines (Ragland-Sullivan 305; see chap. 2).

16. The association of the mother and madness also plays a key role in Cardinal's alternative maternal narrative: "It seems to me that the thing took root in me permanently when I understood that we were going to assassinate Algeria. For Algeria was my real mother" (112). The narrator's symptomatic bleeding not only repeats her real mother's desire to abort her but the terrible bloodletting of the Algerian civil war as well. The mother informs her daughter of the attempted abortion as the latter stares down at "the same sidewalk on which the blood of hatred will later flow" (161).

17. Furthermore, Cardinal alternatively identifies *la folle* with *la salope*. The inevitable association with *la saloperie* specifically names the mother as the madwoman.

18. In another revealing slip, Cardinal repeats the same sentence twice, at the beginning of two distant chapters, to connect the metaphorical and the literal mothers to each other and to the beginning ("French Algeria was living her agony" [111]) and the end ("my mother was living her agony" [317]) of her illness.

19. The controversy surrounding Jean Laplanche's new French translation of Freud's complete works has recently refocused attention on the issue of Freud's cultural specificity. In defense of his claim to return to a more "literal"

Freud, Laplanche notes that what his detractors critique as an "'*ethnocentric*' translation is the natural penchant of almost *all the translators of French culture: to turn the original text around to suit oneself*" ("Mot à mot" 159).

20. In my view the film version of *Les Mots pour le dire* repeats many of the same errors. For example, the film imposes the visual presence of the analyst in ways that grant him far more authority than his novelistic counterpart. During the therapeutic sessions, he frequently appears in the frame with the female patient (now called Marie); often, in fact, he dominates the image. Furthermore, he is also young, handsome, and *tall,* in contrast to Cardinal's "little puppet," and played by Daniel Lagache, a professional psychoanalyst. Moreover, the camera stays with him after Marie's departure and first shows us the male doctor in the act of writing the case study. In the novel, on the other hand, the narrator frequently verifies the crucial absence of male writing: "Often I had abruptly turned towards him, in the middle of one of my ramblings, thinking I would surprise him in the act of writing. . . . He wasn't writing, he was listening. I would have hated for there to be any sort of instrument—a piece of paper, a pencil—between him and me." (173).

21. As I noted earlier, such a comparative context has been strongly characteristic of an Anglophone feminist approach to Francophone texts; all previous studies of *Les Mots pour le dire,* in particular, follow this pattern. Thus, the repetitiveness of feminist criticism echoes that which is discernible in its fictional practice. However, since repetition always involves difference as well as identity, I have chosen not to return to the same texts considered by my predecessors: Sylvia Plath's *Bell Jar* (Martin, Yalom), Margaret Atwood's *Surfacing* (Yalom), Jeanne Hyvrard's *Mère la mort* (LeClézio), and Marie-Thérèse Humbert's *A l'autre bout de moi* (Lionnet).

22. Turkle makes essentially the same point: "In its susceptibility to cultural influence, psychoanalysis is not unique. Most intellectual movements undergo some form of cultural adaptation to different national settings." She does believe, however, that the fact that psychoanalysis encompasses a "therapeutic strategy" as well as an intellectual position results in its special sensitivity to cultural context, since the effectiveness of therapy depends upon its relevance to "a culture's prevailing modes of making sense of experience" (49). Feminism, of course, can be expected to work the same way, not only because its project also depends upon a "therapeutic strategy" of social transformation but because the analysis of gender relations can only make convincing sense of experience when the actual conditions of men and women in a particular culture are taken into account.

23. In this respect, the importance in the semantic spectrum of the term *fantasy* of the domains of both literature ("literary or dramatic fiction characterized by highly fanciful or supernatural elements") and psychology ("an imagined event or condition fulfilling a wish") is revealing. Although fantasy

theoretically differs from its synonyms (e.g., imagination, fancy) by connoting those "mental representations having little similarity to the real world," psychoanalysts have tended to confuse female reality with romantic fiction. Thus, Bettelheim assumes that fairy tales prepare children for their respective adult roles (*Uses of Enchantment*). Similarly, Allen here inscribes the romantic dream of the princess passively waiting for Prince Charming to "save" her.

24. When asked about a phrase in *Les Grands Désordres* ("*la clé sur le porte*"), which appears to refer to an earlier work, Cardinal described this particular textual repetition in explicitly psychoanalytic terms: "In essence, it's a freudian slip that doesn't really surprise me. When you are involved in a writer's life, you always dig the same hole. The unconscious works overtime" (Cahoreau 122).

I began by echoing Suzanne Juhasz's query "What happened?" and listening with her to hear the response en-gender itself. I end by recalling Patrocinio P. Schweikart's question "What does it mean?" and seeking with her to en-gender an answer. "What does it mean," asks Schweikart, "for a woman, reading as a woman, to read literature written by a woman writing as a woman?" (51). What does it mean, I am tempted to repeat, for a woman, (re)reading and (re)writing as a woman, to (re)read and (re)write literature, (re)read and (re)written by a woman (re)reading and (re)writing as a woman? Such a paren-thetical and palimpsestic repetition, such a self-reflective and self-gen(d)erative inter-rogation, offers an appropriately bilingual ré-sumé, both a conclusion and a new beginning, to the *contexture* of *feminism*.

I have discovered that contemporary written feminism en-genders it-self as a *lingua franca,* as a language that by definition escapes defini-tion: *"lingua franca.* Any hybrid language used as a medium of com-munication between peoples of different languages." (That *Lingua franca,* when capitalized, refers more specifically to a multilingual mix-ture of languages spoken in the Mediterranean area would surely not displease Marie Cardinal. Nor is it irrelevant that the French connection embedded in *franca* reminds a woman reading and writing as an Amer-ican of the Francophone context of her own feminism.) Re-viewed as a "hybrid," feminism names our heritage ("the offspring of genetically dissimilar parents"), our hope ("something of mixed origin or compo-sition"), and the role that language plays in the actualization of both ("a word whose elements are derived from different languages"). More-over, etymology (Latin *hibrida,* mongrel) identifies the disparagement with which "unnatural" efforts at recombination must often contend.

Schweikart further suggests that "a feminist reading—actually a rereading—is a kind of therapeutic analysis" (50); and I seem to have repeated Jane Gallop's own experience with textual, linguistic, and psychoanalytic repetition: I too "have had a transference onto the dictionary" and I too find that "this is neither so silly nor so precious as it might sound" (108). As I reread my own text, I realize that I have taken to heart Cardinal's injunction (her en-joinment) to "open words"; the pages of this book are en-joined by my own recurrent practice of this procedure. At some point, asking questions became an *interrogation,* a "formal," an "official" methodology—appropriately characteristic in that case of feminist theory as a whole. With an equally suitable self-referentiality, *interrogation* precisely identifies a means of asking questions ("to examine by formal questioning") and not (at least not necessarily) a way of finding answers. As my own practice indicates, the linguistics of feminism appears to me to fall within the realm of etymology rather than that of definition. Roland Barthes' conception of the inherently multilingual text describes the verbal "openness" of written feminism: "the text borrows from the dictionary not the (closed) definitional power but the infinite structure" (*S/Z* 126). If etymology, by its own derivation, focuses not only on the "origins" but on the "truth" of words (from Greek *etumos,* true, real), the process that it names—that is, "the historical *development* of a word"; "the study of its *changes* in form and meaning"; "semantic *evolution*" (my emphasis)—is one better designed to reveal linguistic "passage" and to highlight the interconnections (the en-joinments) of words than to fix their precise meaning or to distinguish each of them from all others.

Curiously, what surely has to be conceived as a purely arbitrary selection process, by virtue of which some words and not others called themselves to my attention (for, with perhaps two or three exceptions, the words that I "open" in the preceding pages are the only ones that ever drove me into lexical "analysis"), turns out in retrospect to reveal a remarkable degree of ideological consistency. I have inadvertently adopted a vocabulary that writes an embedded feminist narrative. To begin with, I have re-created both Cardinal's palimpsestic text and her dialectics of subversion and conformity. Upon scratching the surface of words, I have consistently discovered that the presence and the importance of gender lies beneath. Thus, *héroïne* shows us that women can hide in the most unlikely of places; *nightmare* exposes what appeared to be the generic horror story—and perhaps the unconscious itself—as specifically female "plots"; *vernacular* describes the everyday speech of humanity in terms of a usage characteristic of women; *vague* and *réglé* encode the very dynamics of sex and gender relations. At other times, the general language of literary culture writes women into the origins of a reality from which their history and experience have appeared to exclude them. *Text, fabrication,* and *fiction* embed the same artisanal activity by virtue of which *embroidery* transforms writing into a female craft. Both *literary* and literary *perversions* contain typically female practices, as does the textual activity of the *ghostwriter* and the *nègre.* Elsewhere, the male surgical activity of the *graft* conceals one of the definitional procedures of *écriture féminine,* and *luce* turns classical (and so classically male) knowledge itself over to women.

At the same time, my interest was repeatedly captured by words that in some way represent the very process of repetition that is equally central to Cardinal's textual practice and to feminist narratives of women's writing and of female culture. Indeed, *culture* itself originates in a *revolve* that now seems particularly reminiscent of feminism's own "revolutionary" potential. *Rhythm* too encodes the recurrent mobility that connects my own linguistic progression (my attention to such terms as *citation, discourse,* and *translation,* among others, that all help keep my text "in motion") to that of *écriture féminine* in general. Moreover, I now realize that I have in fact invaded the realm of definition quite as consistently as that of etymology and that I have found repeated therein a similar female capacity for "duplicity," for the "reconciliation" of multiple and plural meanings.

This re-presentation of the dictionary, from which my own words now appear to derive, offers one metaphor for "the complex process of reinventing, relearning, or reviewing the alphabet" that Sandra Gilbert and Susan Gubar describe as "a crucial act of self-definition and self-assertion" for women writers ("Ceremonies" 46). Ironically, given a literary history throughout which men writers have based their place of privilege on privileged access to language and particularly to its various sciences (see, for example, Gilbert and Gubar, *No Man's Land*), the text that encodes the general process by which human beings use language to understand and to structure the world seems uniquely designed to represent the *difference* of women's discourse. The dictionary, in which language simultaneously replaces and encodes reality, defines language as intrinsically self-referential and self-generative *and* as literally so, as capable, therefore, of engendering and representing an authentic female reality. Etymology reintroduces our foreign and forgotten ancestors into language, as feminism rewrites women into culture. The definition itself, like feminist scholarship as a whole, posits both unity and opposition only to mediate between them by grouping different meanings, drawn from different fields of knowledge and different spheres of reality, into a single common category.

I suggested earlier, in a different context, that a careful attentiveness to the intersections of words might help us create an authentic interdisciplinarity by allowing us to discern the similarities of thought that have been isolated and imprisoned within traditional boundaries of knowledge. When I now pay attention to my own textual practice, I discover with considerable interest that language itself appears to respect contemporary feminism's most fundamental intercultural relationship. The words that have aroused my curiosity re-create in miniature a structure of interconnected parts; they organize the contexture of feminism. In almost every incidence, my interest has been captured by terms that are cognates in French and English; moreover, in the rare instances when this is not the case (e.g., ghostwriter, *nègre*), the nonparallel terms nonetheless remain equally (and similarly) revelatory.

The prefix *inter-* signifies not only "between or among" but also "mutually or together"; and, indeed, the desire to open words appears upon reflection to unite Anglophone and Francophone feminist writers in some unexpected ways. We are, of course, hardly surprised to encounter verbal playfulness and discourse on language among Francophone practitioners and theorists of *écriture féminine*. Moreover, I have already commented on the close resemblance between Cardinal's textual practice and that of Cixous, Leclerc, Chawaf, or Irigaray. More importantly, as we also know, the critical essays of Lamy, Garcia, or Auffret, for example, illustrate as well as describe the very same techniques, characteristic of women's writing in general, that also surface repeatedly in Cardinal's work. Of more interest is an Anglophone phenomenon whose significance I had certainly, at the very least, underestimated until I began to see signs of it in my own writing.

We might still explain (away) the provocatively visible word play of Jane Gallop's essays in terms of their Francophone context; by provoking the interaction of content and form, Lacan's discourse would generate among his commentators a Lacanian discourse in its own image. On the other hand, the structural similarity between the functioning of language in psychoanalytic theory and in women's writing, a parallel that Cardinal signals to our attention, may already be of considerable importance to an effort to understand "what it means" to read and write as a woman. Despite the consistency with which men introduce Freud or Lacan into their discussion of narrative theory, they still seek for the most part to maintain a clear-cut distinction between the respective linguistic conceptions of psychoanalysis and of literature (cf. Skura).

More recently, however, even the discourse of Anglophone critics of female culture appears to have been "contaminated" by linguistic play (made impure by "mixture," by "mongrelization"). To be perfectly frank, I have sometimes reacted with irritation to the constant punning that characterizes Gilbert and Gubar's current work (e.g., *No Man's Land*, "Sexual Ling."). It was as if they had taken on a stylistic tic that appeared to be designed to create a superficial appearance of postmodernist chic but that functioned in the process to distract us from the seriousness of their textual and contextual analysis of female modernism. But my own experience now tells me that the feminist need to interrogate words should not be dismissed on either side of the Atlantic as a frivolous game or a private indulgence.

The etymology of *paronomasia* (from Greek *paronomazein*, to call by a different name, to name besides) presents women's word play as yet another strategy of subversion, an effort to follow Emily Dickinson's advice to "Tell all the Truth but tell it slant— / Success in Circuit lies" ("Tell" 1–2). Like the feminist parentheses, word play functions as an aside, not a digressive nor an expendable remark, but one that gets right to the point—at least for those who are meant to hear it.[1] Moreover, any such defensive function no doubt conceals a complementary offensive measure; the derivation of *pun* (from Latin *punctum*, hole, point, from *pungere*, to prick, pierce) suggests that a practice that allows women to introduce the question of gender into the very heart of language—and to inter-rogate one another in the process—may also act as a thorn in men's sides and leave a visible tear in the text of the dominant culture.

If, like Leclerc and Ronfard before me, I have ended up (once again) repeating Cardinal beyond my conscious (or, at least, my consciously acknowledged) intentions and producing a critical discourse that responds to some extent to her call for a feminist collaboration, I should perhaps not be surprised to discover that my own text also echoes her challenge to the conventional distinctions that even we as feminists have been willing to make between feminists and among feminisms. Through all the diverse ways in which these mismatches have been formulated—

autobiography/fiction; realism/modernism; gynocritics/gynesis; female culture/*écriture féminine;* literary criticism/textual theory; content/ form; ideology/formalism; Anglophone/Francophone—we hear the insistent repetition of the same apparent need to choose between women's actual experience and its textual means of expression.

Yet, my own effort to read written feminism has taught me that, "for a woman, reading as a woman, to read literature written by a woman writing as a woman," means the seemingly inevitable collapse of all such false dualisms and oppositions and, in addition, of the implicitly hierarchical framework within which they are necessarily contained. At no point in my analysis have I been able to consider separately the formal characteristics of women's writing and the thematics of women's reality, precisely the two issues that are supposed to prevent the hybridization of Francophone and Anglophone feminism. Linguistic experimentation, generated by the sign of the female body, generates in its turn a political discourse of gender relations; so does the "free" association (lingua *franca*) of analytic language. Self-referential narrative continues emphatically to refer to the female self, in part, no doubt, because the text referred to is so often the woman's own. Repetition writes textuality into existence at the same time as female culture. There are differences, of course, repeated ones; still, as Adrienne Rich so appropriately puts it, "We are translations into different dialects / of a text still being written / in the original" ("Sibling" 5.20–22).

This ability to transcend boundaries and/or this inability to be contained within acceptable limits reminds us once more of the need to conceptualize written feminism as an interwoven structure of texts, as a contexture in its own right. Notably, although feminism seems increasingly tied to a theory of language, speech, and discourse, twentieth-century feminist writing can apparently not be made to fit into any other context, neither that of realism (language is at once inadequate, untrustworthy, and insistently visible), nor that of modernism (language repeatedly refers to the reality of women's lives), nor that of postmodernism (language's recurrent failures have a precise ideological meaning).

At the same time, and for similar reasons, feminist theory and criticism (from Greek *kritos,* separated, chosen; from *krimein,* to separate, choose) clearly choose not to be separated from women's literary (in the case at hand, fictional and autobiographical) writings, for these texts serve precisely to inscribe the voices and the lives of real women into the contexture of feminism; moreover, female literature's analytic dimension makes an observable difference in how we are able to perceive theoretical discourse itself (from Greek *theoretikos,* able to perceive; from *theoretos,* observable). Rather than *mis*using literature, as I had initially feared, I think that my work and that of others creates or respects what may be a distinctively feminist model of usage (a *ms*-use?). Cardinal's work, perceived as a primary context (the oeuvre that it is), not only allows access to female reality, but its own diversity and repetitiveness (such that the originality of any particular idea perhaps matters less than the particular position in which it is placed in a system of thought) have allowed me to approach it from a variety of directions and so to explore more fully what reading and writing from a feminist perspective might mean. As Nelly Furman argues: "from a feminist viewpoint the question is not whether a literary work has been written by a woman and reflects her experience of life, or how it compares to other works by women, but rather how it lends itself to be read from a feminist position" (Greene and Kahn 69).

In light of this last concern, let me offer a final consolation to the many people who have repeatedly sought over the past few years to replace Marie Cardinal with Marguerite Duras. In some sense, a palimpsestic substitution, a repetition, has indeed taken place. To begin with, there are interesting parallels between Cardinal and Duras, in terms of biographical facts and textual interests; moreover, the two texts whose echoes make this particularly clear, *Autrement dit* and *Les Parleuses,* are precisely the female dialogues on which Suzanne Lamy bases her theory of the specificity of *écriture féminine.* Duras, for example, scarcely knew her father. She has lived "in reprieve" since her arrival in France in early adulthood; she cannot view France as her home, but the Vietnam where she grew up and whose language she spoke as a child epitomizes the "horror of colonialism." Duras attaches great importance to the female voice and consistently associates madness and women's speech. She cites menstruation among the many specifically female subjects that society views as taboo; still, she receives letters that insist "*I'm* Lol V. Stein," suggesting that her readers find their own female reality repeated in her works.

Moreover, Duras's *L'Amant* (1984) openly presents itself as a text that repeats—but differently ("Before, I spoke of the transparent periods. . . . Here I speak of the hidden periods" [14])—her earlier work and, in particular, *Un Barrage contre le Pacifique* (1950). Autocitation serves Duras as well as Cardinal to fuse fiction and autobiography and to write a discourse that is at once realistic and lyrical. Both versions of the same story combine the three elements that most often resurface in Cardinal's own repetition: passionate love for a mother who is not only mad but who loves only her eldest child; a girl's childhood and adolescence in a French colony where she is caught between the worlds of the colonialist and of the colonized; a will and a desire to write that is stronger than anything else. In terms of the inscription of femaleness, Duras uses in *L'Amant* (as elsewhere) an alternance of "I" and "she," the latter associated at times with female madness and the transformation of the narrator into a literary character; Duras also en-genders proper names in ways that allow a playful reflection on L (*elle*).[2] Finally, Duras and Cardinal are included among the women writers who bear witness in *La Création étouffée*. Just as Cardinal once again tells the story of her mother's abortion attempt and of her own subsequent struggle against madness—the same narrative that eventually informs *Ecoutez la mer, La Souricière, Les Mots pour le dire, Autrement dit,* and *Le Passé empiété*—Duras recalls the events repeated in *Un Barrage* and *L'Amant*.

I like to think, then, that I might indeed have begun where I concluded and that I conclude by pointing out the possibility of beginning again—and again.[3] Such repetitions suggest that concentration on a single writer may not only help us to understand women's writing in general but other women writers in particular. As Garcia notes at the end of an intercultural comparison between Colette and Virginia Woolf, the texts of different women consistently coincide to create the impression of "the writing of a single woman" (1:350), of an "eternal repetition, writing always begun again in a continual echo" (1:347).

NOTES

1. Thus, my analysis comes full circle (see chap. 1). According to Juhasz, you will recall, women provide contextual detail and narrative background while men get right to the point. The female text now appears to do both simultaneously.

2. Janice Morgan offers an excellent analysis of the textual relationships between *L'Amant* and *Un Barrage contre le Pacifique* that suggests remarkable similarities between Duras and Cardinal. The examples of textual repetition in Duras extend far beyond these two works, of course. In perhaps the best-known case, the story of Anne-Marie Stretter reappears in *Lol V. Stein, Le Vice-consul, India Song,* and *L'Amour*.

3. Hélène Cixous shares the same personal background (e.g., a fatherless childhood, Algerian upbringing) and textual interests ("Sorties" in *La Jeune Née* incorporates long passages of integral self-quotation from "Le Rire de la Méduse") that characterize Cardinal and Duras. See Conley and Moi (102).

WORKS CITED

Abel, Elizabeth. "Editor's Introduction." *Critical Inquiry* 8 (1981): 173–78.
———. "(E)Merging Identities: The Dynamics of Female Friendship in Contemporary Fiction by Women." *Signs* 6 (1981): 413–44.
Allen, Carol, with Herbert S. Lustig, M.D. *Tea with Demons.* New York: Ballantine, 1985.
Andrew, J. Dudley. "The Structuralist Study of Narrative: Its History, Use, and Limits." *The Horizon of Literature.* Ed. Paul Hernadi. Lincoln: University of Nebraska Press, 1982. 99–124.
Aptheker, Bettina. *Tapestries of Life: Women's Work, Women's Consciousness, and the Meaning of Daily Experience.* Amherst: University of Massachusetts Press, 1989.
Arcana, Judith. *Our Mothers' Daughters.* Berkeley: Shameless Hussy, 1979.
Ardener, Edwin. "Belief and the Problem of Women." *Perceiving Women.* Ed. Shirley Ardener. New York: Wiley, 1977. 19–27.
———. "The 'Problem' Revisited." *Perceiving Women.* Ed. Shirley Ardener. New York: Wiley, 1977. 1–17.
Armstrong, Nancy. *Desire and Domestic Fiction: A Political History of the Novel.* New York: Oxford University Press, 1987.
Auffret, Séverine. *Nous, Clytemnestre.* Paris: des femmes, 1984.
Badinter, Elisabeth. *L'Amour en plus: histoire de l'amour maternel.* Paris: Flammarion, 1980.
———. *L'Un est l'autre: des relations entre hommes et femmes.* Paris: Jacob, 1986.
Bal, Mieke. *Narratologie: essai sur la signification narrative dans quatre romans modernes.* Paris: Klincksieck, 1977.
Barnes, Mary, and J. Berke. *Mary Barnes: Un Voyage à travers la folie.* Paris: Seuil, 1973.
Baroch, Christiane. "Au Féminin." *La Quinzaine littéraire* 16–30 juin 1978: 7.
Barthes, Roland. *The Pleasure of the Text.* Trans. Richard Miller. New York: Hill and Wang, 1975.

281

—. *S/Z*. Trans. Richard Miller. New York: Hill and Wang, 1974.

Beauvoir, Simone de. *Le Deuxième sexe*. 2 vols. Paris: Gallimard, 1967.

—. *La Femme rompue*. Paris: Gallimard, 1967.

Bellour, Marie. *Le Jeu de l'origine: récit d'une auto-analyse*. Paris: des femmes, 1985.

Benjamin, Walter. "The Storyteller." *Illuminations*. Trans. Harry Zohn. New York: Schocken, 1969.

Bensaid, Norbert. "Un si bon divan." *Le Nouvel Observateur* 7 juillet 1975: 51.

Benstock, Shari. "The Feminist Critique: Mastering our Monstrosity." *Tulsa Studies in Women's Literature* 2 (1983): 137–49.

—. "From the Editor's Perspective." *Tulsa Studies in Women's Literature* 3 (1984): 5–27.

—. *Women of the Left Bank*. Austin: University of Texas Press, 1986.

Benveniste, Emile. *Problèmes de linguistique générale*. 2 vols. Paris: Gallimard, 1966.

Bernheimer, Charles and Claire Kahane, eds. *In Dora's Case: Freud—Hysteria—Feminism*. New York: Columbia University Press, 1985.

Betensky, A. "Aeschylus' *Oresteia:* The Power of Clytemnestra." *Ramus* 7 (1978): 11–25.

Bettelheim, Bruno. *The Uses of Enchantment: The Meaning and Importance of Fairy Tales*. New York: Knopf, 1976.

Bloom, Harold. *The Anxiety of Influence*. New York: Oxford University Press, 1973.

Bogen, Nancy. *Klytaimnestra Who Stayed at Home*. New York: Twickenham, 1979.

Boose, Lynda E., and Betty S. Flowers, eds. *Daughters and Fathers*. Baltimore: Johns Hopkins University Press, 1989.

Breen, Katie. "Marie Cardinal retrouve ses racines." *Voyelles* février 1981: 12–14.

Breuer, Joseph, and Sigmund Freud. *Studies on Hysteria*. 1895. *The Standard Edition of the Complete Psychological Works of Sigmund Freud*. Ed. James Strachey. London: Hogarth, 1953–74.

Brooks, Peter. *Reading for the Plot: Design and Intention in Narrative*. New York: Knopf, 1984.

Brownstein, Rachel. *Becoming a Heroine*. Harmondsworth: Penguin, 1982.

Bullfinch, Thomas. *Bullfinch's Mythology*. Ed. Edmund Fuller. New York: Dell, 1959.

Cahoreau, Gilles. "Au Peigne fin: Marie Cardinal." *Lire* octobre 1987: 119–22.

Canestrier, Edith. "Marie Cardinal: De Retour en Algérie." *Marie-Claire* novembre 1980: 300.

Cardinal, Marie. *Autrement dit*. Paris: Livre de poche, 1977. (AD)

—. *La Clé sur la porte*. Paris: Livre de poche, 1972. (CP)

———. *Devotion and Disorder.* Trans. Karin Montin. London: Women's Press, 1990.

———. "Les Dossiers de l'écran." *Antenne* 2, Paris. 14 juin 1988.

———. *Ecoutez la mer.* 1962. Paris: Julliard, 1978. (EM)

———. *Cet Eté-là.* 1967. Paris: Livre de poche, 1979.

———. *Les Grands Désordres.* Paris: Grasset, 1987. (GD)

———. *La Médée d'Euripide.* Montreal: VLB, 1986. (ME)

———. *Les Mots pour le dire.* Paris: Livre de poche, 1975. (MD)

———. *Les Mots pour le dire.* Dir. José Pinheiro. With Nicole Garcia and Marie-Christine Barrault. Belmont, 1983.

———. *La Mule de Corbillard.* 1963. Paris: Julliard, 1979. (MC)

———. *Le Passé empiété.* Paris: Grasset, 1983. (PE)

———. *Au Pays de mes racines.* Paris: Grasset, 1980. (PR)

———. *La Souricière.* 1965. Paris: Julliard, 1978. (S)

———. *Une Vie pour deux.* Paris: Livre de poche, 1978. (VD)

———. *The Words to Say It.* Trans. Patricia Goodheart. Preface and Afterword by Bruno Bettelheim. Cambridge, Mass.: VanVector and Goodheart, 1983.

Chambers, Ross. *Story and Situation: Narrative Seduction and the Power of Fiction.* Minneapolis: University of Minnesota Press, 1984.

Chapsal, Madeleine. "Deux femmes sur un divan." *Express* 9 juin 1975: 44–45.

Chatman, Seymour. *Story and Discourse: Narrative Structure in Fiction and Film.* Ithaca: Cornell University Press, 1978.

Chawaf, Chantal. *Fées de toujours.* Paris: Plon, 1988.

———. *Maternité.* Paris: Stock, 1979.

———. *Retable.* Paris: des femmes, 1974.

Chesler, Phyllis. Review of *The Hungry Self,* by Kim Chernin. *New York Times Book Review* July 13 1986: 34.

———. *Women and Madness.* Garden City, N.Y.: Doubleday, 1972.

Chicago, Judy. *The Birth Project.* Garden City, N.Y.: Doubleday, 1985.

———. *Embroidering Our Heritage: The Dinner Party Needlework.* Garden City, N.Y.: Doubleday, 1980.

Chodorow, Nancy. *The Reproduction of Mothering: Psychoanalysis and the Sociology of Gender.* Berkeley: University of California Press, 1978.

Cixous, Hélène. "L'Approche de Clarice Lispector." *Poétique* 40 (1979): 408–19.

———. *La Jeune Née.* Paris: 10/18, 1975.

———. *Portrait de Dora.* Paris: des femmes, 1976.

———. "Le Rire de la méduse." *L'Arc* 61 (1975): 39–54.

Clifford, James. *The Predicament of Culture: Twentieth-Century Ethnography, Literature, and Art.* Cambridge: Harvard University Press, 1988.

Compagnon, Antoine. *La Seconde main*. Paris: Seuil, 1979.

Conley, Verena Andermatt. *Hélène Cixous: Writing the Feminine*. Lincoln: University of Nebraska Press, 1984.

Corddry, Mary. "Looking into Abyss of Self." *U.S.Sun* 1983, C2.

Cott, Nancy. *The Bonds of Womanhood*. New Haven: Yale University Press, 1977.

Crowder, Diane. "Amazons and Mothers? Monique Wittig, Hélène Cixous and Theories of Women's Writing." *Contemporary Literature* 24 (Summer 1984): 117–44.

DeKoven, Marianne. *A Different Language*. Madison: University of Wisconsin Press, 1983.

de Lauretis, Teresa, ed. *Feminist Studies, Critical Studies*. Bloomington: Indiana University Press, 1986.

Démeron, Pierre. "Marie Cardinal, sa fille et la drogue." *Marie-Claire* octobre 1987: 66–74.

Dickinson, Emily. "Tell all the Truth but tell it slant." *The Complete Poems of Emily Dickinson*. Ed. Thomas H. Johnson. Boston: Little, Brown, 1890.

Didier, Béatrice. *L'Ecriture-Femme*. Paris: Presses Universitaires de France, 1981.

Dinnerstein, Dorothy. *The Mermaid and the Minotaur: Sexual Arrangements and Human Malaise*. New York: Harper, 1976.

Doubrovsky, Serge. *Fils*. Paris: Galilée, 1977.

———. "L'Initiative aux maux: écrire sa psychanalyse." *Cahiers Confrontation* 1 (1979): 95–113.

Duchen, Claire, ed. and trans. *French Connections: Voices from the Women's Movement in France*. Amherst: University of Massachusetts Press, 1987.

DuPlessis, Rachel. *Writing beyond the Ending: Narrative Strategies of Twentieth-Century Women Writers*. Bloomington: Indiana University Press, 1985.

Duras, Marguerite. *L'Amant*. Paris: Minuit, 1984.

———. *The War: A Memoir*. Trans. Barbara Bray. New York: Pantheon, 1986.

Duras, Marguerite, and Xavière Gauthier. *Les Parleuses*. Paris: Minuit, 1974.

Durham, Carolyn A. "Feminism and Formalism: Dialectical Structures in Marie Cardinal's *Une Vie pour deux*." *Tulsa Studies in Women's Literature* 4 (1985): 83–99.

———. "Patterns of Influence: Simone de Beauvoir and Marie Cardinal." *French Review* 60 (1987): 341–47.

Eisenstein, Hester, and Alice Jardine, eds. *The Future of Difference*. New Brunswick: Rutgers University Press, 1980.

Eliot, T. S. "Little Gidding." *The Complete Poems and Plays 1909–1950*. New York: Harcourt, Brace & World, 1934.

Fehervary, Helen. "Christa Wolf's Prose: A Landscape of Masks." *New German Critique* 27 (1982): 57–87.

Felman, Shoshana. *La Folie et la chose littéraire.* Paris: Seuil, 1978.

"Feminist Readings: French Texts/American Contexts." *Yale French Studies* 62 (1981).

Fetterley, Judith. *The Resisting Reader: A Feminist Approach to American Fiction.* Bloomington: Indiana University Press, 1978.

Fink, Laurie. "The Rhetoric of Marginality: Why I Do Feminist Theory." *Tulsa Studies in Women's Literature* 5 (1986): 251–72.

Flax, Jane. "Re-Membering the Selves: Is the Repressed Gendered?" *Michigan Quarterly Review* 26 (1987): 92–110.

Fowler, Roger. *Linguistics and the Novel.* London: Methuen, 1977.

Freud, Sigmund. *A General Introduction to Psychoanalysis.* 1920. Trans. Joan Riviere. New York: Washington Square, 1952.

———. *De la Technique psychanalytique.* Paris: Presses Universitaires de France, 1953.

———. "Fragment of an Analysis of a Case of Hysteria." 1905. *Standard Edition of the Complete Psychological Works of Sigmund Freud.* Ed. and trans. James Strachey. 24 vols. New York: Macmillan, 1953–74. 7:3–122. (*SE*)

———. "Female Sexuality." 1931. In *SE.* 21:225-43.

———. "On Femininity." 1933. In *SE.* 22:112–35.

Friday, Nancy. *My Mother/My Self: The Daughter's Search for Identity.* New York: Dell, 1977.

Friedan, Betty. *The Feminine Mystique.* New York: Dell, 1963.

Friedman, Norman. "Point of View in Fiction: The Development of a Critical Concept." *PMLA* 70: 1160–84.

Frye, Joanne. *Living Stories, Telling Lives.* Ann Arbor: University of Michigan Press, 1986.

Furman, Nelly. "The Politics of Language: Beyond the Gender Principle?" In Green and Kahn. 59–79.

Gallop, Jane. "Annie Leclerc Writing a Letter, with Vermeer." In Miller, *Poetics.* 137–56.

———. *The Daughter's Seduction: Feminism and Psychoanalysis.* Ithaca, Cornell University Press, 1982.

Gallop, Jane, and Carolyn G. Burke. "Psychoanalysis and Feminism in France." In Eisenstein and Jardine. 106–22.

Garcia, Irma. *Promenade femmelière: Recherches sur l'écriture féminine.* 2 vols. Paris: des femmes, 1981.

Gardiner, Judith Kegan. "On Female Identity and Writing by Women." *Critical Inquiry* 8 (1981): 347–61.

———. "Mind Mother: Psychoanalysis and Feminism." In Greene and Kahn. 113–45.

Garner, Shirley Nelson, Claire Kahane, and Madelon Sprengnether, eds. *The (M)other Tongue: Essays in Psychoanalytic Interpretation*. Ithaca: Cornell University Press, 1985.

Geertz, Clifford. *The Interpretation of Cultures: Selected Essays*. New York: Basic, 1973.

Gelfand, Elissa D., and Virginia Thorndike Hules, eds. *French Feminist Criticism: Women, Language, Literature: An Annotated Bibliography*. New York: Garland, 1985.

Genette, Gérard. "Discours du récit." *Figures III*. Paris: Seuil, 1972.

Gilbert, Sandra. "Life's Empty Pack: Notes toward a Literary Daughteronomy." *Critical Inquiry* 11 (1985): 355–84.

Gilbert, Sandra M., and Susan Gubar. "Ceremonies of the Alphabet: Female Grandmatologies and the Female Authorgraph." *The Female Autograph*. Ed. Domna Stanton. New York: New York Literary Forum, 1984. 23–52.

———. *The Madwoman in the Attic: The Woman Writer and the Nineteenth-Century Imagination*. New Haven: Yale University Press, 1979.

———. *No Man's Land: The War of the Words*. Vol. 1. New Haven: Yale University Press, 1988.

———, eds. *Norton Anthology of Literature by Women: The Tradition in English*. New York: Norton, 1985.

———. "Sexual Linguistics: Gender, Language, Sexuality." *New Literary History* 16 (Spring 1985): 515–43.

Gilligan, Carol. *In a Different Voice: Psychological Theory and Women's Development*. Cambridge: Harvard University Press, 1982.

Gillman, Linda. "The Looking-Glass through Alice." *Women and Literature 1: Gender and Literary Voice*. New York: Holmes and Meier, 1980. 12–23.

Gilman, Charlotte Perkins. *The Yellow Wallpaper*. New York: Feminist Press, 1973.

Goury, Gérard-Humbert. "Une Manière de transexualité littéraire." *Le Magazine littéraire* avril 1983.

Greene, Gayle, and Coppélia Kahn, eds. *Making a Difference: Feminist Literary Criticism*. New York: Methuen, 1985.

Gubar, Susan. "'The Blank Page' and the Issues of Female Creativity." In Showalter, *New*. 292–313.

Hammer, Signe. *Daughters and Mothers: Mothers and Daughters*. New York: Signet, 1975.

———. *Passionate Attachments: Fathers and Daughters in America Today*. New York: Rawson, 1982.

Harding, Sandra. "The Instability of the Analytical Categories of Feminist Theory." *Signs* 11 (Summer 1986): 645–64.

Harding, Sandra, and Merrill B. Hintikka, eds. *Discovering Reality*. Boston: Reidel, 1983.

Hardy, Barbara. "An Approach through Narrative." *Towards a Poetics of Fiction*. Ed. Mark Spilka. Bloomington: Indiana University Press, 1977. 31–40.

Hartsock, Nancy. "The Feminist Standpoint: Developing the Ground for a Specifically Feminist Historical Materialism." In Harding and Hintikka. 296–304.

Hébert, Anne. *Kamouraska*. Paris: Seuil, 1970.

Heilbrun, Carolyn G. *Reinventing Womanhood*. New York: Norton, 1979.

———. "A Response to *Writing and Sexual Difference*." *Critical Inquiry* 8 (1982): 805–11.

Herrmann, Claudine. *Les Voleuses de langue*. Paris: des femmes, 1976.

Higonnet, Margaret R. "Introduction II." *The Representation of Women in Fiction*. Ed. Carolyn G. Heilbrun and Higonnet. Baltimore: Johns Hopkins University Press, 1983. xiii–xxii.

Hirsch, Marianne. "A Mother's Discourse: Incorporation and Repetition in *La Princesse de Clèves*." *Yale French Studies* 62 (1981): 67–87.

Homans, Margaret. *Bearing the Word: Language and Female Experience in Nineteenth-Century Women's Writing*. Chicago: University of Chicago Press, 1986.

———. "'Her Very Own Howl': The Ambiguities of Representation in Recent Women's Fiction." *Signs* 9 (1983): 186–205.

Horer, Suzanne, and Jeanne Socquet. *La Création étouffée*. Paris: Horay, 1973.

Hunter, Dianne. "Hysteria, Psychoanalysis, and Feminism: The Case of Anna O." In Garner, Kahane, and Sprengnether. 89–115.

Hutcheon, Linda. *Narcissistic Narrative: The Metafictional Paradox*. New York: Methuen, 1980.

Interview with Marie Cardinal. *Parispoche*. Grasset, Dossiers de presse.

Irigaray, Luce. *Le Corps-à-corps avec la mère*. Ottawa: Pleine Lune, 1981.

———. *Et l'une ne bouge pas sans l'autre*. Paris: Minuit, 1979.

———. *Ce Sexe qui n'en est pas un*. Paris: Minuit, 1977.

———. *Spéculum de l'autre femme*. Paris: Minuit, 1974.

Jacobus, Mary. *Reading Women*. New York: Columbia University Press, 1986.

———. Review of *The Madwoman in the Attic*, by Sandra M. Gilbert and Susan Gubar. *Signs* 6 (1981): 517–23.

Jardine, Alice A. *Gynesis: Configurations of Woman and Modernity*. Ithaca: Cornell University Press, 1985.

———. "Opaque Texts and Transparent Contexts: The Political Difference of Julia Kristeva." In Miller, *Poetics*. 96–116.

———. "Pre-Texts for the Transatlantic Feminist." *Yale French Studies* 62 (1981): 220–36.

Jelinek, Estelle C., ed. *Women's Autobiography.* Bloomington: Indiana University Press, 1980.

Jossin, Janick. "Le Cyclone héroïne." *Le Nouvel Observateur* 18–24 septembre 1987: 65.

Juhasz, Suzanne. "Toward a Theory of Form in Feminist Autobiography: Kate Millett's *Flying* and *Sita;* Maxine Hong Kingston's *The Woman Warrior.*" In Jelinek. 221–37.

Kazantzis, Judith. "The Queen Clytemnestra." *Flame Tree.* London: Methuen, 1988.

Keller, Evelyn Fox. *Reflections on Gender and Science.* New Haven: Yale University Press, 1985.

Keller, Evelyn Fox, and Christine R. Grontkowski. "The Mind's Eye." In Harding and Hintikka. 207–24.

Kolodny, Annette. "Dancing through the Minefield." *Feminist Studies* 6 (1980): 1–25.

———. "The Lady's Not for Spurning: Kate Millett and the Critics." In Jelinek. 238–59.

Lacan, Jacques. *Ecrits.* Paris: Seuil, 1966.

Lagache, Daniel. *La Psychanalyse.* Paris: Presses Universitaires de France, 1985.

Lamy, Suzanne. *d'elles.* Montreal: Hexagone, 1979.

Langland, Elizabeth and Walter Gove, eds. *A Feminist Perspective in the Academy: The Difference It Makes.* Chicago: University of Chicago Press, 1981.

Lanser, Susan. *The Narrative Act.* Princeton: Princeton University Press, 1981.

Laplanche, Jean. "Le Mot à mot de Freud." *Le Nouvel Observateur* 13–19 mai 1988: 159.

Laplanche, Jean, and J.-B. Pontalis. *The Language of Psycho-analysis.* Trans. Donald Nicholson-Smith. New York: Norton, 1973.

Lauder, Estella. *Women as Mythmakers: Poetry and Visual Art by Twentieth-Century Women.* Bloomington: Indiana University Press, 1984.

Leclerc, Annie. *Parole de femme.* Paris: Livre de poche, 1974.

LeClézio, Marguerite. "Mother and Motherland: The Daughter's Quest for Origins." *Stanford French Review* 5 (1981): 381–89.

Lefkowitz, Mary R., and Maureen B. Fant. *Women in Greece and Rome.* Toronto: Samuel-Stevens, 1977.

Lejeune, Philippe. *Je est un autre.* Paris: Seuil, 1980.

———. *Moi aussi.* Paris: Seuil, 1986.

Leonard, Linda Schierse. *The Wounded Woman: Healing the Father-Daughter Relationship.* Boulder, Colo.: Shambhala, 1983.

Lerman, Hannah. *A Mote in Freud's Eye: From Psychoanalysis to the Psychology of Women.* New York: Springer, 1986.

Lerner, Gerda. *The Majority Finds Its Past: Placing Women in History.* London: Oxford University Press, 1979.

Lionnet, Françoise. *Autobiographical Voices: Race, Gender, Self-Portraiture.* Ithaca: Cornell University Press, 1989.

———. "*Métissage,* Emancipation, and Female Texuality in Two Francophone Writers." *Life/Lines: Theorizing Women's Autobiography.* Ed. Bella Brodzki and Celeste Schenck. Ithaca: Cornell University Press, 1988.

Lipking, Lawrence. "Aristotle's Sister." *Critical Inquiry* 10 (1983): 61–81.

Lodovici, Danielle. "La Psychanalyse au cinéma." *Psychologie* octobre 1983: 71–77.

Lotman, J. M. "Point of View in a Text." *New Literary History* 6 (1975): 263–86.

MacKinnon, Catharine. "Feminism, Marxism, Method, and the State: An Agenda for Theory." *Signs* 7 (1982): 515–44.

Makward, Christiane. "To Be or Not to Be . . . A Feminist Speaker." In Eisenstein and Jardine. 95–105.

Marcus, Jane. "Still Practice, A/Wrested Alphabet: Toward a Feminist Aesthetic." *Tulsa Studies in Women's Literature* 3 (1984): 79–98.

Marks, Elaine, and Isabelle de Courtivron, eds. *New French Feminisms.* Amherst: University of Massachusetts Press, 1980.

Martin, Elaine. "Mothers, Madness, and the Middle Class in *The Bell Jar* and *Les Mots pour le dire.*" *The French-American Review* 5 (Spring 1981): 24–47.

Mauss, Marcel. *Oeuvres.* 2 vols. Paris: Minuit, 1969.

Mayne, Judith. "Feminist Film Theory and Criticism." *Signs* 11 (1985): 81–100.

Mercier, Michel. *Le Roman féminin.* Paris: Presses Universitaires de France, 1976.

Messer-Davidow, Ellen. "The Philosophical Bases of Feminist Literary Criticisms." *New Literary History* 19 (1987): 65–103.

Miller, Nancy K. "Arachnologies: The Woman, the Text, and the Critic." In Miller, *Poetics.* 270–95.

———. "Emphasis Added: Plots and Plausibilities in Women's Fiction." *PMLA* 96 (1981): 36–48.

———, ed. *The Poetics of Gender.* New York: Columbia University Press, 1986.

———. "Writing (from) the Feminine: George Sand and the Novel of Female Pastoral." *The Representation of Women in Fiction.* Ed. Carolyn G. Heilbrun and Margaret R. Higonnet. Baltimore: Johns Hopkins University Press, 1983. 270–95.

Millett, Kate. *Sexual Politics*. Garden City, N.Y.: Doubleday, 1970.

Mink, Louis O. "History and Fiction as Modes of Comprehension." *New Literary History* 1 (1970): 541–58.

———. "Narrative Form as a Cognitive Instrument." *The Writing of History*. Ed. Robert H. Canary and Henry Kozicki. Madison: University of Wisconsin Press, 1978. 129–49.

Mitchell, Juliet. *Psychoanalysis and Feminism: Freud, Reich, Laing, and Women*. New York: Vintage, 1974.

Mitchell, W. J. T., ed. *On Narrative*. Chicago: University of Chicago Press, 1980.

Moers, Ellen. *Literary Women*. Garden City, N.Y.: Anchor, 1977.

Moi, Toril. *Sexual/Textual Politics: Feminist Literary Theory*. London: Methuen, 1985.

Morgan, Janice. "Fiction and Autobiography/Language and Silence: *L'Amant* by Marguerite Duras." Ms., Murray State University, 1988.

Muller, Catherine. "Marie Cardinal 'Au Pays de mes racines.'" *Femina* 4 mars 1981: 14–18.

Mulvey, Laura. "Visual Pleasure and Narrative Cinema." *Screen* 16 (1975): 6–18.

Ostriker, Alicia. *Stealing the Language: The Emergence of Women's Poetry in America*. Boston: Beacon, 1986.

Owen, Ursula, ed. *Fathers: Reflections by Daughters*. New York: Pantheon, 1983.

Parker, Rozsika. *The Subversive Stitch: Embroidery and the Making of the Feminine*. London: Women's Press, 1984.

Paterson, Janet M. "Reflet(s) et Rupture dans l'écriture d'Anne Hébert." *Québec Studies* 2 (1984): 118–24.

Pednault, Hélène. "Entretien avec Marie Cardinal." *La Vie en rose* 17 (mai 1984): 18–20.

Poiret-Delpech, Bertrand. "Le Droit à la première personne." *Le Monde* 21 avril 1978: 13.

Poovey, Mary. *The Proper Lady and the Woman Writer: Style as Ideology in the Works of Mary Wollstonecraft, Mary Shelley, and Jane Austen*. Chicago: University of Chicago Press, 1984.

Pratt, Annis. *Archetypal Patterns in Women's Fiction*. Bloomington: Indiana University Press, 1981.

Prince, Gerald. "Introduction à l'étude du narrataire." *Poétique* 14: 178–96.

Racine, Jean. *Iphigénie*. 1674. *Théatre Complet*. Paris: Garnier, 1960.

Radway, Janice A. *Reading the Romance*. Chapel Hill: University of North Carolina Press, 1984.

Ragland-Sullivan, Ellie. *Jacques Lacan and the Philosophy of Psychoanalysis*. Urbana: University of Illinois Press, 1987.

Review of *Les Mots pour le dire*, by Marie Cardinal. *Esprit* décembre 1975.

Review of *Le Passé empiété*, by Marie Cardinal. *Le Nouveau F* avril 1983: 37.

Rich, Adrienne. "Sibling Mysteries." *The Dream of a Common Language: Poems 1974–1977.* New York: Norton, 1978.

———. *Of Woman Born.* New York: Norton, 1976.

———. "When We Dead Awaken: Writing as Re-Vision." *On Lies, Secrets and Silence: Selected Prose 1966–1978.* New York: Norton, 1979. 39–49.

Rimmon-Kenan, Shlomith. *Narrative Fiction.* New York: Methuen, 1983.

Robbe-Grillet, Alain. "Discussion." *Robbe-Grillet: Analyse, Théorie.* Vol 1. Ed. Jean Ricardou. 2 vols. Paris: 10/18, 1976. 1:131–72.

———. *Le Miroir qui revient.* Paris: Minuit, 1984.

Romberg, Bertil. *Studies in the Narrative Technique of the First-Person Novel.* Lund, Sweden: Almquist & Wiksell, 1962.

Russ, Joanna. *How to Suppress Women's Writing.* Austin: University of Texas Press, 1983.

Schafer, Roy. *A New Language for Psychoanalysis.* New Haven: Yale University Press, 1976.

Schneider, Michel. *Voleurs de mots: Essai sur le plagiat, la psychanalyse et la pensée.* Paris: Gallimard, 1985.

Schweikart, Patrocinio P. "Reading Ourselves: Toward a Feminist Theory of Reading." *Gender and Reading.* Ed. Elizabeth A. Flynn and Schweikart. Baltimore: Johns Hopkins University Press, 1986.

Sherman, Julia A., and Evelyn Torton Beck, eds. *The Prism of Sex.* Madison: University of Wisconsin Press, 1979.

Showalter, Elaine. *The Female Malady.* New York: Pantheon, 1985.

———. "Feminist Criticism in the Wilderness." *Critical Inquiry* 8 (1981): 179–205.

———. *A Literature of Their Own: British Women Novelists from Brontë to Lessing.* Princeton: Princeton University Press, 1977.

———, ed. *The New Feminist Criticism: Essays on Women, Literature, and Theory.* New York: Pantheon, 1985.

———. "Piecing and Writing." In Miller, *Poetics.* 222-47.

———. "Women's Writing and Women's Culture." National Endowment for the Humanities Summer Seminar Description. 1984.

Skura, Meredith Anne. *The Literary Use of the Psychoanalytic Process.* New Haven: Yale University Press, 1981.

Smith-Rosenberg, Carroll. "The Female World of Love and Ritual: Relations between Women in Nineteenth-Century America." *Signs* 1 (1983): 1–29.

Spacks, Patricia. *The Female Imagination.* New York: Knopf, 1975.

Spender, Dale, ed. *Men's Studies Modified: The Impact of Feminism on the Academic Disciplines.* Oxford: Pergamon, 1981.

Sprengnether, Madelon. "Enforcing Oedipus: Freud and Dora." In Garner, Kahane, and Sprengnether. 51–71.

Stanton, Julie. Interview with Marie Cardinal. *Chatelaine* avril 1981.

Stewart, Grace. *A New Mythos: The Novel of the Artist as Heroine 1877–1977.* Montreal: Eden, 1981.

Suleiman, Susan. "(Re)Writing the Body: The Politics and Poetics of Female Eroticism." *The Female Body in Western Culture.* Ed. Suleiman. Cambridge: Harvard University Press, 1986. 7–29.

Taylor, Anne Robinson. *Male Novelists and their Female Voices: Literary Masquerades.* Troy, N.Y.: Whitson, 1981.

Thompson, Clara, ed. *An Outline of Psychoanalysis.* New York: Modern Library, 1955.

Treichler, Paula A. "Escaping the Sentence: Diagnosis and Discourse in 'The Yellow Wallpaper.'" *Tulsa Studies in Women's Literature* 3 (1984): 61–77.

Turkle, Sherry. *Psychoanalytic Politics: Freud's French Revolution.* New York: Basic, 1978.

Vernant, Jean-Pierre. *Mythe et pensée chez les Grecs.* Paris: Maspéro, 1965.

Wakerman, Elyce. *Father Loss.* Garden City, N.Y.: Doubleday, 1984.

Westkott, Marcia. "Feminist Criticism of the Social Sciences." *Harvard Educational Review* 49 (1979): 422–30.

White, Hayden. *Tropics of Discourse.* Baltimore: Johns Hopkins University Press, 1978. 81–100.

———. "The Value of Narrativity in the Representation of Reality." In Mitchell. 1–23.

Williams, Raymond. *Marxism and Literature.* Oxford: Oxford University Press, 1977.

Winnington-Ingram, R. P. "Clytemnestra and the Vote of Athena." *JHS* 68 (1948): 130–47.

Wittig, Monique. "The Mark of Gender." In Miller, *Poetics.* 63-73.

Wolf, Christa. *Cassandra.* Trans. Jan Van Heurck. London: Virago, 1984.

———. *A Model Childhood.* Trans. Ursula Molinaro and Hedwig Rappolt. New York: Farrar, 1980.

Wolfromm, Jean-Didier. "Le Syndrome de Clytemnestra." *Express* 25–31 mars 1983: 44.

Woolf, Virginia. "Mr. Bennett and Mrs. Brown." *Collected Essays.* Vol. 1. London: Hogarth, 1966.

———. *A Room of One's Own.* 1929. New York: Harcourt, 1957.

Xenakis, Françoise. "Ainsi sont les femmes..." *Le Matin* 28 mars 1983: 2.

———. "'Au pays de mes racines' de Marie Cardinal." *Le Matin* 8 décembre 1980: 25.

Yaeger, Patricia. "'Because a Fire Was in My Head': Eudora Welty and the Dialogic Imagination." *PMLA* 99 (1984): 955–73.

Yaguello, Marina. *Les Mots et les femmes*. Paris: Payot, 1978.

Yalom, Marilyn. *Maternity, Mortality, and the Literature of Madness*. University Park: Pennsylvania State University Press, 1985.

Zeitlin, Froma. "The Dynamics of Misogyny: Myth and Mythmaking in the Oresteia." *Arethusa* 2 (1978): 149–81.

culture, 20, 23, 47–48, 56–71, 74–75n.21, 108, 146, 194, 273; and female literary tradition, 23, 26–27, 58, 159; identity and difference in, 20, 27, 30, 56, 61, 64, 94, 103, 151; and women's reading/writing practices, 19–20, 27, 33–34, 37, 39–40, 65, 68–71, 73nn.13–14, 90–91, 147, 164, 179, 194, 271, 273. *See also* Autocitation; Psychoanalysis

Rhythm, 94–95, 101, 118, 123n.14, 133, 204n.35, 263, 265, 273

Rich, Adrienne, 39, 62, 67, 160, 203, 276

Rimbaud, Arthur, 135, 138, 143, 146

Rimmon-Kenan, Shlomith, 198n.4

Robbe-Grillet, Alain, 52, 71, 121–22n.2, 131

Romberg, Bertil, 130

Ronfard, Bénédicte, 164, 202, 275

Russ, Joanna, 33, 203n.32

Sand, George, 95, 198n.2

Schafer, Roy, 208, 217, 231, 266–67n.5

Schneider, Michel, 246–47

Schweikart, Patrocinio P., 72, 271

Self, female. *See* Identity, female

Showalter, Elaine, 10, 12, 16n.4, 17n.15, 27–28, 31, 53, 58, 64, 96, 109, 111, 119–20, 132, 150, 197–98n.1, 200n.16, 227, 240

Skura, Meredith Anne, 208, 275

Smith-Rosenberg, Carroll, 23

Spacks, Patricia, 64

Sprengnether, Madelon, 249

Stein, Gertrude, 102

Stewart, Grace, 64, 153, 169, 203n.32

Taylor, Anne Robinson, 149

Treichler, Paula A., 127

Turkle, Sherry, 215, 246, 256–57, 265, 269n.22

Vernant, Jean-Pierre, 159

Vision: in Western culture, 30–31, 111–13, 116, 143, 199n.10, 225–27, 229, 244, 261–62, 267–68n.11

Wakerman, Elyce, 200n.15

White, Hayden, 122, 138, 140–43, 192–93, 204

Williams, Raymond, 133

Winnington-Ingram, R. P., 159

Wittig, Monique, 78, 139, 199n.6

Wolf, Christa, 136, 151, 162, 199n.6

Wolfromm, Jean-Didier, 200n.17

Women's studies, 13–15

Woolf, Virginia, 9–10, 42–43, 56, 58, 74n.16, 131, 159, 278

Writing, women's practice(s) of, 89, 242; and the body, 89, 93–95, 104–5, 107, 109–21, 124n.21, 125nn.24–25, 152, 163, 177, 200n.14, 201n.18, 204; and collaboration, 39, 40, 91, 118, 149, 152, 163–64, 166, 168–69, 171–72, 180, 186, 195, 259–60, 275; theoretical importance of, 12, 132, 192–97 passim, 205n.40. *See also* Culture, female; *Écriture féminine;* Language; Repetition

Xenakis, Françoise, 73n.9

Yaeger, Patricia, 9, 122n.4, 204n.39

Yaguello, Marina, 97, 104, 123n.12

Yalom, Marilyn, 6, 16n.7, 72n.7, 218, 231, 267n.10, 268n.14, 269n.21

Zeitlin, Froma, 159

CAROLYN A. DURHAM is Inez Kinney Gaylord Professor of French and the current coordinator of the Women's Studies Program at the College of Wooster. She is the author of *L'Art romanesque de Raymond Roussel.* Her essays on a wide range of topics in American and French literature and film have appeared in a number of edited collections and professional journals, including *French Forum, French Review, Twentieth Century Literature, Jumpcut, Tulsa Studies in Women's Literature,* and *Women's Studies.*